Balkan Spaces

Selected Writings 10

While the core of this first selection of Richard Berengarten's essays and prose-pieces is his thinking about his own practice as a poet and the sources of his inspiration, the ground this book covers is marked by his sustained involvement in the Balkans over a period of more than thirty-five years, especially the territory of former Yugoslavia. He first visited Yugoslavia in 1982. In 1987, he lived in Split, and between 1987 and 1990, in Belgrade. Since then, he has travelled widely in the republics of the former Federation, all of which are now separate nation-states. He has also lived in Greece and Italy and has travelled in Bulgaria and Romania.

While reflecting his personally lived experience of Yugoslavia before, during and after that country's break-up, *Balkan Spaces* tracks and celebrates aspects of history, folk tradition, literary culture, educational practice, politics and poetry. By means of intimate explorations, detailed insights, caring reading and careful research, Berengarten discovers some of the patternings, varieties and bounties of the Balkan and Yugoslav heritage. *Balkan Spaces* also complements the books of poems in Berengarten's *Balkan Trilogy*: *The Blue Butterfly*, *In a Time of Drought* and *Under Balkan Light*. Overall, it offers a coherent commitment to the values of Balkan civilisation, to the poetic imagination, and to the poet's vocation and craft.

RICHARD BERENGARTEN was born in London in 1943 into a musical family. He has received the Eric Gregory Award, the Wingate-Jewish Quarterly Award for Poetry, the Keats Poetry Prize, the Yeats Club Prize and the Xu Zhimo Silver Willow Award. In 1975, he founded the international Cambridge Poetry Festival. He has been Writer-in-Residence at the international Eliot-Dante Colloquium in Florence, Visiting Associate Professor at the University of Notre Dame, and Royal Literary Fund Fellow at Newnham College, Cambridge. In Serbia, he has received the international Morava Charter Poetry Prize, and in Macedonia, the Manada Prize. In 2007, his book *The Blue Butterfly* served as the oratorio for the annual 'Great Lesson' memorial event in Kragujevac, where in 2011 he was elected an honorary citizen. His books are translated into Macedonian, Serbian and Slovene, and he is the only British writer to have been elected a full member of the Serbian Writers' Association. Berengarten is currently a Fellow of the English Association, a Bye-Fellow at Downing College, Cambridge, and an Academic Associate at Pembroke College, Cambridge.

Also by Richard Berengarten:

SELECTED WRITINGS, SHEARSMAN EDITION

Vol. 1 *For the Living : Selected Longer Poems, 1965–2000*
Vol. 2 *The Manager*
Vol. 3 *The Blue Butterfly* (Part 1, *The Balkan Trilogy*)
Vol. 4 *In a Time of Drought* (Part 2, *The Balkan Trilogy*)
Vol. 5 *Under Balkan Light* (Part 3, *The Balkan Trilogy*)
Vol. 6 *Manual, the first hundred*
Vol. 7 *Notness, metaphysical sonnets*
Vol. 8 *Changing*
Vol. 9 *A Portrait in Inter-Views*

OTHER POETRY

The Return of Lazarus
Avebury
Double Flute
Learning to Talk
Half of Nowhere
Against Perfection
Book With No Back Cover

OTHER PROSE

Keys to Transformation: Ceri Richards and Dylan Thomas
Imagems 1
Imagems 2

AS EDITOR

An Octave for Octavio Paz
Ceri Richards: Drawings to Poems by Dylan Thomas
Rivers of Life
In Visible Ink: Selected Poems, Roberto Sanesi, 1955–1979
Homage to Mandelstam
Out of Yugoslavia
For Angus
The Perfect Order: Selected Poems, Nasos Vayenas, 1974–2010
IDEA and ACT

RICHARD BERENGARTEN

Balkan Spaces

ESSAYS AND PROSE-PIECES (1) 1984–2020

SELECTED WRITINGS
Volume 10

Shearsman Books

First published in the United Kingdom in 2021 by
Shearsman Books Ltd
PO Box 4239
Swindon
SN3 9FN

Shearsman Books Ltd Registered Office
30–31 St. James Place, Mangotsfield, Bristol BS16 9JB
(this address not for correspondence)

ISBN 978-1-84861-753-7

For Vera V. Radojević

ΑΜΦΙΩΝ

ἐγὼ μὲν οὖν ᾄδοιμι καὶ λέγοιμί τι
σοφόν, ταράσσων μηδὲν ὧν πόλις νοσεῖ.

Ευριπιδης

Without contraries is no progression. Attraction and Repulsion, Reason and Energy, Love and Hate are necessary to Human existence.

William Blake

Les événements sont poussière: ils traversent l'histoire comme des lueurs brèves; à peine naissent-ils qu'ils retournent déjà à la nuit et souvent à l'oubli. Chacun d'eux, il est vrai, si bref qu'il soit, porte témoignage, éclaire un coin du paysage, parfois des masses profondes d'histoire.

Fernand Braudel

Mann wird aber nicht hell dadurch, daß man sich Helles vorstellt, sondern dadurch, daß man Dunkles bewußt macht. Letzteres aber ist unangenehm und daher nicht populär.

C. G. Jung

All I have is a voice
to undo the folded lie

W. H. Auden

Contents

References

Illustrations

Pronunciation Guide

Spelling	*Approximate English Pronunciation*
c	*ts*
ć	like *ti* in *station*
č	like *ch* in *church* or *tch* in *hatch*
đ, dj	like *d* in *endure*
dz	like *dg* in *lodger*
e	close to *e in bet*
lj	like *l* in *lure*
j	like *y* in *year*
u	close to *oo* in *look*
š	close to *sh* in *show*
ž	close to *s* in *fusion*

Abbreviations

AV	*The King James Authorised Version of the Bible*
CW	*Collected Works* (of C. G. Jung)
ed. / eds.	editor(s), edited by
Encyc. Brit.	*Encyclopaedia Britannica*
OED	*Oxford English Dictionary* (online)
TEFL	Teaching English as a Foreign Language
trans.	translator(s), translated by
vol. / vols.	volume(s)

Preface

> [W]hat we have written in many ways remains essay-like. On none of the topics selected for discussion can we claim to have come anywhere near to completeness, although we have certainly not avoided detail.
>
> —Peregrine Horden and Nicholas Purcell

This selection of essays and prose-pieces reflects a sustained involvement and interest in Balkan life and culture over a period of more than thirty-five years, especially in the areas of former Yugoslavia. Since I first visited Yugoslavia in 1982, I've consistently experienced the Balkans as a site of intimate and quickened inspiration for my poems. For this reason, this book isn't only about the Balkans and my experience of the region. It's equally, even if sometimes tangentially, about my poetic practice and thinking about poetry and poems, as well as their mysterious sources in the human psyche, or heart-mind, or imagination.

Within these thematic parameters, the book is discursive. Its contents move through and gather in a variety of themes and topics that have caught my interest, attention and involvement. For this reason, the pieces in the book draw on and deploy multiple styles and registers, as they hint at, touch on or glide in and out of various genres and modes of writing – including personal narrative and anecdote, autobiography and introspection, historical and biographical exploration, etymological and philological enquiry, literary essays and reviews, reportage, feature, memoir, ruminations on educational theory and practice, and two pieces on politics. Approaches range from the discursive to the argumentative, from narration to analysis, and from excavation to surmise; and several poems and translations of poems are included. For possible documentary interest, and to localise details in time as well as place, I've also risked including some pieces that I know to be ephemeral and, strictly speaking, 'dated'. Yet even though a book such as this is bound to be a miscellany, and even though it's doubtful whether every part of it will interest any one individual reader, I hope that its variegated motifs and treatments move through it coherently enough to suggest not merely collage or contiguity, but connected threads and patterns, and that these in turn may reveal unexpected correspondences and, even, perhaps, multi-dimensional perspectives.

Apart from these considerations, many intimate threads run beneath and through all of the pieces in this book, including quirks, idiosyncrasies and obsessions. The outlines of a personal story are no doubt readily traceable. I'm aware that these include several repeating motifs, for example: perspectives arising out of overlapping and variegated identities in my own make-up, including being both English and Jewish; the deep and pervasive influence of C. G. Jung's theories on my thinking and practice; a worldview that combines internationalism and multiculturalism with an attentiveness to what William Blake called *the minute particulars*,[1] and Gerard Manley Hopkins, *instress* and *inscape*,[2] all in the context of making poems and mapping a viable poetics; and a corresponding view of the need for history to track and understand details among panoramic expanses of time and space, as for example in the writings of Fernand Braudel and Traian Stoianovich.

A multiculturalist and internationalist worldview, of course, is inevitably political and social as well as poetic and psychological. As an ideology, it necessarily involves opposition to the kinds of stereotyping, ethno-nationalism and racism that swept through Yugoslavia and exploded in the conflicts of the 1990s.

There are no doubt other patterns too that I'm not and probably can't be aware of.

ꟹ

The 'I' that says *I am* is never quite the same as the 'I' that was or says or said *I was* – or, indeed, *I were*.[3] Every writer is a self-reader, and retrospectively, it's been curious to discover that the process of collecting these pieces has itself prompted and marked further personal discoveries, some of which I attempt to track and outline in the following pages. Recursive thinking is in any case an integral part of all creative composition, including writing; and since themes and motifs intersect and interbreed here, some repetition has been unavoidable.

---

[1] See Foster Damon: 280-281; and 'Universalism and Particularism', in RB 2019: 21-24.

[2] See Hopkins 1959: 572; and Hopkins 2013, vol. 2: 1039 (indexes).

[3] See also the reference to Rimbaud, with commentary, 56 below, note 5.

Following this preface, the book is organised into seven parts. These are arranged thematically rather than chronologically, although some temporal patterning occurs within each. Their sequence represents an entwining of autobiographical account and explorative enquiry. The earliest piece was written in 1984 and the latest in 2019–2020. Dates of composition are indicated at the end of each essay and, other than Cambridge (where most of these pieces were written), so are places. As for style, I've deliberately decided to use informal abbreviations such as *I'm*, *it's*, *doesn't*, etc., simply because they're (rather than *they are*) closer to speech.

Apart from the introductions to each section and 'Sketches from Memory', all the pieces included here are occasional. A few were commissioned, but most were generated spontaneously: which is to say, I wrote them simply because I wanted to. Since these writings span the period in which Yugoslavia imploded and collapsed, political themes are inevitably present, usually as a pervasive and persistent background hum, but at times as one that's insistent, a cacophony that forces itself to the fore.

Now that the details of this book have fallen into place, almost as if they were pieces in a jigsaw, I'm glad to discover that, surreptitiously and almost of its own accord, my *Balkan Trilogy* has turned itself, at least for the time being, into a tetralogy: three books of poems and one of prose.

∽

Writing this book hasn't involved only multiple discoveries and realisations, but also ever-richer and ever-more-equivocal uncertainties. Here I list four of these, all inter-related. First, how the two terms *Balkan* and *the Balkans* themselves are to be defined and understood is highly debatable.[4] Second, I've found over the years that a characteristic of the Balkans is that every generalisation that it's possible to make about life and culture will sooner or later find at least one direct and absolute contradiction, usually followed by reams of others. Third, this *resistance to generalisation* in turn means that any attempt to 'interpret' or 'explain' the Balkans is likely to involve taking on a task that can't possibly succeed – especially if this is in the 'light' of a single theory, and even more so if the theory is to be put forward by a non-native. Fourth, because the Balkan region is a world of such rich uniquenesses, subtly graded nuances, fuzzily bordered distinctions, and polarised contradictions – even statements such as those in this paragraph

[4] On this point, see Maria Todorova's ground-breaking book, *Imagining the Balkans* (2nd ed. 1997): 21-61.

must remain open to being queried, modified, countermanded, contradicted. So let no-one trust anyone who claims to be an 'expert'. Such people, both trusters and experts, fool only themselves.

Even so, the sense that a particular place does possess, emanate or, indeed, is possessed by a unique *spiritus loci* or *genius loci* is universal, and anybody may discover this sense just as well in a huge peninsula as in a small patch of ground. At this point, in approaching and trying to talk clearly and coherently about something at once as complex, intractable and evanescent as *the sense of a spirit of a place*, I find I can only speak (it only becomes meaningful for me *if* I speak), however stumblingly, in and through my own *first person singular*.

While I obviously need to be wary of projecting this-or-that particular set of qualities onto any place or space – and, likewise and even more so, onto those who inhabit it, I find I can never stop making, modifying and remaking complex images about it. In poems and stories, as in landscape painting, myth, legend and history, projected images inevitably characterise places and will always go on doing so. And a *spiritus loci* or *genius loci* always resides in and is discoverable through images, or, as T. S. Eliot would have it, in an "objective correlative" that links a specific interior mood or feeling with an exterior 'source'.[5]

How, then, if I'm to be honest and true to myself, should I approach my own images of a *locus*? While both the best and worst of travel writers tend to jump in, and often make utter fools of themselves, sensible scholars may well fear to tread at all, being wary of entrapment in stereotype and cliché, even though they too have no choice but to work with and through what they call 'narratives' or 'constructs': i.e. ideologies.

Since a poet has no choice but work in images, first, I believe, I need constantly to query and challenge my own stereotypes, by which I mean the collectivised and culturally approved caricatures based in and on my personal projections, which by definition are partial, emotive, and necessarily *exclude their opposites*. Second, I should *own up to my projections*, whether positive, negative or mixed, and I should take them back (withdraw them) into myself, rather than allow myself to pretend in *any way* that they're 'objective'. Third, I should be equally careful to avoid replacing these with alternative and contradictory stereotypes by means of some conventionally clever but simplistically suspect game of intellectual dialectics. Fourth, *if and only if* I can remove stereotypes, I run the risk of quite possibly being deflated, disillusioned, depressed, and, what's

[5] Eliot 1961 [1919]: 145.

more, overwhelmed by *details* in vast arrays. But fifth, out of these details, patterns do begin to emerge that *aren't* stereotypes. Simultaneously more and more variegated and individualised, they may perhaps paradoxically reveal features of universal depth. Apparently secure but inevitably falsely superficial stereotypes may yield way to intimations and reflections of complex archetypes.

As in poetry, then, polysemy and paradox are to be followed, respected, rejoiced in, and relished.

September 2019–February 2020

PART 1

IN BALKAN SPACE

This part contains three prose-pieces and three poems, all of which derive directly or indirectly from personal biography. Four of the prose pieces are connected with the composition of *The Blue Butterfly* (1985–2006), whose point of departure in 1985 was an event that lasted no more than a few seconds. Its deeper roots, however, belong to an atrocity of the Second World War. In October 1941, at Šumarice, just outside the city of Kragujevac in central Serbia, a massacre was perpetrated by Nazi occupiers in reprisal against an attack on German troops by local resistance fighters. Nearly 3,000 people, mainly men and boys, were murdered, all of them inhabitants of Kragujevac and its surrounding villages.

Nearly forty-four years later, in May 1985, while I stood in a queue in Šumarice Park with my then-seventeen-year-old daughter Lara, waiting our turn to enter the Memorial Museum, a small blue butterfly suddenly came to rest on the forefinger of my left (writing) hand.

For me, there was a sudden, immediate and resonant connection between the massacre and this butterfly: a chiming, a discovery, a recognition. That fleeting event turned out to be life-changing. Following this butterfly, in 1987 I successfully applied for a job in Serbia. After two months in Split, I spent three years in Belgrade. If it had been possible to stay longer, I would have done so. But my contract couldn't be renewed, so I returned to Cambridge. Gradually, *The Blue Butterfly* emerged. It was completed and published in 2006, twenty-one years later.

The first piece, 'A Synchronistic Experience in Serbia', was written in 2018 and amplified in 2019. As its title clarifies, I've retrospectively interpreted the conjunction of the 1941 massacre with the butterfly landing on my finger in 1985 and my inner state at that time, as an instance of *synchronicity*, or in C. G. Jung's best-known definitions of his own coinage, "meaningful coincidence" and "acausal connection".[1] Varying Jung's term, I suggest that equally appropriate coinages might be *syntopicity* (i.e. 'coincidence of place at and across different times'), and, indeed, *synkairicity* (i.e. 'coincidence of moments considered *qualitatively* rather than merely *sequentially* – from Greek καιρός (*kairos*).[2]

[1] Jung *CW*8, 2014 [1960]: 417-531.

[2] Beekes defines Greek καιρός as follows: "a due measure, fitness, opportuneness" and "the right, suitable, opportune time, good opportunity, critical moment".

Three poems from *The Blue Butterfly* are added here.

The second essay, 'A Grove of Trees and a Grove of Stones' (1989), is a meditation on a separate but related Nazi massacre of nearly 2,000 men and women, also in October 1941, in the town of Kraljevo, around fifty kms from Kragujevac.

The third, 'A Model of Truth-Telling' (2010) was written as a postscript for the historiographical book, *Jevreji u Kragujevcu* ('The Jews of Kragujevac') by Staniša Brkić and Milomir Minić (2011). Staniša's earlier book, *Ime i broj* ('Name and Number', 2007), is a painstaking investigation into the details of the Nazi massacres at Šumarice and the villages surrounding Kragujevac. In writing my postscript to *The Blue Butterfly*, I relied extensively on his researches.[3]

While these prose-pieces are meant to stand in their own right, I also hope that, in various ways, they'll throw light on themes and motifs in *The Blue Butterfly*.

September 2018–January 2019

---

[3] See the memoir of Staniša Brkić, 398-402 below, and *The Blue Butterfly* (RB 2011b): 125-135.

A Synchronistic Experience in Serbia

> I was saying that only I could reach to the other's (inner) life. My condition is not exactly that I have to put the other's life there; and not exactly that I have to leave it there either. I (have to) respond to it, or refuse to respond. It calls upon me; it calls me out.
>
> Stanley Cavell

In May 1985, I visited Serbia from my home in Cambridge, England, to run a series of poetry writing workshops for pupils in Serbian schools, mostly in their early teens. With my daughter Lara, who was then seventeen, I travelled to Belgrade and some smaller towns and villages in the central and western region of the republic, known as Šumadija (*šuma*, 'wood', 'forest'). The project, which included a group of local teachers of English, was set up and led by my friend and colleague Branka Panić, director of a language teaching centre in Belgrade, in collaboration with a Serbian publisher of children's books and magazines.[4] As I didn't know Serbian at that time, when conducting these workshops, I spoke in English and the teachers translated for me. The boys and girls wrote their poems in Serbian. Our group travelled from town to town in a minibus.

One of these poetry workshops took place on a sunny morning on May 25 in a school in the city of Kragujevac (*kraguj*, 'vulture'). A large number of pupils were involved in several sessions, and the events filled the school hall. There was a bright, enthusiastic, expansive atmosphere and a sense of novelty and pleasure about these workshops. Afterwards, with Branka and Lara, I visited the city's memorial museum in Šumarice ('woodland, 'spinneys'), a hilly park of 350 hectares just outside the town.[5]

ᔓ

[4] The publisher was Dječe novine, based in Gornji Milanovac. We ran poetry workshops in Belgrade, Čačak, Šabac, Kragujevac, and in the village of Tršić, birthplace of Vuk Stefanović Karadžić.

[5] See *The Blue Butterfly* (RB 2011b): 123-125.

Nothing could have contrasted more strongly with the mood of these poetry workshops than the history of Šumarice. Here, on 21 October 1941, 2,672 people were massacred. Most of these victims were male Serbs, including boys pulled directly out of classes from one of the main schools.[6] Victims included forty local Jews, an unregistered number of Roma, as well as prisoners from local jails, and some Serbian women and girls.[7]

Following their whirlwind invasion in April 1941, the Nazis had fully occupied Serbia by the beginning of May. The massacre was a punitive reprisal for a night-time ambush by a Serbian resistance group, near the village of Ljuljaci, on the narrow hilly road between Kragujevac and Gornji Milanovac, at a spot lined by woodland on both sides, on October 16. Nine German soldiers were shot and twenty-seven wounded, of whom one died later. A ruthless edict had been published by the occupiers, stating that in the event of a single German being killed, one hundred members of the Serbian population would be executed. For a single wounded German soldier, the toll would be fifty executed.[8]

Three days after the ambush, the reprisals were swift and merciless. On 19, 20 and 21 October 1941, 2,797 people were massacred at Šumarice, in Kragujevac itself, and in the four nearby villages of Maršić, Mečkovac (*aka* Ilićevo), Grošnica and Beloševac. Those killed included at least 27 women, 217 children of secondary school age, and 25 children aged between twelve and fifteen. The largest killing site was at Šumarice.[9]

ഗ

Our visit to Kragujevac coincided with a national holiday linked to the birthday of the former Yugoslav president, Josip Broz Tito. Five years after his death, May 25 was still being observed as *Dan mladosti* ('Youth Day'). Because our entire focus had been on the poetry writing workshops, Lara and I had been given no advance knowledge by my Serbian colleagues either of this event or of the wartime massacre, so we had no idea at all of what to expect. Our friends had told us after the workshops that we really ought to visit the museum, but excused themselves from coming with us. They had already been there; and a repeat visit would be "too upsetting".

---

[6] *Prva kragujevačka gimnazija* ('The First Kragujevac Grammar School'). Several years later, around 1988–1989, I taught another poetry workshop in that school.

[7] See: Brkić undated; and RB 2011b: 125-128.

[8] See RB, *ibid.* 4, 127.

[9] Brkić, *op. cit.*; Brkić 2007; and RB, *ibid.* 4, 5, 125-135.

But Branka kindly agreed to accompany us. I'd never visited the site of a massacre, and nor had Lara. I was curious to visit Šumarice, even though I knew nothing about it and the visit hadn't been envisaged in any way, let alone prepared.

As we arrived, the memorial park presented a curious and completely unexpected scene. The place was thronging with people on special outings. Groups were arriving from many other Serbian towns and villages. Children and teenagers poured out of various hired buses, and pensioners out of others. Many families were coming in by car. Hundreds of people milled around us, and in the queue outside the museum there was a good deal of noisy chatter and friendly jostling. The weather was balmy, and the area around the museum brimmed with youthful energy. In extreme contrast, the memorial park itself, a green area of 350 hectares expressly dedicated to the commemoration of the massacre, retained its own underlying, passive calm. It would be hard to visit this place at any time and not be reminded of the events that had taken place there in 1941.

On both sides of the straight road leading from the town to the museum, large banners had been strung up, on which fluttered phrases inscribed in Cyrillic script. Branka explained to us that these were blow-ups of short messages that had originally been scribbled on scraps of paper by some of the men and boys who'd been selected by the Germans for execution. They'd been interned overnight in a disused barracks before being marched out to be shot the next morning. They'd known or at least expected the fate that was awaiting them. These short messages, written in and through communal and individual terror, overwhelming panic, utter helplessness, and extraordinary bravery, were remarkable documents. Much later, when I tried to render some of them into English, I discovered that they had a heartrending, tragic poignancy, a dignity that utterly defied adequate translation.[10]

Eventually, Lara, Branka and I found ourselves in a queue of people waiting to get into the museum. The building was quite small and, once a hundred or so people had entered, the keepers closed the glass doors to prevent overcrowding inside. The previous group needed to be allowed to percolate through the building to the exit, before we could be admitted. We stood outside, in a crowd of strangers, waiting our turn.

ꟷ

[10] For three of these messages, see RB, *ibid.* 116-119. See also 'Don't send bread tomorrow', *ibid.* 6-7.

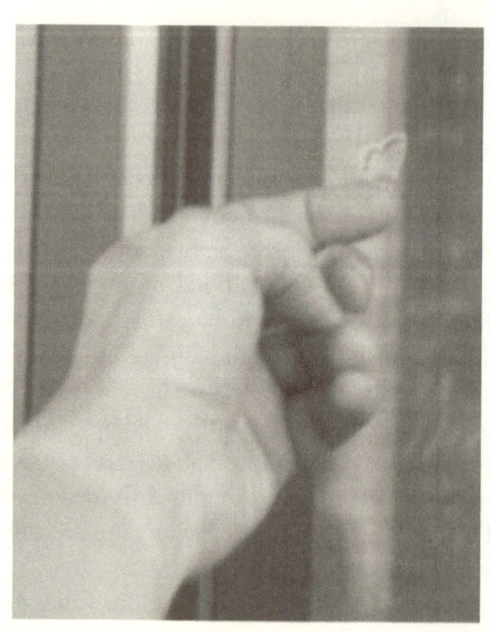

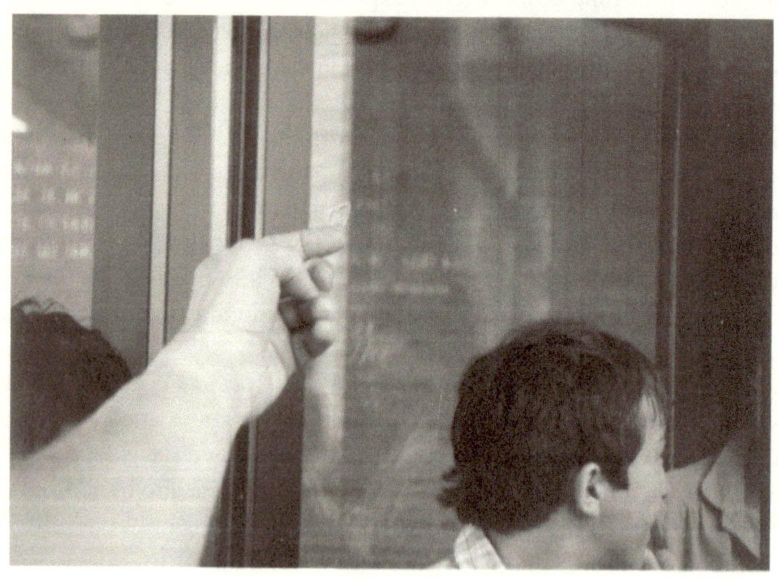

The blue butterfly: enlarged image and full photo
Šumarice, Kragujevac, May 1985 (original photo in colour)

Thirty-three years later, I still have a crystal-clear memory of what happened next, in all its detail. Lara and I were standing close to the glass doors of the museum, slightly bemused by the chatter and bustle around us. I had my arms folded in front of me, so that my right hand cradled my left elbow and my left hand was slightly raised. Lara stood to my right, holding our camera. My eyes were focused on the statement printed in large letters on the partition wall inside the museum, facing through its glass doors so that it could be read from outside: *Machen Sie mir dieses Land Deutsch* ("Make this land German for me"). Beneath it was attached the name *Adolf Hitler*. At that moment, out of the corner of my eye, I noticed a small movement on my left hand.

Looking down, I saw that a small blue butterfly was perched on my left forefinger, its wingspan hardly more than the size of my thumbnail. I gazed at it in disbelief for a second and nudged Lara with my right elbow. "Look," I said. "Quick, take a photo."

Lara pulled out our camera and took the first of two photos. In my astonishment, a vast number of impressions and ideas flashed (flooded) across my mind at once, as the horizons and boundaries of 'normal' perception, thought, and observation suddenly opened wide. Then the tiny butterfly lifted off my finger but, rather than flying away, flittered around in front of my face and just above it. It seemed to be performing a little aerial dance. Then, it settled back down on my finger again, the same finger as before. "It must *like* me," I thought. I asked Lara to pass me the camera, slowly stretched my left arm out in front of me and, using only my right hand, managed to focus the apparatus so that I could take a slightly better close-up shot. I had to manipulate the camera carefully because I'm left-handed, and my right hand isn't as flexible as my left. In terms of clock-time, although all this must have happened in a few seconds, I remember it as a moment in and through which the here-and-now expanded into a kind of timelessness, and time and space either stopped, or stopped being relevant. Time itself seemed to expand (disperse) and collapse (implode) simultaneously, and while 'things' were transformed because of this – somehow (and paradoxically) they also remained entirely 'normal': that is, exactly as they'd been previously. I've captured, or at least suggested, some of these complexities of response in 'The telling, first attempt',[11] although the word *attempt* in the title clearly indicates my sense at that time that language itself – even language, the richest, finest, clearest of our communicative gifts – wasn't adequate to expressing the fullness and

[11] See RB, *ibid.* 10-11; and 40 below.

subtlety (essence?) of such an experience, which leaks away, as it were, through minute cracks in language's jar.

I don't remember much, if anything, of what happened immediately after that. I know that I retained some immediate visual and spatial impressions of the museum's interior, because I recalled them later on, when they became relevant to me as triggers for research. But the incident itself, of the butterfly perching on my finger – and then returning, and then flying away again – together with everything that had led up to it, has been engraved into my memory ever since, with a cut-glass clarity, scattering multiple refractions.

ꟹ

Our tour of Serbia continued and we moved on to other towns. As soon as Lara and I returned home to Cambridge, I had both our photos developed. Although these were of nowhere-near-professional standard, especially by comparison with the extraordinarily fine detail of modern digital photography, the first shot that Lara had snapped and the second that I'd taken both yielded quite clear images of the little blue creature astride my finger, almost as if it had been posing there, sunning itself, waiting – even somehow wanting (?) – to be photographed. Our camera had contained a colour film, so the butterfly's delicate blueness came out clearly enough: wings edged in lacy whiteness, and a black contoured band, a kind of wavering border, between wingtips and the inner dominant blue.

Around that time, I wrote two poems to record the experience. They arrived spontaneously and effortlessly: first, 'The blue butterfly', followed by 'Nada: hope or nothing'. The second poem contains two lines ("A blue butterfly takes my hand and writes / in invisible ink across its page of air…"),[12] which express my acute sense at that time that, rather than *my* writing *them*, both of these poems were *writing themselves* through and out of me. That's to say, rather than my own will, intention (ego) being in control, the butterfly had somehow entered my imagination (psyche), and was guiding and guarding my hand in, through and along the entire compositional pathway.

It was hardly surprising that after the arrival (delivery) of these two poems, I realised that there was considerably more to be said – and done.

---

[12] See: 38, 39 below. See also RB, *ibid.* 7-9, and the interview with Sean Rys, 'I Must Try This Telling' in RB 2017a: 110ff. For an astute critical commentary, see Wilson 2009 and 2016.

As it turned out, these two poems eventually became the core of a book.

Thanks to the resources of Cambridge University Library, one of the great libraries of England, I was able to do some preliminary research into the Second World War in Yugoslavia. I began to delve into this subject from as many angles as possible, including records of German war documents. During this period, I also received and accepted several further invitations to various parts of the then-Federation of Yugoslavia, in Croatia, Slovenia and Serbia. These visits were short, usually lasting no more than one or two weeks: I went either to train English teachers on residential courses sponsored and planned by the British Council or to attend literary events organised by the Serbian Writers' Association. As a result, by 1986 I had a good number of friends among both teaching and literary communities in Belgrade and in Split.

In my early twenties, I'd lived in Italy and then in Greece, and knew both countries well. Now, in my mid-forties, I was discovering that the more I learned about Yugoslavia – which, at that time, I first thought of as the 'space between' Italy and Greece – the more curious I became, the more attracted, and the more I wanted to discover about it as an entity in its own right.

ග

Then a new possibility emerged. Branka Panić's language centre in Belgrade needed a qualified native-speaker to teach English, and a job was to be advertised in the UK through the British Council. By this time, I'd already given poetry readings and run several poetry workshops at this centre, and had several friends there. If I went to live in Belgrade, I'd have the chance to experience Yugoslav – and more specifically, Serbian – culture first-hand, learn some Serbo-Croatian,[13] and work on *The Blue Butterfly*. I decided to apply for the post, and was interviewed by a laconic mandarin at the British Council's head office in Davies Street, London. "I see no reason," he drawled, snootily and almost absentmindedly, "why we can't accept you."

[13] The expressions *Serbo-Croatian* and *Serbo-Croat* are no longer politically correct, either literally or in terms of taste. I use *Serbo-Croatian* non-controversially here and in accurate historical context. Since the demise of Yugoslavia, the term has been systematically suspended and superseded by the separate linguistic designations *Serbian*, *Bosnian*, *Croatian* and *Montenegrin*, each of which claims its own separate identity despite almost total mutual comprehension and, in terms of both grammar and vocabulary, many more points in common than differences. See 'Declaration on the Common Language', 63 below, note 13.

In this way, a new phase in my life was set in motion.

In 1987, Yugoslavia didn't figure especially prominently in the consciousness of most of my English literary acquaintances. I found myself being asked sceptical questions: "Yugoslavia? Why on earth are you going to live in *Yugoslavia*?" But I didn't feel like arguing, and in any case, had always been attracted by edges, borders, and zones of intersections, criss-crossings and crossovers, rather than self-appointed, self-important, big-time 'centres'. So, I took the quick way out and answered, "I'm going to chase butterflies," thinking of Georges Brassens's song, 'La chasse aux papillons'.

I lived in Yugoslavia from 1987 to 1990. I was 44 when I arrived and 47 when I left. During that time, I wrote many poems that would eventually find their way into *The Blue Butterfly*. Following my return to Cambridge in June 1990, I worked sporadically on the book, doing more research, following up various themes, and writing more poems as and when they appeared. I wasn't in a hurry. I knew that this book, with its inception in the synchronistic event of 1985, needed to gestate, emerge, and ripen in its own way and in its own time. I thought of this book as a single composite poem, an organic whole, rather than as a collection of disparate shorter pieces. As things turned out, it took me twenty years to complete. (Another way of putting this is that my little butterfly turned out to be a particularly heavy specimen, and that it took me twenty years to free myself from the almost weightless weight of its momentary touch on my finger.) The first English edition was followed by the Serbian,[14] and the translation was utilised as the oratorio for the open-air choral and dramatic commemoration at Šumarice in the same year.[15]

∽

After writing 'The blue butterfly' and 'Nada: hope or nothing' in 1985, very soon after my return to Cambridge from Serbia, I began to realise that something larger was gestating in me (gesturing to me), of which these two small poems were only indications (forerunners, harbingers). What this something was, or where it came from, I didn't understand at all. Even so, I did trust its source and its impetus, and did so instinctively. I also fully

---

[14] RB 2006a and RB 2007.

[15] *Veliki školski čas* (the 'Great School Lesson'), an event commemorating the massacre, held at Šumarice each October since 1957. See also RB 2011b: 136-137 and 140.

recognised what it was *doing* – which was *calling me* (*calling on me, calling me out*): to write. And while I could scarcely help recognise that these two small poems possessed their own intrinsic qualities of authenticity and depth, it dawned on me that they were also glimpses of a vastly larger and more extensive inner seam, which, so long as I was attentive and patient, I might possibly be capable of exploring and mining. This seam, I realised at the time, and expressed later, ran deep into and through my own personal psyche, both as a Jew and as a poet, entwining these two lodes. And from responses to these poems in Serbia, later on I also realised how deeply it runs through the intersubjective identity and history of the Serbian people too. This set of discoveries surfaced very slowly and gradually: it assembled itself piecemeal, during and along with the composition of the book itself, evidently incorporating (embodying) my full volition, while somehow appearing of its own accord and revealing the whole of itself only in its own good time.

Evidently, my job was to listen, watch, scry, follow, delve – and keep listening and watching for the deeper sources of these two initial poems. Eventually, my butterfly-experience and the poems that flowed out of it would touch and activate (resonate) an archetypal chord not only in myself but in others.

☙

In the Greek tradition, the paradigmatic call to the poet to compose and to sing is delivered, mysteriously, by one of the Muses, daughters of Mnemosyne, goddess of Memory, and of Zeus, king of the Gods. The nine daughters of Memory are the nurses, guides, and guardians of poetic inspiration. In the opening of his epic masterpiece, *Paradise Lost*, John Milton calls on his Muse, Urania: "Sing heavenly muse."[16] Urania, highest of the Muses and patroness of astronomy, is named after the heavenly god Uranus, or Ouranos. Even in Modern Greek, the word *ουρανός* means 'sky'. Who, then, was calling me, on me, calling me out? Certainly, not Urania.

I had felt, even during or immediately after the event, that the butterfly landing on my hand was a message that involved the soul. I knew, too, that in ancient Greek the single word *ψυχή* (ancestor of our word *psyche*) meant *both* 'butterfly' *and* 'soul'. What's more, in my mind, as I stood outside the museum gate at Šumarice, it wasn't so much that

[16] Milton 5: Book 1, l. 6.

the butterfly symbolised the soul in any conventional modern sense, but that *butterfly and soul were one*. And this integral cognitive and linguistic connection between butterfly and soul, through the word *ψυχή*, occurred to me at that time. Whether this recognition happened simultaneously with the butterfly landing on my finger or in the nanoseconds after it, I can't be sure; but, certainly, this meaning (meaningfulness) was key to both the core-event and the entire experience. And as for this *particular* butterfly, I was now coming to think of it as 'my' butterfly, sensing that I had a special bond with it. And I began to have extensive discussions with myself about the creature; and in some of these, I found myself addressing the creature as *part of myself.*

Clearly, then, my Muse was *ψυχή*, the butterfly-soul. And this entity or being had already 'chosen' me, simply by sitting on the forefinger of my writing hand. Equally clearly, this Muse of mine scarcely belonged to the Empyrean (aetherial) heights, but rather to the lower air, and to the gates between life and death. I recognised, too, that these gates had been opened up to me – in me, and through me – gradually and progressively, ever since 1957, when as an Anglo-Jewish boy of thirteen growing up in London, I had first learned about the Nazi Holocaust.[17]

Nor did I need anyone to explain to me that, in Greek mythology, the gates between life and death are those between this world and the Underworld, ruled over by Hades and his queen, Persephone, daughter of Demeter. I knew too, that the myth of Persephone enacts (re-enacts, embodies, encapsulates) the natural annual cycle and the theme (motif, imagem, symbol – and also archetype) of *rebirth*,[18] even though it didn't occur to me consciously at that time to connect this intellectual (bookish, theoretical) knowledge with the fullness of the emotional (heuristic, transformational) experience that I was undergoing in the wake of this synchronistic event.

Thinking of this (and thinking it through) in retrospect, as I write this account in 2019, thirty-four years later, it's clear to me that the meaning of the proximity of the massacre and the butterfly-soul or soul-butterfly in the synchronistic event, involves *rebirth*. And at the time, to me at least, an immediate, direct coincidence (connection, link, mesh, merging, bind, bond) was established between the butterfly and the massacre. This involved a *metamorphosis* – perhaps even a *metempsychosis*.

[17] See RB 2020a, 'My Anne Frank'.

[18] Jung *CW8* 2014 [1960]: 439, §845. See also the 'Afterword' to this essay, 36-37 below.

Even so, if I were to interpret the creature as a perfectly articulated materialisation (embodiment, incarnation, appearance, epiphany) of the soul, the question was, *whose*? At some point in this inner debate with myself, now indiscernible and unrecapturable, I developed the sense that the butterfly's message to me wasn't only personally directed *at* me – *to* me, *for* me – but that it was entirely clear and very simple. After all, the creature had come, whether by chance, accident, or 'of its own accord', to sit on the forefinger of my writing hand, no-one else's. Wasn't there, then, at least according to the mode of thinking that I was applying then – and am also and still applying here – that is, the ancient, Neolithic, symbolic, mythical, mythopoeic mode of poetry, rooted in correspondences and their accretions – wasn't there at the very least a kind of *elective affinity* between my writing hand and this soul-butterfly or butterfly-soul?

As for the inner meaning of my butterfly's message, my sense developed that I was being directed (asked, tasked), *called* (*called on*, *called out*), told (and even tolled – almost as if I were some kind of bell) – to write about (and to write out) the massacre. This calling to me at least was as clear as any call (or call-out or call-up) possibly could be, delivered in the soul's own code-language,[19] a code that had no need of human words. Its meaning and meaningfulness were self-evident, in the blue butterfly's arrival on my writing hand.

January–February 2018

[19] See Hillman 1975 and 1979.

Afterword: the Butterfly, the Soul and Rebirth

Any child who has watched any one of the mysterious transitions in the life-cycle of a butterfly – from egg to caterpillar, from caterpillar to chrysalis, and from chrysalis to flying adult (imago) – is likely to be enthralled by the experience. And it's a small leap from this natural observation to an adult's understanding of how in ancient Greece this creature should have become identified with ψυχή, the soul, and to have evolved as a symbol for both emergence and transformation. For, since the transformations in a butterfly's life are visible embodiments of natural metamorphoses, by extension and analogy they're evidently interpretable in terms of both rebirth and metempsychosis.

C. G. Jung introduces the key theme of rebirth into his famous discussion of his patient's dream of a scarab, which was followed by a similar insect flying in through the window of his consulting room during an analytical session with the same patient. This episode has almost come to be read as a paradigm for his theory of synchronicity itself:

> It was an extraordinarily difficult case to treat, and up to the time of the dream little or no progress had been made. [...] Evidently something quite irrational was needed which was beyond my powers to produce. The dream alone was enough to disturb ever so slightly the rationalistic attitude of my patient. But when the "scarab" came flying in through the window *in actual fact*, her natural being could burst through the armour of her animus possession and the *process of transformation* could at last begin to move. Any essential change of attitude signifies a *psychic renewal* which is usually accompanied by *symbols of rebirth* in the patient's dreams and fantasies. The scarab is a classic example of a rebirth symbol.[20]

In commenting on the transpersonal or archetypal nature of this episode, Roderick Main writes:

> Whether or not the patient in the incident [...] had prior exposure to images of scarabs, and whether or not she could have acquired from her personal experience a disposition to produce symbols of rebirth, the synchronicity suggests that *some factor larger than her personal psyche has been involved in the organisation of the events* – a factor that *encompasses the external world of nature* in addition to her psychic world.[21]

---

[20] Jung *CW8* 2014 [1960]: 439, §845; emphasis added.

[21] Main 2014: 133; and see also 18-19 and 22; emphases added.

And he adds:

> Further, as Jung's example of the scarab beetle indicated, the content of synchronistic events is often *mythic*. This is not surprising if we bear in mind that, for Jung, *synchronistic events are based on the activation of archetypes and myths are the narrative elaboration of archetypal motifs.*[22]

Jung's and Main's perspectives richly inform my 'understanding' of the incident of the blue butterfly landing on my hand. Experientally, this event involved both the process of transformation and of psychic renewal. It included a factor larger than the personal psyche in the organisation of the events, and this factor not only encompassed the external world of nature, but did so in ways that activated archetype and myth. And even though the word 'understanding', with all its connotations of logically presented, rationally argued, causally derived, and consciously motivated and directed interpretation, is hardly the right one here – since the core of whatever I do 'understand' remains richly incomprehensible, radically inexplicable, ineluctably acausal, and ineffably mysterious – in short, entirely beyond me – I still can't think of any better word. This event changed my life, and it still resonates in and through me. I return to it again and again, and it won't let me go. But that's all right. The blue butterfly binds me into joy. For whatever may come after it, to have been visited even just once by the muse in a form that the Greeks designated as that of the soul itself, can scarcely be construed as anything less than a blessing.

June 26–28, 2019

---

[22] *ibid.* 163; emphases added.

Three poems from *The Blue Butterfly*

The blue butterfly

On my Jew's hand, born out of ghettos and shtetls,
raised from unmarked graves of my obliterated people
in Germany, Latvia, Lithuania, Poland, Russia,

on my hand mothered by a refugee's daughter,
first opened in blitzed London, grown big
through post-war years safe in suburban England,

on my pink, educated, ironical left hand
of a parvenu not quite British pseudo gentleman
which first learned to scrawl its untutored messages

among Latin-reading rugby-playing militarists
in an élite boarding school on Sussex's green downs
and against the cloister walls of puritan Cambridge,

on my hand weakened by anomie, on my
writing hand, now of a sudden willingly
stretched before me in Serbian spring sunlight,

on my unique living hand, trembling and troubled
by this May visitation, like a virginal
leaf new sprung on the oldest oak in Europe,

on my proud firm hand, miraculously blessed
by the two thousand eight hundred martyred
men, women and children fallen at Kragujevac,

a blue butterfly simply fell out of the sky
and settled on the forefinger
of my international bloody human hand.

NADA : HOPE OR NOTHING

Like a windblown seed, not yet rooted
or petal from an impossible moonflower, shimmering,
unplucked, perfect, in a clear night sky,

like a rainbow without rain, like the invisible
hand of a god stretching out of nowhere
to shower joy brimful from Plenty's horn,

like a greeting from a child, unborn, unconceived,
like an angel, bearing a gift, a ring, a promise,
like a visitation from a twice redeemed soul,

like a silent song sung by the ghost of nobody
to an unknown, sweet and melodious instrument
buried ages in the deepest cave of being,

like a word only half heard, half remembered,
not yet fully learned, from a stranger's language,
the sad heart longs for, to unlock its deepest cells,

a blue butterfly takes my hand and writes
in invisible ink across its page of air
Nada, Elpidha, Nadezhda, Esperanza, Hoffnung.

The telling (first attempt)

In that moment, I remembered nothing
but became memory. I was being.
And as for *before*? *Before* – a mouthing
of half-dumb shadows had been my hearing
and tunnels sculpted and bored through fearing
the whole bolstered scope of my seeing.

Now my ears awakened in an alert
attentive and percipient listening
to scoured shells of voices, wholly prised apart
from those dead mouths, pouring their testament
onto spring wind, stirred by the instrument
of the butterfly at rest on my finger, glistening.

And I saw the May morning sun shoot fire
on the hillsides, which still glowed green, intact,
and those massed children, I heard as a choir,
although still only schoolkids, who chattered.
Nothing was marred or maimed. Everything mattered.
Matter was miracle. Miracle was fact.

As though an index to the infinite
library of nature and history
had tumbled into me, and a fortunate
finding of buried keys, of forgotten
reference and disappeared quotation
had filled my sight, as gift, as mystery,

all was ordinary, still – and, yet, otherness
without seam. The world didn't sheer away
but was its very self, no more nor less
than ever, but tuned now to its own being,
and the heard and seen were hearing, seeing,
spirit within spiral, wave within way.

A Grove of Trees and a Grove of Stones

In Kraljevo, the visitor approaches the site of the 1941 massacre across a narrow iron pedestrian bridge that spans the main railway line. The afternoon I went there, workers from the nearby train-carriage factory, where the Nazis' victims had been assembled, were pouring over this bridge and thronging the station platform on the other side of it, on their way home from their day-shifts. At first sight, the setting seems ordinary, humdrum, workaday, typical of any small town in Šumadija, in Yugoslavia, in Europe.

Then, from the top of the bridge, one catches sight of a massive, stepped semicircle, carved into the facing hillside like an ancient Greek theatre, and below that, a grove of trees and a grove of stones. The trees are poplars: tall, slender, their branches finger the sky in constant, quiet motion. It was a sunny day in early September, and against the foot of one tree, a young couple leaned, arm in arm in the shade: a picture out of any park in the world. Only the stones stand inanimate and fixed, carved into the shapes of waist-high truncated pillars, bleak whitened monoliths proffering their silent, brooding commentary on the movement all around. They represent felled trees: individual lives brutally cut down.

A grove of trees and a grove of stones. No combination of physical forms could more simply and fittingly symbolise what occurred here. This is a place of which there are too many in Yugoslavia, where life and death meet and merge. If Kraljevo is to mean anything to the world for the atrocity that took place here in October 1941, our human responsibility is surely to try, as best as we can, to understand the significance of this meeting point. It's one thing to respond with strong feelings here. That isn't hard. Understanding, though, is more difficult, perhaps even impossible. Yet if the Kraljevos of the world are really to be prevented from ever happening again, this challenge has to be met. Understanding is necessary, crucial. Civilisation depends on it.

It's in the nature of memory to dig and forage in the past: that's its operational zone, its field of exploration. Its passage is always downwards and back, as far as consciousness can carry us, even to our individual births. Here what's normally called consciousness comes to a full stop. Yet memory itself knows no barriers here, but is willing to take us still further back, through history, through the stages of evolution, even deeper down – through the realms of the dead – and then, patiently to escort us back up to the healing surface of the present.

This being so, memory tends to attach itself to the irrevocable and irrecoverable. So memory all too easily undergoes a kind of transference in our thinking, until we see it as a property belonging only to the dead, with as little bearing on our present lives as a fossil. And so, memory, to some people, simply conjures up the image of a monument, a still and lifeless block, an impassive sculpted slab – a finality.

Yet memory belongs to the living, the sentient. It's a function of life, continuously in movement – and if it's attributed to the dead this can only be so because the dead live on, in us.

We, who are living, all have our own dead: our loved ones, our friends, our family, tribe, people – a whole series of concentric human circles, expanding in us with years like the rings inside a tree. And though our dead often seem distant from us, and although their deaths have inevitably made them strangers, still they belong to us so intimately, and still they seem to regard us with such gentle familiarity, that it might almost be said: we belong to them. Even if there's an almost impermeable membrane between us and them – or perhaps a one-way screen, which on our side, at least, is opaque – we know all too well that, one day, we shall join them, and to those we leave behind us, as well as to the unborn, we shall become what our own dead are to us now.

Whenever the dead speak to us, it's always as a private voice heard inside us, from the depths of our own selves. The dead know nothing of statistics. Their voices are always warm, human, loaded with multi-layered meanings: *alive* – whether they seem passionate or detached, close or distant, fleshed or disembodied – and even if we can't always decipher the codes of their messages, they're carried to us through the underground mazes of memory. We know that certain objects can act as powerful receivers and transmitters for them: things, for example, that belonged to our dead in their lifetimes, which have since passed down to us: a ring, a locket, a photograph; an armchair, a room, a whole house. And the entrance to those labyrinthine channels and tunnels can open anywhere, anytime, often taking us by surprise, because it's located precisely in objects and occurrences we hardly even notice any longer, for the simple reason that they're so familiar: a mirror, a cup, a stone; a melody, a perfume, a word. Constantly the dead remind us that whatever is around us is also inside us, that the mysterious stuff we're made of is shared with all other things and beings – wind, flowers, butterflies – and that this intimate connectedness threaded through creation really is the common miracle.

This community among things makes the dead belong to all of us. The dead have no property and know no possessive pronouns. They observe none of the silly frontiers that obsess the living. Your dead and my dead are one kin. Their peaceful, quiet, impossibly simple language is universal, and its name is: Memory. So, full possession of the faculty of memory is a necessary condition for claiming the title: human being. Memory of the dead, as a constant presence among the living, and memory of the living, unafraid to listen to the voices of the dead, are interconnected links in the chain of being. Not for nothing did the Greeks call Mnemosyne, their goddess of memory, 'Mother of the Muses' – of the poet's inspiration. If for poet we read 'human', and for inspiration 'life' and 'liberty', this ancient myth makes all too poignant sense in our own century: Memory as mother of human life and liberty, insisting on honouring her dead, relentlessly opposing all artificial attempts to reduce her children to ciphers.

Perhaps this helps us towards understanding the mentality of those who perpetrated the atrocities at Kraljevo, and so many other places. Such a mentality not only directs its total attention and energy to separating one living human person from another whether according to race, religion, nationality, or whatever criterion – but also to denying access between the living and the dead. The denial of these natural connections, based on a limited and therefore distorted view of the universe, results in a carefully planned attempt to 'reprogramme' it according to some apparently more convenient, but always reductive theory. Beneath the superficially efficient and cool military exterior, which is meant to operate is a totally effective armour, such a mentality is frightened, spineless, group-dominated, and easily organisable to utterly ruthless behaviour; and it finds the silent voices of the dead either irrelevant or intolerably threatening and disturbing. They must be shut out at all costs. And shutting out the dead means the abolition of memory. An African proverb says, "When a human being dies, a whole great library goes up in flames." So it's no accident that two of the most common expressions of this mentality, which frequently occur together, are the reduction of human beings to numbers, records, statistics, all meticulously tabulated to mask the underlying reality – tattoos on forearms, gassings in trucks and death factories, mass round-ups and executions – and the burning of books, of libraries. But it says something for humanity that even in our bloody century, all the mechanistic and reductionist social experiments conducted by such mentalities eventually collapse. The dead cannot be wiped out of us, the living. They refuse to be silenced. They go on speaking in and through us. They insist on it. Even so, the mentality of those who committed the atrocities at Kraljevo can creep up unawares on any one of us, like an 'emotional plague'.[23] There are still plenty of people who are afraid or have forgotten how to listen to the dead. Remembering the dead is a necessary guardianship of our freedoms, of all we most cherish. Another name for memory is: History.

In Yugoslavia, ordinary people still look each other directly in the eyes when they talk to each other. This frank, clear look occurs ritually, for example, whenever two people toast one another, raising their glasses not just with a wish for 'Good Health', as in my country, but for life itself (*'Živeli!'*).[24] Foreigners don't always notice this, but when they do, this simple, courteous acknowledgement of the full humanity of other people is seen as a radiant grace, a great treasure, a complete recognition of connectedness. But in these eyes, a blacker light also shines. For in Yugoslavia, the dead aren't only buried all around beneath us, but they seem very close to the surface. The land still brims so unbearably with these recent dead, and the memories of the living are still so, paradoxically, alive with images of them, that I can't help almost physically seeing and hearing their gone presences. George Seferis, twentieth century Greek, Balkan and universal poet, wrote: "It's painful and difficult, the living are not enough for me / first because they do not speak, and then / because I have to ask the dead / in order to go farther. / There's no other way… / The dead must guide me."[25] The dead should guide us, everywhere.

A grove of stones and a grove of trees. Memory isn't just a monument: cold, detached, immortal. Memory is a living tree: it has its roots, sap, bark and its inner ring of years, its knotty boughs and sturdy hardwood trunk, and its greenwood shoots that bend and sway in the wind. Like a tree, memory withers only to live again, it hibernates to bloom. And from this tree of memory, when it's cut down, we can make woodwind

---

[23] The phrase was coined by Wilhelm Reich. See, for example, Reich 1975 [1971]: 14, 54; Reich 1973: 401, 403, 410; and Boadella 392 (index).

[24] *živeti* 'to live', *živ* 'alive', *život,* 'life'. See also Skok 1973, vol. 3: 681-682.

[25] 'Stratis Thalassinos among the Agapanthi', in Seferis 281.

instruments for music, tables for bread and wine, furniture to stock our homes with, and gates and doors and windows.

As the workers of this small town go home across the railway bridge, Kraljevo reminds us that we the living, are the gatekeepers of memory, fully formed and informed by the voices of the dead. In remembering them we're the forest keepers, guardians of the tree of life which gives oxygen to the born and the unborn, protectors of the future. At the foot of this tree, a pair of young lovers embrace. Theirs is the common miracle.

Belgrade, 1989

A Model of Truth-Telling

Jevreji Kragujevcu ('The Jews of Kragujevac'), a historical monograph by Staniša Brkić and Milomir Minić, is a book that carries far greater weight and importance than its slimness might at first suggest. Its theme is the history of the Jews of Kragujevac in the context of Serbian history. Inevitably, its most intense focus is on the obliteration of that community during and after the massacres of October 1941. So the book combines the widest possible panoramic perspectives ('Jews on Serbian soil', 'Jews in Serbia', 'the Second World War in Serbia', etc.) with close-up views of one particular small minority in one particular Serbian town, leading up to precisely the moment of that minority's destruction in October 1941, continuing with its aftermath in the terrible fates of Jewish women and children in the Staro Sajmište and Banjica concentration camps in Belgrade in early 1942, and concluding with the consequences today.

Close-ups are the book's core. So we learn snippets of information about where the Jews of Kragujevac came from, their names, families, jobs and professions, their wealth or lack of it, their education and training, their clubs, sporting and leisure pursuits, the names and dates of birth of their children, how they behaved when they were captured and taken to be shot, and how a very few escaped. And we learn of their own desperation and heroic bravery, and the heroic bravery of some Serbs who helped and hid them.

The result of these interwoven perspectives is profoundly insightful and there are wider implications of many kinds for readers. For one thing, from the wealth of detail, from the piling on of fact after incidental fact, one can hardly help thinking – how real these people of Kragujevac were, in some ways so fine, so brave, so heroic, and in others so inconsequential, so typical, so ordinary. In short, how very much like most of us.

While the roll call of names and families is always modestly stated and dignified, it's never just a catalogue. In much of the genealogical writing, the undertone of mourning is ever-present, and at times even the unmistakable burden of a kind of slowly mounting drone, like that of an unstoppable Old Testament lamentation, seems to arise from somewhere deep down within the book's limpid and transparent language. And in all the detail there's always a discernible pattern: the details of the lives and deaths reveal the pattern, and vice-versa. So the double sense of intimacy and monumentality criss-crosses the entire book.

Of course, under this fabric, behind the writing, in order to reveal such richness of detail, a kind of archaeology has been performed. A huge field of collective memory and interpretation whose superficial texture may seem familiar has been excavated and re-excavated by the authors with meticulous and painstaking precision. Their evidence includes artefacts, photographs, official documents, and oral and written testimonies of victims, witnesses, survivors and their families. All existing 'facts' have been examined, re-examined and re-combined with new findings. Both as normative 'good historical practice' and specifically because of the tortured knots, twists and tangles of Serbian history and the shifts in ideologies over the last sixty years, the interpretations of all previous commentators and analysts have had to be tested and revalued.

Such a deconstructive method is of course necessarily slow, patient, quiet, and modest. Nor is such an endeavour easy to carry out and there are no short cuts. Stamina and dedication are needed. So is constant and disciplined application of the intellectual constraint of doubt to the passionate and sometimes unruly desire for truth-at-all-costs.

ꟾ

Backed by the wider historical contextualisations provided by Milomir Minić, who used to work in the Library of the National Museum in Belgrade, the previous works of Staniša Brkić as researcher, historiographer and curator have direct bearings on our understanding of this present book.

Staniša Brkić is the leading and the most distinguished contemporary expert in the world on the Kragujevac massacres of October 1941. As Head of the 21st October Memorial Museum since 1992, and as a senior scholarly researcher at the Kragujevac October Memorial Park at Šumarice since 1982, his professional job has first and foremost necessitated detailed factual knowledge of the massacres themselves and of all relevant events surrounding them. It might fairly be said, then, that the duty of historical research that has been placed upon Mr. Brkić has led him inexorably to examine and investigate what happened to the town's Jews, as one component in the overall tragedy.

Even so, focus on the fate of the Kragujevac Jews as a major topic of study in its own right was by no means demanded of him and less still inevitable. Yet in terms of both human values and scholarship, Mr. Brkić's decision to devote a book to the Kragujevac Jewish tragedy combined with the specific qualities of the result provides an important model for future historical research, as I'll now show.

ശ

Among many passages from Staniša Brkić's previous publications that might be quoted to cast light on his research methods and on the values upon which these are founded, two short extracts seem particularly apposite. The first comes from his bilingual Serbian and English information leaflet entitled *Kragujevačka tragedija / the Kragujevac Tragedy.* With the utmost carefulness and precision, Mr. Brkić writes:

> In our unofficial sources, estimates of the number of people killed range from 3,000 to 8,000. The State Commission for war crimes in Kragujevac, which was set up in 1945, verified that 2,324 people were shot on 20 and 21 October 1941. This figure does not include the victims who were killed in the surrounding villages. [...] Basing its figures on research into all available sources, the 21st October Memorial Museum has at its disposal the data that 2,797 men, women and children were executed: 411 victims on 19 October, 114 on 20 October and 2,272 on 21 October. According to the research so far completed, 61 people survived the executions.[26]

In this passage, Staniša Brkić has simply stuck to the facts that he has verified by his own personal research. By doing so, he has gently, firmly and once-and-for-all exploded the myth of the 'magical' number 7,000 that by now has been linked all over the world to those who perished in the Kragujevac massacres. Furthermore, in exploding this particular myth, he has implicitly challenged the repetitive and familiar cycles of all those myths built on hearsay, hearsay built on lies, lies built on myths (and so on) that are the perennial weapons of the moulders of public opinion who 'require' the compliance, complicity and conformity of 'ordinary' folk.

In the second passage, from his longer study *Ime i broj* ('Name and Number'), we see exactly the same kind of quiet, definite, authoritative statement, but with implications that are even more trenchant:

---

[26] Brkić (undated), trans. Vera V. Radojević and RB.

> A number of historians have written about the massacre in Kragujevac within the framework of other, wider topics. A very small number of them have dedicated their writing to this topic alone. Even though both German and Serbian historical sources have been either fully accessible or fully available to them, they have chosen not to use them. Instead they have remained imprisoned in symbolism and therefore in default of historical science and historical truth. Not one single objective study on the shooting in Kragujevac has been written to this day: that is, no study free from the fetters and errors of ideologies and myths, based on documentation, and thus fully and properly honouring the requirements and principles of historical science.[27]

What's notable here isn't only Staniša Brkić's commendable reticence, but his total commitment to "historical science", that is, to history as a scientific discipline, and thus to historical truth, despite (and even in the face of) "oppression, ideological prejudice and myth". Clearly, then, none of the constrictions and excesses of ideologies, whether of religious creed or political affiliation, affect Staniša Brkić's cool judgement. As for his own values, it might well be argued that these consist, precisely, in his determined, even dogged loyalty to the objective truth that must necessarily underpin honest scholarship, just as it must underpin justice itself.

All of this of course inspires our confidence: that Staniša Brkić is independent, unbiased and therefore reliable. And connected and interwoven into our sense of authorial trustworthiness is yet another sense: how cleanly the language of these two Serbian historians embodies Vuk Karadžić's advice, "Write as you speak." It's well known that the achievement of a transparent style (a style that isn't a style) is no mean technical feat. But such an achievement isn't simply 'literary'. This book's clarity of diction itself reveals qualities of mind and character. From the transparency of their language, the reader immediately realises how dignified, how respectful and how humane is the world-view of these two Serbian historians.

As far as Staniša Brkić's work in and around Kragujevac is concerned, the humanity that he brings to his research, inspiring trust and confidence among the many individuals in Šumadija with whom he has come in contact in the course of his work, above all when he has had to present searching painful questions to survivors and families of victims. Those of us lucky enough to know him personally will readily attest this combination of qualities.

∽

[27] Brkić 2007: 9; trans. Vera V. Radojević and RB.

I think it's no exaggeration to say that Staniša Brkić has brought about a quiet revolution in our overall understanding of the Kragujevac tragedy. Though this achievement is by no means his alone, his work has been at the forefront of much needed post-Tito and post-Titoist revaluation. This is important for many reasons, not least because the Kragujevac massacre marked a crucial turning point in the Second World War in Yugoslavia. Today, the results of Staniša Brkić's day-to-day research into the 1941 massacres are clearly visible. They've involved: first, reorganisation of the exhibits in the Šumarice Memorial Museum; second, the publication of several new and revised information brochures; and, third, his authoritative study *Ime i broj: Kragujevačka tragedija 1941* ('Name and number: the Kragujevac Tragedy 1941', 2007).

With regard to the tragedy of the Kragujevac Jews, his achievement is no less remarkable, even though in this present book, with typical modesty he has taken pains to avoid mentioning his own crucial role. First, there was the establishment of the *Kragujevac Serbian-Jewish Friendship Association* in 1989, which was founded only thanks to his dedicated and persistent work behind the scenes. Second, again through his efforts, relations were established in 1991 between the Kragujevac October Memorial Park and the Yad Vashem Holocaust Museum in Jerusalem. And third, thanks again to his work and advocacy, despite institutional lethargy and some degree of local bureaucratic opposition, fifty years to the day after the first Nazi massacre of Jews and Serbs in Kragujevac, on October 20, 1991, a monument was dedicated at the site with inscriptions in Serbian and Hebrew. And, fourth, now there is this book.

We await further developments from his research whenever the time is ripe, for many important questions about the Kragujevac tragedy still remain unanswered. Furthermore, owing to an extraordinarily complicated history over the last sixty years, Serbia is a field that's still full of puzzling, hidden, and disturbing secrets concerning the tragic fates of thousands of individuals during and in the immediate aftermath of the Second World War. Many of these secrets are likely to remain forever buried. The work of historians of the calibre of Staniša Brkić and Milomir Minić gives us at least hope that some areas of this field, however small, may one day be excavated.

ᘓ

This book points out clearly that in the history of Serbian-Jewish relations, anti-Semitism did exist. Nineteenth century travellers to Belgrade from other countries pointed out the miserable conditions in the Belgrade Jewish community. However, to the credit of the Serbs, the point is also carefully made in the book that at no point in history did Serbs ever of their own accord organise pogroms of the kind that are the shame of many other countries in Europe. As far as local conditions were concerned shortly before the Second World War, we learn that:

> [b]ecause of Kragujevac's strong industries, members of many ethnic and religious groups lived there: Russians, Czechs, Germans, Slovenes, Croats, Muslims, Jews, Arumonians (Vlachs) and others; and among them harmonious relations were the general rule. It may be fairly stated too that relations towards the Jews were correct, indeed they were much more than that: there were a number of mixed marriages, [...] and many joint businesses and medical practices; and children got to know one another in games, sport, parties and entertainment, as adults did in politics and café life, on trips and outings, and through various local committees and philanthropic groups. [...] From the point of view of Kragujevac citizens, anti-Semitism seemed like something faraway and foreign.[28]

In contrast to this, the point is made at the end of the book that, despite a few mixed marriages:

> [...] in Kragujevac there are no longer any Jews left alive who were born before the War. Nor are there any young people who have both a Jewish mother and a Jewish father. There are a few descendants who were born in mixed marriages. Naturally they respect both Serbian and Jewish traditions and customs.[29]

In their perverted and depraved way, the Nazis and their collaborators all over Europe seem to have genuinely believed that the 'elimination' of their Jews would bring them 'purification', even ennoblement. But we know now that every country in Europe from which Jews were eradicated has suffered not only a loss of diversity, talent and depth but also an immediate brutalisation from which it has still not fully recovered. For such coarsening always involves an insidious, long-term malaise: a thinning, narrowing and cheapening of human values, and a corresponding thickening and constricting of racial and tribal myths around clarity of judgement. The same truth applies, of course, to every society in which any kind of racism is condoned. In the face of all such

[28] Brkić and Minić 59; trans. Vera V. Radojević and RB.

[29] *ibid.* 87; trans. Vera V. Radojević and RB.

tendencies, the work of Staniša Brkić and Milomir Minić stands firm, upholding universal human dignity, civility and reason.

These last remarks may perhaps also suggest why, when one is reading *The Jews of Kragujevac*, gradually and almost without realising it one begins to realise that this book stands for far more than it says. The hidden thread that runs through it, which never even needs to be stated by its authors, shines through it so clearly that any reader with even the most basic knowledge of the material can scarcely avoid tracing it. For from its interweaving of meticulously researched historiographical detail with wider, fuller humane perspectives, the realisation dawns that this book could and should become a model, indeed a paradigm, for the work of future historians. As a model of historical truth-telling, this book by Staniša Brkić and Milomir Minić shows that the act of telling the truth, however late it comes, always brings relief to the living, offering clear breath, new life and renewed courage and hope.[30]

February 2010

[30] For my personal sketch of Staniša Brkić, see 398-402 below.

PART 2

MYTHS, HISTORIES, PRESENCES

The four pieces in this part of the book emerged from the writing of *In a Time of Drought*. I composed this poem in an intense, continuous burst through several months of the summer of 2000, at my home in Cambridge, in the immediate wake of both the Millennium and the NATO bombing of Serbia (March 24–June 10, 1999). It was completed before the arrest of Slobodan Milošević by Yugoslav federal authorities (March 29, 2001).

The multilayered themes of this long poem – or lyrical sequence of poems – were woven out of several distinct strands: the Balkan rainmaking rituals; contemporary politics; my approach to myth and symbol and belief in their 'deep' relevance to poetry and poetic composition; and my own personal life. As soon as I discovered the Serbian 'Dodola' figure, I recognised that here was the 'objective correlative' for these diverse motifs.[1] During composition, the ingathering and clustering of these multiple themes were entirely unexpected. The image of the Balkan rain-maiden magnetised and gripped me and, as if governed by a subterranean flood, the poem welled up through me. Based on the Balkan Dodola and Peperuda songs and customs, and dedicated to my then-ten-year-old daughter Arijana and "all my friends throughout and out of Yugoslavia", *In a Time of Drought* was both a response to the traumas of those years and an expression of hope and faith in the future.[2] I dedicated various sections of this poem to some of the writers – mainly poets – who had given me hospitality, welcome and friendship during my time in Yugoslavia, whom I'd been lucky enough to know in those years: Vasko Popa, Miodrag Pavlovic, Desanka Maksimović, Oskar Davičo, Ivan V. Lalić and Danilo Kiš, as well as to the English scholar E. D. Goy.[3]

☙

[1] Eliot 1961 [1919]: 145.

[2] See RB 2006b, 2008c, 2011c. The Serbian version (RB 2004, trans. Vera. V. Radojević) appeared two years before its first English edition. It received the *Morava Charter* international award in Mrčajevci in 2005 (see 242-243 below).

[3] For sketches of these friends and others, and tributes to them, see 'Sketches from Memory', 309ff below.

My post-compositional querying of *In a Time of Drought* and puzzling over its source materials have turned up what, for me, has been a treasure trove, both from studying the Balkan material itself in increasing depth and detail, and from further introspection. While the former procedure has yielded pan-Balkan historical connections and questions about cultural transmission across millennia, especially vis-à-vis comparative linguistics and comparative mythology, the latter has also led to a different *quality* and *degree* of understanding of some of the mental and psychological patterns involved in poetic composition itself.[4] With respect to the latter, I believe that any form of composition involving inspirational experience and material inevitably draws on archetypal layers. I also think a kind of poetic archaeology is involved in both aspects of this kind of exploration. While the ground one digs is singular, its dimensions are both external and internal; and any resultant discoveries are both exogenous and endogenous.

Images and symbols that occur in poems are rarely if ever consciously premeditated. Because they well up spontaneously from sources deeper than deliberative thought, they embed layers that are mysterious, polysemic and, invariably, surprising and unpredictable. The *I* that writes poems combines a 'self' that's apparently more-or-less identifiable, limited and directed, with an 'inner *other*' whose identity is impossible to cognize fully, if at all. This inner *other* is approachable only through partial hints, momentary inklings and tangential glances or soundings. What's more, over time, this *other* is likely to take on many forms and, for this reason, may well need to be recognised as plural: *others*. The *je* ('I') who writes poems, then, is likely to be not just *un autre* ('another, someone else'), as Arthur Rimbaud discovered in the first flash and flush of his genius, but *des autres* ('others, some others'), perhaps *plusieurs autres* ('several others') or, indeed, *many* others.[5] And whatever the source or sources of these *others*, during composition itself one often has the intuition that the images and symbols that get generated are *right*, in the sense that they *fit*, that they're *apt*, *apposite* (that they belong perfectly to their occasion, their *kairos*), and that they can't be evaded, altered or replaced. During

[4] Here, I use the present perfect (*has, have*) rather than the simple past tense because, as I write this (December 2019), this material is still alive in me. I still have notes on further material to explore.

[5] As a sixteen-year-old schoolboy, Rimbaud first formulated the statement *Je est un autre* ("I is another, I is someone else") in a letter dated 13 May 1871, addressed to his former teacher, Georges Izambard, also a poet (see Rimbaud 304-305). This single sentence was the seed of poetic modernism.

and after composition, their expression often seems impelled, propelled, compelled. Even so, retrospectively, they tend to defy analysis, for by their nature they aren't and can never can be rooted in reason alone. This vivid experience of 'another' voice or 'other' voices happened to me distinctly and noticeably in composing *In a Time of Drought.*

ᔕ

In the penultimate section of this poem, I found myself writing a group of stanzas about the *hajduk* or Balkan brigand. Rereading these lines later, I was astonished at the intensity with which this sardonic voice had risen up in me to challenge the 'heroic' aspects of this tradition:

> Whose daughter   whose daughter
> Shall heal this madness and this slaughter
>
> Shall it be sister of potter or miller
> Farmer or butcher or baker turned killer
>
> Orphaned child of woodman or ranger
> Or *hajduk* and ancient honour-revenger
>
> Or future bride of pig breeder or herder
> Turned gangster in rape   reveller in murder?[6]

Whose was this voice? And why these questions? I didn't know then and I still can't really say I do now. But as I realised that I needed to understand the *hajduk* tradition more fully, the first of the following essays, 'Edge-Dwellers, Bandit and Heroes', began to evolve out of my querying of these lines. In 2001, very soon after completing *In a Time of Drought,* I made a first version. But I sensed that there was more to be said, because numerous layers and aspects of understanding still eluded me. I reworked the essay in 2004 and 2008, and then, from time to time, modified it and added more detail, especially after reading books by various English travellers to the Balkans, and writings by the historian Traian Stoianovich. The present version received its very final additions and changes while I was editing this book in February 2020.[7]

---

[6] RB 2006: 24.

[7] The final version incorporates critical suggestions offered by Vesna Goldsworthy (email, Sept. 9, 2019) and Maria Todorova (email, Oct. 31, 2019). I'm very grateful to these scholars.

'Edge-Dwellers, Bandit and Heroes', then, explores the Balkan equivalent of what we would understand in English-speaking countries as the 'Robin Hood syndrome'. It does so mainly through investigation and analysis of the varied and often polarised meanings and associations, both heroic and villainous, carried by the term *hajduk* (pl. *hajduci*) itself; as well as by other names relating to similar groups and entities in the Balkans and elsewhere. In the course of these explorations, I gradually discovered that these terms configured an extraordinarily complex web, consisting of highwaymen, bandits, robbers, pirates, adventurers, outcasts, ne'er-do-wells and persons-of-no-fixed-abode, not to mention mercenaries, state-servants, policemen, enforcers, border-guards and private armies. Not only did I realise that this nexus included both 'villains' and 'heroes' – and many intermediate shades and gradations between them – but also that its connections were spread diffusely among and across various Balkan languages and cultures, as well as others, in an apparently haphazard, rhizome-like profusion, of the sort identified by Gilles Deleuze and Félix Guattari in *A Thousand Plateaus*. The basic premise underlying this essay, then, is that comparative linguistic exploration can yield insights into social and historical conditions, and vice-versa; and all the more so in this case, because many of these terms occur in more than one Balkan language, mainly through appropriation and assimilation owing to contiguity.

Gradually, I also found myself developing a deepening understanding of the complex political, economic and social conditions that led (tempted, enticed, forced, goaded) men into brigandage. And in this way, an increasing awareness of the figure of the 'part-time' bandit also emerged, who by degrees was moved to episodic rebellion and, eventually, to organised uprising. And once I had realised that, a further factor prompting me to research and write this piece was the gradually developing belief that, in every detail of the highly complex conflicts among the southern Slavs that culminated in the collapse of Yugoslavia at the end of the twentieth century, patterns of behaviour had come into play that were deeply rooted in the traditions of the *hajduk* and other similar groups.[8] What's more, since the destruction of the Twin Towers by Al-Qaeda on 11 September 2001, I've also come to believe that exploring the *hajduk* tradition can inform and possibly even illuminate aspects of our understanding of contemporary rebel movements far beyond the Balkan context.

Figures such as the *hajduk*, then, intrigued me for many reasons: poetic and linguistic, historical and contemporary, social and economic,

[8] The name 'Yugoslavia' means 'land of the southern Slavs', from *jugo* 'south'.

not to mention personal-infantile, for pirates and highwaymen had fascinated me since early boyhood. As one piece of information led to another, I found myself growing more and more curious about them.

ഗ

The other three essays in this part of the book are even more closely connected to *In a Time of Drought.* These pieces developed directly out of that poem and my fascination with the Balkan rainmaking customs themselves, which the process of composition itself, far from exhausting, served only to stimulate, so much so that my explorations have extended long after completing the poem itself, right up to the time of compiling this present book more than fifteen years later. The three completed essays I include here are: 'Dodola and Peperuda: The Balkan Rainmaking Customs (2004, 2006); 'Rain and Dust: Correspondance and *In a Time of Drought*' (2004, 2007); and 'How naked?' Notes and Queries on Vuk Karadžić's Dictionary Entries on *Dodola*' (2004, 2007, 2018, 2019).

Since Sir James Frazer mentioned the Dodola/Peperuda customs in his first instalment of *The Golden Bough* (1911),[9] followed by A. J. B. Wace and M. S. Thompson in their study of transhumant Vlachs (1914), so far as I know no other authors writing in English have explored or examined this Balkan ethnological material in any depth or detail, even though plenty of first-rate ethnologists, anthropologists, historical linguists and mythographers writing in Slavonic languages have done so. These include, most notably: in Bulgarian, Mikhail Arnaudov (1921); in Russian, Roman Jakobson (1950, 1964, 1985a, and 1985b), V. V. Ivanov and V. I. Toporov (1974), and Ana Plotnikova (1999); and in Serbian, Mila Bosić (1996), Dražen Nožinić (1998), as well as many others. My research relies on, sifts through, and synthesises the findings of these and earlier authors – including the pioneering Serbian scholar, Vuk Karadžić (1818, 1854, 1867), the Englishmen, Edward Tylor (1871) and W. R. S. Ralston (1872), the German, Jakob Grimm (1875, 1876), and the Serb, Dragutin Djordjević (1901) – all of whom have made major contributions to this field of study.

Quite apart from their connection to *In a Time of Drought*, what all four essays in this part of the book have in common is that, without my consciously planning in advance to apply any particular method or discipline to their making, I gradually found myself developing what

[9] Frazer 1911: 272-275.

could perhaps be called a kind of 'explorative hermeneutics'. If to the non-specialist this phrase sounds over-abstract and somewhat highfalutin, the way in which the process actually evolved was anything but that – and, anyway, I am (and decidedly remain) a non-specialist myself. What method there *was* consisted, rather, of a fumbling, clumsy, uncertain, and often even bungling process of trial-and-error that, in its preliminary stages, could scarcely deserve to be called any kind of 'procedure' at all. But by following my nose, and through discursive reading in various fields, I gradually found my way into comparative philology, along with all its delights, temptations, traps, and pitfalls.

All these essays are research-based.

December 2019–February 2020

Edge-dwellers, Bandits and Heroes[10]

In memory of Zygmunt Bauman (1925–2017)

> Ever since the sea gave shelter to coherent societies, banditism made its entry, never to disappear again. Isn't it still alive today too? Terribly alive?[11] —Fernand Braudel

In the brilliant essay from which this epigraph is taken, whose title 'Misère et banditisme' is itself a powerful statement, Fernand Braudel paints a picture of ubiquitous banditry, brigandage and outlawry around and across the entirety of Europe, the Mediterranean, North Africa and the Middle East from the fourteenth to the seventeenth centuries. He describes a hidden war that few spoke about, one that was *always present*, always being waged at some low level.

This is true today too, except that the level is scarcely low, the terminology has changed, the danger-zone is global, and the 'war against terror' is on everyone's lips, especially those of politicians and journalists. Depending where you are and who you are, for 'bandit' or 'brigand' read *terrorist* or *freedom fighter*; for 'highwayman' read *hijacker*; for 'vagabond' read *refugee*, or rather, for 'refugee' read *illegal immigrant*; and so on.

ᔕ

In the context of the global scale of current social misery, injustice and inequality, I believe that the combined history, sociology and folklore of

[10] Shortly before finalising this essay, in December 2019, I came across Professor Wendy Bracewell's paper '"The Proud Name of Hajduks": Bandits as Ambiguous Heroes in Balkan Politics and Culture' (2003). This short study explores ways in which, historically, the *hajduk* has been interpreted (i.e. stereotyped and evaluated) inside and outside Balkan territories. While there are many points in common between Dr. Bracewell's paper and this essay, I haven't tried to integrate her very fine insights here.

[11] Braudel 1947: 43; trans. RB; and see also Braudel 1995, esp. vol. 2: 1369-1370 (index).

banditism over the ages presents not just a fascinating and highly complex phenomenon but a huge contemporary challenge. I think it may be helpful, and possibly even illuminating, to glance at some aspects of this nexus in the Balkans, and to attempt to tease out some threads and sketch out some patterns, especially in the wake of events such as: the break-up of Yugoslavia, fostered and hastened by the imperialistic war between NATO and Serbia, which resulted in an almost uncannily predictable illustration of the cliché *Balkanisation*; the continuing Israeli-Palestinian conflict, ever-present and frequently exploding, as in Gaza in winter 2008–2009, and at predictably regular intervals since then; the bombings in Washington and New York on September 11, 2001, followed by the American-led war against the Taleban, the invasion of Iraq and overthrow of Saddam Hussein by the so-called Coalition of the USA, the UK, and others; the Israel-Lebanon conflict of 2006, and ongoing conflicts relating to Palestine; the establishment and apparent defeat of the Islamic State, *aka* ISIS or *Daesh* (1999–2019); and the ongoing struggle against *Boko Haram*.[12] Any such list needs to be updated quite regularly. This monograph may also have bearings, even if small ones, on the prevalent phenomenon of suicide bombing in the context of 'Western' ('rich', 'powerful') and 'Non-Western' ('poor', 'powerless') cross-national, national, social, ethnic and religious groups.

ꟹ

The procedure I'll adopt will first involve exploration of a number of words, concepts and associations in several languages, some though not all of which are etymologically related, and mainly, though not exclusively, in the Balkans. The premise is that the exploration of words and their meanings and associations is capable of at least illuminating and possibly even unlocking 'hidden' aspects of history – across linguistic borders, just as within them. To some extent, the procedure will also involve checking, comparing and at times even challenging those apparently most authoritative (and authoritarian) of sources: dictionary definitions. To build up patterns, there will be some hopping and jumping, and some drifting too, from term to term. In these respects (those of *hopping*, *jumping*, *drifting*, etc.), the procedure for enquiry will re-enact aspects of the history itself.

I must add that what follows has no claims to be exhaustive but is

[12] The word *haram* here means 'forbidden'. Derived from Arabic, it's cognate with *harambaša* and Eng. *harem*: see also 96-97 below.

intended rather as a sketch: a preliminary exploration both of a field and of a comparativist method of enquiry. In this respect I'm strongly aware of my own personal limitations as a linguist. Richer and deeper exploration of linguistic associations in Albanian, Arabic, Bulgarian, Hungarian, Macedonian, Romanian, Romany and Turkish needs to be brought together for a more thorough investigation – not to mention Arabic, Kurdish and others.

ഗ

First, some examination of a knot of relevant and related words and concepts, beginning from within the perspectives of former Yugoslavia.[13]

---

[13] In 1945 the Yiddish linguist Max Weinreich wrote, "A shprakh iz a diyalekt mit an armey un a flot" ("A language is a dialect with an army and a navy"). Before the break-up of Yugoslavia in the 1990s, when it came to the official and respectable designation for the majority national language, which was (and still is) mutually comprehensible across Bosnia and Herzegovina, Croatia, Montenegro, and Serbia, terms such as Serbo-Croat, Serbo-Croatian, Croatian-Serbian, etc. were generally considered adequate and acceptable. Following the collapse of the Yugoslav Federation – at least partly thanks to the presence of various armies (and navies), both public and private, officially recognised and otherwise – it became unacceptable to speakers of any one republic to identify the name of their own language variety with that of another group. Hence the separation of the terms Bosnian (*bosanski*), Croatian (*hrvatski*), Serbian (*srpski*), all of which have become politically correct in the exact and narrow meaning of that term. This is clearly neither a resolved nor an easily resolvable matter. For further amplification, see Djurić (2016): xx-xxi.

However, very recently, there has been an attempt by writers from Bosnia and Herzegovina, Croatia, Montenegro and Serbia, to recognise that one mutually comprehensible language is indeed spoken in all four countries. With its focus on cultural reintegration and political reconciliation, this cultural movement produced a declaration in 2017. It also organises meetings and seminars. See 'Declaration on the Common Language', *Wikipedia*. In the wake of the disintegration of Yugoslavia in the last decade of the twentieth century, this is obviously a welcome development. Centrifugal patterns give way to at least some that are centripetal. An observation by Arthur Evans in 1877 comes to mind:

> [W]herever we turn our gaze, our search reveals the still existing bonds of union, of which the strongest and most binding is a common mother tongue, spoken alike by Bosnian Christian and Bosnian Mahometan, and spoken, too, beyond the frontier by Serb and Montenegrin, Croat, and Dalmatian [...]. (Evans 2005: 130)

The common Serbian, Croatian and Bosnian word *hajduk*, pl. *hajduci* (pron. *high-duk, high-dutsi*) meaning, first, 'highwayman, bandit, brigand, outlaw' and, second, 'fighter against Ottoman authorities for national liberation') has cognates in Arabic, Turkish, Hungarian, Albanian, Bulgarian, Romanian, Romany, Polish and German. As often occurs, there have been conflicting explanations for its origin, which is hardly surprising, given the proximities and intermingling of speakers of different languages in and around south-east Europe and the so-called Near East. It's interesting to try to untie this tangled knot. Even in English, one finds a long entry for the word in the *Oxford English Dictionary* (*OED*) under the (almost comical) spelling *heyduck*. Here's the entry in the online edition:

> Heyduck (hai·du*k*, hē'·duk). Forms: heyduque, -duke, -duck, heyduc, heiduc, -duck, haiduk, hayduk. Boh., Pol., Serv., Roman. *hajduk,* Magyar *hajdú* pl. *hajdú*, in Bulg. *hajdutin*, mod. Gr. *chaitoutes*, Turkish *haidūd* robber brigand.
>
> A term app. meaning originally 'robber, marauder, brigand' (a sense still retained in Serbia and adjacent countries), which in Hungary became the name of a special body of foot-soldiers (to whom the rank of nobility and a territory were given in 1605), and in Poland of the liveried personal followers or attendants of the nobles.
>
> 1615 *Satyr. Ess.* 87 Like the Hungarian Heyducks their wrath is prone to mischief, and their amity is worth nothing.
>
> 1684 *Scanderbeg Rediv.* iv. 54 First Marched five Companies of Heyduques.
>
> 1685 *Lond. Gaz.* No. 2072/1 The Heydukes of Cattaro had made an incursion towards Goza, and had destroyed all that Country.
>
> 1729 *Brice's Weekly Jrnl.* (Exeter) 16 May 3 A Dwarf..is to attend on his Royal Highness in the Dress of a Heyduke.
>
> 1772 *Ann. Reg.* 82* Two Heyducks who were behind the coach, bravely exposed their lives to save the King [of Poland].
>
> 1832 *Blackw. Mag.* XXXII. 13 The richly costumed heydukes and chasseurs of the Hungarian lords.
>
> 1847 *Mrs. A. Kerr Hist. Servia* 49 Such as refused to appear before the Kadi [...] fled into the forests and turned *Heyducs* or robbers.
>
> 1858 *Carlyle Fredk. Gt.* VI. iii. II. 158 Carried by two shining particoloured creatures, heyducs so-called, [...] in a sublime sedan.

1889 *Athenæum* 15 June 768/1 One of that extinct species of servants, the heyducs, holds the horse of the fat monarch.

Even from this entry for a term describing a little known 'foreign curiosity', it's clear that the meaning varies widely, depending who is or has been using it and where, for the word has occurred in widely varying contexts. But what isn't apparent from this entry is that this word has also aroused strong (and strongly contradictory) responses. Abdulah Škaljić says that the word *hajduk* ('outcast from authorities, highwayman or thief') passed into Serbo-Croatian from Turkish *haydud, haydut* 'highwayman', which in turn, according to him, came from the Arabic verb *haydud*, whose infinitive form *hada* means 'to stray (from the right path)'.[14] Škaljić's 'explanation' is that this derivation accounts for (the rich and complex connotations of) the Serbo-Croatian term *odmednuti se* (i.e. with its associations of 'fleeing, casting oneself out, becoming a deserter, renegade, or outlaw'). However, he doesn't clarify how this verb might be connected etymologically with *hajduk*. In passing, Škaljić also mentions Hungarian *hajdú* 'soldier', pl. *hajdúk*, but doesn't go so far as suggesting this as the source for the Serbo-Croatian or Turkish word. The same *OED* entry quoted above lists the following cognates: "Boh., Pol., Serv., Roman. *hajduk*, Magyar *hajdú* pl. *hajdúk*, in Bulg. *hajdutin*, mod. Gr. *chaidoutes*, Turkish *haidūd* robber, brigand."

Fahir Iz confirms Turkish *haydut* as 'brigand, bandit',[15] as does similarly Godward, 'brigand, outlaw'.[16] But the latter suggests a different Arabic derivation, from *hhiyatta* 'guarding, protecting', and *hhatta* 'guarded'. However, no connection is suggested between the two Turkish words *haydut*, 'brigand' and *haydar* 'lion' or 'brave or courageous man'. It's illuminating, too, to consider the connotations of the Turkish word *haydut*: I've been told by contemporary native speakers that this has strongly pejorative associations, in direct (and predictable) contradistinction to the romanticised and even heroic associations of the word in Serbian and Croatian. H. C. Hony explains Turkish *haydud* as 'brigand', with the compounds and derivatives *haydudyatağı* 'brigand's den' and *haydudluk* 'brigandage'.[17] He also defines *haydalamak* as 'to drive on animals with loud shouts' and *haydamak* as 'cattle lifter, marauder, vagabond'. Does

[14] Škaljić 300.

[15] Iz 219.

[16] Godward 134.

[17] Hony 19.

this notion of 'loud shouts' relate in any way to the Turkish colloquial vocative imprecation *haydi, hadi, haydin* ('Come on! be off!' etc.), or to the Serbian and Croatian *hajde, ajde, ajd, hajdete, hajdemo*, etc. ('Come on! Let's go! Let's…', etc.)? Or does the connection of some of these Turkish terms and concepts with both cattle-drovers and cattle-thieves link to a similar knot of semantic associations in Hungarian? In Bulgarian, Maria Todorova points out a double usage:

> *hajduk* (*хайдук*), pl. *hajdutsi* (*хайдуци*) and *hajdut* (*хайдут*), pl. *hajduti* (*хайдути*). The first corresponds to the official use in Ottoman Turkish (which uses both forms synonymously), namely robber, rebel, bandit, alongside other descriptors. The second, used in the folksongs, is reserved for the "nobler" hypostasis as protector of the Christians.[18]

Albanian has both *hajduk* and *hajdut,* meaning 'brigand, robber',[19] 'thief, robber, pickpocket, burglar' and 'renegade outlaw, mountain brigand, synonymous with *kaçak*').[20] Under *kaçak,* the same dictionary has '1. *nm* (old) renegade, outlaw, mountain brigand' and '2. *adj.* (old) contraband, illegal.[21] These words and explanations are consistent with both Serbo-Croatian and Turkish.

Noel Malcolm, however, presents a different argument for the origin of the Serbo-Croatian and Albanian words: "the very word *hajduk* – from the Hungarian *hajtó,* cattle drover – developed as a term for a sort of freebooter soldier used on the Hungarian and Serbian sides of the Habsburg-Ottoman frontier."[22] George Gömöri confirmed that the Hungarian word *hajdú,* pl. *hajdúk,* derives from *hatjó,* pl. *hajtók,* 'drover, herdsman', from *hajt* 'to drive' (object: animals).[23]

Petar Skok builds up this complex picture of linguistic loans, borrowings, adoptions and adaptations:

> *Hàjdūk,* gen. – *ka* masc. (Vuk, 16. v.) with fem. in *-ica hajdùčica* = *ajdûk* (Kosmet [Kosovo]); 'synonyms: 1. robber, bandit, thief, 2. pandur

[18] Email, October 31, 2019.

[19] Mann 152.

[20] Newmark 297.

[21] It would be interesting to explore the associations between *hajduk, hajdut* and *kaçak* in more depth, in the Albanian linguistic context. For a further possible etymological connection for Alb. *kaçak,* see also 75 below, note 52.

[22] Malcolm 199 and 382 n. 17.

[23] In conversations, Autumn 2001.

> (=police-functionary, hist.), court official (Hungary, Vojvodina, Srem), 3. četnik, Hungarian foot-soldier, infantryman [...]. A Balkan Turkism of Hungarian origin from the military region (a Hungarian tribal name, ethnic: *haidú*, pl. *hajdúk*, acc, sing. *Hajdút*): Romanian, Bulgarian *hajdúk* and also *hajdút*(*in*), Albanian *hajdût* < Turkish *haydud*. The original meaning of the Hungarian word was 'paid soldier on the Turkish frontier against the Turks, 1. foot-soldier, infantryman, 2. court functionary or servant, (pandur), 3. functionary or servant of the Hungarian magnate, lackey'. At the time of [Stevan] Batory the word was taken into the Polish and German languages, with this meaning. In the Balkans it became pejorative because Hajduks made up the majority of the contingents fighting in the struggle against the Turks.[24]

A reading between the lines here hints at much that's fascinating. In particular, there are the same extreme shifts of meaning, already noted, for the same word across languages: from 'bandit, outlaw' on the one hand to the very opposite on the other 'court-servant, pandur', i.e. 'law-keeper'. These transitions and oscillations suggest the complexity of underlying social and political histories. Don't these apparent contradictions strongly imply, for a start, that ranks of criminals and of police, of renegades and of guards, of state enemies and mercenaries paid by the state, and of outlaws and the state's spies, may be drawn from identical or at least similar social groups? In this respect, Skok's last sentence above seems tautological and curiously simplistic: tautological because the term *hajduk* itself *meant* 'fighter against the Turks' in any case; simplistic because the degree to which the term was 'pejorative' (or otherwise) depended on the perspective of the speaker vis-à-vis that struggle.[25] Furthermore, while from a broad Balkan perspective Skok confirms the view that there's a Hungarian origin for the loanword *hajduk* in Serbo-Croatian, he fails to examine its history within Hungarian, and so misses at least one of its connotations.

---

[24] Skok 1971: 649-650; trans. RB.

[25] The same is clearly true of the highly ideologically loaded word *četnik* in Skok's third definition (etym. *četa* 'troop'), especially if one considers its meanings and associations during the Nazi occupation of Serbia, as well as in the Titoist period and, later, during the break-up of Yugoslavia between 1989 and 1995. See 112-113 below.

The Hungarian historical context is fascinating and worth elaborating. George Gömöri pointed out to me in conversation and emails that the Hungarian verb *hajtani* 'to drive (obj. cattle)', and the plural noun *hajtók* ('drovers, cattle-drivers') were applied in medieval times to herdsmen who drove their cattle to the great seasonal markets in such German towns as Magdeburg.[26] These men developed a reputation for hardiness, toughness and loyalty; and, gradually, armed bands were formed. By the sixteenth century (and perhaps well before), the word had yielded the derivative, *hajdú*, pl. *hajdúk*, 'soldier, footsoldier, trooper'. The term became strongly associated with the Transylvanian Protestant revolt against the Catholic Habsburgs, which served to introduce a new phase in the power balance between the Ottoman and Austrian empires. To put this into a time-frame familiar to English-speaking readers, these events took place over the period when Elizabeth I was on the throne in England and James (I) in England and (VI) in Scotland. And to be clear about the connotations of this term in Hungarian: in the late sixteenth and early seventeenth centuries, it already belongs to the 'register' or semantic zone of *conflict* – religious, political, linguistic and nationalistic.

In brief, the Hungarian story is as follows. The Habsburg Emperor Rudolf II, who reigned in Vienna from 1576 to 1612, was a strict Catholic who had been educated in Spain and, on his accession, soon set about eliminating all Protestants from court service. In 1591, on his orders and those of his close advisers, some of whom despised Magyar culture and history, his army entered Transylvania and Northern Hungary. Under their commander, Giorgio Basta, these troops behaved with extreme cruelty toward the Hungarian Protestants. Their repression led the Transylvanian Protestant prince and general, István (Stevan) Bocskay (1557–1606), who had previously been a Habsburg supporter, to embark on a revolt against Vienna in 1604–1605 and to ally himself instead with the Ottoman. Bocskay drove out Basta and in 1606 concluded the Peace of Vienna with Rudolf II, followed in the same year by the Treaty of Zsitvatorok with the Ottomans. These events served to tip the delicate balance of power-control throughout the region in favour of the Hungarians and away from the Turks. Half a century of prosperity for Transylvania was ushered in, despite Bocskay's sudden and untimely death in 1606 in Cassovia (i.e. Kassa in Hungarian or Košice in Slovakian), which his supporters blamed on a murder involving poison perpetrated by his chancellor, whom they then summarily put to death in the town's marketplace.

[26] George Gömöri's insight prompted my further research.

The relevance of this story to Balkan *hajduks* is that Bocskay's victories are said to have been largely due to the fearlessness and blood-thirstiness of his "army of wild herdsmen (hajduks)".[27] This passage of history is reflected by many place-names in north-eastern Hungary, around the city of Debrecen near the modern Slovakian, Ukrainian and Romanian borders. The fairs in Debrecen were well-known for horses and livestock even in the Middle Ages, and the region is still famous for its cowboys, cattle and cattle-ranches. Bocskay rewarded his militarised population with lands, privileges and title exemptions. Around Debrecen lies the *megye* ('county') of *Hajdú-Bihar*,[28] and within this is the *Hajdúság* region. The prefix *Haidú* is further echoed in the names of a whole network of towns which were developed as military settlements along this loosely strung 'military frontier', such as *Hajdúnánás*, *Hajdúdorog*, *Hajdúvid*, *Hajdúszovát*, and the largest of these fortress-towns, *Haidúböszörmény*. These Hungarian *hajduk* (pl.), then, were the defenders of the Austro-Hungarian Empire against that of the Ottoman Turks.

This rather oversimplified account at least partly suggests how in Hungarian the *hajtók* ('herdsmen') may have become *hajdúk* ('warriors') and then patrollers of fortresses along the shifting borders between the Ottoman Empire, Protestant Hungary and Catholic Austria. Although it doesn't clarify in which directions the word passed among Hungarian, Turkish, Serbian, Albanian, Bulgarian and Polish, it's worth noting that the ethno-linguistic origins of Bocskay's foot-soldiers were mixed, and included not only local Magyars, cattle-drovers and their heirs, but also Serbs and other refugees who had started fleeing in the fifteenth century from the westward expansion of the Ottomans. Since the accession of Rudolf II's predecessor Emperor Ferdinand I in 1553, Croats, Serbs, Vlachs, Albanians and Bulgars had in any case been operating as border-patrollers and guards along various of the Habsburg Empire's southern and south-eastern 'Military Frontiers' (*Vojna krajina*, pl. *-e*) against the Turks.[29]

ꟾ

[27] *Encyc. Brit.* (CD edn.) 2001.

[28] Vesna Goldsworthy kindly pointed out to me that the Hungarian word *megye* derives from Serbo-Croatian *medja* 'boundary, border' (email, Sept. 10, 2019). This word has cognates in Indo-European languages, e.g. Latin *medius* 'medium', Sanskrit *madya* and Avestan *maidya*. See Skok 1972, vol. 2: 398-399.

[29] See 78-79 below.

I'll return later to ancillary relevant information about the transhumant Vlachs themselves (also known as Arumins, Arumonians or Aromanians); but as an aside here on the ethnic or tribal identities of these border-patrollers and guards, it's worth noting that the use of the word *Vlach* in this context is wholly unreliable. *Vlach* (*Vlachos*, *Wallachian*, etc.) derives from a widely distributed set of terms that's evident in most Germanic languages. With all its equivalents in Balkan languages, *Vlach* is cognate with names attributed to a wide variety of ethnic and tribal groupings: for example, Eng. *Welsh*, *Walloon*, Fr. *Wallon*, Fr. *Gaule*, Eng. *Gaul*.[30] The meaning of this Germanic term, 'foreigner, stranger, other' fits well into our theme of edges and borders. It also implies 'speaker of an incomprehensible and therefore inferior and uncivilised language', and so conforms entirely with the etymology or the word *barbarian*, from ancient Greek *βάρβαρος* (*barbaros*, 'inferior foreigner, nonsense blabberer', etc.). Skok's long entry on *Vläh* also demonstrates clearly how movable the term is. On the one hand, it might be applied to groups of people "bez obzira na vjeru i narodnost" ("regardless of religion or ethnicity"). On the other, it could be applied *to* neighbouring ethnic groups *by* different ethnic groups, usually disparagingly. Hence: to Ukrainians, *woloh* designates (or designated) Romanian; to Croats, *vlah*, an Orthodox Serb; and so on.[31] Especially along the Military Frontier between the Habsburg Empire and the Ottoman-held lands, Vlachs and Serbs were hard to distinguish.[32] In 1877, the Scottish traveller Georgina Muir Mackenzie writes:

> To this day the greater part [...] speak their own language, which some call a barbarian dialect Latinized others a Latin dialect barbarized.[33]

Not surprisingly, then, the term 'Vlach' was (and in some regions still is) often used in the Balkans, all the way down through Greece, as a pejorative term for an individual, or member of *another group*, whom a speaker might consider inferior, less cultured, less civilised, etc.[34] When I lived in Thebes and Athens (1967–1968) I regularly heard the word *βλάχος*

---

[30] Onions, 1966: 391, 984, 990 and 999; and *OED* (online).

[31] Skok 1973, vol. 3: 606-608.

[32] Judah 2009: 10-14.

[33] Mackenzie and Irby, vol. 1: 106.

[34] However, Maria Todorova reports that among Bulgarian-speakers, she isn't aware of pejorative elements in use of the term *Vlach*, which simply designates speakers of the Aromanian language (email, Oct. 31, 2019).

(*vláhos*) used to mean something like 'peasant, thick person, stupid person'. This stereotypical opprobrium occurred not just in Greece. In former Yugoslavia, the term often came to be applied exclusively to Serbs. From his research on epithets used by a mixed population in Kordun, Banija and Moslavina in Croatia between 1989 and 1991 – just before the break-up of the Yugoslav Federation – Dražen Nožinić retrospectively remarks:

> The population of Kordun, Banija and Moslavina differed ethnically, culturally, linguistically and in religion (and the entire picture was once again changed by the civil war in former Yugoslavia). Those differences were reflected in the existence of a large number of names which particular groups used for one another. Those nicknames were offensive, resentful, ironic and disparaging. [...] The most widespread group within the three examined regions were Serbs of the Orthodox religion. All surrounding Croats (and Muslims) used to call those Serbs *Vlasi* (*Vlahi* or *Vlaji* – i.e. Vlach). According to my tellers *the rural Serbs used those names themselves* until the Second World War, though, after 1945, the term *Serbs* become widely accepted and established. Many of them also said they considered the term 'Vlach' offensive. According to the area, there were also other names for Serbs and all of them were considered offensive and disparaging. [...] The only name noted in Moslavina for Serbs was 'Vlach'.
>
> One particular group among the Serbs are those in Žumberk belonging to the Greek-Catholic religion who call themselves *Uskoci*, while the surrounding Slovenians and Croats call them *Vlasi*.[35]

Interestingly, considered in terms of projection, introjection and differential evaluation of both *self* and *other*, the first set of names applied by these Serbs to themselves (*Vlasi*, *Vlahi*, *Vlaji*) reflects an often-observed socio-linguistic pattern among neighbouring ethnicities. *A neighbour's term of opprobrium is defiantly adopted by its recipients and converted into a badge of pride.*[36]

What's more, the second epithet, *Uskok*, is similar to the traditional Serbian sense of the word *hajduk*, *hajduči*, both in positive historical reference and, at least in their own eyes, in compensatory heroic and glamorous emotional connotation.

ఌ

[35] *Vlasi* (Vlachs, Arumonians). Nožinić 1998: 77ff; trans. Vera V. Radojević and RB; emphasis added.

[36] Variants of emotively loaded terms often swing between laudatory and pejorative extremes: for example, English *awe, awful, awesome*, etc.

Sea-banditry or piracy, including rapine and raids on coastal settlements from the sea, is attested in the Mediterranean as early as the first Homeric 'Hymn to Demeter'.[37] This poem was composed "not later than the end of the seventh century B.C."[38]

George Mylonas, the archaeologist who not only excavated much of Eleusis but made doing so his life-work,[39] puts the date of composition "in or after the Hesiodic period"[40] and "around 600 BC". Piracy has an ancient heritage:

> The Greeks who sailed to Egypt about 660 [BCE] were pirates who found respectability; Polycrates of Samos was *a pirate with a state behind him*; even the early campaigns of the Delian League in the 470s were against pirates as well as Persians, and some have even linked the League itself to pirates. The best comment is a list of those whom the little coastal city of Teos decided (about 470) to include among its annual official curses: mass poisoners, dissidents, revolutionaries, traitors – and pirates.[41]

To jump forward by around 2,000 years, this comment is as good a guide as any to the *uskoks* of Dalmatia, a localised group who in some respects might be thought of as 'maritime *hajduks*'. In *The Uskoks of Senj* (1992), the most detailed and authoritative historiographic study of them in English to date, Wendy Bracewell explores their history, their multi-ethnic composition, their social and military codes and their lifestyle in fascinating and brilliant detail. The *uskoks* of Senj certainly were pirates "with a state behind" them, even if a small one. And almost half a century earlier, in the course of a description of her own visit to the little Adriatic port of Senj, Rebecca West devotes five pages of brilliant writing to their history. "These are not

---

[37] This occurs in the passage in which Demeter, disguising herself as the harmless crone Dos or Doso, tells the daughters of the king of Eleusis that as a younger woman she was abducted by pirates from Crete:

> Doso my name, for my reverend mother imposed it upon me:
> Recently over the breadth of the sea I unwillingly crossed from
> Crete – yes, unwillingly: pirates abducted me forcibly, using
> Strength of necessity. (Homeric 'Hymn to Demeter', trans. Hine: ll. 122-125.)

[38] Nilsson 1961 [1940]: 45.

[39] Mylonas 1942: 5-8; and 12-13: 1969 [1961].

[40] *ibid.* 11.

[41] Forrest 214; emphasis added. For similar documentation of piracy in the ancient Mediterranean, discussed in the context of the history of slavery, especially of women, see Hordern and Purcell 389-391.

animals invented by Edward Lear," she affirms. "They were refugees. They were refugees like the Jews and Roman Catholics and liberals driven out by Hitler."[42] And she elaborates on how the uskoks had fled west from the invading Ottoman Turks who were sweeping northwards through Bulgaria, Serbia and Bosnia; how they had transformed themselves into a highly organised naval power, first controlling the narrow straight between Senj and the long, narrow island of Krk; how they then "chased the Turkish ships up and down the Adriatic, stripped them, and sank them"; how "for nearly thirty years they lived in such a state of legitimate and disciplined warfare that they attacked only Turkish ships"; and how, following their sense of betrayal after the Venetian-Turkish deal in the 1530s, from 1566 on

> [t]hey became gangsters of the sea. They developed all the characteristics of gunman: a loyalty that went unbroken to the death, unsurpassable courage, brutality, greed and, oddly enough, thriftlessness. Just as a Chicago racketeer who has made an income of five figures for many years will leave his widow penniless, so the Uskoks, who helped themselves to the richest loot the sea ever carried, always fell into penury if they survived into old age. Also they were looted, as thieves often are, by the honest."[43]

As for dictionary definitions and translations of the word or name *uskok*, while the Croatian scholar Željko Bujas rather unsatisfactorily lists 'deserter, fugitive, runaway',[44] Morton Benson has '(hist.) *Uskok*, guerrilla (who invaded Turkish territory)'; and also he mentions the *uskočki ciklus*: 'Uskok cycle (of epic poems)'.[45] The linguist Jasna Levinger-Goy reminded me in conversation (January 2004) that the term *uskok* is cognate with the verbs *skočiti* 'to leap, to jump', whence *uskočiti* 'to leap or jump into, at, to, towards; to step in', etc. with the underlying image of 'a sudden ambush-like *pouncing*, followed by rapid retreat'. This derivation is confirmed by Wendy Bracewell, the historian Traian Stoianovich,[46] and the author of the major Serbo-Croatian etymological dictionary, Petar Skok, who in a well-documented entry derives his own surname from *skočiti* and points out that it's widespread in Istria, Slovenia and Serbia. Then he adds, somewhat gingerly: "The surname *Skok* may also be connected with *uskok*, who are

[42] West 124-128.

[43] *ibid.* 126.

[44] Bujas 1999a: 1536.

[45] Benson 1980: 675.

[46] Stoianovich 1994: 327.

called *gli Scocchi* in Italian documents, whence the Istrian-Italian surname *Scocchi*."[47] Still, I can't help wondering exactly when the term *uskok* began to be applied: whether it was during the course of the earlier migration westwards across the Balkan peninsula to escape the Turks, 'jumping' as it were from place to place, or later, when the persecuted became 'pouncers' themselves, i.e. pirates.

Interestingly, in a broader discussion of piracy, Hordern and Purcell point out that rather than merely being the *other* of maritime commerce – that is, its destroyers – pirates necessarily depend on trade. Nor, these authors argue, should pirates be thought of as mere parasites. Indeed, they function "in profound symbiosis" with official trade, and contribute to it. These authors also compare pirates to pastoralists: "[L]ike pastoralism, piracy is not an exclusive calling: one season's predator is next season's entrepreneur."[48]

As for the role in English history of sea-bandits, in Elizabethan times their daring exploits across the Atlantic were tacitly sanctioned and encouraged by the crown, even if not quite 'officially approved'. The careers of Sir Francis Drake (1540–1596) and Sir Walter Raleigh (1552–1618)[49] give clear evidence of the ways in which Transatlantic colonialism, trade (including slavery) and piracy were intermeshed. Both these Devon-born men, who still have heroic status in English popular mythology, were privateers. Piracy for them was not only patriotic but a business.[50]

Although the 'land-piracy' of the hajduks could scarcely be said to have resulted in great wealth for the vast majority of its practitioners, the suggestion of an analogous link with pastoralists is insightful. And the status of the *hajduk* was ambivalent.

ᔓ

Stoianovich examines all these groups together, directly comparing the *uskoks* of Senj with the *hajduks*, the Russian and Ukrainian *Cossacks* and the

---

[47] Skok vol. 3, 1973: 263; trans. RB.

[48] Hordern and Purcell 157; and see the ref. to Aristotle, 93-94 below.

[49] Raleigh was also a wonderful poet, and a historian and scholar. For poems on his execution by beheading at Westminster, see RB 2020c.

[50] The English word *buccaneer* (first recorded in 1661) enters the language via the circuitous route of Spanish *bucanero* and French *boucanier*. It derives originally from the Caribbean Arawakan word *buccan*, 'a wooden frame on which meat was roasted or smoked'. See 'Buccaneer', *OED* (online) and *Wikipedia*.

Greek *klephts*.[51] The words *cossack* (Eng.), *cosaque* (Fr.), *kazak, kozak* (Russ. < *Kazakhstan*), etc. mean 'one of the, or descendants of, early Russian people who sought free life on steppes, noted for warlike qualities etc". The Turkish source-word *quzzäq*, 'vagabond, nomad, adventurer, guerrilla', itself comes from Turkish *qaz* 'wander about' (all this from Onions: 218).[52] The *OED* (online) amplifies:

> 'In India it became common in sense of predatory horseman, freebooter' (Yule). 1. Name of a warlike Turkish people now subject to Russia, occupying the parts north of the Black Sea. From them the Poles organized a body of light horsemen, in which capacity they formed an important element of the Russian army. Also *attrib.* or *adj.*
>
> 1598 *Hakluyt Voy.* I. 388 The Cassacke beares his felt, to force away the raine.
>
> 1687 *Rycaut Hist. Turks* II. 231 The Piracies and Depredations of the Cosacks in the Black Sea.
>
> 1698 *J. Crull Muscovy* 126 The Cossacks [...] were a certain Body of Soldiers, Established for the Guard of the Frontiers.
>
> 1753 *Hanway Trav.* (1762) I. II. xv. 64 The Cossacks are a species of Tartars; their name signifies free-booters.
>
> 1822 *Byron Juan* VIII. lxxiv, The Kozacks, or, if so you please, Cossacques. *Ibid.* X. li, The parries He made 'gainst Cossacque sabres.
>
> 1855 *Tennyson Charge Light Brigade* iv, Cossack and Russian Reel'd from the sabre-stroke Shatter'd and sunder'd.

As for *klephts*, the Greek word *κλέπτης* (*kleptis*) or *κλέφτης* (*kleftis*) (pl. *-tra*) also means 'robber, highwayman, guerrilla'. The verb *κλέβω* (*klévo*) means 'to rob, to steal'; hence Eng. *kleptomania.* Like the *uskoks*, the *klephts* have their celebrated cycle of heroic songs named after them. And again, with regard to the *hajduk* tradition in the southern Balkans, Stoianovich points out other connections with traditions of song and oral poetry:

> By 1573, according to Stephen Gerlach, chaplain of the Habsburg legation to Istanbul, Serbian and Bulgarian peasants of the districts between Niš and Sofia were already in the habit of singing *hajduk songs* or *Räyber Lieder* (robber songs) while wending homeward from their fields.[53]

[51] Stoianovich, *op. cit.* 166-168; 327.

[52] I can't help wondering if the Albanian *kaçak* is a cognate, from the same Turkish source-word. See 66 above, note 20.

[53] Stoianovich, *op. cit.* 167-168.

It isn't clear from this passage whether Gerlach actually used the term *hajduk* to describe these peasant songs or whether this conflation or identification has been made by Stoianovich himself. In this instance, the latter doesn't elaborate the detailed analysis that comparative etymologies are capable of providing, as he often does elsewhere,[54] and it's a pity that he doesn't explore the Hungarian history in depth. Nonetheless, if this information is accurate, it's clear that these long robber songs in the Ottoman-occupied central and southern Balkans *preceded* Bocskay's military deployment of *hajduks* further north.

With regard to the Greek klephtic tradition, Peter Mansfield points out that "another name for *kleftis* is *andartis*, with the same span of meanings. The term *andartis* was the form revived for the anti-German Resistance in the Second World War. Its etymology, rather interestingly [...] is 'taker back'." Mansfield adds:

> Going back to the end of the first millennium we find the grandfather of these terms, with strong semantic ties to at least one of the groups you mention: *akritas*, lit. 'edge dweller': used of the fighter-farmers and bandit-like frontiersman who lived in the Cappadocian and Western Armenian mountains in the 9th–13th centuries, forming a kind of *maquisard* fifth column for the Romans (= Byzantines) against the Seljuk Turks. The hero of the greatest (or anyhow best known) Byzantine epic. Dighenis Akritas, is one of these.[55]

The word *andartis* (*αντάρτης*) actually goes back further than the Second World War. Like *hajduk* and associated terms further north, it appears towards the end of the eighteenth century in the context of rebellions against the Ottomans. As for the name *Ακρίτας* (*Akritas*), this is cognate with the feminine noun *άκρη* (*akri*, 'end, edge, tip, summit; cape; corner') and the adjective *άκρος* (*akros*, 'extreme, complete, utmost; last'; and 'terminal, outmost, topmost', etc.).[56] This term covers the same semantic field as Slavic *kraj*, *krajina*, etc.,[57] and is probably a direct cognate. In his translation of one of the versions of the Byzantine Greek epic poem, Denison B. Hull renders the name *Dighenis* or *Digenis* as "Two-Blood". The combined name of this glorified fictional heroic character, *Dighenis Akritas*, therefore means something like 'Half-Breed Borderer'. In reality,

[54] e.g. on coffee. See Stoianovich 1995a, vol. 3: 73-74.

[55] Email, February 17, 2003.

[56] Pring 6-7; Onions 10; see also Hall.

[57] Stoianovich, 1994: 329.

however, the insecure, impoverished existence of edge-dwellers, borderers, refugees, tramps, waifs, vagabonds, criminals, released jailbirds, persons of no fixed abode, and dispossessed, exiled and banished people, underlies the entire historical reality not just of brigandry and banditry, but also of several of the other linguistic terms in the various languages that we're exploring here. This observation may be compared with Braudel's comment:

> According to epoch and circumstances, brigandry has managed to change its name or form, but whether *mandrini, masnadieri, ladri, fuorusciti* or *banditi* (the *masnadieri* are primitively soldiers, and the *fuorusciti* and *banditi*, the banished), it's always in fact to do with brigands.[58]

ꕥ

The English word *bandit*, which has close equivalents in many European languages, might at face-value be mistaken to be connected with the word 'band'. In fact, *bandito* (pl *-i*) is the past participle of the medieval Latin verb *bandire* or *bannire*, meaning 'to ban, proscribe, banish, outlaw'.[59] And here, too, the Italian coinage *fuorusciti* means, literally, 'those gone outside': while *masnada* means 'set, gang'; *una masnada di ladri* 'a gang of thieves, armed band; group, company; family'; hence *masnadiere* 'highway robber; brigand; bandit; feudal retainer; trooper'.[60] This covers almost exactly the same semantic range as *hajduk*. And it's precisely at and along borders, edges and frontiers, and in those 'difficult' zones where government powers are weakest, that banditry has most thrived. Braudel continues:

> It's true that it (banditism) is always ranged against the State. And I'd add unhesitatingly that it's always lodged in those zones where the States are weakest. In the mountains, where a troop can scarcely act in force and where the State has lost its rights. And often too at the junctures of States, in frontier zones: along the Dalmatian high country, between Venice and Turkey; in the frontier region of Hungary, one of the major zones of banditism in the 16th century; in Catalonia, in the Pyrenees bordering on France; at Messina, which is a frontier too, in so far as the free city of Messina was in fact a refuge; around the Benevento, the Papal enclave within the Kingdom of Naples; between the Papal State and Tuscany; between Milan and Venice; between Venice and the

[58] Braudel 1947: 133; trans. RB.

[59] Onions 72.

[60] Reynolds 467.

hereditary States of the Archdukes. All these border-junctures between States made admirable HQ's.[61]

Similarly, the French term *maquis*,[62] which in the Second World War came to mean 'underground', has an entirely consonant etymology. The word originates in Latin *macula*. It came into French, via Corsican, from Italian *macchia*, meaning 'spot, mark, stain' and hence 'dense growth of small trees and shrubs'; 'copse, thicket, scrub' [...] "after the spotted appearance of hillsides dotted with such thickets".[63] Obviously, this kind of hilly terrain is ideal for outlaws to hide out and move around in. So the French Second World War freedom fighters named themselves after the wild, 'difficult' terrain that Corsican bandits and guerrillas had been forced, or had chosen, to inhabit, with the added 'deep' social and moral connotations of being 'marked, set apart' – as outsiders who, like Cain in Genesis, had consciously and voluntarily taken on the ambivalent burden, the double-edged status, of being 'stained', 'tainted', 'marked', 'stigmatised'. Traditions of heroism and sacrifice become all the more comprehensible when explored through the complexities of such densely packed verbal histories.

ශ

The Croatian and Serbian word *kraj*, as suggested above, is probably etymologically related to Greek *akri, akros* and *akritras*. This word has its own powerful role in our story. The word means 'edge' and 'end' in both spatial and temporal terms, and also 'area, region, place, zone'. Skok paints a picture of how this term itself has shifted and changed in the geographically adjacent languages of Serbian and Albanian, slipping and flitting backwards and forwards across the border, as it were, with each language influencing and re-influencing the other, in a kind of inter-lingual mirroring:

> Krâj, gen. *kràja* m. [...] Old Slavonic, without parallel in the Baltic group or in other languages. [...] The old derivative in *-ina* is also noteworthy: *kràjina*, with the adjective *kràjinski* (Serbia, Vuk), meaning a territorial end: "1. land on the borders (Bosnia, Montenegro), and 2. war (struggle, fighting) in that land / terrain", and from this the denominal *kràjiniti* (Serbia, Vuk) "*to fight, to wage war*". [...] The semantic and phonetic

[61] Braudel, *op. cit.* 135: trans. RB.

[62] See *maquisard*, 76 above.

[63] *OED* (online).

change (*ai* > *ae*) in Kosmet [Kosovo] *kràešnik* "hero" is also noteworthy, with the adjective *kràešnička pesma* "heroic folk song /poem", because this can help explain the Albanian terms *kreshnik –u* "hero" and *këngë kreshnikë* "heroic poem/song (*cantica heroica*). In fact, these are the poems / songs which sing of heroic warriors in the *Krajina*. This expression was borrowed by Serbs from Albanians in Kosmet (Kosovo) *krèšnìca* < *krajišnìca "heroic folksong/poem". The Albanians borrowed *krajina* > *Kraja* (a territorial 'end' in Bara), *krahinë*. Compare also: Ukr. *Ukrajina* "Grenzland" ('borderland') and Alb. *ukrajë* "wood" < *ukrajina.[64]

Here, in the very vocabulary itself, the same etymological root provides an entire conceptual map for the cluster 'end', 'edge', 'war', 'warrior' and 'hero'; and there are songs and poems to prove it. Varying from one stretch of the Austro-Hungarian Military Frontier to another, names for the warriors employed along it include *krajišnici*, *hajduci*, *uskoci* ('borderers, border-guards', haiduks, uskoks), *Grenzern* (Germ. 'frontiersmen, border-guards') and *graničari* (Srb.),[65] as well as *martolosi* or *armatolosi* ('armed men').

Words intermingling or intermeshing, of course, signal intermingling or intermeshing lives. From her journeys in North Albania into Kosovo in 1908, the English traveller Edith Durham (1863–1944) brings home the reality of the simultaneous blurring and sharpening of identities along border-zones, in intimate and down-to-earth terms:

The Hagi himself visited me, so soon as he had concluded service in the church.

He was a tall, fair, handsome man, very friendly, and much relieved to find I understood Serb. Marko, who knows but little, asked him if he understood Albanian.

He laughed heartily, and replied, "I am an Albanian." Born of Albanian parents, he explained he had spoken Albanian only as a child. But having joined the Orthodox Church, he was now a Servian, and Servian was more familiar to him than his mother tongue.

So it is in the Debateable Lands. The Serbs have a converted Albanian as head of their monastery, and conversely, one of the most patriotic Albanian priests at Djakova was a Serb by birth – had spoken Serb only as a child, and now had almost forgotten it.[66]

---

64 Skok 1972, vol. 2: 176; trans. RB.

65 Stoianovich, *op. cit.* 327. The German word derives from Slavic (Polish) *granica*, 'border'.

66 Durham 2000 [1909]: 252-253

This is Durham in her early mode of writing. However, later, she takes a far less cheery view. In an increasingly sharp and high-handed dismissal of everything and everybody with any connection to Slavs, she points out how the tradition of singing epic poems itself both epitomises ethnic disunity and celebrates conflict:

> The ballads of Montenegro are almost all either war songs or tales of brigandage. Brigandage was, till 1870, the main livelihood of the country. My guide's great uncle was a pirate who plied between Cattaro and the Aegean. The Muslims on the Montenegrin borders of the Herzegovina were mainly Serbs who had turned Turk, and we find in the songs the Montenegrins alternately swearing brotherhood with them and plundering them. [...] In the historic ballads one thing stands out sharp and clear. It is that *the Balkan troubles have nearly all been due to Balkan inability to cohere.* Over and over again is the mournful tale repeated? May the poets of the future have a less disastrous policy to sing about?[67]

The recent tragedy (1995) of the Serbian inhabitants expelled from the Balkan zone called the *Krajina* is also part of this story,[68] and there are clearly links here to the *uskoks* of Senj, which almost falls within the coastal zone this term describes. In the sixteenth century, the *Krajina* or more properly *Vojna krajina* ('Military Frontier') referred to the long border between the Austro-Hungarian Empire and the Ottoman Empire.[69]

The toponym derives from the common Slavonic word *kraj*, 'edge, end, frontier, limit, corner, *quartier*', as does the country-name *Ukraine.* In the Balkans, the Military Frontier stretched all the way from the Adriatic coast just south of the current Slovenian-Croatian border, eastwards across Croatia and Slavonia, as far as Transylvania. In 1630, the Habsburg Emperor Frederick II proclaimed the so-called *Statuta Wallachorum* ('Vlach Statute'), which regulated the status of the 'Vlach' settlers (in fact Vlachs, Serbs, Croats, and others). These were emigrants, refugees and displaced persons who had escaped from the Ottoman Empire. The document defined their military command, their obligations, and their rights to internal self-administration. The Serbs, i.e. 'Vlachs', settled as border-

---

67 'The Serbs as seen in their National Songs' (1920); emphasis added, in Durham (2014): 120-121. For a fuller discussion of Durham's changing assumptions and prejudices about particular ethnic groups, see 101 below.

68 See Judah 2009: 405 (index).

69 See Bracewell 1992: 326 (index); Ćirković 312 (index); Glenny 1992: 5-6; Judah 2009: 13-16; Stoianovich, *op. cit.* 326-328.

guards, protectors and patrollers of the frontiers against the Turks. This was also the frontier between Christian and Islamic dominated regions. The Orthodox soldier-colonists who were granted settlement rights were also called *kmetovi*, meaning 'peasants, landless peasants, farmhands, serfs'.[70]

This designation perfectly reveals the origins of these borderers. They were refugees from what nineteenth century travellers called *European Turkey*,[71] *La Turquie d'Europe*,[72] and *Turkey-in-Europe*.[73]

In the wake of the collapse of federal Yugoslavia, the final savage and forced expulsion of these Serbs in 1995 by the independent Croatian government headed by Franjo Tudjman was the outcome of an agreement made in London between Warren Christopher, the sixty-third American Secretary of State, the German Foreign Minister Klaus Kinkel, and the Croatian diplomat Miomir Zuzul.[74]

ᔓ

To make matters still more complicated, the term *Morlach* was also used along the Dalmatian coast: Croatian *Morlak*, *Morovlah* pl, *Morlaci*, and Italian *Morlacco* 1536, pl. *Morlacchi*. According to the *OED* (online), the term originates in Byzantine Greek, combining the roots *mavros* 'black' and *vlachos* 'Vlach'. The name passed into twelfth century Latin as *Morovlachus*, with variants *Moroblachus*, *Morolacchus*, and from 1420, *Morlachus*, *Morlacchus* and the Latinisation *Nigri Latini* ('Black Latins'). The *OED* suggests that these 'Black Vlachs' were so named because of the colour of their clothes. The term is explained as follows:

> A member of a Vlach people centred originally on the eastern Adriatic port of Ragusa (modern Dubrovnik), and later inhabiting more northerly parts of the Dalmatian coast and its hinterland, the whole region being known at one time as Morlacchia.

The *OED* entry lists usages of the term indicating that it carried many if not all of the connotations and loadings of the word *Vlach* itself. That's to say, it could be used to refer both to the borderers and to the border guards, or paid *hajduks*, between the Austrian and Ottoman empires:

---

70 Benson 1980: 207.

71 Boué 1838a and 1838b.

72 Boué 1840.

73 Mackenzie and Irby.

74 See: Elich (online); and Judah 2009: 2-5, 293ff.

1649 *C. Walker Hist. Independ.* II. 145 The Morlachy [...] have lately preferred the Turkish Government before theirs.

1685 *London Gaz.* No. 2070/2 The Vayvode Janco was drawing together a great Body of Morlacks with a design to attack some place in the Province of Bosnia.

1778 tr. A. Fortis *Trav. into Dalmatia* 56 The Morlacchi, in general, have little notion of domestick œconomy [...]. Yet the Morlack is a great œconomist in the use of his wearing apparel.

1778 tr. A. Fortis *Trav. into Dalmatia* 65 It rarely happens [...] that a Morlacco carries off a girl against her will.

1793 *Universal Mag.* Oct. 268/1 The people called Morlacks, or Morlacchi, inhabit Morlacchia, which is among the inland mountains of Dalmatia.

1837 *Mirror* 9 Dec. 383/1 At the death of a Morlach..the family weep and howl. 1849 A. A. PATON *Highlands and Islands of Adriatic* II. iii. 33 The Morlack is the best soldier and the worst citizen in the Austrian empire.

1881 *E. A. Freeman Sketch Subj. Lands Venice* 184 Are we to believe that the Morlacchi used the turban as their head-dress before the Ottoman came?

1904c *L. Villari Republic of Ragusa* xii. 322 The Morlachs in the Venetian service made raids into Turkish territory.

1920 *M. E. Durham Twenty Years of Balkan Tangle* i. 12 They are known as Morlachs, [...] and historically are in all probability descendants of the pre-Slav native population.

1994 N. Malcolm *Bosnia* vi. 73 The borderers on the north and northwestern frontier of Bosnia [...] were known as 'Vlachs' or 'Morlachs'.

More recently, in a detailed exploration of attitudes to the Slavs among Venetians, Larry Wolf has clarified that there can be no clarity about any precise designation of the term *Morlach*, since it applied first to one group, then another.[75] In particular, he refers to the Venetian traveller Abbé Alberto Fortis (1741–1803), whose book *Viaggi in Dalmazia* was published in 1774 and, as cited in the *OED* above, in English only four years later.[76]

❧

[75] Wolff, espec. 126-227.

[76] *ibid.* 176-177; Fortis 44-89. Both these authors also have a good deal to say about hajduks. See Fortis 52ff and Wolff 399 (index).

Now let us return to the *hajduk*. In Serbo-Croatian, Bulgarian and Macedonian, usage of this word relates closely to its history in Hungarian, although with subtly different associative shifts and complex variations. Most of the pointers indicate that in the Balkans, as elsewhere, what might be loosely called the 'hajduk phenomenon' or 'hajduk tradition' developed first among people living in rural communities; and underlying its history there's a constant echo of that background. The keeping (and moving) of livestock according to patterns dominated by seasonal necessities and rhythms is also implicit.

At various points during the Ottoman occupation between the sixteenth and nineteenth centuries, many young Serbian, Bosnian, Montenegrin, Macedonian, Bulgarian, and Albanian men in rural and hilly or mountainous areas, as well as Thracians, Epirotes and others, alternated seasonally between living as farmers or herders (tillers of the soil or keepers of animals) and taking off into the woods and forests to join male-bonded, quasi-military or military 'outlaw' groups, with strict codes of loyalty and honour, each one with its own leader and set of rules. Over this long period of Ottoman rule, many varied factors were involved in the formation of these bands, including poverty, poor harvests, heavy taxes, religious persecution and social oppression, real or purported crime against the authorities, accusation of crime by the authorities, family custom or tribal tradition passing from father to son, blood-feuds, vendettas, personal squabbles, quarrels, matters of honour (such as Albanian *besë*, definitive *besa*, with its huge and complex range of meanings), as well as protest, rebelliousness and sheer dare-devilry, and even millenarian longings for a leader or saviour to lead the oppressed against their occupiers.[77] Incidentally, Edith Durham attributes to the word *besa* the following varying connotations in her *High Albania*: "oath of peace"; and the same meaning, referring to a period of truce, when "a week's *besa* had been sworn [...] so that all blood foes could meet as friends".[78] Earlier, in connection with the complex Albanian code of honour and revenge, Peter Mansfield also points to the Greek noun *μπέσα* (*bésa*) 'trust' and adj. *μπεσαλής* (*besalís*) 'trustworthy', both derived from Albanian.[79] For the Greek usage he suggests the connotation, "trustworthy in a tribal sort of way; ally in a vendetta over years?" See also Pring, *μπέσα* 'trustworthiness'.[80]

---

[77] For a pertinent discussion on millenarianism, see 108-111 below.

[78] Durham, *op.cit.* 32, 52.

[79] Email, February 17, 2003.

[80] Pring 125.

Numerous accounts by European travellers all over the Balkans between the early sixteenth and early twentieth centuries confirm Braudel's picture. In 1589, two Englishmen, Mr. Harrie Cavendish and his servant Fox, travelled from Dubrovnik to Istanbul. Fox writes:

> [W]e past by Novabazar [Novi Pazar] but went not into the toune for our genysary [janissary] sayd that yt was a thevyshe plac and that many robbaryes and murthers had byne comytted ther. The XXIXth we past by Nyza [Niš] but left the toun for the like causes.[81]

Henry Blount in 1634 also describes alarming incidents, for example, on the road between Belgrade and Niš:

> In the way, wee passed by [...] a Village fortified by mud walles against Theeves; where we found a small Caravan to have been assaulted the day before, and divers remaining fore wounded: for through all *Turkie*, especially in places desert there are many *Mountaineers*, or Outlawes, like the wild Irish, who live upon Spoile, and are not members of the State, but enemies, and used accordingly.[82]

In 1657, the geographer and historian Peter Heylyn writes of Dalmatia:

> The countrey at the time of the Romans was full of Woods who from thence issued out to make spoil and booty.[83]

In 1717, Lady Mary Wortley Montagu, wife of Edward Wortley Montagu, British Ambassador Extraordinary to the Court of Turkey, and a friend of Alexander Pope, wrote to the Abbot and Italian dramatist Antonio Conti from Adrianople (now Edirne) in north-western Turkey:

> The desert woods of Servia, are the common refuge of thieves, who rob fifty in a company, so that we had need of all our guards to secure us; and the villages are so poor, that only force could extort from them necessary provisions.[84]

---

[81] Cavendish 14; quoted by Stoianovich, *op. cit.* 166.

[82] Blount 1666 (3rd edn.): 13. By 'Turkie' he means all areas under Ottoman rule.

[83] Heylyn Peter. 1669 [1652], Book 2: 173.

[84] Wortley Montagu 1993: Letter XXVIII, to the Abbé Conti, Adrianople, 1 April 1717: 60; quoted by Mackenzie and Irby, vol. 2: 319-320; and Stoianovich, *op. cit.* 167. Here *desert* means 'uninhabited, wild'.

And more than a century later, English travellers reporting incidents include Archibald Paton (1845); Arthur Evans (1875 and 1878), later knighted for his archaeological work at Knossos in Crete; Georgina Muir Mackenzie and Paulina Irby (1877);[85] Edith Durham (in many books, published from 1904 onwards); and A. J. B. Wace and M. S. Thompson (1914). They all write dramatically of the risk of being attacked by bands of thieves, bandits, and highwaymen as a danger that goes with the terrain and has to be guarded against.

Oddly, all these British writers seem to take banditry for granted. They apparently assume, unquestioningly, that it 'goes with the territory'. None of them enquire deeply into its historical causes.

ꕤ

Although not all Balkan bandits called themselves by this name, broadly speaking, the *hajduks* were fierce and often unscrupulous bands of outlaws who, in all the Ottoman-occupied Balkan regions, nevertheless possessed a popular reputation and mystique not dissimilar to that of Robin Hood and His Merry Men in English and Scottish oral tradition. Like Robin Hood, individual *hajduks* – some of whose exploits were rooted in historical fact, and others of which were later embroidered into tales of semi-mythical heroes – progressively became associated with and woven into a whole genre of folk-ballads, stories and poems: just as also with the *Krajišniks, Klephts, Uskoks, Cossacks*, etc. Even today in Serbia, Montenegro, Macedonia, and Bulgaria, and in parts of Croatia, Bosnia, Kosovo and Albania, the *hajduci* conjure up images that combine romance, adventure and sentimental reverence. These days, there's a *Hajduk* football club in Split, Croatia, whose supporters are called *Hajdukovci*, which is perhaps unsurprising if one thinks of similar totemic or folk-historical names given by other cultures, including our own, to the highly-paid teams of performers in neo-tribalistic sports rituals such as football or rugby. In Serbia and Montenegro, glamorised historical accounts of *hajduks* continue to be set books for reading (*lektira*) in schools. A popular Serbian children's book by Branislav Nusić, which has gone through more than six editions, is entitled *Hajduci*: the connotations in the title being comparable perhaps to Richmal Crompton's *William and the Outlaws*, though the book is nowhere nearly so funny. In Romania, a group of Romany *lautari* ('traditional musicians')

[85] Throughout both volumes of their *Travels*, Mackenzie and Irby emphasise the seriousness of these dangers and identify robbers and highwaymen with "haïduks".

from Clejani, a village southwest of Bucharest, calls itself *Taraf de Haïdouks* ('band of brigands').

ᔕ

During the centuries-long Ottoman occupation of the Balkans, depending on the particular period, attitudes to *hajduks* among the Christian *raya* population[86] could be scaled on a graph measured between the extremes of outright fear, insecurity and suspicion, along the turning of a blind eye and a kind of benevolent tolerance or guarded approval towards young men who needed to 'sow their wild oats', to the other extreme of openly declared support and revolutionary or nationalistic fervour. Far from being something to be ashamed of, 'having a *hajduk* in the family' operated in close-knit communities as a guarded but nevertheless shared mark of pride or respect. Quoting Stendhal travelling in Italy and Gautier visiting Spain, Braudel indicates clearly that the Balkan examples were part of a far wider phenomenon:

> The peoples' heart was for them (the brigands) and the village girls preferred over all others the lad who, once in his life, had been forced *d'andar alla macchia.*" (lit. 'to take to the bush', i.e. 'join the *maquis*'). In Sicily the exploits of brigands were sung by *urvi*, blind wandering singers who lifted their voices "rather like dusty little violins", and were eagerly surrounded by the crowds along the promenades, under the plane trees. Théophile Gautier noted too that Spain, and above all Andalucia, "has remained Arab on this point and bandits easily passed for heroes there." All of Yugoslav and Rumanian folklore is equally full of stories of *haiduks* and outlaws [...] revenge against the master, against gammy justice: banditism, a little everywhere and in every age, has taken on this allure of redressing wrongs.[87]

Stoianovich analyses the formation of these groups particularly well:

---

[86] Ottoman Turkish *raya, rayah*, pl. of *raiyye*: lit. 'flock, herd, cattle', from Arabic رعايا *ra'aya*, meant 'members of the flock', i.e. 'subjects of the Ottoman Empire'. The term included all who paid taxes, including Muslims, Christians and Jews, as distinct from the *askeri* 'upper class' and *kul* 'slaves'. While keeping this generic meaning, the term came to be particularly used for "non-Moslem subjects" (Hony 294), "non-Muslim subjects (under Turkish rule)" (Benson 1980: 511).

[87] Braudel, *op. cit.* 134-135; trans. RB.

> The members of such men's societies were not ordinary thieves and cut-throats. In essence, they symbolised a variant value pattern that the gerontocracy frequently allowed as a means of diverting hostility from parents, household, kinfolk, community, and clan to other objects and as a vicarious expression of their own hostility to the same objects.[88]

Interestingly, in some areas which weren't subject to Ottoman rule, members of these groups of young fighting males were even 'officially recognised'. So, in Senj, along the Dalmatian coast, there were registered *uskoks*; in Ukraine, registered *Cossacks*; and in Hungary and Poland, registered *hajduks*, who, as has already been noted, settled and founded fortress-towns along the border. We'll return later to the phenomenon of official 'recognition', indeed, of official exploitation, in an uneasy cycle involving postures and policies that varied according to the authorities' own needs: the turning of a blind eye, positive collaboration, rejection, and outright persecution.

ග

Stoianovich's combination of a broad synthesis with documentation of detail reflects a depth of insight that's intimately and intuitively informed by his personal upbringing in a small village in former Yugoslav Macedonia. It's clear that he feels and has experienced the *hajduk* tradition as well as understanding it conceptually. He was born in Gradešnica in northern Macedonia, around fifty kilometres from Poreče, the birthplace of *Hajduk* Chieftain Micko Krstić.[89] With a complex background, education and professional life that spanned Balkan, French and American cultures and languages, Stoianovich's consciousness is that of an 'edge-person' himself.[90] This contrasts markedly with all descriptions of the *hajduk* tradition that I've so far come across in texts by American and British writers, among whom I've not yet found one single insightful attempt to relate either their political history or their romantic popular image to underlying patterns of rural life. This failing applies equally to experienced foreign commentators

[88] Stoianovich, *op. cit.* 165.

[89] See photo and text: 107 below.

[90] Stoianovich (1921–2005) was born in a Serbian village in Macedonia. After obtaining his doctorate under Fernand Braudel in Paris, where he became a key member of the *Annales* group, he emigrated to the USA. He was Professor of History at Rutgers University for four decades. See Vryonis 1992: ix–xv; Stoianovich 1976; and 'Traian Stoianovich', *Wikipedia*.

and journalists in the Balkans, to travellers, and to writers who claim authoritativeness thanks to their academic credentials and established respectability.[91]

The Cambridge academic Noel Malcolm, for example, offers sketchy information on etymology and limited political contexts,[92] but suffers not only from oversimplified reconstructions to suit his overall purpose of debunking Serbs and belittling their culture and history, but also from the snide and transparent pretence that he's being fair and objective in doing so.

In Eric Hobsbawm's *Bandits*, there's a chapter entitled 'Haiduks'.[93] This is one of the most respected 'popular scholarly' accounts of banditry by an English writer. But, despite this book's virtues, its account of the Balkans painfully lacks authority and authenticity. It contains scarcely any references to the Ottoman Empire, only patchy mention of the Christian Greek *klephts* and the very different Muslim *krdžali* in Bulgaria, and none at all to any of the hugely documented Serbian or Macedonian historical and folk material. Astonishingly, the role of the *hajduci* in the various Serbian national liberation movements isn't mentioned at all, and his failure to trace any link between the term *četa* and the political *Četnik* movement clearly indicates the perfunctoriness and shallowness of the treatment.[94]

---

[91] The exception is Bracewell.

[92] Malcolm 118ff.

[93] Hobsbawm (2nd edn.) 2000: 77ff.

[94] *ibid.* 84. Hobsbawm's earlier *Primitive Rebels* (1959), with its acknowledged sources in Fernand Braudel, contains brilliant and pioneering insights on millenarianism and the rituals associated with secret revolutionary brotherhoods. However, this earlier book makes no reference to Eastern Europe, the Ottoman Empire or the Balkans. In hindsight, the title itself, combined with a constant harping on terms like 'primitive' and 'backward', smacks of a naïvely linear view of history which seems to derive as much from the cultural imperialism of such nineteenth century English writers as Edward B. Tylor (*Primitive Culture*, 1871), as from the assumptions about 'progress' that he claims for himself, from within the west-European 'enlightened-socialist' tradition. On this peculiarly British attraction to the word 'primitive, the German historian of ancient Greek religion Walter Burkert comments in a very different context:

> [...] the ethnologists were almost all missionaries. Whatever was alien was understood as primitive, as the 'not-yet' of a beginning which contrasted with the Englishman's own self-conscious progressiveness. (Burkert 2)

To take Rebecca West as a contrary example, while she comments perceptively and charmingly on the handsomely costumed appearance and heroic bearing of descendants of *hajduks* whom she comes across in Bosnia, and although (as we've already seen) she writes in brilliant and powerful detail on the *uskoks*, she nowhere attempts to connect or compare the two traditions. She describes 'Haiduks' as:

> [...] the Christians who after the Ottoman conquest took refuge in the highlands, and came down to the valleys every year on St. George's Day, because by then the trees were green enough to give them cover, and they could harry the Turks by brigandage.[95]

West seems to have spent most of her time in the Balkans talking to witty and sophisticated people from the politer social echelons; or, at least, that's the impression she gives, perhaps due to the incomparably assured elegance of her own writing style, combined with our knowledge of her wealth and privileged social status. Apart from a sneaking doubt whether it's one hundred percent true to insist that *hajduks* were all or even predominantly Christian – a doubt in the mind of this reader at least – West's delicately sharp though limited *aperçu* in connection with Saint George's Day, so typical of her style and approach, is capable of being developed more interestingly by taking up hints and observations from other studies of custom, ethnology and folklore. For example, Olive Lodge, another Englishwoman who writes equally fascinatingly on the Balkans, mentions that:

> At daybreak on St George's Day everyone goes for a picnic (*uranjak*) [*sic*] in the mountains, to gather lilies-of-the-valley – in Old Serbia known as St George's flowers – bathe in certain sacred mountain springs, and roast lambs.[96]

This may be collated with a comment from the American ethnologist Joel Halpern, who points out that the *uranak*, meaning 'getting-up-early' or 'early-rising', was also known as the *hajdučki sastanak*, i.e. 'hajduks' gathering' or 'meeting of the hajduks'.[97]

Putting these references alongside one another does provide interesting clues which suggest patterns even more deeply ingrained in language and custom. They indicate that in Balkan villages, rules governing the

---

[95] West, *op. cit.* 327; and see also 434.

[96] Lodge 255-256. Serbian informants from Belgrade have pointed out to me that the word should be *uranak*, not *uranjak*, i.e. that it should be spelt and pronounced in the *ekavski* rather than *ijekavski* regional variant.

[97] Halpern 242.

behaviour of *hajduks* were wholly integrated into wider patterns of rural tradition and consciousness. Throughout the Slavonic-speaking Balkans, as well as among non-Slavonic Balkan language-groups such as Vlachs and Romanies, the precise date for the transition from winter to spring was irrevocably fixed in the calendar as St George's Day (Serbian *Djurdjevdan*, Bulgarian *Gergiovden*; compare Russian *Yurief Den* or *Yegorief Den*, etc.): that is, April 23 in the 'Old Style Calendar', and May 6 in the new. This was ritually marked as the date when young males could take off to join their *hajduk* bands.

St George's Day also corresponds exactly to the Turkish Spring Festival, *Hizirellez, Hidirellez* or *Hidrellez*, which falls on precisely the same day. The Balkan (Kalderash) Romany name for St George's Day, *Ederlez, Ederlezi* or *Herderlezi*, derives from the Turkish. So in the Balkans the date marking the beginning of Spring was identical for both Christians and Muslims.[98] Furthermore, the strict traditional control exerted by the seasons over the formation and disbanding of these *hajduk* groups strongly suggests their origins in a culture of herders and shepherds – possibly cutting across distinctions of language, tribe and 'ethnicity'. According to a masterly

---

[98] For more on St. George's Day, see *In a Time of Drought* (RB 2011c): 95-98. The Turkish names *Hizirellez, Hidirellez* or *Hidrellez* and the Romany names *Ederlez, Ederlezi* or *Herderlezi* (derived from the Turkish) offer fascinating parallelisms and syncretisms in meaning. The second half of all these names derives from *Ilyas* (*Elias, Ilija, Ilias,* etc.), that is, the Old Testament prophet Elijah, who is the usually accepted 'post-Christian' Balkan and replacement for the pagan Slavonic storm and thunder god Perun – although this of course doesn't apply to Greeks. The first part of the name of this Turkish festival is equally fascinating. It derives from the ancient *Hizir*, better known in Islam as *Khidr* or *al-Khidr*, who is the typological equivalent of St. George, especially in his aspect as Green George. See '*Khidr*', *Wikipedia*. According to Walker and Uysal (1973):

> Hizir may well be one of the oldest gods of the Middle East – pre-Moslem, pre-Christian, pre-Roman, pre-Greek – a vegetation god and a water deity. The Turkish name *Hizir* is transliterated from the Arabic *Al-Kidr*, an epithet that means, literally, 'The Green One' or The Green Man'[…]. Hizir is the Moslem equivalent of Elijah, but, curiously enough, the Turkish folk mind, influenced here as much by the Jewish as by the Arabic tradition, has refused to allow the image of Elijah to be completely assimilated by that of Hizir. Instead, the two exist side by side as doubles, a situation most noticeable in the naming of the Hizir celebration on May 6. It is always called Hizir-Ilyas Day – the Turks usually shorten this name to *Hidrellez* – the Ilyas being the Turkish form of the word Elijah.

study of the Vlachs of Northern Greece, who were traditionally a people of transhumants (that is, shepherds who move their flocks between winter and summer pastures, settling seasonally in both locations), St George's Day was the first day of the year when, like all other such groups in the Balkans, they set about packing their mules and whole extended families set off for their new quarters:

> About St George's Day [...], the shepherds who winter in the Thessalian plains round Trikkala, or between Larissa and Tirnavos or in the Potamia district near Elassona prepare for moving to the mountains for the summer. The lambs which have been born during the winter in December or January are by this time weaned and capable of standing the journey.[99]
>
> The earliest day for families to start to go to Samarina is St George's Day [...], when the shepherds first leave the plains on their way up to their summer camping grounds near their native villages. [...] The shepherds stay on till the day of St Demetrius, October 26th (November 8th N. S.) on which day they start to go down to their winter quarters. From then till next St George's Day the village is all but deserted and inhabited only by those who have made up their minds to stay there as guards or for other reasons.[100]

These passages may be compared with Stoianovich's illuminating synthesis of seasonally based patterns of social and economic mobility in the Balkans. Based partly on Braudel's *magnum opus* on the Mediterranean (1949, 1966), Stoianovich's discussion fully incorporates the *hajduk* into the overall Balkan picture. The passage deserves quoting at length:

> Such population movements were more or less regularized, occurring at stipulated times of the year. In his epochal study of the Mediterranean, Fernand Braudel sketches a remarkable portrait of the role of St. George's Day (April 23, Old Style) and St. Demetrius's Day (October 26, O.S.) as the terminal dates of the winter and summer seasons throughout the eastern Mediterranean and the zone of Byzantine and Ottoman civilisation. As St. Demetrius's Day drew near, the Turks brought their campaigns to a close. From then until St. George's Day, navigation diminished, epidemics were sometimes appeased, war yielded to diplomatic negotiations and correspondence, and rumors abounded. Between St. George's Day and St. Demetrius's Day, commerce and agriculture were reactivated, war was resumed, and epidemics threatened

[99] Wace and Thompson 77-78.

[100] *ibid.* 48.

> again. Rents and debts became payable on one or both the two holidays. Apprentices quit their homes on one of the two occasions to enter the service of a master craftsman. Village craftsmen departed from their homes at the time of the spring festival to offer their services in distant towns and provinces, generally returning for the autumn festival. Farmhands hired out their labor on St. George's Day, returning home for St. Demetrius's Day. Depending upon climatic differences, shepherds and shepherd folk abandoned their summer pastures on the occasion of one of the two festivals and their winter pasture on the occasion of the other festival. The two feasts, along with the feast of the Assumption (August 15) were also occasions for group marriages. A Serbian proverb attests, moreover, to their importance in the life of the outlaw (commonly called *hajduk*), so characteristic a feature in Balkan society between the mid-sixteenth and the mid-nineteenth centuries.
>
> On St. Demetrius's *hajduks* disband,
> On St. George's *hajduks* together band.
>
> War, shepherds' migrations, agriculture, commerce, and marriage were thus endowed with a regular rhythm. Bandits, marriageable girls, farmhands, craftsmen, apprentices, shep-herds, mariners, and warriors moved from one home, from one community, from one kind of activity to another on the occasion of the two feasts. The Balkan peoples of the premodern era, notably during the resurgence of pastoralism between 1400 and 1800 or 1830, were extraordinarily mobile.[101]

These common patterns of custom and behaviour, and especially those regarding seasonal mobility, of course, applied to most and probably all of the ethnic and linguistic groups in the region. It makes sense, then, that these patterns should have been reflected in a pool of words with related and overlapping meanings in neighbouring languages, and many borrowings.

Stoianovich goes on to suggest that under Ottoman rule there were three types of outlaw bands or classes of actions by bands. In the first category, there were the 'tame' *hajduks* or *klephts* who usually collaborated with political authorities and, in contradistinction to these, in the second, the 'wild' *hajduks* or *klephts* who, without being revolutionary, were opposed to the existing order of things or took advantage of the local order for their own personal of family benefit. In fact, a band could be 'wild' or 'tame' – 'cooked' or 'raw', to set the polarity in a Lévi-Straussian *culture-nature* framework – depending on the occasion. We'll come to the third grouping shortly.

---

[101] Stoianovich 1994: 63-64. See also *ibid.* 338-340.

Despite these elegant theorisings, however, in her typically crisp and observant way Edith Durham cuts to the chase when she tells the story of four murderers who were to be taken to be shot at the scene of their crime between Kragujevac and Čačak. She's invited to watch, but after debating with herself, decides to avoid the grisly scene. The account is from her visit to Šumadija in 1902, during the first of her many Balkan journeys:

> I was urged to go, and offered special felicities. Taken aback, I listened, speechless, while the plan was unfolded. I was to rise very early and to drive for three hours up the mountains with the condemned men and the file of soldiers who were to carry out their sentence. I said to myself that it was my duty to see everything, but searched my brains for a decent way out of it. [...] Then I recollected that if I went, for the next fifty years it would be said that all Englishwomen were in the habit of seeing men shot before breakfast. I had not come so far to see Servians killed. My reply caused disappointment and I was strongly urged to go. The murder had been a particularly atrocious one, so that I need not mind seeing the punishment; for the murderers, after cutting the throats of the victims, had gouged out their eyes and otherwise barbarously mutilated the corpses. Twenty men had been arrested, *the last gang of Hayduks* that side of Servia. Four were to die tomorrow.[102]

Even in 1902, then, the term *hajduk* was still being applied not only to heroic patriots and brave freedom fighters, but to gangs of wild and villainous robbers. In the same book, however, Durham writes with matronising relish of a tall Montenegrin youth, "clean-limbed, clear-eyed, and the pink of courtesy, who told me with great earnestness that he wished to be '*a hero like Hayduk Veljko.*'"[103]

ശ

Approval or at least tolerance of brigands is very ancient. In his *Politics*, which he wrote between 336 and 322 BCE, Aristotle designates brigandage as a working profession along with various others. He first categorises it as a subset of hunting: "[D]ifferent people [live] from different kinds of hunting, for instance some from brigandage, others from fishing [...] and others live on wild birds and animals."[104] He then lists various

[102] Durham 2015 [1904]: 151; emphasis added.

[103] *ibid.* 191; emphasis added, RB.

[104] *Politics* I. iii. 4: 35; trans. Rackham.

"modes of life", all of which he regards as entirely proper and acceptable – "the herdsman, the husbandman, the brigand, the fisherman, the hunter" – and he combine this entire absence of approbation of any kind with the clear understanding that people need to take on different kinds of work in order to make ends meet. While pointing this out, he associates brigandage with pastoralism:

> Others also live pleasantly by combining some of these pursuits, supplementing the more deficient life when it happens to fall short in regard to being self-sufficing: for instance, *some combine a pastoral life and brigandage*, others husbandry and hunting, and similarly with the others – they pass their time in such a combination of pursuits as their need compels.[105]

ꕤ

Before we leave the topic of shepherds and herders, here, as it were in parenthesis, is a linguistic conjecture on the possible origins of the ancient tribal names of proto-Serbs and proto-Croats from the second century AD. Marija Gimbutas cites Ptolemy (c. AD 100–178) as the first known source of names:

> Ptolemy may have known another branch of the Slavs, whose name seems undoubtedly related to that of the present-day Serbs. Describing Sarmatia (*Geography* V, 8), Ptolemy enumerates thirteen tribes, among them the *Serboi,* as follows: [...] between the Keraunian mountains [identified with the north-eastern foot-hills of the Caucasus) and the river Ra [Volga] live Orineoi, Valoi, Serboi. [....] Moszynski sees the name derived from the Indo-European root **ser*, **serv-* 'guard, protect', making it cognate with Latin *servus*; the v being interchangeable with b in pronunciation. The original meaning of *Serboi* was probably 'shepherds', 'guardians of animals'.[106]

ꕤ

Other Balkan bandits were known as *kirjali,*[107] or *kirjalii, kurjalii, kirdjalii, kurdjalii, krdžali, daalii.* The Bulgarian anthropologist Milena Koleva suggests two possible etymologies, both from Turkish: *kir* 'field' and *daag* 'mountain'. She adds that they were "[...] real gangsters. This

[105] *ibid.* I. iii, 5: 35.

[106] Gimbutas 1971: 58-60.

[107] Stoianovich, *op. cit.* 166.

phenomenon originates in the decentralisation of the Ottoman empire at the end of the 16th century, which led to the great authority of power being concentrated in the hands of local feudal lords who cared for nothing else but their own political and economic prosperity."[108] The *kirjali*, who were "overwhelmingly Muslim",[109] were employed by landowners as enforcers. Stoianovich suggests that their background of was often urban:

> To integrate their frequently disconnected land possessions and widen their economic power, the new landlord recorded to the use of armed irregulars or *kirjalis*, some of whom had been driven to banditry or service as irregular troops by the decline of sufficient home market for urban production.[110]

Andrejčin *et al.* explain the Bulgarian *kirdjalii* as 'a word of Turkish origin; a gang of runaway soldiers (probably mercenaries) and robbers (brigands) at the end of the eighteenth century, who attacked villages and caused ravage and fires'.[111] Romanian has *kirdjali* and *carjalii.*[112] Apparently, the *kirjalii, kirdjalii* or *daalii* first operated in the Rhodope Mountains in Bulgaria and then spread to other areas in the late eighteenth and early nineteenth centuries. They were portrayed in folksongs and poems of that time as evil and dangerous bandits. The Romanian scholar Răzvan Voncu adds:

> The *kirdjali* (in Bulgarian) or *carjalii* (in Romanian) were Turkish (Islamic) robbers, belonging more to banditism than anything else. They gained a slightly better name when they rose up against the Ottoman power, disturbing its rule in Bulgaria, and so permitted the Bulgarians to organize in the wake of their liberation. Unfortunately, by dismantling the Ottoman power in the Balkans, they were not at all positive to the Romanians. In our history, they left the memory of a number of bloody attacks across the Danube. In fact, coming from Bulgaria after they eliminated the Ottoman regular army and the official border-points on the river, when they crossed the Danube to Romania (Wallachia), they looted everything they could, then returned with their spoils to Bulgaria to continue their mutiny.[113]

---

108 Email, October 17, 2006.

109 Todorova, email, Oct. 31, 2019.

110 Stoianovich 1952, vol. 1: 2.

111 Andrejčin *et al.* 382; trans. Anelia Tapp.

112 Răzvan Voncu, email, November 13, 2006.

113 Răzvan Voncu, email, January 8, 2007.

Similar brigand gangs were formed of both Christians and Muslims. They tended not to be recruited so much from among youths in rural areas, but to be brought together from the ranks of the disaffected and deprived riff-raff of rough urban and semi-urban environments, for example, demobilised soldiers and mercenaries, layabouts, propertyless bachelors and unemployed servants or workers. These men were liable to get jobs as rent collectors, bodyguards or security guards, shift allegiances to new bosses, and move around through various parts of the Ottoman empire – Albania, Bosnia, Serbia, Bulgaria, Macedonia, Thessaly and the Morea – either selling their services to the highest bidder or forming gangs of their own. They seem not unfamiliar in the context of patterns of criminality, business, smuggling, politics, and spying today.

Clearly, as Stoianovich points out, these three different conceptual groupings must be regarded as 'ideal categories', and in reality a single bandit-group might at differing times contain elements or adopt the behaviour patterns of each category.[114] Equally clearly, although the very fact of their formation indicated disaffection and rebelliousness, they weren't always or primarily motivated by nationalistic urges or beliefs. Even so, there's evidence that from the late sixteenth century on, at least among certain clan-chiefs in rugged areas of Albania and Montenegro, that co-ordinated political plans did get formulated from time to time to eject the Ottomans from the region once and for all. These plans were even communicated by emissaries to Western European powers, including Venice, Austria and Russia, with requests for assistance.[115] So when the Ottoman Empire did begin to disintegrate in the Balkans, such bands came to play an important part. The mid-nineteenth century founders of both Serbian royal dynasties, Karadjordje ('Black George') and Miloš Obrenović, both periodically led lives as farmers and as insurrectionary *hajduk* warrior-chiefs.

It therefore seems almost paradoxical that one of the Serbian words for a senior *hajduk* commander or chieftain (i.e. warlord, guerrilla leader) who fought against the Ottomans should have a Turkish derivation. The title *harambaša* comes from *haram* (Turk. 'illicit, unlawful'), hence with the connotation 'banned, taboo, outlaw'. Here, unsurprisingly, is yet another rich word-cluster that crosses the multiple and shifting borders that have alternately divided and connected Balkan peoples and languages. It also further illustrates the point already made: that the targets of negative stereotypes often take on the precise terms cast upon them

114 Stoianovich 1994: 164ff.

115 Malcolm 120-1.

by their abusers, and convert their labels into positive symbols. Turkish *haram* itself also embeds a contradictory polarity, meaning *both* 'forbidden by religion (i.e. Islam)' *and* 'sacred, inviolable', as does the word *taboo* itself.[116] The word *harem*, meaning 'women's enclosure', clearly combines both opposites. The combination of *haram* with Turkish '*baş*' (lit. 'head, chief')[117] yields *harambaša* and the verb *harambašovati*. Skok confirms that Serbian *haram* ('inadmissible, forbidden, unlawful') derives via Turkish from Arabic حرام (*harām)* 'forbidden, taboo'.[118] Cognates include: Bulgarian *harám*, Romanian *hâram*, modern Greek *χαράμι* (*harámi*), and Arumonian (Cincar or Vlach) *harame* ('illicit thing'). Skok adds that Vuk Karadžić lists *harámija* as a synonym for *hajduk*, with the variant *(h)áramija* in Kosmet (Kosovo and Metohia). He also mentions various derivatives and idioms that contain the idea of 'untrustworthiness, cunning, offensiveness', including swearwords and curses, such as Serbian *haramzada*, *aramzada* 'Lying Bastard' and Albanian *aramzade* 'Bastard'.[119] For Serbian *haram*, Škaljić adds the colourful curse *Haram ti bilo materino mlijeko* ('Damned be your mother's milk').[120] As is so often the pattern, a word and its derivatives can come to occupy emotive and evaluative connotations that are diametrically opposite, depending on who's talking to and about whom.

During the Serbian uprisings against the Turks, the word *harambaša* eventually overlaps with the term *vojvoda*, although the two have very different origins and connotations. Whereas the former suggests forest and frontier, outlaw and transgression, and wildness and independence, the latter carries the weight of official authority, respected position and high military rank. The title first appears in the tenth century work *De Administrando Imperio* ('On Administering the Empire') by the Byzantine emperor Constantine VII Porphyrogennetos,[121] where it identifies Hungarian military leaders.[122] As for the Serbian word *vojvoda*, this has cognates in all the Slavonic languages, as well as in Romanian, Hungarian and Latvian. Its etymology is, simply, 'military leader', from *vojnik* 'soldier, warrior' and

[116] Freud, 'Taboo and Emotional Ambivalence': 19ff.

[117] Hony 134 and 33.

[118] For the connection with the militant Islamist movement in Africa, *Boko Haram*, see 62 above, note 12.

[119] Skok 1971, vol. 1: 656 (trans. RB).

[120] Škaljić 312-313 (trans. RB).

[121] Porphyrogennetos, lit. 'born to the purple'; hence 'born of the blood Royal'.

[122] 'Voivode', *Wikipedia*.

voditi 'to lead'.[123] The meaning also includes high-ranking administrative command and responsibilities over a particular territory, so that it takes on an honorific sense close to and identifiable with *gospodar* ('duke, lord'). In an 1869 entry, the *OED* cites "the Hospodars or Voyvodes of Wallachia and Moldavia" as synonyms. In English, the term first occurs in 1589 in Richard Hayklut's *The Principall Navigations, Voiages and Discoveries of the English Nation* [...].[124] In his *Cosmographie* (1652), the learned Peter Heylyn writes about "the Vaivods and Princes of Transylvania. He adds: "the word Vaivod signifying as much as *Praefectus Militiae*, or a Lord Lieutenant; [...] a man by reason of the greatnesse of his place and power, of most Authoritie in that Kingdome".[125] Travelling in Greece in 1812 and 1813, Henry Holland uses the Slavonic word when describing a location as far south as Thebes, Boeotia: "The house of the Vaivode is the only considerable building in the place."[126] In 1877, Georgina Muir Mackenzie writes:

> A rank of military origins was that of voivode, leader in war, a name which has found its way through German into English under the meaningless cacophony of "waywode". Under the monarchy, the voivodes appear as companions in arms of the sovereign; and this office was bestowed on a talented general, whatever might be his descent or social rank.[127]

As for the word *vožd*, closely related to *vojvoda*, this means 'leader'.

By the nineteenth century, the *hajduk* tradition has contributed to numerous Balkan revolts and uprisings. So the tradition of the *hajduk* is integral to the fact and spirit of Serbian and Yugoslav national independence, giving these figures a heroic, flamboyant image in popular imagination, which has lasted to this day.

ও

As these criss-crossed and intermeshing linguistic and historical complexities clarify, under Ottoman rule, there was no way in which the subject peoples in the Balkans could improve their lot, especially the Orthodox Christians living at the lowest level of rural communities. Travellers to the Balkans

[123] Skok 1973, vol. 3: 612-613.

[124] *OED* (online).

[125] Heylyn (1669 edn.) Book 2: 169.

[126] Holland (1819 edn.) vol 2: 108.

[127] Mackenzie and Irby, vol. 2: 294.

from the early eighteenth to the late nineteenth century repeatedly report both on the abuses suffered by the Christian *raya* at the hands of their Ottoman rulers and on the complex patterns of corruption and complicity exacted by the many kinds and degrees of servants, henchmen and stake-holders in the *status quo* – including born Muslims, converted Muslims (*Janissaries*, etc.), Christians (especially *armatoles* and Greek *Phanariots*, i.e. residents in the Greek quarter of Istanbul), and Jews. Thus the *raya*, the agricultural workers, were the lowest of the low in a complex hierarchy. For centuries, Balkan villagers were subject to taxation, bullying, persecution, reprisals, imprisonment, torture and execution. They had few if any rights under the law and their miserable fates all too often depended, randomly, on the whim of their rulers. As Henry Holland writes of his tour of Greece in 1812–1813, treatment varied widely from time to time, from place to place, and the proportion and numbers of settled Turks in a given area in relation to those of Christians:

> In larger towns, the population is usually of a mixed character; and here the relation of Turks and Greeks depends in part upon the numbers of each class; the more active and cultivated genius of the latter people giving them a facility in eluding or opposing *the sluggish tyranny of the Turks*, and this facility being increased by their numerical strength. Where the population is wholly Greek, there is a still further exemption from *the direct evils of personal oppression* [...].[128]

Here we note the typical and spurious tendency to assign particular 'intrinsic' qualities to this or that ethnic group, evident later in both Evans and Durham. Even so, the evident pattern of "tyranny" and "oppression" is constantly reiterated by observers. Of the many examples of observations by English travellers that could be given, three further quotations will suffice. These span almost two entire centuries.

Nearly one hundred years before Holland, in letter dated one day before the previous one quoted above, Lady Mary Wortley Montagu writes to the Princess of Wales, Wilhelmina Caroline of Ansbach, consort to King George II, and later Queen of England:

> We crossed the deserts of Serbia, almost quite overgrown with wood, though a country naturally fertile and the inhabitants industrious.[129] But the oppression of the peasants is so great, they are forced to abandon

[128] Holland *op. cit.* 11; emphases added.

[129] Here, *deserts* clearly means 'uninhabited spaces'. See 84 above.

their houses and neglect their tillage, all they have being a prey to the janissaries, whenever they please to settle upon it. We had a guard of 500 of them, and I was almost in tears every day to see their insolencies in the poor villages through which we passed.[130]

Although by the time she reached Istanbul, Lady Wortley Montagu's fascination with Ottoman *haute couture* came to outweigh these sympathies, her remarks here are just as astute economically as they're convincing in moral outrage, proving her to be a brilliant observer and analyst. Her comments about the fertility of the land and the industriousness of the local people reveal the clear and immediate implication that, given a different regime, these peasants' lives might well have been fulfilling and prosperous.

Nearly one hundred and seventy years later, in 1875, the young Oxford graduate Arthur Evans, later known as the excavator of Knossos, offers many descriptions of the sufferings of Bosnian peasants at the hands of Phanariot Greeks (i.e. Greeks from Istanbul) who act as Ottoman tax collectors. This passage is one of his milder descriptions:

> No considerations of honour, of religion, or humanity, restrain these wretches. Having acquired the right to farm the taxes of a given district, the Turkish officials and gendarmerie are bound to support them in wringing the utmost farthing out of the *misera contribuens plebs*, and it is natural that this help should be most readily forthcoming when needed to break the resistance of the rayah.
>
> These men time their visitations well. They appear in the villages before the harvest is gathered and assess the value of the crops according to the present prices, which, if course, are far higher just before the harvest than after it. But the rayahs would be well contented if their exactions stopped here. They possess, however a terrible lever for putting the screw on the miserable tiller. The harvest may not be gathered till the tax, which is pitilessly levied in cash., has been extorted. If the full amount – and they often double or treble the legal sum – is not forthcoming, the tax-gatherer simply has to say 'then your harvest shall rot on the ground till you pay it! And the rayah must see the produce of his toil lost, or pay a ruinous imposition which more than swamps his profits.[131]

Evans, like Muir Mackenzie and Irby, is strongly anti-Ottoman, although not anti-Muslim. His attack here is on Christian Greeks who contribute essential services to Ottoman rule.

---

130 Wortley Montagu, *ibid.* Letter XXVI, 1 April 1717: 55-56.

131 Evans 1875: 257.

In extreme contrast to these two passages, in an essay based on a visit in 1906 and first published in 1920, Edith Durham diverts responsibility for the conditions of the Balkan populace from the Ottoman overlords to their feudal Christian predecessors and, later, to the Turks' converted local henchmen:

> In pre-Turk days the rule of the chieftain *seems to have been* severe. Under the Turk the system continued, and the "Turk" of many a ballad who oppressed his Christian peasant was *in fact* the Slav feudal nobleman who, having turned Muslim carried on the ancestral tradition, and to the tyranny of the feudal noble added religious intolerance.[132]

This analysis is transparently spurious. The foundational assumption in the phrase *seems to have been* is a clear give-away, and on this slender premise the term *in fact* is erected. Durham continues with strong disapproval of the *hajduk* tradition. The tone of irritable condemnation and outright dismissal of all Slav culture, especially of Montenegrins, disfigures all her later writings:

> There was *little organized government under the Turks.* The traditional ballads give us a vivid picture of the heyduks or brigands. Highway robbery up till, and well into, the nineteenth century was both a lucrative business and a sport which well suited the lazy but adventurous *spirit of the people.* It perpetuated *in fact* the everlasting raids of one noble against another in pre-Turk days. To this day a Montenegrin "junak" delights in pillaging a village. But continuous work is abhorrent to him.[133]

Here, the idea that there was *little organized government under the Turks*, if superficially plausible, is a distortion, whether naïve or specious, or both. The filtering of absolute Ottoman power over the subject peoples of the Balkans through layers of intermediaries such as janissaries, armatoles, *kiryalis* and Phanariots was a deliberately cultivated, assiduously organised and subtly administrated method of control that, for all its failings – including strong moral objections – worked more-or-less effectively for more than four centuries. Here again, Durham's term *in fact* is supported not by evidence but by prejudice, leading to the suspect notion of *the spirit of the people.* And while the *hajduk* tradition may well have developed before the arrival of the Turks, that is, in a medieval and feudal society

[132] Durham 1920: 123; emphases added.

[133] *ibid.* 123; emphases added.

not so different from the England of the Robin Hood tradition, Ottoman rule over the Balkans can scarcely be adequately analysed in terms of *class*. The term *caste* would perhaps be more apt. What Durham signally fails to do is to think through *how* and *why* brigandage was perpetuated for so many hundreds of years in the Balkans. Nor was it carried out solely by Slavs. Male members of most *raya* populations, including Albanian, might become bandits. The Serb sociologist Nebojša Popov clarifies that war was "part of everyday life", that "*the vocation of warrior* was very highly regarded", and that "that profession was the most convenient channel of vertical mobility for individuals and their families, *even regardless of religious and ethnic allegiance* [...]."[134]

ꕥ

Once again, for an adequate analysis, we turn to the historian Traian Stoianovich – who also uses the term *vertical* – especially his two essays entitled 'Factors in the Decline of Ottoman Society in the Balkans' and 'The Social Foundation of Balkan Politics, 1750–1941'.[135] He argues that Ottoman society "was not a class society but [...] an imperial and estate society".[136] His discussion is finely tuned, but at the risk of oversimplification, I quote several key passages, if only to give the gist:

> Every society has an image or several images of itself. One of the Ottoman self-images was a view of society, theirs as well as the wider society of human kind, as a vertically structured social order of four pillars or estates: the men of the pen, the men of the sword, the men of business, and the husbandmen.[137]

In approaching this quadripartite set, we note, first, that all these categories are for men and that the status of women isn't even recognised, a view consistent with the wholly subservient role of women throughout Ottoman society – as extensively and intimately explored and fascinatingly portrayed, for example, by Lady Mary Wortley Montagu in many of her letters – as well as in the Balkan Christian world. What's more, since the 'vertical' Ottoman worldview was structured in a manner

[134] Popov 1996b: 82; emphases added.

[135] Stoianovich 1995, vol. 3: 103-110 and 111-138.

[136] *ibid.* 103.

[137] *ibid.* 103.

so rigid and exclusive as to be more-or-less absolute, it admitted no way in which 'husbandmen' (i.e. peasants, *raya, rayah*) or their families could either improve or escape their miserable condition. Stoianovich argues that the term *class* involves factors such as a common law for all and at least some mobility between levels, neither of which applied to the Ottoman regime, especially at the bottom of the social scale. In this respect, the term *caste* might well have been used, but Stoianovich seems deliberately to have avoided it, perhaps in order not to confuse a reader's understanding by suggesting any direct comparison with the structures of Indian society. Even so, his quadripartite set is reminiscent of Émile Benveniste's exposition of traditional Indo-European social structure in terms of its traditional three 'colours': "priests, warriors and farmers".[138] Benveniste does use the term *classes*, though rather loosely.

In writing of demarcations in rural society, Stoianovich distinguishes attentively between the producers of meat and of grain: that is, between transhumant herders and shepherds, who were mainly Macedo-Vlachs and Greeks, and the landed Slavonic-speaking agricultural workers. And observing the latter in still more finely grained detail, he goes on to distinguish between Muslims and Christians:

> Unlike the privileged Christian raia, who were almost invariably herdsmen, the pariah raia were generally tillers of the soil, bound in many districts by the seventeenth or eighteenth century to land or master. Some of the raia were the descendants of non-Turkish peasant converts to Islam. But unlike the unprivileged Christian raia, the Muslims could be assimilated into the *asker* (military and governing estate). The unprivileged, or pariah rayah, were Orthodox Christians (and, in the western provinces, Roman Catholic) peasants of South Slavic ethnicity. *They could escape their dependent or servile condition in life only by fleeing into the hills and woods and becoming outlaws or by running away*, in violation of the law, to some distant town or region and seeking the protection of friendly notables or of other lords.[139]

This analysis of servitude in 'Turkey-in-Europe' is strongly supported by many other travellers' accounts, for example, Evans's observations in 1875 and 1877.

Equally interestingly, Stoianovich analyses how, in rural non-Muslim

[138] Benveniste 1973: 227ff.

[139] Stoianovich, *op. cit.* 112; emphasis added.

families, "alternative behavior patterns" were evolved "to compensate for the lack of security in life and property under Ottoman rule".[140] These include features that can still be recognised in Balkan and East Mediterranean life today, extending from northern Serbia to the Peloponnese, Crete, Cyprus and other Greek islands:

> (1) *kumstvo* (*compaternitas*), or godfatherhood, affiliations of several different kinds; (2) *probratimstvo* or *adelfopoias* (*aderfopoitoi*, *bratimoi*) and *posestrimstvo* – foster-brother and foster-sister patterns of behavior; (3) brothers of the cross (*stavraderfoi*); (4) *prijatelstvo*, or friendship, associations; (5) *katun*, or pastoral communities, and *tselingas* (*tselingata*, *čelnik*) or associations of shepherds bound by kinship or quasi-kinship as well as economic tries; and (6) *rod*, *bratstvo*, and *pleme* (kin, phratry, and clan associations).[141]

Anyone with some experience of Balkan and east Mediterranean life and customs will recognise the functional importance of at least some of these social categories, even in our own time. For *kum* 'godfather', Skok specifies Latin *compater* and *commater* as direct cognates.[142] The Greek equivalents, masculine and feminine, are *κουμπάρος* and *κουμπάρα* (*koumbaros* and *koumbara*), terms that sound similar to those occurring in Sicily. These later migrate to the USA as *kumba* or *goomba*, which, thanks to Hollywood gangster movies, are well-known in the West for their importance in Mafia family structures. In Turkish *kuma* means 'the second of two wives'.[143] The term *bratstvo* was used (and, arguably, abused) in Communist Yugoslavia in the slogan *Bratstvo i jedinstvo* ('Brotherhood and Unity'), probably with implicit additional echoes of the French revolutionary slogan *Liberté, égalité, fraternité.* A seventh socially significant Serbo-Croatian term that Stoianovich might well have mentioned in this context is *društvo*, 'society, association, club, gathered group of friends'. This word has a huge range of cognates including the noun *drug* 'friend' and, in the Communist period, 'comrade' (fem. *drugarica*) and the adjective *drugi* (*-a*, *-o*) 'other, second'. The word *zadruga*, meaning a traditional Serbian communal household, is also part of this web.[144] The term *rod*, meaning 'genus, species', which is cognate with English *root*, and has a wide range of derivatives such as

140 *ibid.* 107.

141 *ibid.* 107.

142 Skok 1972, vol. 2: 232.

143 Hony 212.

144 See 237-240 below.

rodjenje 'birth', *rodjendan* 'birthday', *roditelj* 'parent', is no less rich and variegated.[145]

Considered separately, the emotive and moralistic force of each one of these terms can't be underestimated. Considered together, they evoke complex interacting systems of both loyalty and conflict. They not only underpin and contextualise the entire *hajduk* tradition, but also help to clarify that under Ottoman rule, there were few realistic alternatives for many young men to adopt other than to follow the way of the *hajduk*. All in all, then, the *hajduk* tradition emerges as an integral part of a highly complex web of social, economic, political and religious inter-relationships. And while this tissue, as presented here, is characteristically and perhaps even specifically Balkan, understanding its patterns has further and wider ramifications, at least some of which are contemporary.

ও

I've already suggested that law-keepers ('police') and law-breakers ('outlaws') tend to originate in identical or closely similar social groups.[146] The resultant ambivalence of some categories of Christian subjects towards their Ottoman rulers, especially in its Greek-speaking lands, is particularly well illustrated in the figure of the *αρματολός* (*armatolós*, anglicised as *armatole*). This word is defined by Pring as 'armed Greek having police duties under Turkish occupation'.[147] These men were low-level local Christian officials, taken on in the Empire's Balkan provinces and peripheries, who were "charged with local security functions – fortress defense, route watch, and defense of mountain passes – in a territory known as an *armatolik* or captaincy". In the seventeenth and eighteenth centuries, many armatoles were

> goaded into becoming klephts or bandits [...]. The *armatole* /klepht thus became an *ambiguous man – by turns, defender and interpreter of authority and a social rebel.*[148]

The very ambivalence of such men towards their careers as upholders and enforcers of Ottoman law can be generalised across all the Balkan territories under Ottoman rule. But these armatoles weren't lone rangers. Com-

---

[145] See Skok 1973, vol. 3: 151-153; and also 149 below, note 227.

[146] See 69 above.

[147] Pring 27. See also 'Armatoles', *Wikipedia*.

[148] 'Prospective Third and Fourth Levels of History' in Stoianovich 1995, vol. 4: 107; emphasis added.

manding their own retinues, each had "a contingent of armed retainers, his braves or *pallikaria*".[149] Living "in houses resembling fortresses, they practiced a ruinous hospitality [...]".[150] As the Ottoman Empire grew larger and more and more corrupt and decadent, and, correspondingly, as its central control over its far-flung corners grew less and less effective, so the Greek *armatoles* gradually became klephts, while their equivalents in Slavonic-speaking areas, the *martolosi* or *armatolosi* became hajduks. While terms varied, the social realities were similar if not identical. Economic and social conditions ranging from relative poverty to oppression and desperation led these men and their retainers alike to see themselves as "marginal persons, 'masterless men' in search of a new identity".[151] Viewed short-term, close-up and from one individual to another, their detachment from the *status quo* occurred in fits and starts and was often reversible; resulting in the phenomenon of the 'part-time' or seasonal klepht/hajduk. But seen over a long period, a slow but sure transition occurred. Once the balance had tipped, the roles of 'outlaw', 'bandit' and 'rebel' gradually transformed into a new and revised mode of action and behaviour, with corresponding shifts and modifications in self-image: that of a revolutionary working for and towards the future goal of an independent nation-state.

These revolutionary movements developed not in the metropolitan heart of empire, but rather at its far-flung edges, around and close to its border-lands. The three main reasons for this are closely interconnected. First, in border-areas the geographical terrain was often mountainous, tougher, more intractable. Second, central governmental control was weakest at these points. And, third, on the other side of these borders, alternative social and governmental models were more visible and, therefore, appeared not only more attractive and definite but also realistically attainable:

> In an empire, or great-territorial state, change of this kind is easier at certain well-situated peripheries – especially if the proponents of the new discourse are present nearby – than at the core. For imperial power is concentrated at the core, whereas, in the event of defeat, peripheries offer the hope of sanctuary or escape to neighboring countries.[152]

---

[149] *παλληκάρι* 'courageous, bold young man, young brave'.

[150] Stoianovich, *op. cit.* 107.

[151] *ibid.* 107.

[152] *ibid.* 109.

Hajduk Chieftain (Harambaša) Micko Krstić, with comrades and associates from Poreče, Macedonia [153]
National Ethnographic Museum, Belgrade

Micko Krstić was born around 1855, and possibly earlier, in the Poreče region of what's now the Republic of Macedonia. Identifying himself as a Serb, between 1876 and 1881 he was an instigator of rebellion against the Ottoman Empire, a prominent harambaša *or* arambaša *(hajduk leader, warlord) and then* vojvoda *or* vožd *(commander). Sentenced by the Turkish authorities to twenty years' imprisonment in 1882, he served his full term until 1901. He was assassinated in 1909.*

This rare photo, from the National Ethnographic Museum, Belgrade, is tagged without enclitics "Porecani i Micko arambasa" ('Men from Poreče and Haramabaša Micko'), and with no identification of either the date it was taken or which of these six men is Krstić. From comparison of this image with Micko Krstić's features in other known photos, my belief is that he's the third figure from the left, although this isn't 100% certain. If this hunch is correct, while the date of the photo is uncertain too, it seems likely to have been taken before his imprisonment in 1882.[154]

---

[153] For etymologies of the words *harambaša*, *vojvoda* and *vožd*, see 96-98 above.

[154] I'm grateful to Mladen Radulović for discussing this issue with me. The opinion is my own.

It isn't hard, then, to see how the uncomfortable and dangerous reality of these marginalised and alienated groups could be romantically glamorised in the popular imagination, especially when they occupied a heroic and legendary status in songs and poems that had themselves developed organically out of the tales of the Kosovo cycle, or in their mould.[155]

ᔓ

A further phenomenon connecting these motifs with Balkan banditry, at a 'deep' level, is less likely to be quite so obvious. This is millenarianism.[156]

Following Stoianovich, I've noted above that throughout the Ottoman Empire, social structures were based on strict and complex divisions of its ruled populations into 'estates'.[157] These were determined largely by religion, ethnicity and language, with very few opportunities for movement across these cadres except by the most versatile, inventive and ingenious subjects, such as the Empire's mainly Christian and Jewish merchants and traders, whom the Ottoman rulers viewed with varying degrees of disdain even though they couldn't manage their affairs without the service of these vassals, as well as the Janissaries and Phanariots.[158] Once again, then, the point needs re-emphasis: that the ranks of the *raya* most systematically exploited and persecuted were those at the lowest level, the landed Christian peasants.

Dreams of salvation, often articulated in stories, songs, poems and prayers, and loaded with symbolic and religious themes and images, are among the few prerogatives of the oppressed.[159] If in practice one can do nothing oneself to change one's own life for the better, one's hopes and desires are likely to transform into idealised compensatory substitutes. These may range from motifs of individual fulfilment in a paradisal after-

---

[155] For selected English translations, see for example, Locke, espec. his introduction: xii-xxxvi; and 'Ballads of the Border Raiders', 'Ballads of the Montenegrins' and 'Ballads of the Nineteenth Century Uprisings': 164-212. See also Matthias and Vučković; Lord; Parry.

[156] See Stoianovich 1995, vol. 4: 'Les Structures millénaristes sud-slaves aux XVIIe et XVIIIe siècles', 1-13.

[157] See Stoianovich 1995, vol. 3: 103; and also 102-103 above.

[158] For a detailed study of these groups, see 'The Conquering Balkan Orthodox Merchant' in Stoianovich 1994, vol. 2: 1-78.

[159] Compare, for example, spirituals, the song tradition of Afro-American slaves in the southern States of the USA.

life to the projection of presently unfulfillable hopes onto an imagined future resolution for one's children or children's children, combined with apocalyptic ambitions for one's tribe or people (Serbian: *pleme*, *narod*) to be saved by an external agency, whether in the form of a fated and prefigured person or event, or both – such as the coming of a saviour. Under such a rigid system as that of the Ottoman Empire, it's hardly surprising that in a region as ethnically mixed as the Balkans, there were tendencies towards millenarian and mystical movements. From the seventeenth century onwards, the Balkans became a breeding ground for multiple expressions of this kind; and these occurred in variegated manifestations among Christians and Jews alike, and even within Islam itself.

Millenarianism and salvation cults in general tend to latch onto whatever mythemes are available at a particular place and time and to convert them to their own ends, in a process of *bricolage*. At first glance, this process may seem merely opportunistic and accidental, but closer examination usually reveals that the particular mythologems and symbols that get 'triggered', 'hooked', and thus 'empowered', are always organically rooted in a group's collective history and unconscious. They correspond powerfully to the felt needs of an entire group *because* they surface ('well up') from such deeply intersubjective sources. My generalised argument, then, in practice, is that when the social, economic and political conditions that underpin traditions of banditry are energised by millenarianism, the popular sense of a higher or deeper 'cause' grows. The result is likely to be revolt and eventually revolution.

∽

In the Balkans, the eventual conversion of millenarian tendencies of one religious group into nationalistic ideology is clearly evident in Orthodox Christianity, the majority faith of the subjugated *raya*. Christian millenarian cults in the Serbian-speaking lands assimilated material from several sources. One of these was the idealised motif of the return of Marko Kraljević, the mythicised hero of the epic poems of the Kosovo cycle. This theme bears direct comparison with that of the return of Arthur in the medieval English tradition:

> Yet som men say in many p[art]ys of Inglonde that kynge Arthure ys nat ded, but h[ad] by the wyl of oure Lorde Jesu into another place; and m*en say that he shall com agayne, and he shall wynne the Holy Crosse*. [...] And many men say that there ys wrytten upon the tumbe thys:

Hic iacet Athurus, Rex quondam Rexque Futurus.[160]

Like the Arthurian promise, with its explicit overtones of messianic redemption and salvation, couched in a suggestive ethno-nationalist mould, Marko Kraljević embodies the ideal of the hero-leader who will be resurrected or reborn. What's more, the name *Kraljević* itself embeds the word *kralj* 'king'. Could it be, then, that the variant but equivalent motifs in these Serbian and English stories suggest that they both draw on a common Indo-European tradition? Or that these two mythologems share archetypal resonances? Or both of these patterns? For example, Marko's breaking of his lance before his incipient death and his hurling of his cudgel into the sea is closely paralleled by the above quotation, combined with Arthur's instructions to Sir Bedivere to throw his sword Excalibur into the lake:

> [S]eyed King Arthure unto sir Bedwere, 'take thou here Excaliber, my good swerde, and go with hit to yonder watirs syde; and whan thou commyste there, *I charge the throw my swerde in that water*, and com agayne and telle me what thou syeste there."[161]

These passages evidently bear comparison with the less adorned Serbian motif:

> [...] Marko then broke his lance
> In seven pieces, and he threw them up
> Into the branches of the slim fir-tree.
> Then in his strong right hand Marko took up
> His mighty bludgeon, armed with many spikes
> And, from the very heights of Urvina,
> He hurled it down into the azure sea.
> Cried Marko: "*When it rises from the sea*
> *A hero such as I will be reborn.*"[162]

---

[160] Malory 717: "Here lieth Arthur, king once and king in the future." Curiously, it might well be said that Malory (1415–1471) was himself a kind of English *hajduk*. Originally a country gentleman, for reasons unknown he turned to a life of banditry. He wrote his mammoth prose book on the stories of King Arthur in Newgate Prison, London, between 1468 and his death three years later. This was less than eighty years after the Battle of Kosovo (1389) and at a time when the oral poems in the Kosovo cycle were forming and proliferating.

[161] Malory, *op. cit.* 715; emphasis added.

[162] 'Marko's Death', in Locke (trans.): 107; emphasis added.

In Greece, another appropriated source of inspiration was ancient pagan myth. In an outbreak of revolutionary millenarianism in Epirus, in 1616,

> a certain Dionysos, former Bishop of Trikkala [...] returned to the convent of Saint Demetrius, whence he toured the countryside with a wooden vessel of wine on his shoulders. Pouring out drinks to the local shepherds and cultivators, he spread a message of rebellion among them. Causing disorders as they scurried from village to village, his band of rebels fell upon the hamlets. [...] They slaughtered the local Turks and burned their houses.[163]

This rebellion was mercilessly and brutally quashed. In such sporadic, spontaneous and eruptive outbreaks as this, both chthonic and 'daemonic' symbols surface frequently, including that of *blackness* or *darkness*. This motif recurs later in the name given to the farmer and *hajduk* Djordje Petrović (1768–1817), leader of the first uprising against the Ottomans (1804–1818) and eventually founder of the first Serbian royal dynasty. He was called *Karadjordje* 'Black George'.[164]

∽

In summary, multiple social and economic factors are discernible in the background to the nationalistic movements of the Balkans in the nineteenth century. These include: the Ottoman regime's decadence, corruption and its ruthless oppression of the Empire's subjects; the influences of alternative and visible contemporary social and political models from across frontiers; the ambiguous roles of functionaries such as *armatoles* and *kiryalis*; increasingly difficult social and economic conditions, leading to the gradual conversion of these men from outlawry and banditry, as well as of previously relatively peaceful farmers and village chiefs, to take on roles as leaders of rebellion and revolution; and the eventual materialisation of all of these factors into organised military uprisings. Intimately enmeshed into this nexus are deeper, more intersubjective and less 'visible' cultural and ideological factors, rooted in religious, ethnic and linguistic identities. In Serbian-speaking lands, these include the longevity, over centuries, of songs and poems of the Kosovo cycle in the popular epic tradition; millenarian

[163] Stoianovich 1995, vol. 4. 'Prospective: Third and Fourth Level of History': 106.

[164] See *ibid.* 'Les Structures millénaristes sud-slaves aux XVIIe et XVIIIe siècles': 1-13, esp. 6-7.

longing, contained and fostered by the mythologems and imagems of these songs; their continuation into songs and poems romanticising and glamorising *hajduk*; and the development of all of these motifs into a revolutionary nationalistic ideology, combining religion, language and perceived ethnicity.

ɞ

As this discussion draws towards a close (though not to a conclusion), it becomes clear that what I've called 'the *hajduk* tradition' was one of the various directly linkable historical factors underlying and contributing to the doggedness and ferocity of the many fighting units making up both Tito's communist partisans and the royalist *četnici* ('chetniks', a term derived from *četa,* 'military company, detachment, troop, band', from *četati* 'to fight, wage war'), loosely held together though not controlled by Draža Mihailović, in their guerrilla campaigns and complex to-ings and fro-ings during the Nazi occupation of Yugoslavia, as well as against each other during and after it.[165] Skok's dictionary lists *četnik* as one of the meanings for *hajduk.*[166] The *vojvoda* ('leader, duke') led a *četa* (a 'troop' of hajduks).

The term *četi* had an earlier revolutionary connection too, and this provides further clear historical links between the *hajduk* tradition, rebellion against the Ottoman Empire, and nationalistic ideologies and uprisings in the Balkans. The Internal Macedonian Revolutionary Organisation (IMRO) called its guerrilla groups *četi.* Originally a secret society founded in 1893 in Salonica by students and associates of the Bulgarian Men's High School, under the slogan 'Freedom or Death', *Свобода или смъртъ* ['Svoboda ili smrt'], IMRO opposed Ottoman rule and aimed to establish autonomy for Macedonia and the Adrianople region, linked to Bulgarian interests. Obtaining widespread support, in 1903 it fostered the Ilinden-Preobrazhenie Uprising, which the Turks mercilessly suppressed. In his *Fighting the Turk in the Balkans,* Arthur D. Howden Smith, a young American traveller looking for adventure, gives a first-hand account of his involvement in guerrilla action in this campaign. He vividly captures the danger, bravery, camaraderie, male bonding, and subliminal

[165] For widely differing ideological accounts of this conflict in the Second World War, see Deakin, MacLean and Lees. The first two were Churchill's emissaries to Tito's partisans, and the third was a British officer sent out to liaise with the royalist chetniks, led by Draža Mihailović.

[166] Skok, *op. cit.* 649.

homo-eroticism within the *četa*. After the First World War, espousing uncompromising violence, the movement was quashed by Yugoslav, Greek and Bulgarian authorities. In 1934, its members co-operated with the Croatian *Ustaše* in the assassination of King Alexander I of Yugoslavia in Marseille. The highly complex history of this movement, including its transformations and offshoots, is still an undercurrent in Macedonian and Bulgarian politics.[167]

The *Ustaše* are best known as the backbone of the Fascist Croatian regime led by Ante Pavelić in the Second World War. They committed atrocities on Serbs, Jews, Roma and Communists, especially at the complex of concentration camps known as Jasenovac. Their delight in sadism was unparalleled, even by the Nazis. Their name embeds a revolutionary meaning: from *uskočiti* 'to rise up'.

The *hajduk* tradition was also a specific and underrated historical factor underlying the formation, not to mention the resilience, stark codes of honour and loyalty, ruthless determination and frequent mercilessness and savagery of various private, self-appointed nationalist armies which struggled against one another and in doing so, swept up large numbers of civilians during and after the break-up of Yugoslavia in the 1990s – including, for example: the HDZ in Croatia and Hercegovina (*Hrvatska Demokratska Zajednica* 'Croatian Democratic Union); the 'Tigers' led by the ruthless, flamboyant and charismatic Serbian gangster, warlord and one-time international spy Željko Ražnatović, *aka* 'Arkan', who was murdered in 2000 in the lobby of the Intercontinental Hotel, Belgrade; the KLA in Kosovo; and the ethnic Albanian NLA in Macedonia (both anglicisations: 'LA' standing for 'liberation army'). In this period all major ethnic groups in former Yugoslavia produced their own fierce fighting bands, who were regarded as noble, loyal and heroic or as unscrupulous, brutal and barbaric, depending which side one was on.[168]

---

167 'Internal Macedonian Revolutionary Organization', *Wikipedia*. Maria Todorova comments that its role was "pervasive in Greek and Bulgarian history and, if anything, was instrumental in sealing the image of the Balkans as a space of rampant brigandage and violence" (email, Oct. 31, 2019).

168 For documentation on aspects of the wars of the 1990s, including their complex historical backgrounds, many writers can be cited. I've found Judah 2009 particularly helpful. On Serbian views on ways in which the traditional image of the warrior was crudely fostered and exploited by the Serbian government under Slobodan Milošević, see 'War as a way of life' (Popov 1996b: 80-87), 'The use (or abuse) of the Kosovo myth' (Zirojević 202-209), and *The Politics of Symbol in Serbia* (Čolović 2002).

☙

In 2001, in the months before the 9/11 attacks on New York and the Pentagon, with my eye on the disintegration and explosive final collapse of Yugoslavia, and on the dishonest role of all the so-called Great Western Powers in aiding and abetting it, I drafted both the preceding two paragraphs as well as the following one, to 'conclude' an earlier version of this essay:

> Today, the majority of well-meaning, urbanised, consumerised and usually 'shocked' contemporary Americans and West Europeans possess scant knowledge of Balkan history or interest in it, and tend to combine their ignorance with a most powerful and inherently dangerous tendency to impose their own politically correct values onto a part of the world of which they have not the slightest understanding. More sensitive and informed perspectives are needed among the richer parts of the world on the structures and histories of national, ethno-religious and tribal cultures where well-established customs of 'honour' and 'revenge' operate. [...] And not only in the Balkans, or Africa, or Indonesia, but closer to home too, for example in Northern Spain and Northern Ireland.

Eighteen years later, I hardly disagree at all now with what I wrote then. Except for one factor, which is that of degree. For my conclusion was far too mild. Since then, the Taleban and followers of Saddam Hussein have apparently been 'removed', as has ISIS, and Official Western History has moved on in its usual senseless, callous, arrogant way, like Capital itself, trampling not only over tyrants but also over the innocent and the defenceless. The problem to rich westerners now, of course, is that it isn't just *those* countries 'on the edge', somewhere over *there*, in the 'bad borderlands' and 'danger zones' that are no longer safe to visit for pleasure or profit, on business or on holiday, but what were once known as 'well-secured and familiar places' *here* too. "Things fall apart, the centre cannot hold. / Mere anarchy is loosed upon the world," wrote Yeats in 1919.[169] Exactly one hundred years later, there's no more distinction between *edge* and *centre*. Today everyone is on edge and at the edge, and any/everyone is at risk every/anywhere: in the street or road outside one's own home, whether in village or city, just as much as 'abroad'. Terror is as likely to stalk and strike the long-term tenant or home-owner as it is the traveller, whether tourist, tramp, migrant or refugee. In a prophetic essay entitled

[169] Yeats, 'The Second Coming': 210-211.

'Tourists and Vagabonds', Zygmunt Bauman offered a characterology of two opposing aspects of the postmodern condition:

> Many would perhaps refuse to embark on a life of wandering were they asked, but they had not been asked in the first place. If they are on the move, it is because they have been pushed from behind – having first been uprooted by a force too powerful, and often too mysterious, to resist. They see their plight as anything but the manifestation of freedom. Freedom, autonomy, independence – if they appear in their vocabulary at all – invariably come in the future tense. For them, to be free means not to *have to* wander around. To have a home and to be allowed to stay inside. These are the *vagabonds*, dark moons reflecting the shine of bright suns, the mutants of postmodern evolution, the unfit rejects of the brave new species. The vagabonds are the waste of the world which has dedicated itself to tourists' services.[170]

It was from the ranks of the ancestors of such dispossessed people that the *hajduks*, *uskoks*, *kiryalis*, *klephts* and *andartes* emerged. Their heirs and those like them are still poor, as poor as ever. But once they too taste a little hope in their hopelessness, or even just scent it afar – or rather, once they realise that since they possess so little that it seems worthless, less even than nothing – then they realise too that they'll have less than nothing to lose if they fight back against their perceived oppressors, and so from their ranks, in turn, more fighters will arise, and be called martyrs and heroes by some, and fundamentalists, criminals and terrorists by others, and have songs and poems made about them, at least by some people. Their motives twist and smoulder in pain to be understood, their hopes to be released, their curtailed and curtained calls for love and justice to be honoured by us all, until one day we begin to understand, with Octavio Paz that "for

---

[170] Bauman 1997: 92. Zygmunt Bauman wrote 'Tourists and Vagabonds' in 1985, republished it in several variants and with distinct subtitles (e.g. Bauman 1997, 1998 and 2000), but all versions reiterate the same central theme. At the time of compiling and editing this book (2019), this masterly essay reads in retrospect as a prophecy of the ever-swelling global refugee problem:

> But remember – the vagabonds are the rubbish bins for the tourist filth; dismantle the waste-disposal system, and the healthy ones of this world will suffocate and poison amid their own refuse. [...] More importantly yet, the vagabonds – remember that – are the dark background against which the sun of the tourist shines so brightly that the spots are hardly seen. The darker the background, the brighter the shine (Bauman 1997: 94).

the first time in our history, we are contemporaries of all humanity."[171]

That day seems further away than ever – a millenarian dream, a fantasy born of hope and longing that's hopelessly unrealistic.

2001; revised 2004, 2008, 2018, 2019, 2020

[171] Paz 1967: 182. I've changed the word 'mankind' to 'humanity'.

Dodola and Peperuda: The Balkan Rainmaking Customs

In a few eastern and south-eastern areas of the Balkans, especially Bulgaria, the rainmaking rite is still practised, even though vestigially. In other parts of the Balkans, the custom has all but died out, although as late as the 1960s it was very much alive in parts of Yugoslavia too, and well-documented by camera-toting ethnologists and travellers in Serbia and Vojvodina.[172] In 1996, Mila Bosić writes:

> The *dodolas* more or less entirely disappeared in Vojvodina only after the 1960s, probably as a result of the economic development following the Second World War, including [...] the mechanisation of agricultural work and improvements to fields resulting from the construction of ditches and land-drainage, all of which made crop-production possible on a world-scale. Moreover, the rapid increase of education and culture in the population resulted in the loss of many customs and beliefs in magic, including the *dodolas*.[173]

Despite their demise over the course of several generations, the same author clarifies that:

> [t]he *dodolas* [...] are still very much alive in people's memories [...]. Whenever there is a drought in summer, the older women wish for the *dodolas* to appear, firmly believing even today in their magical power to make rain. In the village of Brestač in Srem, the last time *dodolas* appeared was in 1988.[174]

ග

[172] Vojvodina: the northern region whose regional capital is Novi Sad, towards the Hungarian border. The word *vojvod* means 'duke' or 'count': hence 'The County' or 'The Dukedom'.

[173] Bosić 345; trans. Vera V. Radojević and RB.

[174] *ibid.* 341; trans. Vera V. Radojević and RB.

photo: Dr. Dragić

Dodola, Banja Koviljača, near Loznica, Western Serbia, 1957

During a period of spring or summer drought, it was the custom in many Balkan villages for a group of local girls to put on various combinations of leaves, sprigs, blossoms, flowers and herbs to perform the rainmaking ceremony. Early reports, made mostly if not entirely by male observers, describe these girls as 'naked' under their clothing of greenery: although what precise degree of undress this 'nakedness' really constituted is a moot point, since none of the commentators is likely to have witnessed the actual disrobing,[175] let alone the training, preparation or rehearsal of the girls for the ceremony – roles which seem to have been reserved exclusively for mature and sometimes elderly women). At any rate, led by an older girl or young woman who had also been dressed or decorated in this way, the girls then went in procession through their village, and stopped in front of houses to perform dances and sing songs, which included formulaic refrains, all the while calling upon the heavens to send down rain. The housewives poured water over the troupe leader, and sometimes the girls sprinkled water over the courtyards, using bundles of sprigs and leaves. The householders then rewarded them with flour or food and sometimes money. In some areas, especially Dalmatia, Albania and northern Greece, boys or youths were involved as performers.

The custom – or groups of customs – seems all the more interesting in that, while it flowered predominantly in south-east Europe, 'typologically comparable' elements can also be traced much further north, for example among other Slavs, and possibly among Balts, Teutons and Celts.[176] Moreover, even in the Balkans it wasn't confined to any single group. As the Bulgarian ethnologist Mikhail Arnaudov wrote in his survey of Balkan rainmaking ceremonies and songs:

> In name as well as in essence, here we do have a pan-Balkan ritual. The resemblances that indicate such a unity are spread through all elements of the dances, beliefs and spells. [...] With some small variations, everything here points to a single basic type, known equally among all Balkan peoples.
>
> To pose questions about where the ritual sprang up, or what forms it took elsewhere within the large yet relatively closed cultural and historical area occupied by Balkan people, seems almost inappropriate. Not only are the rudiments lost in the remote past but the [...] equalising influences deprive us of any grounds for firm hypotheses.[177]

---

175 On this question, see also 149ff below.

176 Ivanov and Toporov use the term "typologically parallel". See next note.

177 Arnaudov 155-201; trans. Anelia Tapp and RB.

So it seems impossible to trace the ritual's precise lines of development. Yet, despite Arnaudov's commendable reticence in ascribing theories of origin, other scholars appear to agree that it was first practised among Slavic (or possibly Balto-Slavic or proto-Slavic) tribes, and then disseminated to other groups. Even so, since there's no archaeological evidence and a complete absence of artefacts of any kind as far as the rainmaking ceremonies themselves are concerned, and since the first written records about them date only from the early nineteenth century, the best clues available for any kind of historical reconstruction are reports and, more recently, interviews and recordings from travellers, ethnographers and other witnesses and observers, supported by whatever 'circumstantial evidence' may be gleaned – or reconstituted – from comparative linguistics and mythology.

Even though it's clear that all such reconstructions can only be regarded as tentative, they do offer us some clues which amount to more than pure fancy or guesswork. Various scholars have traced fascinating similarities and correspondences between the Balkan ceremonies and far more ancient religious rituals, so that various tantalisingly appealing, attractive and plausible theories have been put forward, all indicating that the names given to the participants in these Balkan ceremonies are likely to reflect archaic mythological motifs and personages. For example, one group of names for the rain-maiden, of the type *Peperuda,* probably links with the name of the Slavonic thunder god, *Perun,* and/or his Baltic equivalent *Perkunas*; and this may apply to the other names too.[178]

Comparative linguists and mythologists have also traced further possible connections with myths associated with rain in ancient India, especially via the *Rig Veda*; not to mention with names of Hittite, Lithuanian, Icelandic, Etruscan, Roman and Greek figures. Some scholars have postulated reconstruction of the origins of the rituals to as far back as the Neolithic period.[179] There's no dearth of fascinating theories, traceries and conjectures, among which the invaluable contributions by Roman Jakobson and the further daring and sometimes fantastic linguistic excavations and conjectures by Ivanov and Toporov are probably the most notable.

Perhaps rather obviously, the customs are readily interpretable as a branch or scion of seasonal fertility rites. Dražen Nožinić, a particularly thorough researcher, writes in 1998:

---

[178] See Jakobson 1985a and 1985b, and *In a Time of Drought* (RB 2011c): 88-90.

[179] Apart from Arnaudov and Jakobson, for other interesting and original contributors to theories of ancient antecedents, see: Skok 1973, vol. 3: 55-56; and Ivanov and Toporov 1974: 104ff.

> The peoples of south-east Europe have until recent times known various customs and magical rituals by means of which they have attempted to influence atmospheric phenomena., i.e. to maintain a balance in nature, particularly in times when there was a threat of drought. It is believed that these customs were born in the Neolithic period, and they have been noted in ethnographic literature in various parts of the world. As far as the Balkan Slavs are concerned, it is not hard to differentiate these customs from those which are performed at particular times of the year. Even so, both these categories possess many common features which suggest far more aspects in common than any indications of external similarities to the forms of either type of enactment taken singly. Throughout the literature, the emphasis has been on the similarities between south-Slavic rainmaking customs and the rural customs which belong to the spring-summer cycle. So, on the basis of these facts, the rainmaking customs may be considered as a sub-group within the wider category of customs which aim to ensure fertility.[180]

ᔕ

Despite the enormous and fascinating variations to be found in details of the rainmaking rituals throughout the Balkans (and not just from region to region but sometimes from one village to the next), the underlying unity among them seems incontrovertible. Nor were they confined to one religious group. In Kosovo, as elsewhere, they were practised by both Christians and Muslims. The leading rain-maiden has been variously described as being from a poor and humble family, as a pauper, an orphan, a non-privileged person and as the youngest daughter of a widow who never remarried and was past childbearing age. There's general emphasis on her lowliness, modesty and purity; and she always went barefoot, perhaps to emphasise her humility or, rather, humbleness and, more simply, her direct connection with the soil. In this way, it might be said, she was 'earthed'.

In many areas, the role passed gradually to the Romanies, until they took it up exclusively. In certain areas, to be a rain-maiden even became a seasonal profession for Romany girls and young women, which involved them in travelling around to perform the ceremonies for various village-communities. It's unclear whether they confined themselves to areas in which their families regularly moved, or went further afield. Far more detailed work needs to be done, and done quickly, in researching the role of gypsies in varying – and carrying on – the tradition. It may soon be altogether too late to discover anything at all about this.

---

[180] Nožinić 75 ff; trans. Vera V. Radojević and RB.

The custom diminished in scale and importance throughout the nineteenth and twentieth centuries, partly because of official disapproval and at times outright censorship, first on the part of the church and later by communist authorities, both of whose proponents and administrators deemed such practices improper, immoral, primitive or degenerate. Rulers, it seems, tend to be prudes regardless of their ideologies.

❧

So far as I've been able to discover, the first person ever to report, document and transcribe the rainmaking songs and ceremonies was the Serbian collector, language reformer, dictionary-compiler and translator, Vuk Stefanović Karadžić (1787–1864). He included an entry on 'Dodola' in the first edition of his *Srpski Rječnik* (*Serbian Dictionary*), published in Vienna in 1815. Through a subsequent edition of the *Dictionary* (1857), the first volume of his collection *Srpske narodne pjesme* (*Folk Songs of the Serbian People*, 1841) and his posthumously published study *Život i običaji naroda srpskoga* (*Life and Customs of the Serbian People*, 1867), the rainmaking customs and songs became well-known to such internationally renowned poets and scholars as Goethe – whom Karadžić actually met. Karadžić travelled widely, especially to Vienna, where his books were published; and from the mid-nineteenth century on, rainmaking ceremonies were documented by travellers to Serbia from other parts of Europe too.

While Karadžić uses the word *djevojke* ('girls'), an English traveller to Serbia in the 1840s, A. A. Paton, took pains to point out that the leading participant was by no means a mere-slip-of-a-girl:

> One of the most extraordinary customs of Servia is that of the Dodola. When a long drought has taken place, a handsome young woman is stripped, and so dressed up with grass, flowers, cabbage and other leaves, that her face is scarcely visible; she then, in company with several girls of twelve to fifteen years of age, goes from house to house singing a song, the burden of which is a wish for rain. It is then the custom of the mistress of the house at which the Dodola is stopped to throw a little water on her.[181]

Following Karadžić, Paton adds: "This custom used also to be kept up in the Servian districts of Hungary, but has been forbidden by the priests."[182]

---

[181] Paton 1845: 270.

[182] *ibid.* 271.

The Serbian writer Dimitrije Nikolajević told me, in Belgrade in October 2000, that in his childhood, in rural areas near Kragujevac, villagers deliberately set out to choose "the most beautiful girls, aged sixteen or seventeen, for the roles of dodolas." Mila Bosić says that in the village of Banatske Here, in Vojvodina, "the *dodola*, who was a gypsy, had to be pregnant."[183] Dražen Nožinić offers further details on the question of the ages of those involved:

> This work is based on the results of the author's own fieldwork between 1989 and 1991 in two hundred and ninety villages in Kordun, Banija and Moslavina as well as in the surrounding areas. [...] The period of time for which the details were collected covers approximately one hundred years (1870–1970). Thus, all the informants interviewed during the course of this research had actually already participated actively in the customs discussed. [...] A few of them were born towards the end of the nineteenth century, and the majority at the beginning of the twentieth century. The youngest were born in the 1920s. The performers were trained and taught by older women, born some 45 to 50 years before the performers themselves. These older women thus transferred their knowledge of traditions in which they themselves had participated. These facts about invoking rain take us back to the last quarter of the nineteenth century. Moreover, certain rites could be and were permitted to be performed only by elderly women, and in this context the 'teachers' appear in a different role, i.e. the informants had themselves participated throughout the whole of their lives in various rites to summon rain. Their fellow villagers, whom they had taught, went on performing these rites right up to the 1980s, when most of the rituals were eventually given up.[184]

This passage not only provides insights into the precarious survival and eventual demise of the rite and the ages of participants but implies that, in many villages, 'inner' knowledge of rainmaking rituals was an integral part of female 'magical' lore, and passed on either in matrilineal fashion or at least solely among women. It's a pity we have no authoritative reports by female ethnographers who have been allowed in on these preparatory rituals. It's tempting to interpret Nožinić's information in terms of a genuine 'mystery' and, what's more, to perceive the rite as a descendant of far more ancient female fertility ceremonies. Perhaps, such as those enacted and performed at Eleusis? A question to be left, for the time being at least, and perhaps forever, dangling. But a question mooted by several scholars,

---

[183] Bosić. 341-345.

[184] Nožinić, *op. cit.* 75ff; trans. Vera V. Radojević and RB.

most notably by Ivanov and Toporov,[185] in suggesting an etymological connection between the name of the rainmaking celebrant in Dalmatia, *Prporuše*, and the goddess Persephone.

ꕥ

On the age of participants, then, there exists considerable difference of opinion, which certainly reflects a wide variety of divergent practices. Some commentators say that the ages of the girls gradually diminished from between around eleven and sixteen to between five and ten years; and others, usually envisioning or interpreting the ceremony in terms of a specific *rite de passage* from childhood to readiness for sexual activity, argue that crucial criteria for the selection of the rain-maiden were prepubescence, and/or virginity/chastity.

While these are certainly oversimplifications which in any case don't fit all the facts, there's little doubt that a specifically 'childlike naivety' does appear through all the recorded rain-maiden's songs, which are recognisably distinct in tone from other genres of folksongs performed by adults in the same geographical areas. It seems at least possible, then, that the rites had always involved young girls, at least as members of the leading rain-maiden's troupe, in much the same way as they may well have done in Minoan and Mycenaean religious ceremonies, at least, that is, if we're to accept the interpretations from seals and similar artefacts offered by Sir Arthur Evans.[186] It's also apparent that the rain-maiden's intimate association with the *pouring* of fresh water in itself provides the clearest possible indication of her 'purity'.[187] Whatever her age, the key factor isn't only that she 'stands on a threshold', but that she herself represents or embodies it. As the Bulgarian anthropologist Florentina Badalanova pointed out to me in London in 2000, in every respect her necessary condition is 'liminal'.

ꕥ

It perhaps also needs to be added here that, by comparison with some of the narrative epics or love songs in the various Balkan traditions, the rainmaking songs in general can hardly be described as 'masterpieces of oral composition' comparable, say, with the Serbian oral epic ballads,

---

[185] See 147-148 below.

[186] Evans 1925: 1-75.

[187] See: Djordjević 401ff; and 142ff below.

as recorded and studied by Milman Parry and A. B. Lord (1964), and as translated by John Matthias and Vladeta Vučković (1984), Geoffrey Locke (2002) and many others, not to mention the love songs as translated by E. D. Goy (1990). In their simplicity of style, their 'naïve' and 'intimate' vocabulary, and their obvious, unsophisticated rhymes, many of these songs are reminiscent of children's jingles all over the world. Shortly before his death in 2000, E. D. Goy, the last teacher of Serbo-Croatian language and literature at Cambridge University, told me that the Balkan rainmaking songs reminded him of children's jingles in the British Isles.[188] He quoted a Welsh song which he remembered from his own childhood:

> A soul cake, a soul cake, a soul cake,
> Please, Good Missus, a soul cake –
>
> An apple, a pear, a plum or a cherry,
> Any good thing to make us all merry –
> One for Peter, two for Paul,
> And three for Him who made us all.

This chant may be compared with some lines in a Dalmatian rainmaking song, sung by boys, youths and unmarried bachelors, quoted by Vuk Stefanović Karadžić:

> Grant us, mistress,
> An oke of flour, mistress,
> A fleecelet of wool, mistress,
> A portion of cheese, mistress,
> A handful of salt, mistress,
> Two or three eggs, mistress,
> God be with you, mistress,
> For you have bestowed gifts upon us.[189]

2004, 2006

[188] I call Ned Goy *the last*, because, after his retirement in 1990, the University of Cambridge closed down all Serbo-Croatian scholarship, teaching and studies.
[189] Karadžić 1957 [1867] 65; trans. Vera V. Radojević and RB.

photo: Dr. Dragić

Housewife pouring water over a dodola in the village of Banja Koviljača, near Loznica, Western Serbia, 1957

Rain and Dust: 'Correspondance' and *In a Time of Drought*

When I first heard about the rainmaking customs of the Balkans, their mythological dimensions and content triggered something in me, snagged, stirred, pulled me in and kept me bound, until a book-length poem had written itself out of me, *In a Time of Drought*. There was an immediate sense of recognition, of discovery, of multiple unfolding connections and 'correspondances'. These struck like lightning. The unfolding went on throughout the process of composition.

As I started working on the poem, an idea that had come to me started unravelling: it began as a hunch, a theme, accompanied by a little (*too* little) knowledge. So, during composition of the first drafts, I set about finding out as much as I could about the rainmaking practices and songs. More than once I was astonished to find that images which had been cropping up spontaneously in my own mind during composition turned out to belong *to the sources themselves*, and even to be part of their stuff or grain.[190] This curious recognition of a spontaneous 'matching' between my inner images and personal compositional processes on the one hand and, on the other, material already 'out there' (i.e. woven, patterned, documented and above all *socialised* in myth, legend, ritual, folk custom, etc.) had often occurred to me before, but rarely with such force. Whenever that kind of heuristic experience arrives, however well prepared one may be, and however well one may have envisaged it, it's always new, surprising, uplifting, expansive: *a gift*. From the experiential point of view, words like *illumination* and *epiphany* are hardly too strong to describe the state of mind, of being, instantly triggered and simultaneously validated by this set of multiple recognitions. There's a numinous element.

My current understanding of this kind of 'correspondance' is that, in certain kinds of 'deep' poetic composition, mythological patternings well up through individual consciousness with a force that a poet learns to

[190] RB 2011c: 76-77.

trust, follow and be bound by. Without this binding, this following and this trust, no poem emerges – unless it's one that's stunted or maimed. It might also be said that it's both necessary and inevitable that, during the act of composing itself, the poet isn't likely to be able to fully understand the powerfully loaded material that surfaces through what may well be subjectively experienced as the most profound and intimate layerings of his or her being.[191] In the first and last resort, the craft (Fr. *métier*, It. *mestiere*: compare Eng. 'mastery') of making poems involves and tracks a *mystery* (in the Greek sense of the word), and necessitates this willed and willing two-way flow between the consciousness of the individual poet and a mode or layering of consciousness that might be called transpersonal.[192]

But the making of a poem isn't an involuntary process. Experientially, for a poet working with, in and through a myth, both volition and intelligence appear to be fully harnessed by the 'other' ('higher', 'deeper', 'magical', 'inspired', etc.) forces – for the *precise purpose*, as it were, of the poem's making. In this context, such mantic and teleological notions as 'inspiration', 'destiny', 'vocation', 'calling', 'divine calling', that have so often been invoked to validate the poet's practice, remind us that the evolutionary origins of poetry are probably shamanic. The poet recognises and participates actively in this harnessing. Indeed, the poet, apparently,

---

[191] Similarly, Michael Polanyi writes: "Scientific discovery, which leads from one framework to its successor, bursts the bounds of disciplined thought in an intense if transient moment of heuristic vision. And while it is thus breaking out, the mind is for the moment directly experiencing its content rather than controlling it by the use of any pre-established modes of interpretation: it is overwhelmed by its own passionate activity" (Polanyi 196). These observations about scientific discovery are comparable to some of Shelley's statements about poetic composition in *The Defence of Poetry*, such as: "[...] the mind in creation is as a fading coal, which some invisible influence, like an inconstant wind, awakens to transitory brightness" (Shelley 1923: 53).

[192] In 1964–5, in Venice, I apprenticed myself to the English poet Peter Russell (1921–2003). In his old age he told me that, in his experience, his own poems that remained most deeply meaningful to him had emerged from material that he "didn't know much about". He said that what was strange (unknown, not-understood, partially understood, mysterious, 'other', etc.) had always held the strongest and most passionate pull for him, and tended to fascinate and bind him. This attraction, he recognised, often included or was akin to erotic longing and desire. See also Eliade 1964: 510-511; and Polanyi 198: "Mystics speak of religious ecstasy in erotic terms."

wants this yoking, this yielding, this involvement with the interiorised and transpersonal other. And, for the poet (Scots. *makar*), the fulfilment and pleasure that are wrought into the *poesis* – i.e. into this making that is equivalently a yielding, a trusting and a following – both reside and are justified precisely in the resultant discoveries that occur, in the mind's heuristic leaps and plunges through the act of creation, in the connections that appear, unexpectedly and 'as if from nowhere'. Such further and later outcomes as the possibilities of publication and recognition, the chances (and fantasies) of acclaim, fame and fortune, and so on, may well be ancillary: as the passionate intentness on reclusiveness that we trace in the lives of such poets as Emily Dickinson and Gerard Manley Hopkins makes abundantly clear, even if such privacies were enforced by circumstances.

Aside from correspondances *during* the making of a poem itself, in the particular instance of *In a Time of Drought*, I've also found it curious that the mythological sources and associations which the poem draws on have been powerful enough to go on quietly working in and through me long *after* poetic composition ended. Indeed, since then, I've found myself continuing to be 'held' by all aspects of the underlying and surrounding material, continuing to want to explore more of its roots and ramifications, and continuing to be astonished and delighted by the emergence of further unexpected details and apparently chance associations. That's to say: this material is still alive for me, it hasn't petered out, it carries a charge, it wields tiny hooks and needles, it won't let go, it won't let *me* go. It might be said: involvement in a myth can have an obsessive quality about it. One can get taken over: *possessed*.

Even so, I think it also needs to be added here that, as far as such correspondances are concerned, this later (secondary) process of 'prosaic' re-analysis and re-synthesis often calls for a course of recapitulations that seems laborious, pernickety and frustratingly slow, by comparison with the insistence of the lyrical flushes, heady flights and heuristic breakthroughs that marked the first phases of composition.[193]

From a psychological perspective, these occurrences and perceptions of pattern make full and coherent sense when viewed through a Jungian lens. Taken together, the theories of Jung, and those of others like Neumann and Hillman who have followed and applied them, are not only consonant with these processes, but can scarcely be seen as anything other than authentic inner mappings of what goes on psychologically during

---

[193] Compare Polanyi on 'Mathematical Heuristics': *op. cit.* 124-131.

poetic composition, that is, at least in my own experience and practice.[194] According to these thinkers, myths, legends and folk tales present and re-present the patternings of archetypes. Their manifestations and influences, their strings, skeins and strands, their webs, meshes and knots surface and sink and re-surface, apparently spontaneously and unpredictably, and according to laws partially but not fully understood. They combine and recombine. They spin and weave constantly new but always recognisable patterns. They're the DNA of myths, legends and rituals.

I think that in my work on *In a Time of Drought*, just as on this essay that follows it, particularly bearing in mind the material's mythic elements, I've recognisably been caught (touched, embraced, moved, transported, etc.) by an archetype, *within* and *through* an archetype, perhaps even *for* an archetype, That's to say, *in the service of* that archetype.[195]

Scope and Modes of Enquiry

In the discussion that follows, on psychological grounds, I've taken the Jungian perspective as given. But because I'm interested here not only in tracking psychological patterns, but in mapping possible historical and evolutionary relationships, I integrate several other methodological models. First, broadly speaking, my approach is diachronic-linguistic. Second, I apply a structuralist analysis to one particularly well-known example of the Balkan rainmaking practice. For all the obvious risks this approach carries – that is, on the one hand, of simplifying and hence misunderstanding the material, and, on the other, of superimposing interpretations on it and so crushing it, rather than delicately teasing them out of it – the unpicking of a composite whole into its parts is nevertheless capable of yielding interesting insights. Within this approach, comparative strands are necessarily interwoven. Third, I take a single feature of one particular rainmaking custom, and to this detail I apply close linguistic examination and comparative contextualisation. Fourth, I throw in some pure fanciful conjecture.[196]

---

[194] Among the many salient titles by these authors, those most pertinent to this discussion of poetry and mythology are: Jung (*CW*9, part 1 and *CW*15), Neumann 1959, and Hillman 1975, 1979.

[195] This is true, too, of the other long poem that emerged out of the same 'deep' mythological nexus, *The Blue Butterfly* (RB 2011b).

[196] What passes as 'scientific' among even major scholars (historians, linguists,

The approach that combines comparative mythology with comparative linguistics has many antecedents among scholars. In this instance, I owe most to Roman Jakobson, who made a striking contribution to the study of the Balkan rainmaking rituals.[197] By submitting the chosen material to analysis and, in the course of doing so, bringing other linguistic, mythological and historical information and conjectures to bear on it, my intention is to open questions for discussion of the rainmaking custom as a whole. Inevitably, this procedure will involve excursions and diversions. These, I hope, will lead back into the material at possibly unforeseen angles and along unexpected declivities – which in turn may reveal further perspectives, layerings and conjectures. Finally, since it's in the nature of myth to enfold and include, I'm aware, too, that both *In a Time of Drought* and this essay not only derive from the mythological material and comment on it, but now come (return) to be part of it.

Source and Text

The finely documented account by Dragutin Djordjević, originally published in 1901, of a version of the Balkan rainmaking custom, performed near the River Morava in south-eastern Serbia near the Bulgarian border, is so well-known that it has almost taken on the status of a classic:

> When there is a period of drought during summer, and rain is withheld over a long period of time, the Dodolas go around the villages even today. In Leskovac, until around ten years ago the Dodolitsas used to go from house to house singing 'dodolitska' songs,[198] praying to God to give rain and wealth. Nowadays, only small gypsy girls go around the town, followed by an older gypsy woman. In some of the villages, one can still see small local girls, although gypsy Dodolitsas appear even there. In Dušanovo, even today, when the rain is 'withheld', four small girls go around as Dodolitsas. Each one is dressed in old and shabby clothing. Each one has a wreath made of nettles and *burjan* ['sambucus', a weed]. They walk barefoot. The first two carry a copper bowl with water which they sprinkle over the houses with a bunch made of *burjan* and nettles.

---

archaeologists, ethnographers and anthropologists) is often no more than conjecture, suitably dressed up to appear accurate, objective and authoritative. Ideology and vanity play tricks with even the best minds.

[197] Jakobson 1985a: 6-7, and 1985b: 22-23.

[198] *dodolitsa*, n. 'little Dodola'; adj. *dodolitska.*

[...] When the Dodolitsas arrive at a house, using the bunch of *burjan* and nettle, they sprinkle water over the yard and sing:

1. Fly, fly, *peperuga*
   Oh, *dodolas*, Dear Lord!
   We go over the fields
   And the clouds over the sky

2. The sun is burning our fields
   The little *dodolitsas* are praying to our Lord
   'Give us, Lord, gentle rain,
   To bedew our fields
   So that gentle grain will grow
   So that two grapes will give us a barrel of wine

3. Fly, fly, *peperuga*
   So huge riches will be born
   So the barns will be full –
   Barns *and* stores
   So white grain will grow
   So the ploughman will have white bread
   Give us, Lord, give, give, Lord, give!

4 So that white hemp will grow
   A thin thread of a bit of hemp
   Don't eke it out in stingy morsels
   But if in bits, with bits of cheese
   Bits of cheese and a bit of flour.'

After each verse the refrain "Oh, Dodolas, Dear Lord" is sung twice, or this refrain once, followed by "Give us, Lord, give, give, give."

Whilst the dodolitsas are singing, the 'lady' of the house, or someone from the family, takes a bucketful of water from the well, and pours it over the wreaths on the dodolitsas' heads and over their feet. The dodolitsas splash their feet in the spilt water and sing. Many housewives add fresh water to the copper bowls, so that the rain may overflow in similar manner onto the dry soil. When the dodolas have finished their song, the housewife brings out corn flour in a sieve and gives it to the dodola who is collecting flour. When the dodola pours some of the flour which has been presented as a gift to her into her bag, she positions the empty sieve on her hip towards the East, and lets it drop with her right hand, saying, "Full, full!" Should the sieve settle in the correct position, as when one is sieving flour, it's believed that rain will come and the crop will be rich. However, if the sieve turns over and falls onto its other side, the opposite will happen. It's customary for the dodolas in the village of Dušanovo to go into the fields. As soon as they have finished calling on the houses, they go through the fields singing and sprinkling water as far as the local quarry. They go into the quarry three times, and sing and sprinkle it with water, and then they return to the village to a widow who, usually, makes them some corn porridge from her own flour.

In other villages, as used to be customary in the town of Leskovac as well, the dodolas take the flour which they have been given to a local widow, who makes a porridge from it in their copper bowl. The porridge is eaten in the middle of the yard and the bowl is placed on a plate which is turned upside down, underneath which they have first poured some fresh water. In Štulac (in the county of Jablanica), the dining table for the dodolas is set above running water, so that a few crumbs of porridge may fall into the running water.

When all this is finished, the dodolas take off their leafy clothing, and take their wreaths and bunches made of *burjan* and nettle with which they have sprinkled the houses and fields, and throw them into running water.

Recently, Gypsy dodolas have collected not only flour, but also other victuals – bread, beans, cheese, paprika, etc.[199]

The names *Dodola* and *Peperuga*

The terms *peperuga*, *dodola* and the diminutive *dodolitsa* that appear in Djordjević's text are among the names for the Balkan rain-maiden. The various names have been elegantly mapped by Plotnikova (1999) to reveal regional variations. Names of the *dodola* type, which I designate as the 'central' group, are more common in Serbia, Bosnia; and names of the *peperuga* or *perperuda* type, designated as the 'eastern and southern group', tend to be more frequent in Bulgaria, Romania, Moldavia, Albania, Thessaly and Epirus.[200] In the border-area of dialect-continua between Bulgaria and Serbia, as in Macedonia, both verbal variants appear in the same song.

Names in the *peperuga* (or *peperuda*) group are related to the Slavonic storm-god *Perun*, cognate with Lithuanian *Pergunas* or *Perkunis*, Latvian *Perkons*, *Perkuns*, Prussian *Percunis*, Norse *Fjörgynn* and, of course, *Thor*. But in Bulgarian, the word *peperuga* (*peperuda*) has two apparently quite unrelated further meanings: 'butterfly' and 'poppy'.[201] While there exists

[199] Djordjević 401-403; trans. Vera V. Radojević and RB.

[200] See *In a Time of Drought* (RB 2011c): 35, 37-38, and 42.

[201] Duridanov 1996: 161-164.

plenty of fascinating theoretical conjecture among scholars on these etymologies, all of it relevant to a depth-study of the rainmaking practices, the key factor to bear in mind for this discussion of Djordjević's account is that, to the villagers actually involved in practising and witnessing the ritual, multiple overlays of meaning and associations were *simultaneously* present in their language and minds. The niceties of scholarly etymology were hardly relevant to them.

Vuk Karadžić, Stevanović and Djordjević

Djordjević's text confirms many of the observations made by the first known commentator on the practices, Vuk Karadžić, 180 years previously, in his first edition of the *Srpski rječnik* [Serbian Dictionary] (Karadžić 1818). A later dictionary entry on the rain-maiden (1989), listed under *Dodola* and giving some of her other titles, along with secondary meanings and literary references, provides further commentary:

> *dodola* f. ethn.; *Peperuda, prporuša, čarojica.* folk-custom in some parts of south-eastern Europe, in which participants (usually girls) go from house to house in time of drought, sprinkle (or get sprinkled with) water, and sing folksongs praying for rain.[202]

Here, a key fact, not mentioned by Karadžić, is that the participants not only 'sprinkle water' but can 'get sprinkled' themselves. Djordjević's account of the Morava version strongly bears out this reciprocity, which progressively takes clear shape as a key structural and thematic feature.

Stages in the Ceremony

From the wealth of specific detail in Djordjević's account, the ceremony can be seen to develop in clearly demarcated stages, each rich in symbolic associations:

1. The girls walk to each house in the village, bringing their own copper water-bowl and bundles or sprays of plants, and use these to sprinkle water over the house.
2. The first words of their songs identify or correlate their own action of walking over or through the fields with that of the movement of

[202] Stevanović 446-447; trans. RB.

clouds across the sky. It's implicit here that the dodolas are (or are *like*) clouds, in that both are dispensers of rain. The first line of the song also means 'Fly, fly, butterfly.'

3. The words of the song call on God to pour down rain, to enable the fields to yield grain for bread, as well as wine, hemp, and basic victuals.
4. The housewife takes water from her well and pours it over the girls' wreath-covered heads and feet.
5. The housewife gives the girls a sieve and some flour.
6. One girl does more pouring or sprinkling of flour on the ground according to a formulaic procedure which involves using the right hand and facing the east. The emphasis on the right hand and on the easterly direction together imply invocation of the sun as the source of light. There follows a "heads-or-tails'" procedure with the sieve. Effective performance and results constitute success and good luck.
7. The girls go to the fields and repeat their sprinkling of water there.
8. They go in and out of the quarry three times, with more sprinkling of water into it.
9. They receive porridge from a widow. In some cases, the bowl from which they eat is placed on a plate which has been turned upside down.
10. Their food is served and they eat it over spilt or running water.
11. At the end they throw their ceremonial leafy clothes and gear into running water.

In this ritual, several distinct natural transformations, reciprocities and interdependences are re-enacted, both sequentially and simultaneously. The most obvious is the set of transitions from the sprinkling and pouring of water, via flour, to porridge, then to the action of eating the porridge over water, followed by more sprinkling on the fields, and the final discarding of their leafy clothes into running water. This sequence in itself represents an entire natural cycle.

The Sieve

The sprinkling of flour from the sieve in stages 5 and 6 of the ceremony is similar enough to the pouring of rain from clouds for the latter to symbolise the former. Flour is the finest of dusts. From this single set of associations, further vivid and evocative correspondences emerge. For example, the word *sito*, which means 'sieve' in both Serbo-Croat and Bulgarian, has many derivatives, all of which indicate smallness or minuteness, e.g. the Serbo-Croat adjective *sitan* (*-na, -no*) meaning 'fine', 'little', and hence *sitno*, meaning 'small change' or 'loose change', as well as words like *sitnarijia*, meaning 'odds and ends'. Thus, a common formula in many of the Serbian rainmaking songs for 'fine rain' (i.e. 'rain falling in small droplets') is *sitna kiša*, more precisely, 'sieved rain, sifted rain' and in Bulgarian, *sitna rosa*, 'sieved or sifted dew'.

Surely, then, the sieve in Djordjević's account actually *embodies* this *sitna kiša* or *sitna rosa*. Bearing in mind the rain-maiden's connection with *Perun*, and the possible link between *Perun* and the Vedic god *Parjánya*, consider the striking similarities evident from the following commentary on the woollen sieve that filters the *soma*, or 'juice of the divine plant', in the *Rig Veda*:

> [...] the woollen sieve through which the juice of the divine plant is filtered is identified with the sky, and the filtering and pouring of the juice into the water and milk that awaits it is made to represent all manner of cosmic processes. Because the juice is liquid it is compared to and identified with the rain, and Soma becomes the Lord of streams and son of the waters. Because the plant is golden in colour it is compared to the lightning and the noise made by the pressing is compared to the thunderstorm. Assimilated to the sun it fills heaven and earth with its rays [...][203]

According to the same commentator, the woollen filter in the *Rig Veda* is by no means a mere metaphor for clouds:

> The sieve which filters the juice, as we have seen, is likened to the sky; indeed it *is* the sky. Soma is 'in the navel of heaven in the woollen filter' (*RV*, 9.12.4), it 'traverses the lights of heaven, the woollen filter' (*ibid.* 9.37.3), or 'purifying himself in heaven [...] he walks with the sun in the filter' (*ibid.* 9.27.5). In none of this is any incongruity felt, for the cultic act creates a magical rapport with the entire cosmos, and the woollen filter thus becomes the centre of the universe and identical with the sky.

Exploring the same example, the commentary by Schrader is pertinent:

---

[203] Zaehner 20-21.

(photo: Dr. Dragić)

Two dodolas, Banja Koviljača, near Loznica, Western Serbia, 1957

"Magic may be practised either by an action or by words, as can be clearly gathered from its terminology."[204] Similarly, the flour (powder) that passes through Peperuga's sieve may be said to stand for (represent, embody, symbolise, etc.) the wished-for rain.[205] This implication in turn opens up still more fascinating and fertile correspondences, which will lead, firstly, in directions away from our text, and then back into it.[206]

---

[204] Schrader 40.

[205] Rain is identified with "heavenly' seed in many cultures: "In Amerindian tradition rain is 'the storm god's sowing'. Rain was the sperm which made fruitful the sacred marriage. All agrarian civilizations attribute the same symbolic properties to it" (Chevalier and Gheerbrant 783).

[206] Melanie Rein has reminded me of a symbolic aspect that hasn't been explored here: the function of the sieve is not primarily to 'refine' but to separate. In some cases, what is of value is 'fine' and so passes through. In other cases, the contrary is true: the sieve 'nets' what is of value and it is the waste or by-product that passes through. See also Chevalier and Gheerbrant: 881-882.

An excursus through rain, mist and dust

Across a wide range of Indo-European languages, there's a fascinating maze of perceptual associations and meanings embedded or hidden under words for *rain, mist, dust, powder,* etc. I'd suggest that this network is present as a kind of mesh of 'deep' memories and associations, whose echoes reverberate dimly but directly beneath all versions of the Balkan rainmaking customs. The following tables contain expressions collated from dictionaries and other sources (listed in the bibliography).

Some words and phrases expressing notions of
'rain', 'dew', 'water', 'vapour', 'mist', 'powder',
'dust', etc. in Indo-European languages

Table 1: some cognates beginning with */θ/, /f/, /d/, /t/*

Ancient Greek	*thymiān*	'to burn so as to produce smoke'
	thymós	'spirit, breath, life, mind, soul, desire, courage, anger'
Latin	*fumus*	'smoke'
	fuscus	'sombre, dark, dusky'
Old English	*dust*	'fine powder, dust'
Old High German	*tunst, tunist*	'storm, breath'
Middle High German	*tunist*	'storm, breath'
Modern German	*Dunst*	'haze, steam, smoke, vapour, mist'
Modern Dutch	*duist*	'meal-dust'
Irish	*tunst*	'vapour, fine dust'
Norwegian	*dusk-regn*	'fine rain, dew' (i.e. 'dust-rain')
Swedish	*regn-dusk*	'fine rain, dew' (i.e. 'rain-dust')
Norwegian	*dysja*	'fine rain, drizzle'
Serbian, Croatian	*dažd*	'rain' (obsolete)
Bulgarian	*dăzhd*	'rain'

Table 2: some cognates beginning with /*p*/

Tocharian	*pärs-*	'sprinkle' (dust, powder), 'splash' (sprinkle, water)
Hittite	*papparš-*	'splash, water'
Czech	*prš*	'rain'
	prchat	'evaporate'
Slovenian	*pršavica, pršec*	'drizzling rain, spray, Scotch mist'
	pršen	'shower'
	pršenje	'drizzle, drizzling, rain'
	pršeti	'to drizzle, to sprinkle'
	pršiti	'to spray, to sprinkle'
	prašen	'dusty, powdery'
Bulgarian	*prah*	'dust'
Bulgarian dialects	*părsholi,prashuli*	'it's raining, drizzling', (derived from *prah* i.e. rain consisting of fine drops, like dust)
	prashasvam	'to cover with dust'
	prashevitsa	'mill'
	praunka	'fine ash from fireplace, wood-ash'
	prashitsa	'water', derived from *prah*
Serbian, Croatian	*prah*	'dust'
	prskati, prsnuti	'to spray, sprinkle, spatter; to gush, pour; to explode, blow up'
	prašiti	'to dust; to spray; to sprinkle with powder'
Croatian	*prašek*	'powder'
Serbian, Croatian	*pepeo*	'ash'
Bulgarian	*pepel*	'ash'
Montenegrin dialect	*prpor*	'water poured over ash'
Croatian (Dalmatia)	*prporuše*	'participants in rainmaking ceremony'

Even a cursory glance at Table 1 and Table 2 indicates gradual metaphorical shifts in meaning within and across languages which, when laid out in this way, not only make 'good sense' in perceptual and cognitive terms, but even suggest several twangs of recognition and delight to a person who is registering these connections for the first time. Moreover, these varied linguistic examples, across many languages, themselves indicate that the obvious 'opposites' – 'dust' and 'rain' – may well be intimately related in human perception.[207] For example, the compound Scandinavian expressions in Table 1, meaning 'fine rain, dew', *dusk-regn* ('dust-rain') and *regn-dusk* ('rain-dust'), find similar counterparts both in the Russian expression, *porošena doždya* ('powdery rain'), and in the formulas of Balkan rainmaking songs: *sitna rosa, rosna kiša* and *sitna rosna* ('sieved rain', 'dewy rain' and 'sieved dew').[208] In one location, at Graovo in western Bulgaria, the rain-maiden is actually called *Rosomanka*, 'dew-caller, dew-bringer'.[209]

Furthermore, the two sets of etymologically and semantically related Indo-European words listed in Table 1 and the semantically related words in Table 2, many of which also have clear etymological links, fall consistently into two *phonological* sets: those beginning with the / *d* /, / *θ* /, / *f* /, / *t* / consonants, and those beginning with /*p* /: comparable, then, to the sets for the / *d* / and / *p* / groups of names for the rain-maiden, *Dodola* and *Peperuda*. Thus, in a number of Indo-European languages, a wide range of words beginning in both / *d* / and / *p* / covers similar fields. Moreover, from a mere glance at the Russian expression, *porošena doždya* ['powdery rain'], with its combination of / *p* / and / *d* / sounds, it's hard *not* to be reminded of the western (Dalmatian) variant of the name for the rainmaker, *prporuša*, whose etymology has been directly related to *prah* ('dust') via the reduplicated *prpor* ('water poured over ash').[210] Nor does it seem entirely coincidental that the Russian expression *porošena doždya* presents a similar combination of / *p* / and / *d* / sounds to the *Peperuda-Dodola* configuration. In the light of these comparisons, one can hardly help wondering, too, if the regularity of occurrence of the reduplicated plosives / *p* / and / *d* / associated with the rain-maiden is more than coincidental.

[207] I wonder if such labyrinthine associations as these may not be present somewhere below the cognitive surface among many (all?) contemporary speakers of Indo-European (and other?) languages and, furthermore, break through the surface occasionally, in much the same way that interlinked subterranean chambers consisting of caves, tunnels and wells supply our overground rivers and lakes. Such a conjecture would be consonant with Jungian theory.

[208] I suggest that, to a reader coming across these phrases for the first time, their striking quality may well consist in the apparent 'unlikeliness' of the analogy between liquid (*dew, rain*) and solid (*dust, powder*).

[209] Plotnikova 101.

[210] Skok 1973, vol. 3: 55-56.

To sum up: I suggest that the specific words used to describe some of the actions and functions in these Balkan songs, along with the phenomenon of 'fine rain', that's to say, 'sieved or sifted rain' (*sitna kiša*), are of direct linguistic relevance to any discussion of the rainmaking ceremonies, as they're integrally bound up with the meanings both of the rituals themselves and of the names of the protagonists.

Water above, water below

To return, albeit lingeringly, from this linguistic excursus to the Morava custom and Djordjević's text: it's equally interesting that his account indicates several intermingling reciprocities between water from above and water from below. The water and flour sprinkled by the girls symbolises rain in the stages that have been numbered above as the 1st, 6th, 8th and 9th, as do the words of the song in the 2nd and 3rd stages. In this context, as a 'pourer' in her own right, the rain-maiden herself is transformed into an agent, representative or embodiment of the clouds which deliver rain, miming their actions and in her song identifying her own movements with them ("We go over the fields / And the clouds over the sky"). Incidentally, more than forty-five years before Djordjević, Frazer had read a very similar account of the ritual, and published an extract from a nineteenth century translation in *The Golden Bough*:

> We go through the village;
> The clouds go in the sky;
> We go faster,
> Faster go the clouds;
> They have overtaken us,
> And wetted the corn and the vine.

Frazer comments:

> The words of the Servian song, however, taken in connexion with the constant movement which the chief actress in the performance seems expected to keep up, points to some comparison of the girl or her companions to clouds moving through the sky.[211]

[211] Frazer 1911: 275. But interpretations of ritual actions and gestures are never interpretable as simple signs. 'Meanings' are multivalent, as in poems. Here, the constant movement might, quite obviously, *also* be intended to indicate the flittering of a butterfly.

Conversely, water from *below* (i.e. from the well, under the plate, and as a stream) is represented in the 4th, 9th and 10th stages. So the dodola herself is the *recipient* of the sprinkling or pouring too, and as such *re-presents* and even symbolically *becomes* the earthly vessel or container into which the rain falls, and/or the growing plant onto and around which it descends, thereby enabling the plant to grow and flourish in the soil.

In all these respects, this discussion clarifies that the 'purity' of the rain-maiden is unquestionable, whether she's momentarily the agent or recipient of the rain that it's her function to promote, invoke or encourage – as well as to represent and embody in her own person by means of her actions and movements. Sky-water is purer and less contaminated than earth-water, or at least, used to be until pollutant acids got into it; and arguably, rain symbolises purity in and of itself. The girl's role as agent thus emphasises her connectedness with 'spiritual' elements: in this aspect, in the rite she becomes, almost literally, 'heavenly'. On the other hand, as recipient, whether as an embodiment of the earth itself or as the mortal symbol of all that will grow from it, live and die on it and be buried in it, she may equally be regarded as a 'pure' vessel or receptacle into which, one might suggest, the equivalent of a libation is poured. As we shall see, this motif in itself suggests further, and much older associations for the rain-maiden.

In the context of this ritual of sprinkling and pouring, all the lowly 'earthly' attributes of the rain-maiden[212] – her barefootedness, her humble social status in the village and her rootedness in cyclic and seasonal change, not to mention her individual mortality – are modulated, blended and uplifted into a 'higher', impersonal, elemental and perennial pattern. And as far the notion of any *rite de passage* is concerned, this discussion at least gives credence to the idea that, whatever the age or maturity of the ritual's leading celebrant, its main accent was always on the onset and arrival of fertility, in the springtime or early summer, as a 'pure' gift from above as well as from below, both for the girl herself and for the community she belonged to or interceded for. In this sense, it might be said that this humble Balkan peasant or gypsy girl fully embodies the Heraclitan and Hermetic principle, "As above, so below."

Furthermore, the idea that the ceremony has elements in common with a kind of pagan 'baptism' shouldn't be ignored. It appears to be not merely a fertility ritual but one of purification and initiation which, for the people

[212] These motifs are well documented by such writers as Kulišić, *et al.* (108-109), Arnaudov (155-201), and Plotnikova.

of the village, needs to take place if fertility (i.e. survival and, hopefully, prosperity) is to occur at all. Such actions of sprinkling and pouring water occur widely, of course, in purificatory and initiatory ceremonies. Christian baptism is just one example. Far earlier evidence is provided, too, by Minoan and Mycenaean seals which, in this context, suggest that the modern Balkan rain-maiden may have very ancient antecedents.

The Pouring of Water in Minoan and Mycenaean Art

In his 1925 paper entitled 'The Ring of Nestor', Sir Arthur Evans, the excavator of Knossos, examines Minoan and Mycenaean seals, including signet rings, which depict female figures. Among these, he correlates designs showing what he calls "the Spring Goddess rising from the earth" and "a female figure [...] rising from the ground". Several artefacts reveal a central, more mature female figure accompanied by two smaller and probably younger females. He asks: "Were these little twin companions and ministrants simply handmaidens of the Goddess? Were they perhaps her daughters?"[213] With scarcely veiled excitement, his discussion then gathers pace towards an interpretation of this central figure, who is holding "poppy heads". Evans sees this figure not only as the "Spring Goddess" but as the goddess who appears "*one thousand years before* [...] *her Hellenic successor Persephonê, at her moment of ascension from the earth*".[214]

Evans then goes on to compare a Mycenaean bead-seal from Thisbe in Boeotia with a Minoan seal-impression from the Domestic Quarter of the Palace of Knossos. As can be seen from the illustrations, both clearly show a female figure pouring a libation:

> On the left side of the field, with one of *her little girl attendants* imitating her action behind, stands the Goddess [...]. Her left arm is raised and her right hand is held immediately over the rim of a large jar or amphora, into which an adult female attendant [...] is pouring some kind of liquid from a jug.[215]

He then introduces the second seal, discovered in 1922 in the Domestic Quarter of the Palace at Knossos:

---

213 Evans 1925: 12-16.

214 *ibid.* 16; emphasis added.

215 *ibid.* 18; emphasis added.

> [...] the substantial correspondence of the major episode in the two designs is such as to necessitate the conclusion that both refer to some ritual function of the same kind.[216]

Then, rejecting the argument that the libation was wine, Evans proposes his interpretation:

> It seems preferable to connect the ceremonial pouring of the liquid content of the smaller vessel into the greater with methods of "sympathetic magic" in vogue *among primitive folk the world over by securing rain in seasons of drought.* [...] The view that these intaglio types present ceremonial acts designed to secure rain in a dry season – a not infrequent contingency in Crete – receives support from the appearance of a whole series of somewhat summarily engraved stones, belonging to a numerous amuletic class, which there is every reason for regarding as rain-charms.[217]

Here, Evans's term 'primitive folk' echoes the patronising terminology and attitude of the redoubtable Victorian scholar Tylor (*Primitive Culture*, 1871).[218] He then inserts a footnote that directly cites Grimm's discussions of rainmaking ceremonies in *Deutsche Mythologie* (1875), and offers a further hint of the survival of ancient rainmaking customs in the Macedonia of his own time, correlated with a shrine to the Roman thunder god:

> A curious instance of such a rain-producing rite was noted by me at Ibrahimovci near the ancient Scupi (Skloplje). I was informed that an altar, with a dedication to Jupiter, which I had observed lying face downwards there on the village green, was set up in its proper position in times of drought, and that villagers, both Christian and Mahometan, with a local Bey at the head, went together to the stone and poured wine over the top, praying the while for rain.[219]

---

[216] *ibid.* 18.

[217] *ibid.* 19; emphasis added.

[218] Incidentally, the youthful and as-yet-unknighted Arthur Evans travelled widely in the Balkans, and wrote a fascinating book, illustrated with his own sketches, *Through Bosnia and Herzegóvina On Foot During the Resurrection, August and September 1875* (1876). For historical insights underlying the state of affairs in Bosnia in our days, as well as revelations of his own superior self-assumptions and patrician prejudices, this text makes enlightening reading (see also: 63, note 13 above).

[219] *ibid.* 19, n. 44.

Mycenaean bead-seal from Thisbe in Boeotia
(Evans 1925: 17)

Minoan seal-impression from Knossos
(Evans 1925: 18)

To summarise: Evans interprets the images of water-pouring figures carved into these seals as those of a goddess who was the pre-Indo-European antecedent of Persephone. Furthermore, when he wrote these passages, I think it likely that Evans had the Balkan dodola at the back of his mind. He knew the work of Grimm, Frazer and others on this theme, and was familiar with Wace.[220]

[220] A. J. B. Wace, among other distinctions, was director of the British School at Athens (1914–1923) and second Laurence Professor of Classical Archaeology at Cambridge (1934–1944). (See 'Alan Wace', *Wikipedia*.)

Is there a link between these images and the rainmaking practices that survived to the end of the twentieth century? In the absence of hard historical evidence, although it's impossible to go further than hypothesis and conjecture, I suggest that these passages are, at the very least, indications of what the Russian scholars Ivanov and Toporov call "typologically parallel" practices in the ancient world. In that sense, at least, the Minoan and Mycenaean images may be interpretable as precursors, even if not as direct ancestors, of the modern Balkan rainmaking practices.

Furthermore, the idea of "typological parallelism" is consonant with a Jungian interpretation: that, at different times and places, similar constellations of archetypes surface, apparently 'spontaneously', yet without necessarily being linked via direct historical cause or even influence. Combining Jung's approach with that of Ivanov and Toporov would suggest that, rather than searching for ancestral lineage, it may be more helpful methodologically to ground the exploration of links in examining similarities both of societal type, structure, ideology, etc., and of patterns among the mythical configurations themselves.

The Rain-maiden and Persephone

The variant 'western' names for the participants in the Balkan rainmaking ceremony are *Prpac* and *Prporuše*. This pair constitutes the third main group of Balkan rainmakers' names. They're found along the Adriatic coastline of Dalmatia and Istria, with only two locations in inland Croatia and one further south on the Montenegrin coast.[221] The name *Prpac* is of masculine gender. The name *Prporuše* occurs only in the plural and is feminine. The variant *Preporuše* also occurs. The two names describe different functions in the ritual. They were first described by Vuk Karadžić:

> In the same way as the *dodolas* go in Serbia, so do the *prporuše* in Dalmatia (Kotari), except that they are not girls but unmarried youths, and they go from house to house with green branches and flowers, and dance and sing. Their master or dance-leader is called the *prpac*, and he is wrapped in *pavetina* [a herb] and brambles. While they are dancing and singing, the women pour water over them, making sure that the prpac is the one who gets [drenched] most; once they have finished singing and dancing, the housewife makes them a gift of wool, salt, cheese, curds, butter, eggs, etc., and

[221] Plotnikova 1999; *In a Time of Drought* (RB 2011c): 35 and 44-45.

in the evening, they make a feast of whatever they have collected during the day and share it among themselves. The *prporuše* sing in front of the houses.[222]

This group of names is geographically separated from the eastern group, to which it shows marked similarities, especially in the reduplication of /*p*/. There are three distinct theories to account for the etymology of these names. First, Jakobson identifies them with the eastern group and with his derivation from *Perun*: "In Dalmatia, Perperuna has the name Prporuše with the substitution *per* > *por* in the second part of the root and with zero grade in the first part."[223] The second theory is Skok's. For *prporuša*, he lists two meanings: first, 'when water is poured on burning ash', and secondly

> [...] a term in folklore made metaphorically from this, on account of the pouring of water: unmarried youths who in drought go from house to house, dancing and singing, so that rain will fall; women who pour water over them (in Kotor and Dalmatia).[224]

The third theory comes from Ivanov and Toporov, who present a conjectural but fascinating argument for a correlation between *Persephone* and *Prporuša*:

> In this connection, one's attention is attracted to the ancient Greek fertility goddess *Persephone*, daughter of Zeus, the god of the sky, and of Demeter, the goddess of the earth. The depiction of Persephone in the form of *a young maiden with ears of corn and/or flowers*, her representation or appearance as the *opener* of Spring, of the earth, the motif of the first *rain* of spring which accompanies her arrival on earth, and finally, the presence of the ritual and cult of Persephone and Demeter in the Eleusinian mysteries, with elements which are reflected in ceremonies among contemporary Balkan peoples – all of this leads one to perceive in the image of Persephone something like a *typological parallel* (emphasis added) to the images which are under consideration here (localised, indeed, at the highest level). Moreover, the ancient Greek *Persephóni*, the Latin *Proserpina*, the Etruscan *Phersipnai* and *Phersipnei* (the Orco tomb/sepulchre) and the like, have not yet received any satisfactory explanation, even though these have been the continuous objects of 'folk etymological' transformations. In so far as any tentative explanation has been put forward about this, i.e. that these genuinely attested names were preceded by a form of the type **Prsepna*, **Prse(r)pona*

[222] Karadžić 1957 [1867], trans. Vera V. Radojević and RB.

[223] Jakobson 1964; and 1985b: 23.

[224] Skok, vol 3, 1973: 55-56; trans. RB. See also Table 2, 139 above.

> and the like, one cannot help thinking about the closeness in sound of these forms to the source of the Balkan names for isofunctional personages such as *Prporuše* < **Pr(s)pors-*; *Perperona, Perperuna* < **Per(s)per-on-*, and so on. The comparison of Etruscan *φersu*, meaning 'underground world', with Latin *persona* is a characteristic example.[225]

Conjectural though this is, and whether one finds the link between Peperuga-Dodola and Persephone acceptable or not, the material gathered in this essay leads to a single incontrovertible conclusion. Hemming the borders and edges of the rainmaking songs and interwoven through the fabric of their linguistic associations, ancient mythological patterns are intricately stitched. This observation would suggest that detailed and in-depth comparative analysis of formulas, set phrases and patterns of imagery in rainmaking songs from *all* the Balkan languages is called for, within the scope of a single systematic study. This, ideally, should include research into etymological, ethnographic, literary-critical, musical and folk-song patternings. There's no doubt that this would yield richly rewarding results.

Fertility and Soulmaking

Finally, to return to the opening words of the Morava song: its opening injunction 'Fly, fly', combined with its invocation of God and its comparison of the young singers and dancers themselves with 'clouds over the sky', must mean that *at this moment* the village girls are given the status of aerial, spiritual beings. From this opening, I suggest, they're to be understood as servants or handmaidens of the all-powerful god who makes the rain fall. And this line of thinking leads to two further willing suspensions of disbelief, both of which should, of course, be entertained simultaneously. The first is that these singing, dancing girls *represent a goddess*, whether as living embodiments of the feminine deity herself, or her aerial ministrants or her mortal priestesses. The second is that they represent *departed souls*, who have vanished like clouds "into air, into thin air" – or who are, perhaps, still present, as if fluttering, close by. We've already pointed out that the words "fly, fly, peperuga" identify the rain-maidens with butterflies. Butterflies symbolise the soul.

2004, 2007

[225] Ivanov and Toporov 106-108; trans. Richard Cook and RB.

'How naked?' Notes and Queries on Vuk Karadžić's Dictionary Entries on *dodola*

The rainmaking songs and ceremonies form a small but integral thread in the enormously complex and intricate web of oral tradition of the Balkans. So far as I've been able to discover, the first person to report, document and transcribe them was the Serbian collector, language reformer, dictionary-compiler and translator, Vuk Stefanović Karadžić (1787–1864).[226] Thanks to him, they became well-known to such distinguished writers as Goethe and the brothers Grimm, through the several editions of his famous *Srpski Rječnik* ('Serbian Dictionary') which appeared in Vuk's own lifetime, as well as the first volume of his 1841 collection *Srpske narodne pjesme* ('Folk Songs of the Serbian People'), and his study entitled *Život i običaja naroda srpskoga* ('Life and Customs of the Serbian People'), published posthumously in 1867.[227] Karadžić travelled widely himself, and from the mid-nineteenth century on, rainmaking ceremonies were documented by travellers to Serbia from other European countries too.

It's interesting and valuable to revisit Vuk's writings on *Dodola*, *Prpac* and *Prporuše*, for a variety of reasons, not least of which is the attention that these figures and customs have received since then, not to mention the ways in which they've been interpreted and deployed by many later international scholars in the construction of ethnographic and linguistic theories.[228]

Examination of the entries on '*Dodola*' in the different editions of Vuk's *Dictionary* reveals a good deal of information about the rainmaking customs as well as minor but interesting differences, some of which have

[226] For an excellent biography of Vuk's life and achievements, see Wilson 1970.

[227] The word *narod* can be variously translations as 'nation', 'folk' and 'people'. The root of *narod* is *rod*, which itself is related to English 'root'. The latter word has a very wide range of meanings, including 'relative', 'family', 'kin', 'clan'; 'gender'; 'harvest', crop', 'fruit', etc. (Benson 1980: 308-309). For further implications of this word's connotations, see also 294, n.1, and 301, n.1 below.

[228] For a list of some of these scholars, see 59 above. See also the previous three essays in this book.

led to interpretations by later writers who cite Vuk, which in fact turn out to be inaccurate readings of the statements he actually made. Here are the relevant passages in English translation (trans. RB):

Srpski rječnik ('Serbian Dictionary'), 1818

> Dodole, f. pl. some girls who, in the summer, when there is a drought, go through the village from house to house, and sing and call on rain to fall. One of the girls gets completely undressed and, thus naked, lines and ties herself up in various grasses and flowers so that not even one small part of her skin is seen, and she is called dodola (she has turned herself into a dodola – is said of a girl or a woman who has adorned herself right up to her head): then they go around from house to house. When they arrive in front of a house, then the dodola dances alone, while the other girls stand in a row and sing various songs; after which the housewife, or some other member of the household, takes a bucket or a pitcher of water and pours it over the dodola, and she meanwhile dances and turns around. In the *dodolske pesme* ['rain-maiden's songs'] they sing at the end of every verse: *oj dodo! oj dodole,* e.g.
>
> Our doda prays to God, oy dodo! oy dodo!
> To pour down dewy rain, oy dodo! oy dodo!
>
> The Dodole dance nowadays throughout nearly all of Serbia from Valjevo down to Timok. Around Srem, Bačka and Banat they danced until quite recently, but the new priests have forbidden and uprooted it [the custom].[229]

Srpski rječnik, 1852

> Dodole, f. pl. When there is a drought, a number of girls go through the village from house to house, and sing and sing and call on rain to fall. One of the girls gets completely undressed down to her shirt, and thus naked, lines and ties herself up with various grasses and flowers, so that no part of her can be seen at all, and she is called dodola (she has turned herself into a dodola – is said of a girl or a woman who has adorned herself right up to her head): then they go around from house to house. When they arrive in front of a house, then the dodola dances alone, while the other girls stand in a row and sing various songs; after which the housewife, or some other member of the household, takes a bucket or a pitcher of water and pours it over the dodola, and she meanwhile dances and turns around. In the *dodolske pesme* ['rain-maiden's songs'] they sing

[229] Karadžić 1818: 135.

at the end of every verse: *oy dodo! oy dodole*, e.g.

> Our doda prays to God, oy dodo! oy dodo!
> To pour down dewy rain, oy dodo! oy dodo!

> In Serbia it used to be our own local [home] girls who went around the village, but nowadays it is mainly Gypsies [female] begging for themselves. In the Vojvodina region the new priests have forbidden the dodolas, as they have also done to the *kraljice*, but they can still be observed in various places. cf. *prporuše*.[230]

The differences between these two texts are small but not all of them are insignificant. Apart from relatively minor alterations in punctuation, typography, word order and emphasis, as well as the elimination of redundant detail (e.g. "in the summer" in combination with "drought") – other changes indicate two further possibilities, namely: that, between 1818 and 1852, Vuk had received or gathered new information, and/or that, in certain respects, he had altered his interpretation, or at least his presentation, of the custom. The main differences are as follows:

First Difference

In the later version, the 'complete nakedness' or 'state of undress' of the girl who plays the part of the *Dodola*, before she's covered in grasses and leaves, is qualified by the phrase "down to her shirt" (*do košulje*). This qualification, however, which is unclear in itself, has led to a good deal of confusion among many later writers, especially from outside the Balkans, who had obviously never actually witnessed rainmaking ceremonies themselves but simply followed or embroidered on Vuk's descriptions. I suggest that this textual change may be interpreted in at least four possible ways:

> 1. For most people in the twenty-first century, 'nakedness' means, literally, 'without wearing any clothing at all'. However, Balkan peasants in the nineteenth century were used to living in cramped quarters, with whole families often sleeping in a single room. For them, being 'naked' may have meant no more than being 'undressed down to one's underwear'. Vuk himself was born into a peasant family. But by the time he came to prepare the later edition, he had travelled widely, and as far as 'nakedness' was concerned, he may have become considerably more

[230] Karadžić 1852: 128.

aware of discrepancies between the customs and habits of city-dwellers and those of countryfolk. However, if his textual alteration does imply any such awareness, this isn't stated very clearly.[231]

2. A simpler if cruder interpretation is that the girls who took part in the ceremonies were indeed 'completely naked' at some unspecified time before 1818, and at some time between then and 1852 were only undressed down to their shift or shirt. However, this interpretation seems far less plausible. The phrase *pa se onako gola* ('and thus, naked') is retained in the 1852 edition, along with the new qualification about the shirt (*svuće do košulje ca svijem*: 'gets completely undressed down to her shirt').

3. A third interpretation is that Vuk was in two minds about the extent to which the Dodola got or was undressed. This might even indicate that he had never actually witnessed a rainmaking ceremony himself. As for preparations for the rainmaking ceremonies, if the question of traditional village morality is considered, especially under the eye of the local priest, it seems entirely beyond belief or possibility that any males would have been allowed to witness either the dressing or undressing of a young village girl, whether before or after puberty.

To elaborate this last point, the special role of older women in the villages is clarified by Dražen Nožinić.[232] Video documentation from older women in Thrace, northern Greece, who remember and re-enact the custom from their youth, strongly confirms what would seem obvious: that preparations for the *dodola-peperuda-perperouna* rituals were not only domains controlled by women but their exclusive prerogative and responsibility, passed down traditionally and in 'matrilineal' fashion (see 'Perperouna Custom' online). Preparing young girls for a ceremony meant caring for them, looking after them, in a motherly, responsible and impeccably respectable fashion.

A further purely practical point is that layering hard twigs and sharp-edged leaves directly next to the skin with no intervening layer of protective material at all would have been extremely uncomfortable for the girls involved. Leaves and twigs carry bugs and insects. A likely result would have been a good deal of itching, scratching and sore skin.

Interestingly, with the single reception of the Russian scholar Ana Plotnikova, all the expert scholarly commentators and interpreters of the

[231] I'm indebted to Jasna Levinger-Goy for drawing attention to the points made in this paragraph, as well as for reminding me about *Crven ban*. See also Weissbort and Longinovic.

[232] See 123 above.

rainmaking rituals that I've so far come across have been male. It's a pity that there has been such a dearth of women ethnographers and anthropologists working in the field. If one considers the wealth of intimate details about life in Yugoslavia collected, for example, by Olive Lodge, it's clear that female ethnographers would be have been far more likely to be trusted, both by the young participants and by their older female carers.[233] In this way, we might have been more intimately informed about many significant details of the custom. Now that it has all but died out, it's unfortunately too late for us to learn from first-hand female perspectives – other than from the reminiscences of older women, as in the Greek documentation mentioned above. Perhaps this essay might be an encouragement for young female ethnographers to interview elderly women, before this folk tradition has been totally lost to memory.

Though certainly no prude himself, Vuk was certainly familiar with censorious disapproval of various aspects of his work by ecclesiastical authorities. Two of his collections of folk-material (of women's songs, and of bawdy and ribald rhymes and songs) were never published in his lifetime, probably for political reasons, perhaps because he was intent on presenting his people as valorous rather than vulgar, and, equally probably, because of his fear that this kind of material might "shock and alienate the Serbian elite in Hungary, who were very much under the sway of the Orthodox Church".[234] To achieve Serbian publication, both these collections had to wait more than a hundred years after Vuk's death: that is, until the 1970s. In that decade, despite the puritanical family ethic imposed by the Communist regime after World War II, official morality in Yugoslavia became more relaxed, partly through the influence of the Western 'sixties phenomenon'. More than one hundred years earlier, because of his acute awareness of what others might find 'salacious' in his work, it's likely that Vuk wouldn't have wished to place too much emphasis on the question of the rain-maiden's 'nakedness', and that he might have deliberately left this point vague and open to interpretation.

Second Difference

In the 1818 entry, Vuk merely distinguishes between the regions of Serbia in which the rainmaking custom was practised in his time and those in

[233] It's a pity that Olive Lodge (1941) didn't observe the dodola custom herself.

[234] Longinovic 16.

which it was dying or had already died out owing to church censorship. His first version uses the rather strong phrase: "forbidden and uprooted", but in the second version the more heavily-loaded part, "and uprooted", has been removed. This could imply that he was doing his best to avoid offending the Church.

Third Difference

In the 1852 entry, Vuk has extended his information in three ways:

1) He mentions the gradual replacement of Serbian girls in the rain-making custom by Roma girls. His use of the words *naše kučevne djevojke* (lit. 'our home girls') may imply regret that the custom was in the process of being discarded by his own people.

2) In the context of church censorship, he now brings in the similar and possibly related custom of the *kraljice*, a folkloric term for another folkloric custom. Benson describes the *kraljice* as "girls who perform ritualistic songs and dances during Pentecost".[235]

3) Vuk realises the integral relationship between the Serbian *dodole* and the Croatian and *prporuše, prpac*, which also has an entry in the 1854 edition. He has certainly acquired new information between the two editions of the dictionary.

4) Vuk's fuller information on the Croatian *prpac* / *prporuše* custom isn't published in his own lifetime but appears posthumously, eleven years later, in *Život i obićaja naroda srpskoga* ('Life and Customs of the Serbian People'), 1867.[236]

[235] Benson, *op. cit.* 226.

[236] See 146-147 above.

Afterword: Scholars' Distortions (Roman Jakobson, 1950)

In the light of the above discussion, and if its premises are accepted, it's worth recording how widely off the mark are scholars who have emphasised the complete 'nakedness' or 'nudity' of the young participants. The description given by even so distinguished and influential a scholar as Roman Jakobson is a good example. Here is one of his commentaries, first published in 1950, and much cited or referred to by others since then:

> The ritual of the rain charm, widespread among Bulgars and Serbs and thence to Greece and Rumania, assigns the paramount role to *a vigorously chaste girl* (*as yet unable to conceive* and born of a mother who since has become unable to conceive). *Nude and draped with flowers, she whirls ecstatically* in the middle of a ring, invoking in song the sky or Elijah to moisten and fructify the earth. She bears the reduplicated name of Perun, whether unchanged (Perperuna) or with hypocoristic modifications. This couple Perunъ- Perperuna recall the Germanic Fjörgynn-Fjörgyn and the Lithuanian Perkúnas-Percuna etc. In another variant of the South Slavic ritual, the main role was performed by a boy assuming Perun's name, reduplicated and altered: the people, whirling and drinking, besought him for rain. To the same cycle refer the old Russian reminiscence of Pereplut, worshiped by whirling and libations, as well as the Magdeburg epistle of 1008 damning the "impudent" god Prigala.[237]

Several points need attention here, even before the main interpretative issue is broached. First, the rain-maiden being "as yet unable to conceive" is by no means general and is quite possibly a fanciful 'poetic' conjecture of Jakobson's. More than a century earlier, in 1845, the English traveller Archibald Paton gives contradictory evidence, when he describes the leading "Dodola" as "a handsome young woman". In Belgrade, October 2000, the Serbian writer Dimitrije Nikolajević told me in conversation that in his childhood, in rural areas near Kragujevac, villagers deliberately set out to choose "the most beautiful girls, aged sixteen or seventeen, for the roles of dodolas". Mila Bosić says that in the village of Banatske Here, in Vojvodina, "the *dodola*, who was a gypsy, had to be pregnant" (341-345).[238]

Second, a detailed questioning of Jakobson's language suggests a version of the custom so fanciful that it might almost have been filmed in Hollywood. The ascription of 'nudity' is an evident oversimplification,

[237] Jakobson, 1985a: 6; emphases added.

[238] See 122 above.

and probably a falsification or fabrication too. For direct counter-evidence, the extent to which the young participants were 'undressed' is actually clarified by Vuk Karadžić, who in 1852 corrects and qualifies his earlier statement about 'nakedness'[239] with the phrase "completely undressed *down to her shirt*".[240] Apart from being inaccurate, the choice of the word "nude" (rather than "naked") has the wrong connotations, for this term properly belongs to the domain of art, especially painting and sculpture, and implies male objectification of the female body, in such a way that the phrase "nude and draped with flowers" can hardly avoid evoking an idealised image of a painting, for example, Botticelli's 'Primavera'.

What's more, the statement that the leading girl whirls "ecstatically" conjures up a vision of a trance-like state akin to that of Maenads in an ancient Dionysian rite or of participants in a modern Voodoo ceremony. Actual ethnographic evidence suggests that any such abandonment on the part of these young village girls would have been highly unlikely, at least in recent times. Finally, what "vigorously" means as an attribute of "chaste", especially in combination with "as yet unable to conceive", is hard to guess, unless it fancifully implies a girl who isn't only prepubescent and a virgin, but also strong, 'well built': i.e. *nubile*. The conclusion is that on the basis of an over-literal and uncritical reading of Vuk Karadžić's first dictionary entry of 1818, Jakobson has indulged in a gentle male fantasy of his own. An enraptured image of pretty peasant girls has got the better of his scholarly judgement, but this has caught the eye of later male scholars and influenced them.

2004, 2007, 2018, 2019

---

[239] Karadžić 1818: 135.

[240] Karadžić 1852: 128; emphasis added.

PART 3

ON WRITERS AND WRITING

Three of the six pieces that follow have arisen out of translating the poets concerned, including the first and most detailed essay here, 'A Nimble Footing on the Coals: Tin Ujević, lyricist; some English perspectives' (2011). This interpretative essay was written after I'd completed a dozen translations from the collection *Kolajna* ('The Necklace', 1926) with Daša Marić (Ujević 2011). So far as I know, our versions and this essay represent the only attempts to date to represent or evaluate this major Yugoslav and Croatian lyric poet in English. Affectionately known simply as 'Tin' (for Augustin), he was born in 1891 and died in 1955.

A word of caution needs to be added here about cultural appropriation in the service of nation-building. Ever since Croatia declared its separation from the Yugoslav Federation on June 25, 1991, Tin Ujević has been acclaimed as Croatia's national poet in much the same way that, for centuries, Scots have celebrated Robert Burns. Understandable though this outcome may be, the historical record belies any such nationalistic claim for Tin. In the 1920s he lived in Belgrade and, from 1930 to 1937, in Sarajevo; and he consistently regarded himself as a Yugoslav and internationalist. When I lived in former Yugoslavia, his poems were as deeply loved by Serbs as by Croats. Andrew Baruch Wachtel notes: "He was equally at home sending his work to Serbian and Croatian journals, an indication that he considered his work at the very least pan-Yugoslav. [...] He proclaimed himself 'Yugoslavia's first and only true European artist'."[1] The essay on Tin is followed by a translation of what I believe to be his greatest lyric poem, 'Daily Lament'.

After this comes 'A Medieval Serbian Poem' (1998), which explores 'A Prayer to the Most Holy Lady, Our Virgin and Mother of God' by Dimitrije Kantakuzin, a Serbian poet who lived from about 1435 to 1500.

Then, two introductions to books of haiku, both multilingual. The first, *Naked Eye*, is by the Macedonian poet, literary theorist and academician Katica Kulavkova (2010). The second introduces *Dreams of Hilandar* by the Serbian poet and publisher Slobodan (Boba) Pavićević. Vera Radojević and I worked on the English version of this book together. But Boba Pavićević died just before the book was due to go to press, and since then no-one has been able to reactivate its publishing process. Perhaps, sooner or later this

[1] Wachtel 123.

short piece may prompt its publication.[2]

Finally, two essay-reviews: an interpretative piece on a long poem by Maja Herman Sekulić, *Gospa od Vinče* / *Our Lady of Vincha* (2017), written after I'd attended a recital of this poem in the stupendous setting of the battlements of Smederevo fortress, overlooking the Danube.[3] This is followed by 'Demons and Daimons: The Dark Vision of Filip David' (2018), a review of his novel, *The House of Remembering and Forgetting*.

November–December 2018

---

[2] For my memoir of Boba Pavićević, see 395-397 below.

[3] On *Poetry Autumn* in Smederevo, see 261-262 below

A Nimble Footing on the Coals: Tin Ujević, lyricist; some English perspectives

For Daša Marić

The Croatian poet Augustin (Tin) Ujević (1891–1955) is one of the finest Southern Slav lyric poets and one of the great poets of Europe in the first half of the twentieth century. What follows is a sketch of some of the qualities of his lyrical poems, from the particular perspective of an English poet who has translated some of them. My intention is to introduce a poet who, so far, has scarcely been registered at all in the English-speaking world[4] The idea here is to pick out strands and suggest possible entry points. I also want to explore some of the reasons why I think he merits the appellation 'great poet', one that's easy enough to bestow, perhaps too easy, but less so to justify.

The procedure I'll adopt will be suggestive and glancing rather than direct and expository. While moving into and around some of Tin's lyrical poems and suggesting paths for critical analysis and interpretation, these notes will follow zigzagging forays and tangential meanderings, some of which will spiral back on themselves, as well as paratactic jumps and juxtapositions with other reference points and contexts, especially in the Anglophone literary tradition, rather than any kind of straightforward march towards a preformulated thesis. The act of writing this involves discovery for me too. *I learn by going where I have to go.*[5]

ꕥ

[4] In the English-speaking world, so far as I know, at the time of writing there has been only one international event to honour Tin. Entitled *Homage to Tin Ujević*, organised by Marilyn Cvitanić, took place at the Bowery Poetry Club, New York, on April 21, 2007. Among the readers was the American poet Anne Waldman. Translations by Daša Marić and myself were included. The event was covered by the evening news programme (*Dnevnik*) on Croatian TV, April 22, 2007.

[5] 'The Waking', Roethke 104.

While Tin Ujević's poems are hardly known in English, they're loved in his native Croatia and throughout former Yugoslavia. I say 'loved' advisedly. I don't mean just admired or respected. At least until the break-up of the Yugoslav Federation in the early 1990s, many of his lyrics were known by heart and quoted by people all over the country, even those who weren't particularly literary, in much the same way that some of W. B. Yeats's early poems, like 'The Lake Isle of Innisfree', 'He Wishes for the Cloths of Heaven' and 'Down by the Salley Gardens',[6] are known and quoted all over Ireland and the UK. This is mainly because people brought up in the various Yugoslav republics learned some of Tin's poems at school. What's more, the sincerity of affection for him as a poet and as a man is evident even today in South-Slavic countries, especially in the tendency still to refer to him by his pet-name: Tin – a practice I'll follow here because of my own affection for his writings. And just as the topics of his poems are intimate, and his poetic personality comes across as endearing and sympathetic, so readers in his own language experience and share an intimate response to his poems and feel that they 'know' the 'real' Tin too. "Not a line does not flow out of genuine feeling," writes the Ch'ing editor Yang Lun of the great Tang dynasty poet Du Fu. His poetry "greatly surpasses others precisely in its sincerity," writes the Sung Buddhist monk Hui-Hung[7]. No less could be claimed for Tin, even though it would be hard for a lyric poet in any language to match the achievement of Du Fu.

Such a popular response as this asks to be unravelled, especially when the character of the man is so conflated with his dominant poetic persona. When I went to live in former Yugoslavia in 1987, the poems of Tin's that I first came across, as might be expected, were his most anthologised pieces. In Split, 1987, Daša Marić asked me to try translating some of these best-known poems, and because my Croatian at that time – or rather, my Serbo-Croatian – was a beginner's, we made literal versions, which we worked from together. Later, in Belgrade and then in Cambridge, I became proficient enough to translate several more poems alone.

Tin's art is delicate, highly crafted, akin to that of filigree. Translation of a poet as intricate as he is sometimes works, sometimes doesn't. You try things out, one after another, you keep your head down, you follow your nose, you fool around, you suddenly wake up in the middle of the

[6] Salley Gardens: *Gort na Saileán*. "'Salley' or 'sally' is a form of the Standard English word 'sallow', i.e., a tree of the genus *Salix*. It's close in sound to the Irish word *saileach*, meaning willow." See 'Down by the Salley Gardens', *Wikipedia*.

[7] Chou 197.

night with a better alternative for a phrase running through your head, you turn the light on and scribble it down for fear of forgetting it, you recheck it next morning, you revise, you polish – and sometimes, if you're lucky, one or two poems do come out right.

Of course, I felt it at all times necessary to transmute Tin's *form*, in both the narrow and broad senses.[8] At the micro-level, his patterns of rhyme, rhythm, melopœia and so on, and at the macro-level, his overall musicality and sense of number, measure and measurement, are integral to his poems and inseparable from their overall meaning – though number and measure come in at all other levels too. At any rate, without rendering all these elements, Tin's genius gets lost. 'Meaning' is in no way reducible to 'literal meaning'.

Between 1987 and 1980, when I lived in former Yugoslavia, translating these poems was part of my introduction to the language then known as Serbo-Croat or Serbo-Croatian. In Monica Partridge's grammar, which I was working through at the time, I even found one of Tin's most famous poems, 'Svakidašnja jadikovka' ('Daily Lament'), quoted as a reading exercise for the Ijekavian (*ijekavski*) variant of Štokavian (*štokavski*), a form of Croatian.[9] Since the conflicts of the 1990s and the splintering and collapse of the Yugoslav Federation, the appellations 'Serbo-Croat' or 'Serbo-Croatian' are no longer 'politically correct'. There has been too much bitterness, on all sides, to allow any of the communal good will that was once inherent in these composite terms to survive. War and politics aside, however, the linguistic point that needs reiterating for English-speaking readers is that Tin's work is entirely approachable and understandable by readers throughout Croatia, Bosnia, Herzegovina, Montenegro and Serbia, just as it always has been.

Between 1987 and 1991, I took part in poetry festivals and gave readings all over Yugoslavia. In Croatia, Serbia and Montenegro, as well as in Macedonia and Slovenia (which have entirely distinct Slavonic languages), whenever I gave a reading of Daša Marić's and my English translations of Tin's poems at these literary events – always of course alongside deliveries of the original versions, whether by friends, students, fellow poets or actors – I had plenty of first-hand opportunities to experience the full extent of his popularity. On these occasions, it was the immediacy and depth of the connection that audiences made with Tin's poems which unleashed the

[8] For insightful explorations of 'form', see Leighton 2007 and Hass 1984. My notes are *in*-formed by these works.

[9] Partridge 66.

fullest pleasure, together with listeners' delight that some of his poems had been translated into English.

ꟼ

Despite – yet also because of – his popularity in the South Slavic zone of language and culture, I do think there's a genuine 'difficulty' in understanding Tin's uniqueness as a poet, as distinct from simply 'responding' to his poems with readiness and sincerity. For the more questions that are asked of the poems, the more does what at first seemed transparent and lucid on their surfaces seem either to mist over or to refract a bewildering array of facets. And while there are plenty of available pointers into the 'interiors' of the poems, these aren't exactly arrow-like, but tend to be so intricately plaited, or criss-crossed, that picking out one from another isn't that easy. Then again, once one has passed through the poems' surfaces into their depths, one is inevitably confronted by a specific and intrinsic literary 'problem': how to read – and configure – Tin's melancholia, which is sometimes discomfiting and can at times arouse a sense of embarrassment.[10] In any reading of his lyrics, this issue can scarcely fail to resonate, as a sort of background hum or *basso* drone. Inevitably, this difficulty will surface in what follows and require at least occasional attention. And if 'embarrassment' is the deep 'ground', the tenderer question of 'sincerity', which sometimes reaches a higher, shriller pitch, will also need occasional focus. Both these issues need to be contextualised, too, within the larger question of how a reading of 'beauty' is to be approached – or not approached – in post-Romantic poetry, including in works being written and published today.

ꟼ

Born in 1891 in Vrgorac, a small town in the Dalmatian hinterland, Tin grew up in Imotski and Makarska, and attended the classical gymnasium in Split. His language and sensibility are indelibly marked by the rugged beauty of the Dalmatian littoral, that narrow, sunbaked, rocky coastline, backed by mountains, facing out on the Adriatic Sea and the islands of Hvar, Brač and Korčula. So, for example, in 'Slaboća' ('Frailty'), he writes longingly of "našem plavom, plavom valu, / […] našem bijelom, bijelom žalu" (translated as "the waves of our blue blue sea, / […] and white

[10] My use of this term follows that of Christopher Ricks (1974) vis-à-vis Keats and English Romanticism.

pebbles"). Although Tin's major achievement is as a lyricist, his *oeuvre* is much broader than lyric alone. He was a writer of profound and discerning intellect, broad and capacious interests, inquisitive appetite and eclectic range. His *Collected Works* number sixteen volumes, including poems in many forms, from free verse to the Whitmanesque *verset*, prose-poems, essays, criticism, aphorisms, a book of thoughts and jottings compiled into a kind of personal 'encyclopaedia', and translations of fiction, plays and poems by authors as various as Poe, Whitman, Verhaeren, Rimbaud, Gide, Conrad, Meredith and Benvenuto Cellini, among others.

Tin spent many years living in Zagreb, as well as periods in Split, Sarajevo, Mostar, and Belgrade. In his youth, his involvement in the Pan-Slav movement to establish a Yugoslav state earned him the disapprobation of the Austro-Hungarian authorities and the close attention of their police. From 1913 to 1919, he lived in exile in Paris (Montparnasse), where he mingled in the same milieu as other radical writers, artists and intellectuals from Croatia, Bosnia and Serbia, as well as such men as Cocteau, Picasso, Modigliani, Ehrenburg, and D'Annunzio. Throughout his life, he lived simply. Well-known as an anarchic bohemian, he was a frequenter of bars and cafés, and always poor. Typical photos show him wearing a battered and ramshackle trilby, cocked at a lopsided angle. Affectionate anecdotes about him abound, whether true or apocryphal, like the one I heard about him from poet-friends in Kragujevac, Šumadija, the Serbian heartland. It goes like this: Tin is sitting in a bar with friends, blindfold, tasting wines from all over Yugoslavia and identifying them. He sips half a dozen samples in turn, swirls each one around his mouth, and names all of them in quick succession without a single mistake. Then someone thrusts a glass of water into his hands. He takes a slurp. "No, I don't recognise that one," he says. Other stories aren't so salubrious. There's one about him taking off his hat, picking two fleas out of his hair, and inviting his friends to place bets on a race between them across a café table. It's also rumoured that he spent five years in the French Foreign Legion, though if this is true I haven't yet found out when or where he served.

∽

Tin's most celebrated lyrics are those in the collection *Kolajna* (*The Necklace*) (1926), the *tour-de-force* 'Svakidašnja jadikovka' ('Daily Lament') as well as several other poems that first appeared with it in *Lelek sebra* (*Cry of a Slave*) (1920). These are the pieces I'll concentrate on in the following notes, because they're the poems I've translated and know best. These poems are anthology classics, and in them Tin achieves an exquisite finesse of craft. In Croatian, at least a dozen of them are no less than perfect. They stand as models of lyrical purity,[11] and I believe will do so unequivocally for all time, whatever the vagaries of literary fashion.

First, then, the surfaces. Curiously, even though these poems were published after World War I, their prevailing motifs – loss, longing, loneliness, nostalgia and regret – seem at face value almost entirely conventional and derivative, as do their traditionally formal patternings, especially to any reader familiar with the poetry of the French Symbolists and the English Victorians, or the paintings of the English Pre-Raphaelites and exponents of 'Art for Art's Sake'. Indeed, for some English-speaking readers, these poems by Tin may have an altogether *too* familiar *fin-de-siècle* flavour. In this context, incidentally, it may seem surprising to discover that Tin read Ezra Pound. So far as I know, there's no indication that he read T. S. Eliot. It'd be interesting to find out whether he did.

It is probably accurate to say that Tin's writing straddles the *fin-de-siècle* and early modernism. In tones of flamboyant enthusiasm, the *Wikipedia* entry for him confirms this view: "Ujević spent his turbulent *Lehrjahre* in the Zagreb bohemian milieu, in the circle of the central figure of Croatian early modernism, the revered and slandered doyen of aestheticism, Antun Gustav Matoš."[12] In an age such as ours, when some aspects of Tin's kind of writing may tend to be undervalued, unvalued, regarded as 'effete' or 'decadent', or simply dismissed as 'dated', inevitably some readers will find Tin's lyrics not to their taste, even irritating, especially those who like their poetry rough-edged or 'experimental'. Only when his formal and thematic constraints have been accepted by the reader can it be recognised that, as a lyricist, Tin is unparagoned. The intense, clear personal voice that he brings to the convention, and what he does with and within it – the depths and resonances that he sounds in it – are the most rewarding.

ᔕ

Tin's poems of the 1920s are immediately approachable in their surface lucidity and simplicity. Every poem is interpretable as a formally composed container or vessel from which an interior feeling emerges. And if it's a truism that exploration and expression of subjectivity are part and parcel

---

[11] I intend 'purity' in the way that Donald Davie (1952) uses the term.

[12] Croatian writer of fiction, poetry and criticism, 1873–1914.

of all lyrical poetry, what particularly characterises Tin is that the feeling itself appears to be allowed 'out' and 'up' in the very instant of being felt; or, rather, it's released, simply and clearly, in the precise act of being apprehended. That is to say, it's 'expressed', or perhaps a better word would be 'ascribed', directly, with neither resistance nor hesitation, and certainly with no need of filtration through the kinds of self-irony, emotional reticence or linguistic gamesmanship that mark a good deal of modernist and postmodernist writing. There's artifice, to be sure, and of a high order: Tin is far too sophisticated a poet ever to be interpretable as a naïf. Once (or, rather, if) this point has been accepted, it then becomes evident that his artifice operates so unobtrusively that it *implies* an effortless spontaneity and sincerity. At this level of reading, then, if there's an impression of transparency in Tin's lyrics, this becomes convincing and genuine thanks to his artifice, although as I hope to show, that isn't necessarily all there is to it. Impressions can be beguiling and misleading.

ౢ

From an English reader's perspective, my first suggestion is that in its direct expression of feeling, its melancholia, and its musicality, Tin's lyric poetry is reminiscent of Tennyson's *In Memoriam* (1850). Consider, for example, the frankness and modesty of the following imagem[13] of the water glass, with flowers in it, from *The Necklace* (XI):

Za mene ipak nešto fali
u voj uzi bez raspeća,
na dragoj usni osmijeh mali
u casi vode kjita cvijeća.

Here's our translation, though not an entirely literal one:

And yet, there's something still I miss
from this crib without a cross,
a smile upon dear lips, the kiss
of flowers in a waterglass.

And here for comparison are two quatrains from *In Memoriam* (from

[13] The term *imagem*, first coined in the context of my own poetics, is deployed here to indicate 'a bundle or nexus of integrated or correlated images'. For fuller delineation, see: *Imagems 1* (RB 2013), *Imagems 2* (RB 2019); and 171-172 below.

sections L and CXX):

Be near me when the sensuous frame
Is rack'd with pangs that conquer trust
And Time, a maniac scattering dust.
And life, a Fury slinging flame [...]

~

I trust I have not wasted breath
I think we are not wholly brain,
Magnetic mockeries; not in vain,
Like Paul with beasts, I fought with Death [...]

And to oscillate further between the two poets, now compare the quatrains above with the following, also taken from *The Necklace* (XI):

laženo jutro koje padaš
sa snopom svjetla u tu sobu,
već nema smrti da mi zadaš,
no vrati ljubav ovom Jobu.

~

Blessed morning, while you dress
this room in your translucent robe,
I've no fear of death's caress.
Only give love back to this Job.

As these examples suggest, from distant edges of Europe and across more than seventy years, Tennyson and Ujević present surprisingly strong similarities. We can't help noting the Biblical references in their punch-lines, while also knowing that neither poet was a believer. We also note their similarities in melancholic theme and tone, the oscillation between yearning, self-pity, regret, suppressed anger, and bitterness. And technically, we note that both poets deploy the tetrameter. Tin's patterns of versification derive directly from the rich tradition of South Slav oral poetry. In Tennyson's rhythms, as in those of many other English poets at least until the end of the nineteenth century, the sounds and echoes of the English and Scottish ballads are never far away. Tennyson's musicality has often been commented on, most famously by T. S. Eliot. In his ambivalent, contradictory essay on *In Memoriam*, Eliot writes: "He had the finest ear of any English poet since Milton"[14] – even though, as Frank Kermode has pointed out, this is something of a backhanded compliment, because Eliot didn't much like Milton.[15] Was Eliot thinking of *Lycidas*? Might George Herbert's *The Temple* have been equally pertinent as a point of reference, with regard to overall structure as well as metrics and musicality? Whatever the case, Eliot's point is amplified, more interestingly, as he approaches his conclusion:

> In ending we must go back to the beginning and remember that *In Memoriam* would not be a great poem, or Tennyson a great poet, without the technical accomplishment. Tennyson is the great master of metric as well as of melancholia; I do not think any poet in English has ever had a finer ear for vowel sound, as well as a subtler feeling for some moods of anguish.[16]

If we replace "English" by "Croatian" here, and add "consonant sounds" to "vowel sounds" to include the dense clusters that give strength and body to the Croatian language, we actually discover an insightful perspective into Tin too, even if it needs to be acknowledged that *Kolajna* is a small collection of poems gathered loosely around a theme, rather than possessing the vaster, overarching structure of a self-cohering elegy such as *In Memoriam*: "a long poem made by putting together lyrics"[17]. Tin is indeed also a "master of melancholia" and the register and connotations of Eliot's terms – "subtler", "feeling", "moods" and "anguish" – combine to fit Tin as aptly, indeed perfectly, as they do Tennyson. As an expression of a certain "mood of anguish", 'Svakidašnja jadikovka' ('Daily Lament') is in a league entirely of its own.

At any rate, as I put these thoughts down, only now do I realise the extent to which the Tennysonian cadence must have underpinned the English versions that Daša Marić and I made more than twenty years ago. Even though it must be recognised that Ujević's expression is 'airier', 'lighter', and more modernistic than Tennyson's, at some subliminal level of awareness, I now see that I must have registered the many similarities between the two poets, not just in pace and rhythm, but in tone, mood, attitude and content. What's more, the issue of *how* to read (understand,

---

[14] Eliot:1961 [1936]: 328.

[15] Kermode (online).

[16] Eliot, *op. cit.* 337.

[17] *ibid.* 333.

configure) Tin's melancholia could scarcely be more aptly approached than by a comparison between these two. But I don't know if Tin ever read Tennyson. From his personal 'encyclopaedia', there's no evidence that he did.

ശ

While Tin's imagems appear to occur 'spontaneously', they can't avoid calling attention to themselves, not by any kind of forced foregrounding but, as it were, just by 'being there'. These imagems are usually as direct and striking as is the interior feeling that they're associated with or embody. This is to say that, at their most effective, thanks to the quality of their artifice, they possess an ease and poise that are almost Zen-like; for so adroitly embedded is the craftsmanship in Tin's poems that craft itself appears to have become second nature to him, so that what comes across isn't 'craft' perceived as high gloss or superficial sheen but the *impression* of transparency, and hence the appearance of naturalness and simplicity. We've already mentioned "u časi vode kjita cvijeća" (translated as "flowers in a water glass") as an imagem typical of Tin, accurate in its aptness and freshness. A similar plant-container appears in 'Star on High', where the observed scene fits the associated feeling so aptly that each might be said to 'define' the other:

> ja sanjam još o cvijetu i sonetu,
> i o pitaru povrh trošne grede,
>
> ~
>
> flowers and sonnets occupy my dreams,
> with plant-pots perched on seasoned wooden beams –

The visual picture is specific, precise, fresh and immediately visualised, in both languages. Furthermore, even if one doesn't know Croatian, one can scarcely fail to register the pithy sonic effect of the combined plosives and four rolled 'r's, in the line "i o pitaru povrh trošne grede", especially from the vocalic */r/* in "povrh". And here, incidentally, our translation has managed to carry over the alliteration on the */p/* ("pitaru povrh"; "plant-pots perched").

This kind of combined aural and eidetic effect illustrates a further crucial point about Tin's language: that the imagem coheres as a *nexus of possibilities*, all of which it unleashes simultaneously. It functions neither merely visually nor merely acoustically, but actively engages all speech organs: lips, tongue, hard and soft palate, and larynx. Can one almost *smell* the flowers too? The effect of a line like this, then, is composed of all these sense impressions at once. And this observation leads in turn to the crux of the matter: richly textured and tissued in contrived artifice, Tin's imagems, while appearing 'simple' and 'transparent', operate *synaesthetically*.

ꕥ

As implied above, Tin's composite verbal patternings are inadequately described as literary 'devices' or 'techniques'. In this respect, they don't subsist just as *images*, which is to say, they don't function 'at a mere subsistence level'. Rather they're verbal embodiments of ways of *actually experiencing and perceiving the world.* To clarify this point further, it's appropriate to delineate my term *imagem* in more detail.

When one is approaching a line like "i o pitaru povrh trošne grede", especially from the world-view of a speaker of English, the difficulty is that, if one is to do it the justice it deserves, the word *image* has become unsatisfactory as a descriptive or analytic tool. I suggest at least two reasons for this inadequacy. First, the word *image* privileges the visual faculty, and in so doing makes (and gives) inadequate 'sense' of the corresponding and equal primacy of all the other human senses: not only the aural and oral, but also the tactile and the olfactory, not to mention the as-yet-under-developed perceptual faculties that conventional registration of 'the five senses' in Western discourse effectively serves to muffle, mask and minimise. Second, through generations of use by teachers and students in literature faculties, the word *image* has grown listless, vapid, effete. If it hasn't entirely lost its meaningfulness, whatever meaning does remain to it has become impoverished.

Therefore, drawing more fully from the working definition outlined in the term's first appearance above ("a bundle or nexus of integrated or correlated images"), I now deploy the word *imagem* to differentiate the kind of immediately apprehensible, composite and *synaesthetic* nexus that occurs frequently in Tin's poems, from the predominantly visual (eidetic) word *image*. Hence, by the word *imagem*, I intend a more comprehensive meaning, as follows: 'a fundamental cohering theme or motif present in and moving through a mental image' and therefore, in poetry, 'a cohering unit of interior consciousness expressed in a word or group of words, relating to the verbalisation of any sense impression or cluster (bundle, knot, group, combination, etc.) of sense impressions'. Founded (grounded, funded, routed, rooted) in and through synaesthesia, the imagem includes the eidetic but neither depends on it nor is limited to it. It necessarily embeds (compacts, engenders and releases) energy: a mood, a tone, a feeling.[18]

ᔓ

As suggested in the previous example, some of Tin's imagems are far from being imbued with anything like a merely vapid or effete elegance. Even in exploring 'decadence' itself, they're capable of unleashing a packed, almost explosive power. Consider these lines from *The Necklace* (XX):

> U ovom mraku mirisavu
> slušajmo kako ječe živci;
> i sjećaju na ljutu travu,
> a našem grču jesu krivci.
>
> ~
>
> Listen how in this perfumed dark
> our nerves' thin wires are twanged to flame
> as if struck by a nettle's spark.
> For wounding us, they'll take the blame.

This imagem's composite artifice is immediately registered. We unpack co-occurring sensations: of smell ("mirisavu", "perfumed"); sight ("mraku", "dark"); hearing ("slušajmo", "listen") and touch, from the suggestion of stinging ("ljutu travu", "nettle's spark"). By their proximate juxtaposition, all these separate sense-words gather with focal precision into a pinpointing of inner sensation ("živci", "nerves"), almost as though an acupuncturist's needle had unerringly located and activated the *qi* (*chi*, 'vital energy') on a series of points along and among the meridians of the 'listener'.

I'm aware, incidentally, that by bringing out these synaesthetic effects even more strongly than in the original (e.g. "our nerves' *thin wires* are *twanged* to flame"), the English version might well be charged with breaking the modest bonds (bounds, double-binds) usually imposed (or self-imposed) on a translator. My reply would be that in this breaking, the

---

[18] Shortly after arriving at the term *imagem*, together with this first, tentative definition, I discovered that it already exists as a word – in Portuguese – meaning, simply, 'image'. In English, though, I think the coinage *imagem* helpful, because it fills a conceptual gap, comparable to the word *mythologem* (meaning 'unit of myth or mythology', or, as defined by the *OED* (online), 'fundamental theme or motif of myth or other discourse'). See also 167 above, note 13.

English remains loyal to the polysemic, multilayered imagem gathered in the Croatian, and even lifts it.

ɞ

Yet even if what this poem is actually 'about' is clearly 'triggered' by the set of sense-responses indicated above, the range of topics in a poem by Tin, as well as the mind's movement through them, is considerably more complex. Approaching this imagem tangentially, I'd add this: my personal response to the lines quoted above (which of course involves their transference or transformation into the English version into which Daša Marić and I have turned them) consists of the accurately recalled revitalisation of a bundle of experiences that are specifically *Mediterranean*. Though this poem's moment is by no means one of 'anguish', at least in this opening stanza, but rather one of plenitude, once again a 'subtle feeling' or 'mood' adheres to the entire imagem, as if it were a kind of sheen or haze around it, belonging to it, and in no way separable or extractable from it. For me, the poem re-evokes the rich, sweet, sad, ephemeral fullness (*tristesse, tristezza, brama, čeznja, spokoj*, etc.) of Mediterranean late afternoons and early evenings: that quiet time of the changing of the light, of *τα δειλινά* [*ta dheilina*], the approach of *sumrak, dusk*, when perfumes of flowers (jasmine?) and herbs (basil? oregano? thyme?) assault the senses, and the hum of cicadas swells against the background thrum of the sea's waves. These, then, are some of the constituents of the imagem which resonates at and through all layerings of my own response. And as all these words leap out at me, they do so at once and together – Italian, Greek, Serbian, Croatian, French, English – brimming, spilling over, a cornucopia. This, then, models the kind of *abbondanza* (*richesse*) that I think Tin's finest poems gather and hold. And what's more, the containing of so *much* 'material' in poems that are so small and delicately carved seems all the more extraordinary. It's a miniaturised version of a Keatsian quality, and it has much to do with music.[19]

ɞ

[19] The only contemporary Anglophone poet I know whose imagems touch and sometimes sustain this quality and range of synaesthetic *tessitura* is Robert Hass. See for example, *The Apple Trees at Olema* (2010).

A further associative note: the composite quality of the imagem in this particular poem, the woof and warp of its particular *tessitura*, is perhaps most closely approached by the strikingly precise and evocative – and wonderfully long – German compound-word *Sonnenuntergangstraurigkeit*: literally, 'sun-undergoing-sadness', i.e. 'sunset melancholy'. If you combine the sense of that with the Greek expression *ο ίλιος βασιλέβει* [*o ílios vasilévei*]: i.e. 'the sun is *kinging*', roughly explicable as 'the sun is in his kingship', i.e. 'the sun is setting', and if you then throw in the English word *longing* – I think you begin to get somewhere close to the overall feeling engendered in Tin's lines.

ᔕ

Furthermore, while this recall is at once ineluctably and vigorously sensual (physical, embodied, palpable, tactile, tangible, etc. – *and* sexual), it's necessarily indefinable as an experience. It can't be pinned down, because doing that would kill it, and it simply won't be killed. It refutes and refuses death, and, that refutation and that refusal of death constitute its ineradicable and irreducible affirmative core. For the imagem itself insists on leaping and diving about, connecting and reconnecting with and into far too many perceptual and experiential zones ever for it to be able to stay still for long enough to be (drearily) 'defined'. So the multidirectional way in which the experience moves, and tumbles back on and into itself, and the only way it can even (ever) be annotated verbally, *has* to be by synaesthetic hints, suggestions, stimuli, associations.

The principle of synaesthesia, of course, is one of the main keys that unlocks the myriad associative patternings that motivate and move both dream (*san, songe, sogno*) and memory (*sjećanje, memoria, μνήμη* [*mními*]). It's no accident that by harnessing synaesthetic principles the philosophers and proto-scientists of the Italian Renaissance developed their art of memory (see Yates 1964 and 1966). A poet such as Tin Ujević is perhaps to be regarded as one of their heirs.

ᔕ

This irrepressible, *vital* quality in Tin's finest poems (among which I personally count *Kolajna* XX) is what I take to be one of his core qualities, because it opens up what I would describe as a huge 'vault' of perceptual potential in the reader. Here, I should like to explore this idea a little further, by means of a brief side-glance at William Blake. In *The Marriage of Heaven and Hell* (1793), he introduces the startling phrase "the abyss of the five senses". He continues:

> How do you know but ev'ry Bird that cuts the airy way
> Is an immense world of delight, clos'd by your senses five?[20]

To Blake, closure *within* "the five senses" involves 'abysmal' limitation (and self-limitation), which prohibits the possibility of experiencing "delight". Imprisonment in the depths of (presumably Plato's) cave is contrasted with the aerial freedom of any flying bird. Furthermore, the precise wording here ("an immense world of delight, clos'd by your senses five") could be taken to imply that synaesthetic connectivity opens up far more than the sum of its component "five senses". As we know from evolutionary biology, when a richer and more intricate connectivity occurs among the parts of an organism, *qualitative* changes follow.

The *image*, I suggest, is a ratiocination that belongs to the Blakean abyss. Founded in a naïve mimetic theory, it limits and suffocates. But the more intricate *imagem*, as deployed by Tin, not only opens and reveals abundance and vitality, but the "implicate order" and harmony within abundance.[21] Hence, Tin's finest poems entirely fulfil the demands inherent in my contention – that a poet's role is to open up *all* the senses, not represent limited perspectives on 'reality' according to narrowly preformulated models of *mimesis*.

ꙮ

Yet, even after all this, there's still more to this particular poem, because it turns out that its theme isn't just to do with the rush of feelings and associations conjured up at and by a certain place at and by a certain time, and reopened. For one's passage through the text's inner *paysage* also opens outwards into a historical attentiveness: as already suggested, to that point at which a civilisation, past its zenith, tumbles into decadence. The time is late afternoon, early evening; and the evening is (and is *at* and defines) the end of an era:

> U ovom muku punom boga
> zalazi rujna epopeja;

---

[20] Blake 183.

[21] The term "implicate order" derives from David Bohm (1980).

nutrašnja kavga i nesloga
otkriva zelen niz aleja.

Umire naša lijepa tuga,
tuga od svile i barš una;
varava kao rosna duga,
zlatna i plava kao Luna.

~

In this deep hush, with glory filled,
our epic dawn sets, lost from view,
yet vision from this strife is spilled
through the green ranks of the avenue.

The beauty of our grieving frays,
its splendid silk and velvet folds
like dewy rainbows, fade in haze
fringed like the moon in blues and golds.

There's no 'I' in these lines: only an "our" / ("naša"), attached to the feminine noun phrase "lijepa tuga" ('beautiful grief', 'lovely sorrow'), a stylised and sophisticated oxymoron, translated here as "the beauty of our grieving". (Aren't *all* oxymorons stylised and sophisticated?) Scarcely noticing this assumption of complicity, perhaps not even registering it other than subliminally, the reader gets drawn into a sadness in which, collectively, 'we' somehow find 'ourselves' resigned, and yet proud and calm for all that. This is an 'attained', 'dignified', even ironic response – all of which adjectives need highlighting between quotation marks, except (ironically?) the last one: because it's the key to the rest. And if I say 'ironic' – a term that may seem unexpected and even misplaced in its attribution to Tin – I mean to imply an irony so subtle and sublime that it, too, is scarcely registered. Such a sophisticated and elegant feeling-response necessarily presumes a good deal of prior training and practice. It assumes civility, civilisation: the *polis* and its shared history. Cunningly, unobtrusively, delicately, this imagem reconstitutes the components of the *fin-de-siècle* into a specific moment, and leaves it there, poised.

ꟹ

As for the formalities of technique in Tin's lyrics, the *mot juste* is always aptly placed; the rhythm is an accurate and correct embodiment of the content; and even though rhyming is easy to achieve, perhaps even too easy, in a language as highly inflected as Croatian, Tin's rhyme-choices are nearly always interesting, often brilliant, rarely merely facile, and never banal. Consider for example the untranslatable pleasure in the chime between *epopeja* and *aleja* in lines 2 and 4 of the poem just quoted.

In the felicitous cohering of all such elements in Tin's most effective poems, form achieves a kind of pearly or jewelled perfection. It appears effortlessly; so much so that, for all his individuality, and for all its pressure, the voice of the individual 'I' in these poems seems to rise *out of* the language itself, and therefore to be interpretable as celebration *of* the language itself: of what's inherent and inherited in it.

I hope the examples already given, at least in Croatian, adequately illustrate this quality. But for an Anglophone reader this last suggestion may need more clarification. What I mean is that the specific character and qualities of the Croatian language are opened up, all at once, in Tin's lines: its compression, its accuracy, its range; its ability to express, precisely and immediately, visual and sonic detail, and sonority, depth and range of feeling. If a language, any language, can be said to possess anything like a genius of its own, then Tin embodies a particular expression of the genius of Croatian that stands and will stand, monumentally. This is one of the keys to his masterly art: the synaesthetic impression of naturalness.

~

Both the pearly, opaque qualities and the associated sparkling and 'jewelled' qualities in these poems are aspects that Tin himself was aware of, as is evident in the title he chose for his 1926 collection. This multifaceted and recurrent imagem calls for detailed focus and exploration. It's obvious that the title *Kolajna* (*The Necklace*) designates the book itself, with the concomitant indication that the individual poems in it are the necklace's pearls and precious gems and metals. Each poem is indeed a small, worked object, crafted to be beautiful, valued and treasured. No less obviously, throughout the sequence the predominant idea is implicit that the maker and giver of the necklace, which is studded with all these precious things, is the decidedly (indeed irreducibly) *masculine* persona of the poet himself, while the implicitly feminised 'you' who is the recipient and 'addressee' of the necklace is the reader.[22]

[22] Tin's neo-Romantic worldview, as expressed in his images of women and femininity – and as explored here – is entirely patriarchal. Approached through the lens of any modern or contemporary reading, this view dates him.

Tin introduces several variations on this theme. In traditional Croatian village costumes, women used to adorn their clothes with ornately embroidered pinafores or waistcoats and with necklaces made of coins and jewellery: their dowries. The dowry itself was worn on the breast and around the neck. Consider the two final verses of *The Necklace* (V):

> Nisam li pjesnik, ja sam barem patnik
> i katkad su mi drage mnoje rane
> Jer svaki jecaj postati će ztanik,
> a moje suze dati će djerdane.
>
> – No one samo imati će cijenu,
> ako ih jednom, u perli i zlatu
> kolajnu vidim slavno obješenu
> ljubljeno dijete, baš o tvome vratu
>
> ~
>
> Though I'm no poet, I do know pain –
> so I must love my human hurt.
> So, from my tears, I'll braid a chain
> to ornament a dowry shirt.
>
> – With pearl and coins of minted gold
> worth more than any poet wrote –
> if only, my beloved child,
> you'll wear my necklace at your throat.

The key word here is the culturally specific, untranslatable, perfectly placed "djerdane" in the fourth line; and we can scarcely fail to underestimate the quality and authenticity it brings to the rest of the poem, even through the over-determined and inadequate English explication, "dowry shirt" (inadequate *because* over-determined).

Djerdan (in the nominative) is a specific and localised term that derives from the Turkish word *gerdan*, meaning 'neck, throat, front of the neck, with the compound *gerdanlik*, 'necklace'.[23] Tomislav Kuzmanović clarifies this etymology, as well as the term's meaning, register and usage:

> 'Djerdan' is a dowry necklace, usually of gold coins. This isn't a word used in everyday speech, so I wouldn't say it's exactly 'standard' Croatian. Nor could I say, though, that it belongs to only one dialect (that of Slavonia).

[23] Hony 119.

I'd be more inclined to view it as an expression of tradition, meaning 'a specific kind of necklace'. Here again, the word is not one that would be used in any context other than in specific relationship to a folk costume: more precisely, the most precious (and prized) part of the costume worn at weddings – which is probably meant to imply 'the happiest moment in one's life'. So, in this respect, the word carries connotations of something extraordinary, precious, extremely valuable, etc.[24]

Clearly, translation of the word *djerdane* can't avoid being inadequate (can't fail to fail), simply because the dowry custom is by and large obsolete in English-speaking countries. Yet by this word's delicate, detailed, aptly-placed and perfectly pitched specificity in Croatian, the entire composite imagem of the folk-wedding that develops in the final stanza is grounded, potentialised, *in*formed: "u perli i zlatu", "kolajnu", "tvome vratu"; "pearls and gold", necklace", "your throat". Kuzmanović's comment makes the entire marriage custom come alive, illuminating how this dense, complex detail (a word-gem in itself) is the key that unlocks the fuller perspectives of the poem in its cultural context, which would otherwise have been all too easily lost in translation. For the necklace is neither merely ornamental nor merely a displayed or displaced 'symbol' of the dowry. Rather, the necklace, whose function and meaning imply and carry the irreducible imagems of 'display' and 'bodily adornment', is *and* constitutes the dowry *itself.*

Furthermore, since it's traditionally the bride's family that provides a dowry, and since the speaker's addressee ("you") is "ljubljeno dijete" (a "beloved child"), the reader is perhaps entitled to assume that the persona in the poem is a father addressing his daughter. If this reading is indeed implicit, the speaking 'I' will then fit the voice of *any father*, that is, any 'typical' family man who upholds the tradition of country-folk by 'giving his daughter away' in marriage. Such a reading re-integrates and makes full sense of the first line, which otherwise would have been lost. So the jaunty, highly idiomatic statement "Nisam li pjesnik, ja sam barem patnik" (translated as "I'm no poet, but I do know pain") is one that can be made by any 'ordinary' man, who despite stereotypical masculine inarticulacy in the sphere of feelings, here endeavours to express the whole complexity of interconnected feelings and thoughts that suddenly flood through him, as he stands beside his daughter at the altar.

What's more, since the first line quoted here (actually belonging to the second stanza of the poem) is clarified by the last stanza, the poem demands to be read several times. Its moment, then, can be read safely as a poignant

[24] Email, June 18, 2011.

and delicate one, which allows a traditional 'masculine' male to open up and express and ponder over his tenderer feelings, and to do so *without embarrassment* – even if he isn't "a poet". The issue of embarrassment, then, is one that's consciously focused on, and addressed here, with decorum. This reading of the poem attains a psychological accuracy which otherwise it wouldn't possess.

The finest comparison from the English tradition to the situation so subtly and – it must be emphasised – tactfully embedded in this poem is to be found, I believe, in a passage by Tin's contemporary, D. H. Lawrence, in Chapter 5 of *The Rainbow*, entitled 'Wedding at the Marsh'. Here, the narration registers Tom Brangwen's thoughts and feelings as his attention drifts to the stained-glass window of the church in which he's giving away his daughter Anna, as he too stands beside her at the altar. Here is the abbreviated gist of the passage, with some phrases highlighted. The italicised phrases are recognisably applicable to Tin, both to this poem and to others:

> Brangwen was staring away at the *burning blue* window at the back of the altar, and wondering vaguely, *with pain, if he ever should get old,* if he ever should feel arrived and established. With *a pang of anguish* he realised what *uncertainties* they both were. [...] *How did one grow old* – how could one become confident? He wished he felt older. [...] *He felt himself tiny, a little, upright figure on a plain circled round with the immense, roaring sky*: he and his wife, two little, upright figures walking across this plain, whilst *the heavens shimmered and roared* about them. When did one come to an end? In which direction was it finished? *There was no end, no finish, only this roaring vast space.* Did one never get old, never die? That was the clue. *He exulted strangely, with torture.* He would go on with his wife, he and she like two children camping in the plains. What was sure but the endless sky? But that was so sure, so boundless.
>
> Still the royal blue colour *burned and blazed* and sported itself *in the web of darkness* before him, unwearyingly *rich and splendid. How rich and splendid his own life was, red and burning and blazing* and sporting itself in the dark meshes of his body: and his wife, how she *glowed and burned dark* within her meshes! Always it was so unfinished and unformed![25]

ᔕ

According to the above interpretation of *Kolajna* (V), the poem is a dramatic monologue, a speech made by a male character in an implied fictional situation. Evidently, such an interpretation is dependent on the

[25] Lawrence 134-135, emphases added.

assumption of a high degree of conscious craft on the part of the poet and a complicit recognition and speed and elegance of response from the reader. For this interpretative facet sits neatly side by side, and without contradiction or conflict, with the macro-imagem of the necklace itself, which applies to the whole collection: every poem in it being 'strung' on the 'necklace' that is itself the book. But when it comes to *Kolajna* (V), the necklace-imagem functions as a micro-imagem too: for *Kolajna* and "djerdan" are one, or rather each is a version of the other. That's to say, this particular poem is at once a precious coin or pearl strung on the chain of the book and an entire dowry-necklace in its own right. In this way, there's a kind of fractal replay (interplay) of the imagem, at both macro and micro levels. The refractions branch multi-directionally and become more and more complex. As I've suggested above, this is the art of filigree.

By the same token, in this poem too, the reader is feminised as the poet's imaginary daughter, the recipient of the "djerdan" (dowry necklace), i.e. the poem itself. And if this is so, and the "I" in the poem is readable as a conflation of two personae simultaneously – first the poet, and second 'any' father addressing his daughter whom he's 'giving away' as bride – then the conceit could also ramify, playfully, into the "you" in the poem being interpretable as the poet's daughter, and the recipient, her bridegroom, who is the receiver of the gift her father 'made' and is now 'giving away'.[26] Structurally, therefore, the concurrent (polysemic, multifaceted) interpretations of the poem that are possible can be represented by means of a table, in which each item within every column may replace and stand for any another.

Polysemic layers in *Kolajna V*: a substitution table

Giver/maker	makes	gift	and gives it to recipient
Jeweller (minter?)	makes	necklace (filigree)	and gives it to woman
Worker	earns ('saves')	coins (money)	and gives them to family
Father / parent	makes ('creates')	daughter	and 'gives' her to bridegroom
Poet / author	makes	book of poems	and gives it to the reader
Poet / author	makes	poem	and gives it to the reader

According to this reading, the 'lie' of the first line, "I'm no poet" – a lie because we know perfectly well that Tin *is* a poet, and an accomplished

[26] In this sentence and subsequently, the term *conceit* means "a fanciful, ingenious or witty notion or expression" (*OED*).

one – inevitably becomes a rhetorical conceit, and, what's more, one through which we're bound, inescapably, into artifice. Here, I can't help being reminded of the seventeenth century English courtier poets Herrick and Lovelace. The poem is readable, then, as an intricate, delicate word-game: at once punning, light, playful, sweet, sad, self-aware, urbane, and self-ironic. Urbane and self-ironic above all. As for the vexed questions of 'sincerity' and 'authenticity', they dissolve into irrelevance. Any notion that the poem is a self-pitying and cloying personal confession disappears.

☙

And yet, such a reading, plausible and appealing though it may be, doesn't really 'solve' the issues of authenticity and sincerity that crop up in readings of many of Tin's poems. While the finest of them are investigations of melancholia, some of the weaker poems do rely so much on a sweet, superficial facility that they fail to achieve emotional complexity. The sentimental chord is undeniably present just beneath the surface of this poem too.

So for this particular poem, a contrary reading, admittedly a rather naïve one, might proceed along the following lines. We know that the opening statement, "Nisam li pjesnik" ("I'm no poet") is a lie, just as the idea of Tin having a child is also (so far as we know) biographically untrue. He lived and died a bachelor. So any impression of 'sincerity' that the second stanza is supposed to give isn't merely contradicted, but vitiated from the start. According to this reading, then, the entire feeling of the poem is inauthentic, weakly sentimental rather than genuinely felt: specious, the epitome of *in*sincerity.

Furthermore, if this kind of interpretation occurs *specifically* in translation, the reader might then reach one of several conclusions: for example, that the original poem is too plangent to 'cross over' into English; that the melancholy in Croatian veers towards a rhetorical self-pity, which somehow doesn't 'fit' or seem 'right' in English, with the result that in English, even if not in Croatian, the blurry line between a pressured containment ('decorum', 'taste') and embarrassment has been breached. An alternative variant of such a reading might be that the English translation itself, rather than the original Croatian, is the vessel that leaks plangency, whether because this particular translation contains too many hair-cracks and is simply not 'firm' enough (not 'good' enough, not 'loyal' enough) to hold the original, or because the 'core' or 'essence' of the 'original' is so culture-specific that it's *inherently* untranslatable. Either way, the entire poem will arouse in the reader something between a mild irritation and the sour taste of having being cheated. According to such a reading, then, the necklace can't be made of gold and pearl: it's an imitation, a fake.

When all is said and done, I think a reading that goes to these lengths of disapproval has to be a misinterpretation, because by failing to register the implications of the word *djerdan*, it doesn't take into account the notion of dramatic monologue explored above, insisting rather on the assumption that the poem's entire function is a naïve kind of self-expression: a naïve assumption in itself. That's to say, such an interpretation involves the reader's *projection* of the vice of naivety onto the poet, a charge which should rightfully be directed back to the reader. So too should similar charges of 'insincerity', 'lapse in taste', etc. Such a reading, it could be argued, posits a failure to respond to the precise quality that makes any poem a poem: its foundation in an art, a craft, or in Italian, a *mestiere*.

Again, and yet again. … it has to be said that it's hard not to trace a tinge of at least some such 'decadence' at some level of response to this poem. This issue recurs in readings of too many of Tin's lyrics to be entirely dismissible: there *is* an ambivalence, and I believe it's one that's necessary and inevitable. … Perhaps the *frisson* discharged by this kind of ambivalence belongs to *all* 'decadent' art, as one of its defining features. … Anyway, I bring in the words "necessary" and "inevitable", because the element of embarrassment or irritation in the reader's response, whether dominant or subliminal, is part of the *risk* that Tin knowingly takes in exploring feelings. He sometimes tumbles into sentimentality, sometimes wobbles and teeters on its edge, and sometimes precariously balances over it without quite falling and, so, steadily or unsteadily, somehow confounds it. Finally, 'exploring feelings' in turn opens up a wider and more significant issue: Tin's constant willingness to remain open to beauty, despite the infinitely repeated paradox of its occurrence in or alongside pain and death.

ᔕ

I take my next cue from the suave and melancholy oxymoron "lijepa tuga" ('beautiful grief' or 'lovely sorrow', which in our translation becomes a line that I'm entirely happy with, "the beauty of our grieving frays") in line 4 of the above poem. And here I turn to the wider question of beauty, and its associations with death and pain in Romantic and post-Romantic poetry. This turn (*βόλτα, volta*) necessarily moves onto a digressive path away from Tin himself, but it's one that will inevitably lead back to his poems, hopefully opening a deeper, richer seam into and through them.[27]

In English, the pinnacle of the tradition that associates and sometimes identifies beauty, pain and death is of course to be found in Keats. Incidentally, there's no evidence, so far as I know, that Tin had read Keats, any more than he had Tennyson or Eliot. Yet Tin's phrase, just pinpointed, can hardly fail to remind an English reader of the masterly 'Ode to Melancholy', of lines like "drown the wakeful anguish of the soul", and the magnificent and unforgettable last stanza:

> She dwells with Beauty – Beauty that must die;
> And Joy, whose hand is ever at his lips
> Bidding adieu; and aching Pleasure nigh,
> Turning to poison while the bee-mouth sips:
> Ay, in the very temple of Delight
> Veil'd Melancholy has her sovran shrine,
> Though seen of none save him whose strenuous tongue
> Can burst Joy's grape against his palate fine;
> His soul shalt taste the sadness of her might,
> And be among her cloudy trophies hung.

Other relevant poems by Keats are the 'Ode on a Grecian Urn', with its line "Beauty is truth, truth beauty" and his eerie 'La Belle Dame Sans Merci'. The tradition then carves a broad avenue through French, sweeping in measured magnificence out of the alexandrines of Racine and Corneille. For a paradigmatic piece, see for example Baudelaire's early poem 'Beauté', in which Beauty herself speaks to humans: "Je suis belle, ô mortels, comme un rêve de pierre" ("I am beautiful, O mortals, as a dream in stone.") The tradition then weaves through pretty well every European language and into a host of other nineteenth century writers, including Walter Pater. And here I draw on Angela Leighton's book, *On Form*, for its sweep of relevant commentary and its insightful and attentive interpretations:

> Like his contemporaries, Pater loves the way that 'form' is itself a conditional word that can touch on abstractions, like 'beauty', as well as on beloved bodies. [...] 'Every moment some form grows perfect in hand

[27] Use here of the Greek word *βόλτα* [*volta*] alludes to the poem of that title in 'Black Light' (RB 2011a): 157-158. See also the 'Volta Project' and its introductory essay (RB 2009b and RB 2009c, both online).

or face', he writes. For Pater, [...] 'form' easily interchanges artistic and physical beauty.[28]

This too is relevant to Tin. A few pages later, exploring Virginia Woolf, Leighton adds:

> Pater's 'gemlike flame' goes on flickering in Woolf's work, appearing here and there in her prose like a sign of her controlling aestheticist yearning. 'Look! What a beauty!' cries Eleanor in *The Years*. 'A flame danced on top of the coal, a nimble and irrelevant flame.' Beauty, the 'irrelevant flame' can still get a 'nimble' footing on the coals in the twentieth century.[29]

This is a brilliant and delicate observation, which will flood its slight, intense beam back on Tin's lyrical poems, illuminating them too. Leighton reminds us that the thread of 'beauty' does run, even though inconstantly and fitfully, through twentieth century English poetry and fiction. To which I think it needs to be added: it runs not only throughout and out of the nineteenth century, somehow or other surviving into and through the twentieth too, but out of it into the twenty-first. In twentieth century literature, however, it isn't a constant flame. Actually, it *is* irrelevant. It's non-functional. And it's also irreverent. It doesn't fit. And for these reasons, it's awkward. It's discomfiting too, because it makes *us* feel awkward. But beauty is tough. Against the odds, it makes a come-back. It survives, even if only in patches and corners. In fits and starts. Fitfully.

Throughout the modernist and post-modernist period, beauty has posed a huge aesthetic problem which refuses to go away. The core of this is already fully present and familiar in the nineteenth century, in Keats and in Baudelaire, where it resides in the detached, aloof *indifference* and, hence, *amorality* of beauty. This view is articulated precisely in Rilke, still writing within the aestheticist convention:

> Denn das Schöne ist nichts
> als der Schrecklichen Anfang, den wir noch grade ertragen
> und wir bewundern es so, weil es gelassen verschmäht,
> uns zu zerstören.

[28] Leighton 81.

[29] *ibid.* 96-97. The last line of this quotation provides the title to this essay, which I gratefully acknowledge.

For Beauty's nothing
But beginning of Terror we're still just able to bear,
And why we adore it so is because it serenely
Disdains to destroy us.[30]

In 'Easter 1916', Yeats writes: "All changed, changed utterly: / A terrible beauty is born." But, as if the First World War weren't enough to bury beauty once and for all in the trenches of Normandy, beauty's absolute nadir arrives for the whole world with the Nazi Holocaust, Stalin's purges and death camps, and the mushroom clouds over Hiroshima and Nagasaki. By the end of the Second World War, the *amorality* of beauty and the horror and pain it arouses is so acutely and directly juxtaposed against adjacent abuse and atrocity, that it becomes, literally, unbearable. Indeed, could it even be said that, perversely, beauty and atrocity at times impinge on each other so closely, so intimately, that they become inextricable? If poetry and beauty are identified, then, to Adorno, both are *so* unbearable, that at one point in his intellectual career he even recommends that there should be no more lyric poetry after Auschwitz.[31] Yet of all the poems in the world, in a poem that's *still* a lyric and still incapable of ending in a full stop, this juxtaposition is pitched most ironically, most bitterly, most excruciatingly, most unforgettably – incomparably and for all time – in Paul Celan's 'Todesfuge' ('Death Fugue'), published in 1952. It ends with its 'lyrical' refrain to end all refrains:

Der Tod ist ein Meister aus Deutschland
dein goldenes Haar Margarete
dein aschenes Haar Sulamith

~

Death is a master from Germany
your golden hair Margarete
your ashen hair Shulamith[32]

We note: there's no shrinking from beauty here. Nor I believe is there any such shrinking in the entirety of Celan's work, all of which addresses this issue, and does so in and through *pain*. Next to this, however, the reaction of modern English poets *against* beauty seems pitifully inadequate and

[30] Rilke 24-25.

[31] Adorno 19.

[32] Celan 52-53.

provincial. Philip Larkin's measly contribution, for example, whose writings for some inexplicable reason remain wholly acceptable to contemporary English taste, is to offer a piece of crude, crass, infantile burbling *contra* Keats: "Ah, beauty, beauty! What is truth? Balls. What is love? Shite. What is God? Bugger. Ah, but what is beauty. Boy, you got sump'n there. I should like to know."[33] It's curious, too, to remember that Larkin's first book, *The North Ship* (1945) was inspired by Yeats, one of the self-confessed "last Romantics". Among poets writing in the English language since Yeats, there have been plenty of waves of fashion and taste – including several predominant contemporary schools on both sides of the Atlantic – which refute, deny or altogether *avoid* beauty, dismissing or ignoring most if not all of the challenges thrown down by the poets quoted above, and doing so, inevitably, to the detriment in quality of the poems they engender and advocate.

Tin's poems, however, are balanced on a high wire of emotional intensity, and although not all of them avoid the occasional wobble – even tumbling into sentimentality – some of them do walk the tightrope with unerring poise and sureness of footing. Tin in the 1920s takes on the whole of the European Romantic tradition.

As I've already noted, we don't know if Tin read Tennyson or Eliot. But we do know that he read Proust and the French Symbolists. And if he might have aspired to the mordant intensity of Baudelaire, the tone he actually attained more frequently turns out closer to the languid melancholy of Verlaine. Tin's most famous anthology-piece is probably this perfect miniature (*The Necklace* XXI):

> Noćas se moje čelo žari,
> noćas se moje vjeđe pote;
> i moje misli san ozari,
> umrijet ću noćas od ljepote.
>
> Duša je strasna u dubini,
> ona je zublja u dnu noći;
> plačimo, plačimo u tišini,
> umrimo, umrimo u samoći.

The apparently unforced musical quality of this highly wrought piece is beguiling, with its moody alliterations and vowel harmonies, its intent and monotonous mimetic repetitions of consonants, words, rhythms

---

[33] Larkin 1992: 26; quoted by Leighton 39.

and syntax, all of which embody and ramify the weight and intensity of its melancholy. For reasons that, once again, I think are less to do with 'language' boundaries in the narrow sense than with variances in cultural attitudes, especially vis-à-vis embarrassment and sincerity (which, as we've seen, in turn embroil issues of decorum and taste), this particular poem may well be impossible to reproduce, or transmute, in modern English. Even so, I hope what follows isn't too distant an approximation:

> Tonight, my forehead gleams
> and sweat drips in each eye;
> my thoughts blaze through dreams,
> tonight, of beauty I shall die.
>
> The soul's core is passion deep
> in night's abyss, a blazing cone.
> Hush, weep in silence. Let us weep
> and let us die. We'll die alone.

However hard I tried to get it right, this was one of those translations that refused ever to come out quite as I wanted, or rather, exactly as I felt I was 'hearing' it, at a kind of 'subverbal' even 'babbling' level, in my head.

Even so, everything about the achieved Croatian original reminds me of Verlaine: its melancholy, of course; but also, its precision of timbre, its finesse of tone, its sonority balanced between tears and fire. It might even be suggested that, within Croatian tradition, this poem epitomises the *fin-de-siècle* 'moment' as perfectly as Verlaine's 'Art poétique' ("De la musique avant toute chose") and "Il pleure dans mon cœur" do in French. More interestingly still, the line "umrijet ću noćas od ljepote", "tonight, of beauty I shall die", succeeds in calling up (or, as Stanley Cavell would put it *calling upon, calling out*) an entire tradition of nineteenth century European poetry, which associates 'beauty' with death. And what's even more striking in this eight-line poem is that more or less every other core-ingredient of that tradition manages, explicitly or implicitly, to be present too. Here, as stated motifs, we find *fire*, *depths*, *passion*, *dreams*, *tears*, and *loneliness*; and, as constant undertows through the poem's movement, *form* and *music*.

Tin's minuscule Croatian poem, a gem in his *Necklace*, gathers up this entire tradition of responsiveness to 'beauty'. Here, as elsewhere, his writing draws directly on the French tradition rather than on any English models. Unfortunately, I'm not well-versed enough in nineteenth and early twentieth-century Croatian and Serbian poetry preceding Tin to be competent to point to specific models in his own language. But actually, for the point I want to emphasise here, the issue of Tin's direct sources doesn't really matter, precisely because the tradition of 'beauty' is pan-European and pervasive, with variations through all its local expressions and examples. Patterns of influence move back and forth and intersect and intertwine. What's more interesting is that Tin's poem, like all the others in *Kolajna*, happens so very late in the story of 'beauty': its year of publication is 1926 – that is, after the *Futurist Manifesto*, after Imagism and Dadaism, after the First World War poets such as Guillaume Apollinaire, Albert Michel, Wilfred Owen, Isaac Rosenberg, Siegfried Sassoon, August Stramm, Georg Trakl, Ernst Toller and Giuseppe Ungaretti, and after the publication of *The Waste Land.* To say the poem is retrospective and nostalgic, then, seems an understatement. The mood is appealing, charming, even seductive.

This anthology piece is immensely popular in South Slavic countries. It's Tin's anthology piece *par excellence.* At this point, however, I want, deliberately, to delineate a contrary response to this poem, one that doesn't 'fall for' its seductiveness, but rather, challenges it. In line with other comments made above, putting forward such a view, I hope, will not only address the ambivalence that Tin's work can call up in his readers, but also eventually spiral back into suggestions of a richer complexity – including a series of fault lines – in his writing, both of which may well be masked by the very fact of his popularity.

ᔓ

According to such a response, this poem, this perfect miniature gem in *The Necklace*, teeters on the brink of sentimentality. For one thing, so intensely beautiful is the "beauty" ("ljepote") the speaker experiences, that he will "die" of it. This statement is over-the-top, self-dramatised to the point of being histrionic; and not just over-the-top, but obviously so, even to the point of parody or, perhaps, self-parody. And could there even be a threatening undertone to the self-pity? From a sober, detached, mature (etc.) point of view, the voice seems akin to that of a breathy teenager's: self-indulgent, self-serious, gasping, impossible to take seriously, even in the very moment of appearing to need to be taken *very* seriously, a message that parents might heed, even if only for safety's sake. Here is the first layer of ambivalence.

What's more, the statement "umrijet ću noćas od ljepote ("tonight of beauty I shall die", line 4) provides the key to the entire poem. It unlocks the final statements in lines 7 and 8: "plačimo, plačimo u tišini, / umrimo, umrimo u samoći." A literal translation of these lines is: 'Let us weep, let us weep in silence, / let us die, let us die alone / in aloneness.' So the first-person singular statement opens into the plural: the extreme condition that applies to the poet's confession about his own present (not only weeping but also *dying* of weeping) heralds the generalised statement that 'we' – actually or potentially or both – are in this condition too, *and* lonely to boot. The conclusion then is that 'we' mortals are all tortured by beautiful moments, that beauty turns us all into miserable, pathetic sufferers, that 'beauty kills us all.' It must be admitted here, too, that the twice repeated injunction "Let us" of our English translation, combined with the predictive "We'll die alone" doesn't quite gather the multiple complexities inherent in the deceptively simple, condensed Croatian.

What's more, apart from the fact that this leap from singular to plural is a non sequitur, it's hard to conclude whether this movement from "I" to "we" is profoundly poignant or pathetically plangent. Here, then, is a second layer of ambivalence in a possible response. Could Tin even have written this tongue-in-cheek? And was this his supreme Hollywood moment?

Probably neither. But consider: the year when Shelley published his most over-the-top line, "I pant, I sink, I tremble, I expire", was 1820. In its context in the long and rambling poem 'Epipsychidion',[34] that line oozes an excruciatingly embarrassing sincerity. Keats's 'Ode on a Grecian Urn' was written in 1819 and published in 1820. One hundred and six years later, Tin's poem is an echo chamber in which all the bells of Romanticism continue to jangle, discomfitingly, awkwardly, and perhaps irrelevantly.

ꙮ

Now for the opposite view, which is the one I actually hold. Within the broad zone of influences and conventions, my first counter-contention is that Tin's poem still, and against all the odds, manages to belong entirely 'to itself'. And I think it does so in quite complicated and subtle ways. Of these, I'll list six.

First, as in *Kolajna* (V), if the 'I' in this poem is considered as a persona, and if therefore the poem is read as a dramatic monologue, and hence as a fiction, the whole functions as a statement of a certain mood that I believe most people over the age of, say, sixteen have experienced and recognise.

Second, according to this line of thinking, from the point of view

[34] Shelley 1919: 418, l. 591.

of psychological insight and empathy, the statement couldn't be more exactly delineated and portrayed.

Third, to expand and justify the first two points, the poem's artifice isn't only perfect but tactfully and discreetly evident as undertone or, rather, as undertow to the waves of feeling that crash across its surface. Hence the first impression of an urbane, polished, plausible veneer is beguiling. The poem's 'deeper' effectiveness resides in its clever impression of physical immediacy. For example, the keyword "noćas" ('tonight') is repeated three times and further heightened by a further indication of night: "u dnu noći" ('the bottom of night', 'the depths of night', translated here as "night's abyss") The effect of these repetitions is to draw the reader back, again and again, into its poised moment. All this suggests that, even in terms that a critic as taxing as F. R. Leavis might have applied as a test of quality, the poem is in his terminology 'realised' (*real-ised*: made real).[35]

Fourth, the poem's entire vocabulary-set resonates a sexual register, which, together with its repetitions and rhythms, combine to suggest a powerful erotic movement. This is traceable from the passionate and soulful isolation of the 'I' in the first stanza, burning and sweating in tears, to the four-times repeated "-imo" verb-ending in the last two lines, indicating 'we': "plačimo, plačimo … / umrimo, umrimo", "we weep, we weep, / we die, we die". If the 'we' here is interpreted as two people together, rather than as a generalised indication of community and communality, the piece becomes readable as a love-poem of extraordinary delicacy and gentleness. While indications of *jouissance*, of *le petit mort*, once drawn attention to, could scarcely be more evident ("umrimo, umrimo"), this layer of meaning, though constantly present, is never overstated. The erotic layering is subtle and tactful. And its very last phrase, "u samoći" ("alone"), also provides the second half of an oxymoron, since grammatically the act or process of 'dying' here is something that involves 'us' both, together ("umrimo, umrimo", "we die, we die"); for, if 'we' "die" 'together', how *can* we be "alone"? Hence, this final "alone" is (means) many things at once. At one level, it's a return to isolation: after the intensity of "beautiful" passion, after its movement and its moment, to post-coital sadness, to the "lijepa tuga" ('beautiful grief' or 'lovely sorrow') already encountered in another poem.

---

[35] To a packed academic audience in the largest of the Mill Lane lecture rooms at Cambridge, in one of his lectures on practical criticism in 1961 or 1962, I remember F. R. Leavis adroitly and mercilessly destroying a line of Matthew Arnold's: "'Planting his steadfast footsteps on the sea'," he quotes. "A poor line. A very poor line. You don't plant *footsteps*. You plant *feet*. Not *realised*, not *realised!*"

At another level, it's a statement about mortality itself. As Derrida has clarified once and for all, it's literally impossible to 'die for another'. Dying by definition is and has to be done, inevitably, by every mortal being, by and for and in oneself, alone. [36] And at yet another level, the finest, purest and most poignant moment of Keatsian music is recalled here, that at which the nightingale abandons him, and he's left with his "sole self":

Forlorn! the very word is like a bell
  To toll me back from thee to my sole self!
Adieu! the fancy cannot cheat so well
  As she is fam'd to do, deceiving elf.
Adieu! adieu! thy plaintive anthem fades
  Past the near meadows, over the still stream,
Up the hill-side; and now 'tis buried deep
  In the next valley-glades:
Was it a vision, or a waking dream?
  Fled is that music: – Do I wake or sleep?

And fifth, quite apart from these kinds of comments, which are, after all, the familiar stuff of traditional literary criticism, a simpler point needs making out of them: this poem's immense popularity throughout former Yugoslavia *itself* suggests that, far from being merely shallow, self-indulgent, sentimental or specious, it touches a chord that's genuinely transpersonal, communal, resonant and deep.

My sixth and final argument, then, which incorporates all the previous ones, is that to interpret this poem as merely conventional can only be a misreading. While being no more or less than what it is, Tin's poem epitomises an entire convention, sums it up, and comments on it. Indeed, I'd make a further claim: that this is a great poem both for what it both is and does, in itself, and also because it stands on a time-threshold, firmly, without faltering or collapsing. In doing so, it looks back across a huge panorama. This minuscule poem, written in Croatian – not French, not English, not German, not Italian – is the entire summation of the nineteenth century tradition. And I don't see how that tradition could be taken any further than this. The last Romantic isn't W. B. Yeats but Tin Ujević.[37]

---

[36] See Derrida 1995.

[37] Another contender for this title might be the Chinese poet Xu Zhimo (1897–1936), who spent a year at King's College, Cambridge, between 1921 and 1922, where he met well-known English writers, artists and intellectuals, such as Rupert Brooke, Roger Fry, and Bertrand Russell. Xu's poem 'Leaving Cambridge

And to a reader reading these lines in any *now* you might care to specify – all readings happen ineluctably in a *now* – Tin's poem issues a challenge for the future. It says: *I looked at beauty. Whatever fears and ambivalences you may have, you have beauty to deal with, too.*

ꝏ

T. S. Eliot's essay on *In Memoriam* contains both unqualified praise and measured though snide qualifications. Taken together, these adumbrate Eliot's own complex and ambivalent response towards Tennyson: his debt, his genuine admiration, his 'emotional' response, as well as his unease as a modernist looking back into the previous century. The remarks already quoted above are quoted often enough. But then Eliot adds this:

> The surface of Tennyson stirred about with his time; and he had nothing to which to hold fast except his unique and unerring feeling for the sounds of words. But in this he had something no one else had. Tennyson's surface, his technical accomplishment, is intimate with his depths: what we most quickly see about Tennyson is that which moves between the surface and the depths, that which is of slight importance. By looking innocently at the surface we are most likely to come to the depths, to the abyss of sorrow.[38]

Whether we agree or not with Eliot's ambivalent, combined denigration and adulation of Tennyson, here again I think we do find insights that are applicable to Tin's lyric poems and profoundly helpful in our attempts to 'understand' them. And just as Tennyson generates an ambivalent response in Eliot, so, I wonder if Tin may also generate an ambivalent response in later readers. If so, it's hard to say, of course, whether such an ambivalence might be 'typical' of readers' responses. My guess is that this isn't so, at least in his own language, especially since Tin's status in Croatia currently approaches that of 'national poet', to the extent that it might be compared with, say, that of Robert Burns in Scotland. It's also a moot point whether such an ambivalence, if consensual, might suggest an inherent flaw in his genius. That suggestion is left open here.

Again', which today is learned at school by every Chinese schoolchild, has a similar formal quality and nostalgic tone to many of Tin's poems. Writing in the 1920s – almost coincidentally and almost eerily, both poets recall and recapture an entire Romantic tradition.

[38] Eliot, *op. cit.* 337.

I conclude these notes with 'Svakidašnja jadikovka' ('Daily Lament'). The waves of emotion released in Tin's poems can often be so raw in delivery that their effect is stunning, sometimes leaping and tumbling, almost as it were *vertically*, through, across and out of the rippling horizontality of his formal rhythms, in a discomfiting, awkward, agonised cry. This is a poem that manifests extraordinary lyrical control while taking every imaginable risk. Its voice assumes the power of an Old Testament Job berating God. It is, in all senses, on the edge. But in terms of modulation, pace and emphasis, the patterning here is flawless. 'Daily Lament' is Tin's lyrical masterpiece. Unrhymed, but with an inescapable, incessant, pounding rhythm, it insists, with slow inevitability, on successive waves of feeling that tumble over one another in rapid succession, oscillating between unease, anxiety, angst, anger, anguish and despair. I think this is a universally powerful poem. I don't believe there's a human being, however sanguine, who hasn't at some time felt something of what it expresses. Finally, what's most astounding about it is the vitality, vigour and dignity that pulse through it: its beat, its breath, is paradoxically most full of life even in the fullness of its diatribe against life.

June 13–20, 2011

Daily Lament

How hard it is not to be strong,
how hard it is to be alone,
and to be old, yet to be young !

and to be weak, and powerless,
alone, with no one anywhere,
dissatisfied, and desperate.

And trudge bleak highways endlessly,
and to be trampled in the mud,
with no star shining in the sky.

Without your star of destiny
to play its twinklings on your crib
with rainbows and false prophecies.

– Oh God, oh God, remember all
the glittering fair promises
with which you have afflicted me.

Oh God, oh God, remember all
the great loves, the great victories,
the wreaths of laurel and the gifts.

And know you have a son who walks
the weary valleys of the world
among sharp thorns, and rocks and stones,

through unkindness and unconcern,
with his feet bloodied under him,
and with his heart an open wound.

His bones are full of weariness,
his soul is ill at ease and sad,
and he's neglected and alone,

and sisterless, and brotherless,
and fatherless, and motherless,
with no one dear, and no close friend,

and he has no-one anywhere
except thorn twigs to pierce his heart
and fire blazing from his palms.

Lonely and utterly alone
under the hemmed in vault of blue,
on dark horizons of high seas.

Who can he tell his troubles to
when no-one's there to hear his call,
not even brother wanderers.

Oh God, you sear your burning word
too hugely through this narrow throat
and throttle it inside my cry.

And utterance is a burning stake,
though I must yell it out, I must,
or, like a kindled log, burn out.

Just let me be a bonfire on
a hill, just one breath in the fire,
if not a scream hurled from the roofs.

Oh God, let it be over with,
this miserable wandering
under a vault as deaf as stone.

Because I crave a powerful word,
because I crave an answering voice,
someone to love, or holy death.

For bitter is the wormwood wreath
and deadly dark the poison cup,
so burn me, blazing summer noon.

For I am sick of being weak,
and sick of being all alone
(seeing I could be hale and strong)

and seeing that I could be loved),
but I am sick, sickest of all
to be so old, yet still be young!

translated with Daša Marić,
Split, 1988–1989

A Medieval Serbian Poem

An unusually fine poem is introduced to English-speaking readers in a recent anthology published by the *Serbian Literary Quarterly*: *Medieval and Renaissance Serbian Poetry* (selected and introduced by Predrag R. Dragić Kijuk, Belgrade 1987). The poem is entitled 'A Prayer to the Most Holy Lady, Our Virgin and Mother of God', and the poet's name is Dimitrije Kantakuzin, who lived from about 1435 to 1500.

Although it must be said that there's virtually nothing in the book that embodies the 'Renaissance spirit' as that term is usually understood, and despite serious flaws in the English translations, there's still a good deal of valuable material here – the highlight of which is Dimitrije Kantakuzin's 'Prayer'. The strength, delicacy and beauty that are materially visible on the walls of Sopoćani, Mileševa and the other great Serbian and Macedonian monasteries, are concentrated here in words. So, quite apart from its own literary merits, a poem like this is invaluable for the insights it gives us into the profoundest inner thoughts and feelings of those master-builders and master-painters: their beliefs, their preoccupations, their torments and their passions. The 'Prayer', translated by Karolina Udovički, is distinguished for its simple directness of language, clear conceptual development and strictly patterned form. As with much devotional and mystical poetry in the European tradition, the poem deploys a precisely formulated numerological symbolism; and a grasp of this opens its depths of meaning. Just as a monastery, in the Raška or Morava style, conforms to a strict building plan, so a single architectonic structure is ramified through every line of the poem.

The key numbers here are three and four: the trinity and the quaternity. Odd-numbered sections all have four verses of four lines, alternating with four verses of three lines in the even-numbered sections: so every idea is developed, through varied but related images, four times in one verse. The result is a controlled, disciplined harmony between incantatory technique and spiritual content. Section 6, which focuses on mortality, is typical of the poem's patterning, with its formulaic repetitions at the beginning of each line:

That is when the eyes are lowered sadly,
That is when the tongue goes mute,
That is when the flames within flare high,
That is when the body's power fails.

Death comes only then, bitter and final,
Death and the soul's departure, joined as one,
Death, the bearer from here to there,
Death in the dark stealthy night.

Darkling I am, and to dark Hell sent,
In darkness serve I Satan best,
Darkly by me, hence, the Angel beloved,
In darkness, choose I the dark, all dark I be.

Of course, in an age when, throughout the English-speaking world, the trend in both church service and Biblical translation is all towards the contemporary demotic, one might well object that the artificial archaisms in the last verse – as in most of the book – serve only to alienate the reader, rather than to elevate the content. And for experienced poetry readers, the choice of the word "Darkling" can only seem a grating cliché: since Keats immortalised that word in his 'Ode to a Nightingale' ("Darkling I listen…"), it's become virtually unusable. Inversions of syntax, and too many 'Thee's' and 'Thou's' smack too strongly of the decadent Romanticism of Swinburne and Rossetti.

Still, the transparency of language in the first two verses just quoted is entirely effective, and the line, "Death, the bearer from here to there" works particularly well – just because of its unpretentious modesty and homeliness. Much of the underlying impact comes through here; and it must be remembered that the poem does speak to us of a period whose world-view was utterly different from our own.

And that note of doom and gloom has been struck time and again in Yugoslav poetry: not surprising, perhaps, considering the history of invasions and occupations over the ages, well into the twentieth century. Consider for a moment the social conditions of Dimitrije Kantakuzan's time; take out the Christianity; forget the archaic diction – and the tragic vision of this passage seems remarkably similar to the voices of many modern Yugoslav poets: Tin Ujević's sonnet, for example (from *The Necklace*, 1926):

Deep in that heart, black wounds he dare not show;
He's wearied, cursed, a being in distress.
That sparkle in the eyes, that starry brow -
You're dead, Tin. All your paths are emptiness.
Death is your love, in every step you take,
Death, in your belly and in every breath,
Death is your drink and daily bread you break,
In expectation and attainment, death.

What use blind love or hope without a goal,
What use desire's wild dash. When there's no cure
Through breathing lungs or heartbeats, for the soul.
And though your loves are beautiful and pure,
Like faded perfume, in as broken bowl,
None of your babbling heartsong can endure.[39]

The *timor mortis* theme, of course, was wholly conventional in the medieval world, and the 'Prayer' catalogues all its ingredients, almost as if it were a *haute cuisine* recipe in a text-book for sinners of all times. The world is a vale of tears; in mortality there's neither hope nor redemption; the supplicant is beset by sins, corruptions, temptations, terrors and devils from without and within. In fact, to say the poet "was much possessed by death" and "saw the skull beneath the skin" would be a delicate understatement. But even in these passages, and despite the distorting glass of translation, the vision comes across with a grim and effective power. In section 7, for example, where the translator's use of alliteration ("flames flaring", "work of worms") inevitably reminds the reader of the similar patterning in the great English medieval religious poem, *The Perle*:

Even before Death appears, in truth am I dead,
Even before the Court speaks, myself I condemn,
Even before the torments begin, teeth gnash at remembrance.
Even before the end comes, I writhe in torment.
Hence fear I the searing flames flaring,
Hence bide I the fierce and angry gnashing,
Hence dread I the prickly work of worms,
Hence sink I into my sheath of darkness.

And so the poem proceeds through eleven dark sections. But, in the twelfth, precisely half way through, the fertile image of bread ("Today

[39] Ujević 213: 31, trans. RB and Daša Marić.

I beg a crumb of salvation") introduces the Holy Virgin, and the tone changes utterly, mounting in hymns of increasing affirmation. As seen by Dimitrije Kantakuzin, the Mother of God will not only intercede for him but, in transforming death into life, will bring him life's central gift and secret: Joy. And the word 'Joy' is repeated constantly in the later sections.

It's also striking how universal, and even at times pagan, are the features of the Blessed Mother, however well veiled she may be by Orthodoxy. As an ancient Mesopotamian creation hymn reminds us, we are all "Sons and Daughters of Earth and of the starry Heavens". And in this poem, the 'Most Holy Lady' is both earthly (chthonic) and heavenly (ouranic). Some of her attributes are outlined in the most concrete of images ("haven", "anchor", "fleece"); and some of her powers are revealed through the kinds of paradoxes which are at the core of all religions. ("By Her, the Infinite was formed.")

She is the ladder seen by Jacob.
She by whom God descended to earth.
She is the Unconsumable Bush in Sinai,
She who received the Divine Fire in her womb.
She, the Fleece which was Gideon's,
She, the soundless receiver of the Father's Word,
She, the sealed scroll which is heard from,
She, by so many names known and extolled.

"Many names" indeed. In Greek, she's called the *Panaghia*, The All-Holy One; and in Jewish Kabbalistic tradition, her equivalent is the *Shekhinah*, the Glory, the feminine aspect of divinity. I wouldn't be at all surprised if there were profound Gnostic elements underlying this poem; and who knows whether Dimitrije Kantakuzin was just a simple monk, or a profound visionary?

But, in the last resort, what's most exciting about this poem is that it runs the whole gamut of traditional liturgical symbolism that one would expect of a poem from this period, yet still comes through, as a minor triumph of passion, purity and intelligence, in celebration of life overcoming death. And it's life that's the bridge between heaven and earth, in any age.

Belgrade and Split, 1998

Katica Kulavkova's *Naked Eye*

In this collection of haiku by the Macedonian poet Katica Kulavkova, presented in a six-language collection,[40] the poems leap from the mundane to the visionary and back again in the splice of an instant. That's what we expect from a haiku. In Kulavkova's poems, we aren't disappointed.

Light creaks, whispers, sings. Voices reach, stretch on tiptoe, touch. A tangle with an unexpected memory makes hairs on forearms stand on end. Desire blows the mind. The sun's graze on the skin is heartbreak. Joy is brushed in a green shadow. The naked eye sees momentarily into and through the stuff of things.

While it's never entirely possible, let alone necessary, to speak of *reasons* when it comes to haiku, I do think there are two aspects (elements, ingredients, modalities, etc.) worth drawing attention to in Katica Kulavkova's poems. For while the manner of their movement is love, their mode of delivery is lightning. The title is *Naked Eye*. The dart of this eye is immediate, sharp and swift, not just for the intensity and longing in the poet's gaze but because of her intelligence and vitality. Kulavkova's eye cuts across and through illusion because it's *quick*. The word *quick* in English incorporates two meanings: it means *fast, swift* – and also *alive, vital*. This is to do with what the Chinese call *qi* and the Japanese *ki*.

Another interesting thing from the semantic point of view is that Katica Kulavkova's poems coin meaning. Or rather, they coin meanings – plural. That's to say: in the wake of every discovery opened by any single one of her eyeblinks (*Augenblicke*), meanings proliferate. They spill out, newly minted, and being unique, each new meaning revisions and revaluates all previous ones. In such an order, there's no tarnishable currency or ready-made code for vision. Meaning is gift: irreducible, priceless, invaluable. In its full and entire *thisness*, each poem is experienced as if it were the first poem ever made. As she looks out at the sea from the

[40] Here only Macedonian and English are quoted, the other translators being Maya Mastnak-Car (Croatian), Harita Wybrands (French), Mariangela Biancofiore (Italian) and Manuel Frias Martins (Portuguese).

Portuguese island of Porto Santo, consider for example Kulavkova's view of waves:

Брановите безбројни а осамени. Бескрајна слика.	Waves countless and unique. An endless story.

Or consider her here, in her own country, Macedonia:

Небото над Македонија	The Sky over Macedonia
Обрач достапни планини и недостапна историја.	Ring of accessible mountains and inaccessible history

Clarity, seam of presence, and complexity, ore of what Hopkins called *inscape*, combine in Kulavkova. She achieves close, accurate and richly detailed observations of real phenomena, immediately juxtaposed against highly sophisticated patterns of intellective abstraction:

Друго око / Différance	Other Eye / Difference
Фотката го фаќа одеднаш, ние го гледаме до крај.	What the photo traps from an eyeblink we'll spend an age looking at.

The blink of the eye and the blink of the camera: moments of vision: miracle and commonplace: timelessness married to a kind of intimacy, almost, even, a domesticity. And as this example shows, the geometries glimpsed by Kulavkova's eye or camera are fractal:

Синегдоха	Synecdoche
Дел во кој се одразува целоста. Филмот е осветлен.	Part. And in it is revealed the whole. The film is exposed.

As the above examples clarify, the Macedonian language is crisp, complex, precise and subtle. It's capable of terse economy, pendant clarity, mordant irony and rippling polysemy. This six-language edition aims both to reveal these original qualities and to transmute them anew. Whether by accident, design or serendipity, the other five languages chosen are: Croatian, which operates as a kind of foil and perfectly echoing mirror, deep inside the same Slavonic family as Macedonian; Italian, with its vast high-walled halls and capacious wells of limpid Romanic reverberations; French, with its economy and succinctness, its perspicacities and sonorities; Portuguese, with its exuberant longings and bittersweet sadnesses, its apertures and closures on huge oceanic vistas; and English, with its hive of busy precisions, coverages, tangles and voids. All of this has meant that translating these poems has been a work of richly textured pleasure.

As for the overall result, the unique quality of each language creates its own *original.* And each original re-casts multiplicities of nuance, tonality, timbre, reference and meaning on all the others. Each meshes delight in precise particularity with universal human scope, hope and aspiration.

Finally, haiku reveal that what we call *knowing* is act and movement, not state. Transmitted, transmuted into any language, any one of Katica Kulavkova's poems reminds us of this, surely, swiftly, simply. At the same time, within this act of knowing, every good poet knows how little s/he knows.

Kulavkova's poems are open secrets. They simultaneously reveal all she does know, in human vision and precision, and all she doesn't, in human longing and passion. Out of the one, many: within the many, one.

June 2010

Gems, Stems, Diadems: Slobodan Pavićević's *Dreams of Hilandar*

In the play of mind around and among sacred spaces and places that are at once familiar and full of mystery, the human spirit opens, dances, flies upwards. This sequence of poems by the Serbian and European poet Slobodan Pavićević invites the reader to enter such zones of quiet, joyful, meditative delight.

Following in the wake of his long poem *Let Peace Be the Name of the Centuries* (2010), an impassioned tour-de-force commemorating the victims of the 1941 massacre at Kragujevac, Pavićević now moves to the opposite extreme in terms of both subject matter and poetic form. Here, he presents a set of thirty-three *haiku*. Even smaller and more finely carved than the poetic jewels of Tin Ujević's *Kolajna*, these tiny, glittering, glistening, meditative poems are strung like monk's rosary beads across the landscape of mortality. Yet, despite enormous differences, both these works by Pavićević share several deeply entwined strands, and these do need to be noted and tracked, for they're no less than central motifs that run throughout his passionate art. First, his *haiku* are steeped in Serbian *loci*, tradition and history, as is the suffering of the victims of Kragujevac, Pavićević's hometown. Second, their reach – or rather, their *outreach* – is universal, as the multilingual aspects of both books clarifies, not to mention the *haiku* form itself. And third, their core theme is love, harmony and peace, achieved through the Herculean task of moral self-examination, through doubt, loss, sacrifice and sorrow, as well as through love and dedicated work. And here, in *Dreams of Hilandar*, Pavićević celebrates his own most personal tradition. Steeping his compressed lines in references to the treasures of Serbian medieval history, art and poetry, he draws his major inspiration from Serbian monasticism.

The word *religion* etymologically means a 'rebinding', a 're-yoking', a 'relinking', a 'rejoining'. These beautiful, simple, moving poems are *religious* precisely in this sense. In their carved and honed simplicity, they rebind and rejoin peace with spacetime, destiny with faith, and harmony with love. They encapsulate and radiate peace won through turbulence and pain. In their intimacy they're universal. They are gems, stems, diadems. They channel and refract light.[41]

October 2012

[41] For the memoir on Slobodan Pavićević see 395-397 below.

Drawing from the Neolithic: Notes on Maja Herman Sekulić's *Gospa od Vinče*

I first came across Maja Herman Sekulić's writing in 1993, when I published a single poem of hers in an anthology that I was guest-editing for an American journal entitled *Out of Yugoslavia*.[42] This was at the time of the collapse of the Yugoslav Federation. I met her work again – and the poet herself for the first time – in October 2017 at the Smederevo Autumn Poetry Festival.

There I heard a recital of the four-part poem *Gospa od Vinče*, delivered by the actor Vjera Mujović, before an audience of Serbian and international poets, in a small, open theatrical space, tucked among the battlements of the huge fortress of Smederevo, perched high over the Danube. The event took place during the Smederevo's annual 'Poetry Autumn' Festival, presided over by Goran Djordjević. October 17 was an exceptionally warm, clear day and the trees along the river blazed in their variegated golds. As we took our seats, a chorus of girls in long dresses formed a row before us, seven in white and one in maroon at each end. They launched into one of those Serbian folk songs whose tonal complexities fire heart and mind and stretch desire into skeins of ever-deepening longing. One slender girl, with a commanding presence and a deep, authoritative voice, led the others through complex harmonies. Firm and clear, their voices meshed and counterpointed multiple chords into spiralling choruses that leapt from note to note on long-drawn-out vowels. The impression was of youth, pride, depth, delicacy and strength. Following the song, the publisher Vesna Pešić stepped forward and made a short speech to introduce the poet. After saying a few words in Serbian, Maja Herman Sekulić read the prologue to her poem in English. Then came the expressive delivery of the poem by Vjera Mujović.

This was a unique experience of poetry and song that combined a high level of intellectual finesse and a sustained pitch of emotional intensity, delivered against a striking panoramic background. In such a setting, *Gospa*

[42] 'Gumbo', *North Dakota Quarterly* 61/1, 1993: 79.

od Vinče came across immediately as a powerful and, I believe, important work.[43] I offer the following notes to explore how and why I admire *Gospa od Vinče*, and to suggest how and why it's close to my own concerns as a fellow-poet.

ಌ

The site of Vinča Belo Brdo itself, which lies 24 kilometres east of Belgrade, was excavated intermittently between 1908 and 1932 by Miloje Vasić. According to the archaeologist and cultural historian Marija Gimbutas: "At Vinča alone, almost 2,000 figurines were discovered, by far the greatest number unearthed at a single site".[44] What Gimbutas rightly calls Vinča civilisation stretched from the lower regions of what we know today as Hungary in the north to modern Kosovo and Macedonia in the south, and from Bosnia in the west to Bulgaria and Romania in the east. This, then, was a pan-Balkan culture that extended as far as the Aegean Sea just above the Khalkidhiki peninsula.[45] According to the same author, other significant sites "are seen to cluster around the modern towns of Belgrade, Vršac-Timişoara, Cluj, Kragujevac, Priština, Kosovska Mitrovica, Skopje and Štip".[46]

Maja Herman Sekulić was born in Belgrade. In exploring Vinča culture, she therefore not only tracks her own personal and cultural roots back into prehistory, but does so within and across a geographical area that corresponds closely and intimately to the location of her own birth. In selecting this particular archaic material, then, the poet is drawing on a psychogeography that already 'belongs' fully to her. There's no question of her needing either to 'lay claim to' such material or to 'occupy' it, and less still 'appropriate' it. The *materia*, in all its profusion and fecundity, is readily available to her, offering itself as a field wide open for poetic exploration and interpretation.

---

[43] In quoting from the English version of the poem, here and there I've needed to alter awkward phrasing.

[44] Marija Gimbutas, *The Goddesses and Gods of Old Europe* (1982): 22. In her 'Prologue' (6), Herman Sekulić doesn't refer to this book, but to two later ones by Gimbutas: *The Language of the Goddess* (1989) and *The Civilization of the Goddess* (1991). Another relevant book by the same author is *The Living Goddess* (1999).

[45] Gimbutas, 1982: 23, map.

[46] Gimbutas, *ibid.* 22.

Confronted by the divisive and retrogressive cultural nationalists who are regrettably to be found all over the world today, including both in Serbia and in my own country, the United Kingdom, I think it needs to be emphasised here that Herman Sekulić has clarified in other writings that her ethnic and geographical heritage is heterogenous.[47] Her family background incorporates both Serbian and central European strands. Nowhere in *Gospa od Vinče* does she lay claim to her material merely on the grounds of being a Serb. The implicit message here, I believe, is that this kind of *materia* belongs to all of us, simply by virtue of our being human. The poet's personal closeness to the material, therefore, is neither merely nor ultimately a matter of ethnicity: it is, rather, authenticated by being part of her biographical, cultural, linguistic and human heritage; and it's intimate to her because she was born and brought up in this *balkanski prostor.*[48]

With respect to Gimbutas, the original title of her major book, first published in 1972, was *The Gods and Goddesses of Old Europe.* For her second edition, ten years later, she revised the ordering – and hence the prioritisation – of the words in her title, to *Goddesses and Gods.* The evident purpose of this change was to maximise her readers' attention to the theory that the Neolithic Vinča culture, and others like it, were matriarchal. This thesis, which Herman Sekulić takes on fully in her preface and her poem, implies that the peaceful cooperativeness of these matriarchal cultures of old Europe was interrupted by successive invasions of patriarchal tribes ('Indo-Europeans') from the east, and then lost for ever. Broadly speaking, and however we may construe it, this theory provides the intellectual impetus and ideological underpinning for her opus.

ᔓ

The Latin word *materia* ('matter') – twice used above – is etymologically cognate with *mother.*[49]

A large number of the anthropomorphic figurines excavated from Vinča are female. Like Gimbutas before her, Herman Sekulić finds major inspiration in these small sculptures in clay and stone, one of which appears on the cover and eight of which are illustrated in the central pages of her book. The poet's identity and aspirations as a poet – and specifically as a contemporary woman-poet – are fully engaged in this material.

---

[47] Herman Sekulić 2015.

[48] 'Balkan space'.

[49] Skeat 358, 359, 379.

As with all books, it's natural to be attracted first by their pictures, and in this case, by the illustrations of these figurines. While these all belong to an overall style that's immediately recognisable, the pieces that the poet has chosen for inclusion vary considerably in detail. And while they're all ancient, they also have a power and resonance that seem quite modern in their appeal. For example, there's a highly schematised, symmetrical, almost abstract form, engraved with deep symmetrical incisions, which is striking in its geometrical purity and erotic suggestiveness.[50] Then there's a slightly forward-bending figure whose slender and delicate head, arms and upper body are explicitly contrasted with the steatopygous lower body. Here the exaggeratedly voluminous hips, buttocks and legs, which are almost reminiscent of some of Niki Saint Phalle's giant female sculptures, celebrate a capacious chthonic fecundity.[51] Then there's a perhaps more clumsily made but no less interesting maternal figure, which could be interpreted in at least two ways. At first sight, she might appear to be holding a child before her, as she sits in her bowl or bath, which itself is supported by four sturdy animal legs. More probably, she might be sitting *on* a four-legged hooved animal, as she gently but firmly holds and guides its head before her.[52] This particular figure might be said to be identified *both* with the containing vessel *in* which she sits *and* with the four-legged creature *on* which she perches.

While aspects of all these figures resonate through Herman Sekulić's poem, the piece illustrated on the book's cover is the one the poet identifies with most actively and acutely. In this refined abstract female figurine, the Neolithic artist has modelled the head and body down as far as the belly, where the base coincides with the broadening hips. The statuette has no more than carved indentations to indicate a rudimentarily smiling mouth and eye socket. There are also various small, neatly incised holes, in the positions of ears, shoulder blades, and elsewhere – perhaps intended originally to attach to a thread or threads, or to hang ornaments on? The colour is black, with dramatically contrasting red diagonal stripes across the head, neck and body. The sculpture's left arm is missing, but most strikingly, the figure has her right arm bent, indicating the position of the undifferentiated hand over her heart, in what the poet calls "a pose of power and prayer" – which, she says, "is the symbol of that Old Europe

---

[50] Herman Sekulić 2017: 43.

[51] *ibid.* 44. I'm grateful to Melanie Rein for introducing me to Niki Saint Phalle's works.

[52] *ibid.* 44, reverse.

and the first human being who recorded her truth. She inscribed it, this autochthonic proto-artist, on pottery and figurines [...]"[53]

The poet's claim, then, is that the pose and gesture of this female figure combine *both* 'active' *and* 'receptive' attributes. While "prayer" indicates supplication to a higher divine authority, "power" necessarily involves self-belief in her own identity and selfhood. Here, let it be emphasised, the poet also ascribes the making of the artefact to a female artist.

ᔓ

From this rich materia (matrix), the four sections and epilogue of the poem take their path, in flowing and at times cantatory free verse. In what follows, I'll try to pick out some of the salient aspects of *Gospa od Vinče* that I've found most interesting, rewarding and puzzling – at times alternately and at times simultaneously. I'll also do my best to hint at possible ways of exploring and interpreting the poem, mainly by offering suggestions and asking questions that focus on the textual details, and by amplifying their motifs and themes.

The female figure celebrated throughout Herman Sekulić's poem is complex and composite, manifold and multi-faceted. At the start of section II, the *Gospa* appears beguilingly as a small, erotic figure, and the poet leaves it unclear whether this is merely a votary artefact or a living woman. Seen idyllically "[a]t the edge of a meadow, in a chaos of stones / [h]idden from view by high blades of grass / [s]he lies naked, shameless, fearless." As this ambiguity indicates, the *Gospa* has many layers, whether explicitly stated or implicitly suggested within the poem's pleats and folds.

In terms of her intellectual and poetic ancestry, the *Gospa* has been generated not only from the poet's readings of the figurines explored by Marija Gimbutas, but also from the imagem of the cold moon goddess who thrilled, frightened and fascinated male English Romantic poets such as Samuel Taylor Coleridge (in 'The Rime of the Ancient Mariner'; quoted in the book's epigraph) and John Keats (in 'La Belle Dame Sans Merci'), as well as the twentieth century English poet and scholar Robert Graves (in *The White Goddess*; referenced in the Prologue).[54]

By a process of accretion, the poet endows her central figure with a large number of the attributes both of traditional femininity and of female divinities. She's chthonic and lunar; lover, mistress and wife; creatrix,

[53] *ibid.* 7, 'Prologue'.

[54] *ibid.* 5 and 6.

harmoniser and destroyer; and the birth-giving, protecting and caring mother embodied in the Orthodox Christian ikon of the three-handed Virgin Mary in the Serbian Monastery of Hilandar on Mount Athos. A strong suggestion of this particular layer in the poem is immediately evident to any reader of a South Slavonic language, since *Gospa* ('Lady') is one of the terms traditionally used to address the Virgin Mary, for example in prayer, in both Orthodox and Catholic traditions, which, equally, sprang up and first developed in the Mediterranean.

Clearly, in English, however, even with the addition of the personalised word "My" attributed to "Lady" in the title, the echoic reverberation of this epithet can't come across with full effectiveness, since for the last five hundred years in northern Europe, Protestantism has been the dominant form of Christianity, in which the feminine element *has been more or less discarded or eliminated.* Indeed, this apparently incidental and minuscule linguistic point might well in itself be regarded as one of the keys to the entire motivation for this poem: that is, *the repression of the feminine in contemporary, globalised, post-industrial society.* To clarify the linguistic and geographical point further, in Italian, *Madonna* means, literally 'My Lady'; while in Serbian, the Virgin Mary is called *Bogorodica*, and in Greek, *Παναγία* (Panaghia). The literal meanings in English of these two latter names are, respectively, 'Birthgiver-to-God' – an enigmatic paradox in itself – and 'All-Holy-One'. And all three of these names, of course, have feminine gender, whereas in English, all nouns are ungendered.

In modern Greece, the annual day dedicated to the *Panaghia*, August 15, identifies her ancient provenance in the pagan harvest festival in honour of Demeter, a goddess whose name itself belongs to the huge set in Indo-European languages that contains cognates for words meaning 'mother'. Thus, in section IV of the poem, which is spoken in the voice of the Goddess herself, the line "I will give birth again when hawthorn trees bloom"[55] embeds the implicit presence of a Demeter type-figure, with a prophetic force perhaps redolent and indicative of the tree in the Book of Revelations: "[O]n either side of the river, was there the tree of life, which bare twelve manner of fruits, and yielded her fruit every month: and the leaves of the tree were for the healing of the nations."[56]

What's more, the *Gospa* is explicitly stated to be linguistically identified with *Maja*, or *Maya*, which Herman Sekulić interprets from Sanskrit as "mother" and "grandmother, the proto-mother of us all". *Maja* is of course

[55] *ibid.* 36.

[56] *AV, Revelations* 22: 2.

the poet's own first name, and she also states that *"I, here, in the poem, assume all these roles."*[57] (There will be more to suggest – and ask – later, about this direct identification of the voices of poet and goddess.) As seen above, the *Gospa* also has an explicit association with the fecundity and protectivity of trees, in particular the willow and white hawthorn, also called the 'May' tree.[58] This kind of learned attention to etymology by the poet produces a dense linguistic polysemy and weaves multilayered and multifaceted symbolism into the poem's fabric: sonic and semantic resonances, curious and suggestive echoes, dim memories' or pre-memories' murmurings: *Maja, Majka, May…*

ᔕ

The poet also offers the challenging statement that, according to her interpretation, the goddess in her primal form precedes human awareness of good or evil. "This is how the inhabitants of Old Europe saw her – the Great Goddess – as the embodiment of the whole life cycle from birth until death and rebirth, *without dividing it into good and bad*, as all later religions have done."[59] In this passage, incidentally, even though Herman Sekulić has set her theme in a mysterious, ancient and mythical past, I can't help wondering whether there might be a corresponding nod or glance, even if in passing, at Nietzsche – and at futurity – with reference to his *Beyond Good and Evil: Prelude to a Philosophy of the Future* (1886). This suggestion will be taken up later.

What does Herman Sekulić mean by "without dividing it (i. e. the life cycle) into good and bad"? Does she mean, simply, that in the Neolithic period the pains and joys of existence, including the condition of mortality itself, were accepted far more fatalistically than today, in accordance with the uncontrollable will of divinities and spirits?

At a slightly more complex level of possible interpretation, the question whether, as readers, we're ready to accept Herman Sekulić's claim that this Great Goddess belonged to an age in which good and bad were undifferentiated is perhaps an issue best left in abeyance. A more qualified and helpful, and less literalist response may well be to accept this statement as provisional, as poetic, and therefore as a cue for the willing suspension of disbelief that's needed in order to understand and respond to the work

[57] Herman Sekulić, *op. cit.* 6: 'Prologue'.

[58] *ibid.* 6.

[59] *ibid.* 5; emphasis added.

itself. Herman Sekulić continues, again adopting the Goddess's own voice: "The womb is life / The womb is the tomb / I am the mistress of both / *Not knowing it.*"[60] The puzzling motif of "*not knowing it*", "*without even being aware*" etc., is repeated throughout the text as a kind of mantra and is always emphasised by being italicised.[61] It occupies the final line of the entire composition ("*without even knowing it*").[62]

Here, we can scarcely fail to wonder what the poet means by "knowing". The registering and recognising of a physical familiarity? An emotional realising? Or a conceptualisation? The word's polysemic resonances here, shrouded or clouded by the narratorial voice's retrospective negation, in the phrase "without even", are curiously dissatisfying. Is this ending a deliberate puzzle?

As we examine this expression more closely, we can scarcely fail to note that the identity of the *subject* who doesn't know – of the one who isn't not aware – varies according to context. The condition of not knowing applies both to "us" (*nous autres*, us others, mere mortals) *and* to the goddess herself. Thus, even though the goddess is gifted with articulate speech, insofar as the condition of "not knowing" is one of her own attributes, the poet takes pains to emphasise that a key aspect or manifestation of her character is that she is *not conscious of herself.*

How else are we to interpret this possible layer of meaning? In evolutionary terms, could it be that the poet believes and claims that Neolithic peoples, living as it were 'just before the dawn of history', weren't morally or ethically 'conscious' at all, or at least, not in ways that modern humans are? And in Jungian terms, might this also indicate that, in Herman's interpretation, the *Gospa od Vinče* inhabits and represents some of the most profound undifferentiated depths within the present-day collective unconscious of both female and male humans?

ꕥ

I would argue that both of the above interpretations may be plausible and valid. Furthermore, with regard precisely to the attribute of "not knowing", might it not also be asked whether this condition could be mirrored back onto the poet herself, so that another pertinent question might be asked – one that has intimate bearings on intrapsychic phenomena, on the artist's

[60] *ibid.* 36; emphasis in original text.

[61] *ibid.* 22, 23, 24 and 36.

[62] *ibid.* 39: 'Epilogue'.

and poet's inner creative process, as well as on the ancient role of the poet as shaman? That is, could the phrase "without knowing it" suggest that *the poet herself / himself may not fully understand the full meaning* of her / his own utterances, when through inspirational, heuristic and possibly synchronistic discovery, s/he is in some way 'inhabited', 'occupied' or 'possessed' by the voice of a 'divinity' or 'spirit', such as that of this goddess?

I think considerable care needs to be taken in exploring and differentiating these inner aspects of poetic composition. In Jungian terms, such personal connectivity to subliminal elements and their energies (i. e. to underlying archetypes) may occur in several ways, some creative, some destructive, and some both. What every true poet knows instinctively is that when these deeper layers are activated, the compositional process is one in which the 'I' *has to acquiesce willingly*, for the sake of the poem, while, at the same time and all along, as far as possible maintaining some degree of conscious detachment. The challenge for all poets and artists, then, is to avoid *totally* identifying one's own individuality and consciousness with the archetypal elements that inevitably surface in and through composition; for to do so would inevitably lead either to inflation, or to engulfment and self-destruction, or all of these outcomes. The condition of a Cassandra isn't an enviable one, and is to be avoided.

Contrarywise, I would also argue that despite all such risks, this kind of "not knowing" is unequivocally the *necessary* mental and emotional state in which a poem (any poem) requires of its maker, in order to get written at all, and, furthermore, that far from providing a merely initial or preliminary impetus that first engages curiosity, desire and longing, the condition of "not knowing" actually motivates and drives the poet on through every stage of the compositional process.[63] The underlying implication here – that a work of art may well have some kind of mysterious will or intentionality of its own – isn't accidental. My own experience of working on long poems that have contained markedly archaic, mythical or symbolic resonances is that I've felt precisely this kind of 'possession' by the latent theme and salient energy of the emergent poem. "I wake to sleep, and take my waking slow," wrote Theodore Roethke, then adding: "I learn by going where I have to go."[64] The condition of "not knowing" also involves the kind of necessary modesty and ignorance that are characterised in Zen and Chan Buddhism as *shoshin* 初心, usually translated as 'beginner's mind'. The word 心 *shin*

[63] For treatment of this theme in relation to *In a Time of Drought* (RB 2011c), see 'Rain and Dust': 127-148 above, esp. 127-129.

[64] Roethke 104.

(*xin*, in Chinese) means not only 'mind' but also 'heart' and 'spirit'.[65] An 'innocent ignorance', combined with one's own modest admission of it, are necessary prerequisites for discovery. This might well be called the necessary preliminary condition for the functioning of the *Eureka Principle*.

ဟ

The end of section IV of *Gospa od Vinče* contains a description of the goddess's divine male consort, whose attributes, complementing those of the goddess herself, include *all* relational aspects of maleness: "My husband, lover, brother, father, friend, embraced me".[66] As an aside here, it's worth noting that in another line, an aspect of this male figure is revealed through a traditional symbol in Serbian poetry, that of the wolf: "His wolf's breath kissing my white face." This motif is repeatedly deployed by the Serbian poet Vasko Popa, especially in *Wolf Salt* (*Vučja so*, 1975).[67] Significantly, Herman Sekulić acknowledges Popa as a mentor, friend, and influence on her work.[68]

Conversely, for male readers, Herman's goddess manifests at least partially as the Jungian *anima* in both creative and destructive aspects – as her references to Coleridge and Robert Graves indicate. But for female readers, the goddess herself is arguably even more complex, because she appears not only as protean and multiform, but also as paradoxical, even to herself. In this connection, another phrase that echoes as a sonorous and puzzling refrain through the poem is "Her-who-was-I", "You-who-were-I", etc.[69] In this identification, the Lady of Vinča transgresses the boundaries that separate first, second and third person singular pronouns, and even eradicates or dissolves their relational identities in such a way that 'I' and 'thou', and 'I' and 'she', bond and merge.

An imagem such as this is richly suggestive in its implications and associations. Could this blending and dissolving perhaps suggest the precognitive 'oceanic' experience of the foetus in the maternal womb? Or

---

[65] "Shoshin (初心) is a word from Zen Buddhism which means 'beginner's mind'. It refers to having an attitude of openness, eagerness, and lack of preconceptions." See 'Shoshin', *Wikipedia*.

[66] Herman Sekulić, *op. cit.* 36.

[67] See also Popa 1997: 215-261.

[68] Conversation with Herman Sekulić, October 18, 2017, Smederevo; and email correspondence, October 30-31, 2017.

[69] Herman Sekulić, *op. cit.* 15, 18, 27, 39.

the blissful dissolution of boundaries in the *jouissance* of reciprocal orgasm? Alternatively, could it be taken as a response to Arthur Rimbaud's famous statement in one of his explosive letters of 1871, which he wrote when he was sixteen years old, and out of which the entirety of poetic modernism unrolled: "Je est un autre"?[70] Or might it resonate with the explorations Martin Buber makes in *I and Thou* (1986), and those of Emmanuel Levinas with regard to the mysterious and inalienable alterity of the human face?[71] From a strict linguistic perspective, the relative interchangeability of pronouns and the semantic and structural arbitrariness of distinctions among them, especially in Indo-European languages, has been brilliantly explored and profoundly and incisively analysed by Emile Benveniste, in 'Relationships of Person in the Verb' and 'The Nature of Pronouns'.[72]

Aside from these expansive associations, however, as soon as we focus more closely and intently on Herman Sekulić's text to examine the precise context of each of the key phrases in this "You-who-were-I" category, it immediately becomes evident that they must indicate one of two motifs. Either the poet herself has entirely identified herself entirely with the goddess; or else she has identified the voice of *her own persona in this particular poem* with the goddess's voice, as a lived experience that continues to resonate in her consciousness. The second of these interpretations is borne out by one of the poet's statements of responsibility already referred to: "*I, here, in the poem, assume all these roles.*"[73]

ഗ

From the above notes, I hope it's by now clear that in *Gospa od Vinče*, I believe Marija Herman Sekulić has taken on a dauntingly large poetic task. By deploying the female figurine of Vinča simultaneously as source, persona and objective correlative, she has attempted to plumb some of the deeper layers in the complex archetype of the feminine. In doing so, I suggest, she has attentively re-opened what Goethe described in *Faust* as the "Realm of the Mothers".[74] To put this another way, in the making of this poem, she appears to have undertaken an inner journey that has not been

---

[70] Rimbaud, 'Letter to Georges Izambard', Charleville, May 13, 1871: 302-303. See also 218-219 below.

[71] Levinas 2000, 2003a and 2003b.

[72] Benveniste 1971: 195-204 and 217-222.

[73] *op. cit.* 6, 'Prologue'; emphasis added.

[74] Goethe, *Faust* Part II, Act 1, Scene 5.

without some of the dangers of identification, immersion, submersion and, ultimately, possession, as outlined above. After all, we know what happened to Nietzsche, who in his final madness signed himself 'Dionysos'.

At the very end of her poem, however, through the last question that the poet poses, the reader is able to trace – with considerable relief – an explicit separation and detachment from the primeval goddess by the author as a twenty-first-century woman poet. "Was it your conscious decision," the poet asks, by now almost prosaically, and in a somewhat sceptical and possibly even accusatory, if regretful tone, "[t]o destroy everything, to burn all traces, / [b]efore the barbarians of the East invaded you, / [o]r did you just want to move on, into the unknown, / [t]o be totally free again, /[*w*]*ithout even knowing*?"[75]

ഗ

Finally, the possibility of being able to make "conscious" decisions but "without even knowing it" is in itself riddling, problematic. As the poem ends on this unanswered question, we may well reflect that if the movement of the poem is full of such puzzles and contradictions, this factor itself evinces the character of this goddess, and does so with considerable accuracy. For being both *complex* (adjective) and *a complex* (noun), the *Gospa* is ineluctably enigmatic to herself. So, it's hardly surprising that she's unlikely to be easily amenable to analysis, whether poetic or psychological. How else could such a poem end, if not on a question?[76]

Furthermore, the poet discovers that rich paradoxes reside in these depths, which *either* have not been fully articulated or assimilated to consciousness at all, *or* have since been repressed in individual consciousness by the successive cultures that have been dominated by patriarchy. What's going on here, then, I suggest, is a kind of poetic archaeology, whose procedures of excavation couldn't be anything other than introspective, since they necessarily explore layers in both the personal and the collective psyche that are closely interwoven, intrinsically mysterious, irrational, and interior. This is far from easy terrain: these layers include passion, celebration, suffering, sorrow, lament, anger, promise, hope, despair and regret.

---

75 Herman Sekulić, *op. cit.* 39.

76 For a possible comparison with a final question in another long poem on a Balkan theme exploring aspects of the feminine, see *Do vidjenja Danica: Goodbye Balkan Belle* (RB, 2012a): 26 and 52; and (RB 2011d): 15.

Mention of promise and hope in this context, however, implies that this archaeological delving, just identified, isn't entirely retrospective or nostalgic. As suggested in various hints above, Maja Herman Sekulić's hearkening back to a Neolithic age is intermeshed with a forward-looking, purposive, directional thrust. This consists of a creative longing and aspiration for "the language of love that we have not yet spoken";[77] and this language, most significantly, is a universal one that *includes women and men together*. This phrase is spoken by the *Gospa* herself, in celebration of rain, the most powerful elemental symbol of the mating of the ancient elemental sky god and earth goddess, which was celebrated in the pan-Balkan rainmaking rituals of Dodola and Peperuda until at least the 1950s: "The rain has come again that is not rain and tears that are not tears / And in the soft clay I have etched the first word in the world: LOVE".[78] In these gentle, moving lines, the core character of this Goddess, then, is revealed: beneath her lunar layers, she's the chthonic creatrix, the Earth Mother.

ᔓ

In approaching closure to this enquiry, it may be helpful to amplify the poet's symbolic language into that of "the psychologist of culture". The longing and the hope embedded in these last quoted lines was clearly recognised in the 1950s by Erich Neumann:

> The problem of the Feminine has equal importance for the psychologist of culture, who recognizes that the peril of present-day mankind springs in large part from the one-sidedly patriarchal development of the male intellectual consciousness, which is no longer kept in balance by the matriarchal world of the psyche [...].
>
> Western mankind must arrive at a synthesis that includes the feminine world – which is also one-sided in its isolation. Only then will the individual human being be able to develop the psychic wholeness that is urgently needed if Western man is to face the danger that threaten his existence from within and without.[79]

In further amplification, to this comment may be added the brilliant and excited intuitions of the sixteen-year-old Arthur Rimbaud, writing in 1871:

[77] Herman Sekulić, *op. cit.* 36.

[78] *ibid.* 36.

[79] Neumann, *The Great Mother* (1972 [1955]): xlii; also quoted in *Keys to Transformation* (RB 1981): 103-104, which also explores this theme. Neumann's book is relevant to all the motifs foregrounded in this current essay.

> When the endless servitude of women is broken, when she lives for and by herself, man – heretofore abominable – having given her her release, she too will be a poet! Woman will find some of the unknown! Will her world of ideas differ from ours? – She will find strange, unfathomable, repulsive, delicious things; we will take them, we will understand them.[80]

And from M. Esther Harding, writing in the early 1930s:

> A woman's creation is not an abstraction; it is a very personal thing, based primarily on her own subjective experience and not on objective experiences of the external world. If a woman is to create in the man's world, she needs not only to bring up into consciousness her masculine qualities, but also to experience deeply her feminine nature.[81]

ꕥ

Finally, since my knowledge of the work of contemporary Serbian women poets is, to say the least, patchy, I'd like to add a remark that's highly tentative. In the USA, a marker for contemporary women's poetry was set down by Anne Waldman in her powerful, beautiful and witty chant-poem, *Fast Speaking Woman* (1974). Here, Waldman contextualises her own modern identity through the modalities of a deep shamanistic past. However, in modern Serbian poetry, I'm not aware that any woman poet has yet laid down such an ambitious and challenging marker as Maja Herman Sekulić in *Gospa od Vinče*, where she takes on a personal responsibility for ancient history, archetype and myth.

October 2017

[80] "Quand sera brisé l'infini servage de la femme, quand elle vivra pour elle et par elle, l'homme – jusqu'ici abominable, – lui ayant donné son renvoi, elle sera poète, elle aussi! La femme trouvera de l'inconnu! Ses mondes d'idées differeront-ils des nôtres? – Elle trouvera des choses étranges, insondables, repoussantes, délicieuses; nous les prendrons, nous les comprendrons," Letter to Paul Demeny, Charleville, May 15, 1871: Rimbaud 308-309.

[81] Harding 77. I'm indebted to Melanie Rein for this reference.

Demons and Daemons:
The Dark Vision of Filip David

The House of Remembering and Forgetting is a profound and complex novel. The central, enormous question broached on each of its mere 130 pages is: what is the nature of evil? And the ancillary question it poses, equally powerfully, is: what is the nature of reality itself?

All its chapters occur during or in the wake of the Holocaust. External events are recounted both directly and through its characters' letters and diary entries, and these are mingled with accounts of their dreams. The unpredictable inter-scenic movement is filmic.

The first narrator, Albert Weisz (White) attends a conference in Belgrade. Its theme is 'Crimes, Reconciliation, Forgetting'. An unnamed stranger begins to speak, arguing that Hannah Arendt's phrase 'banality of evil' is a rationalisation. Evil, claims the stranger, by its very nature can't be so glibly encapsulated. Evil is huge, uncatchable, incalculable, all-pervasive, metaphysical. All individuals and families – "indeed entire peoples" – he argues, have "a mysterious power watching them, a power called a daemon. It guides them, it saves them or it destroys them." Evil is "cosmic, irrational, unrestrainable."[82]

Then, the stranger goes on recount in private to Weisz how as a child, he watched in horror from a hiding place, as German occupiers shot his parents. The chapter closes with Weisz later seeing a TV report about a bus being bombed. One of the victims is this unnamed stranger.

Following one of Weisz's recurring nightmares, and Weisz writing his diary, we jump to the prime childhood trauma that has governed his entire life. He has survived a transport in an Auschwitz-bound train only because his parents managed to prise open a floorboard of the wagon they were travelling in and drop him onto the tracks. They also dropped his little brother Eli, but Albert has never been able to find Eli and is haunted by guilt.

---

[82] David 29.

As these out-takes suggest, the book consists of no single plot-line, but a mesh of apparently disparate events that are gradually seen to be mysteriously connected across space and sequential time. This interwoven quality, it's implied, itself embodies the lurking presence of an invisible overruling "daemon" working behind and through events. While hints of meaningful connectivity are offered through multiple accounts of synchronicities and Kabbalistic insights, precisely how or why this inescapable destiny functions as it does is as incomprehensible as in a Sophoclean or Shakespearean tragedy. Many chapters have ironic subtitles, which themselves function as self-commentating meta-texts. The one that seems to stand most thoroughly for the whole book occurs in Chapter 6: "In which a mysterious event is described but nothing is explained. Everything is in doubt, including life itself."[83]

Similarly, narrators, speaking in both first and third persons, take up all loose threads. Their presence has a similar effect: first, to emphasise the commonality of suffering; second, to expose the tenuousness of the hold on reality of the conscious and rational 'I'; and, third, to indicate the eerie pervasiveness of evil as a mysterious force that can suddenly, ruthlessly affect everyone, including even its perpetrators.

This complexity is woven together by means of a cool, sparse, deadpan prose that barely contains its underlying ambiguities and absurdities. Beneath the rational flatness lie swirling and fathomless depths of irrationality: A closer look at the language shows that highly emotive terms recur and abound: "inner horror", "inner panic", "frightening", "danger", "topsy-turvy", "unknown", "foreboding".

This is a masterly book, at once acutely, mercilessly intelligent, and an uncanny, eerie exploration of "the corridors and labyrinths of many criss-crossing worlds".[84] In its intermingling of tragedy and absurdity with philosophical questions, it queries and challenges the nature of the novel itself. The book belongs to a genre perfected by such great Serbian writers as Danilo Kiš and Milorad Pavić, and if anything, outmatches them in quality. It's steeped in a way of being and thinking that I think of as irreducibly and intrinsically Balkan, in which epiphanic beauty and unmitigated horror can both burst through the seams of humdrum reality at a moment's notice.

December 2017

[83] *ibid.* 61.

[84] *ibid.* 60.

PART 4

ON LITERARY MEETINGS AND FESTIVALS

The following four prose-pieces explore three international literary festivals in Serbia, one in detail. While their main focus is localised, I hope these sketches may implicitly draw attention to the role played by these kinds of gatherings in a more panoramic context: i.e. in the larger cultural and political currents of our time.[1] I also suggest that modern literary festivals deserve more attentive study, for multiple reasons and in many interconnected ways, for example: traditions intrinsic to literature and culture, including hospitality; changes in political and economic orientations, especially hegemony and dependence; shifts in relative world-views; and the availability and exploitation of new forms of media and communications.

The first piece, 'Belgrade, Poetry Capital', is a quasi-journalistic article on the city's international October Writers' Meeting.[2] It was written for the *Serbian Literary Quarterly* in 1988, when the Russian poet Joseph Brodsky was the star guest. He'd been awarded the Nobel Prize in the previous year. He received huge acclaim from Serbian audiences, but not only for that reason. This article, which recalls one of the last of these international gatherings before the implosion of Federal Yugoslavia, is 'dated' in all respects. I include it here mainly for documentation.

This short piece is followed by a longer essay, 'Writing and Meeting Writers in Serbia: The International Writers' Meeting in Belgrade'. Since that event was founded in 1964, its achievements have hardly been noticed, let alone acknowledged or appreciated in the self-regarding English-speaking literary world, even though many Anglophone writers have attended it. The text documents the role and historical development of this 'October Meeting'. By viewing it in the context of other literary festivals in former Yugoslavia and elsewhere, the piece also amplifies some aspects of a more general history of literary festivals since the 1960s.

---

[1] My involvement in events of this kind has been active since I founded the Cambridge Poetry Festival Society in 1973 and co-ordinated the first of its international biennial events in 1975. The Cambridge Poetry Festival ran until 1985. See RB 2009a.

[2] The Serbian name is *Medjunarodni oktobarski susreti pisaca*, lit. 'International October Encounters of Writers'.

Between 1982 and 1989 I was a regular guest at this annual event, and my repeated involvement in it during that decade gradually helped to shape my understanding of Serbian literary life and its patterns and complexities, as well as many other aspects of former Yugoslavia.[3] I often attended this event during and after my three-year stay in Belgrade too. This essay was first drafted in 2013. Since then, although I've elaborated it, I've preferred not to revise the main passages that belong to that earlier version.[4]

Tinged with personal reminiscences, this longer piece is followed by some later retrospective thoughts about the wholly deleterious effects of the Milošević era on Serbian literary life, when the role of the Serbian Writers' Association changed radically to explicit support for nationalism. The concluding short piece offers some brief notes on *Pesnička jesen* ('Poetry Autumn') in Smederevo.

At times, these essays digress from their main themes to expand on related topics.

September 2019–January 2020

---

[3] The long poem '*Do vidjenja Danice* (*Goodbye Balkan Belle*)' draws extensively on impressions of former Yugoslavia, some of which I gained from the tours organised by the Serbian Writers' Association. See RB 2011d: 3-15; RB 2012a.

[4] At the October 1999 Meeting, I was elected a member of the Serbian Writers' Association, thanks in part to my opposition to the NATO bombing of the country in the springtime of that year. To the best of my knowledge, I'm the only British member.

Belgrade: Poetry Capital

When I first attended the Serbian Writers' Association's international October Meeting in 1982, along with Scottish poet Walter Perrie, we read our poems at various venues, enjoyed the company of writers from miscellaneous countries, sat drinking to the accompaniment of 'Old Town Songs' in Skadarlija, visited the frescoes of Sopoćani in stunned silence and, replete with Yugoslav hospitality, flew home. Gazing out of a bus window as we careered through the green hills of Serbia to Novi Pazar, Mr. Perrie remarked, "This landscape reminds me of Scotland."

It isn't just the landscape. In the intense, gossipy intimacy of its literary life, Belgrade is strongly reminiscent of Edinburgh. It's a capital city, but small enough for everybody to know everybody; and, even when writers aren't on speaking terms, they're bound to one another by indissoluble ties and loyalties deeper than personal, or even ideological loves and hates.

In 1982, the conference theme seemed little more than an excuse, but the topic in 1988, 'Exile and Literature', seemed to matter very much. Amid current debates in all echelons of Yugoslav public life, it isn't surprising that the event was packed out, and that many speeches had an urgency about them.

Why, asked the West Berlin poet Olav Münzberg at one of the Round Table discussions, should this theme of exile be chosen in Belgrade this year? One answer, provided by critic Raša Popov, lay in appreciating the gradual liberalisation of literature in Yugoslavia since the Destalinisation of the fifties, and in working out what further steps needed taking. Another answer came from Montenegrin writer, Petar Sarić, who spoke of the plight of Serbs forced to flee from their native Kosovo as "a terrible exile in a free and sovereign state". The entire tenor of the conference repeatedly emphasised that in Yugoslavia today, writers and intellectuals have had as crucial a part to play in shaping the country's future as factory workers or economists.

So, Milan Ranković, Serbian Minister of Culture, argued that despite past censorship, Yugoslavia still had the best record of all socialist countries for freedom of creative expression, and that during this time of revitalisation, articulate criticism through continuing free speech must be upheld. Predrag Palavestra, of the Serbian PEN Centre, stated that when the political colours of exile faded, many writers who had experienced rejection were the next day the pride of their nations. Dr. Nikola Milošević, a member of the Academy of Serbian Arts and Sciences, made a plea for a new tolerant philosophy among socialists: "who is not with us can be for us" – as he opened exhibitions devoted to two Yugoslav writers who had lived abroad: Rastko Petrović in the USA and Miloš Crnjanski in London.

Among writers from over thirty countries, few had much original light to shed on the theme other than discursiveness or autobiography. But there were exceptions. A tactfully worded, moving speech was made, in French, by the expatriate writer living in Montreal, Negovan Rajić, returning to his native Belgrade for the first time in forty-two years. In contrast, the young Chilean poet and theorist, Myriam Díaz-Diocaretz, now teaching in Utrecht, made a remarkable contribution in English, entitled 'The Sites of Silence in the Invisible Cities of Language', a testament to the 'inner listener', rooted in the philosophy of Mikhail Bakhtin.

Then, among all these contrasts and contradictions, the highlight: Nobel Prize-winner Joseph Brodsky, in the evening in his honour at the Yugoslav Drama Theatre in Marshal Tito Boulevard, gave a recital of his poems in Russian and answered searching questions in modulated, elegant English, for two and a half hours. Not a seat was empty, the audience packed the aisles, and he received a standing ovation that was slow, measured and thoughtful in its intensity rather than rapturous in the American mode. This was an event which those present will remember for years, maybe decades to come – of a subtlety that could only be experienced in a country where a Slavonic language is spoken and the Cyrillic script used.

Four, three, even two years ago, it would have been inconceivable for Soviet poets and Brodsky to attend the same literary festival. But Yugoslavia has always been a crossroads, and on this evening of October 20, 1988, the forty-fourth anniversary of the liberation from Nazi occupation by the Red Army and Yugoslav partisans, Belgrade for a few hours became poetry capital of the world. Soviet poets attending Brodsky's reading refused to take their reserved seats and insisted on standing. When asked why, one of them replied to his Yugoslav host: "When a Russian poet of this calibre recites his poems, it's wrong that I should sit. I stand, out of respect for a Master."

Belgrade, October 1988

Writing and Meeting Writers in Serbia: The International Writers' Meeting in Belgrade

The role of the *International Writers' Meeting* in Serbian literary life is best viewed in the context of the history of the Serbian Writers' Association, whose origins go back to various literary and cultural societies founded between 1883 and 1912. The *Srpsko književničko društvo* (Serbian Literary Association) was founded in 1905 to advocate Serbian literature, to bring together Serbian writers, and to help Serbian writers and their families. In addition to these aims, broader international perspectives were explicit from the start. The rising communal consciousness of a South Slav culture was a strong motivational factor, a tendency that was reflected in conerences in Belgrade in 1904 and Zagreb in 1905, when writers took part from Serbia, Croatia, Slovenia and Bulgaria. This impetus grew to be influential in the movement among intellectuals towards the establishment of the Kingdom of Yugoslavia in 1918. Following the First World War, in December 1920, the *Udruženje srpskih književnika* (Association of Serbian Writers) was reconstituted. Necessarily disbanded during the Second World War, it was re-founded on 31 December 1944 as the *Udruženje književnika Narodne Republike Srbije* (Writers' Association of the National Republic of Serbia), with Isidora Sekulić as president, Jovan Popović as vice-president, Oskar Davičo as secretary,[5] and Ivo Andrić as one of its most internationally distinguished members. At the time I write this piece, the *Udruženje književnika Srbije* (Serbian Writers' Association) is chaired by the poet Radomir Andrić.[6]

ഗ

[5] See my personal memoir on Oskar: 360-363 below.

[6] The first draft of this essay was made in 2013. It has been revised and elaborated since then.

The Association's *International Writers' Meeting* was a post-Second World War phenomenon and a child of the 1960s. The event still combines features that echo the informal, experimental, inclusive, buzzy atmosphere of that decade, as well as aspects that have reflected and kept pace, year by year, with contemporary literary, social and political issues. It includes some characteristics that are typical of international literary festivals all over the world, and others that belong specifically to Belgrade and Serbia. As Ivan V. Lalić[7] points out in a two-page memoir written in 1996, ever since its inception the *Meeting* has been an event organised "by writers, for writers"; and it embodies "the effort of amateurs – in the best sense of this double-edged word".

At the time when I write this piece, seventeen years later (2013), in a period of international economic stagnation, Lalić's words seem particularly apposite. In the last four years, all over Europe, cutbacks in funding for literary events have been the norm. For a group of amateurs to have kept a major international event of this kind going for fifty years, through thick and thin and without a single year's break, is an achievement in itself. What's more, the Belgrade *Meeting* has somehow managed to survive the ravages of war and Serbian isolation from the international community, which marked and marred the 1990s, broke up Yugoslavia, and caused untold suffering. It has also survived the rule of Slobodan Milošević. The *Meeting* has inevitably been severely maimed and scarred by these events.

Many internationally famous writers sent messages of support to the very first Belgrade *Meeting* in 1964, which was attended by, among many others, Angus Wilson (UK), Boris Slutsky (USSR), Kazimierz Brandys (Poland), and Oskar Davičo, Predrag Palavestra and Dušan Matić from Serbia.[8] Ivan V. Lalić, who was present at this event, reminds us that the founding of the Belgrade *Meeting* marked the twentieth anniversary of the withdrawal of Nazi forces from Serbia after more than three years of occupation between April 1941 and October 1944.[9]

For historical reasons, then, while the celebration of national identity, independence and freedom underpinned the Belgrade *Meeting*, just as it did the *Veliki školski čas* ('the Great School Lesson') in Kragujevac, which was founded between 1959 and 1962,[10] the anti-Fascist motivation for both these events, combined with their commemorative aspects, inevitably

---

[7] Lalić 1996b: 16. See my obituary for him, 407-410 below.

[8] See Dimić 1996: 6; and Mraović.

[9] Lalić *op. cit.* 16.

[10] See RB 2011b: 136-138 and 140.

gave them an international dimension from the outset.

In the Belgrade *Writers' Meeting*, internationalism and nationalism have always sat side by side, usually balancing moderately comfortably, but at times oscillating steeply, until the Milošević years, when the balance tipped.

ᔓ

It makes sense, too, to situate the Belgrade Writers' Meeting in its international context. In the 1920s, throughout the industrialised world, sound recording and above all public radio broadcasting returned both fiction and poetry to spoken transmission and large audiences. In the UK, for example, the first of Dylan Thomas's famous radio broadcasts took place on April 21, 1937. He delivered *Under Milk Wood* to the BBC in 1953, and his American tours in 1950, 1952 and 1953 attracted huge followings.

In Western Europe, large communal literary celebrations developed in the wake of the Second World War. The thriving Edinburgh Festival, for example, based mainly on drama, started life as early as 1947 in an effort to "provide a platform for the flowering of the human spirit";[11] while the Cheltenham Literature Festival, founded in 1949, lays claim to being "the longest-running festival of its kind in the world".[12] In 1948, the formal acceptance by the United Nations General Assembly of the *Universal Declaration of Human Rights* was a foundation for all subsequent cultural international events.

In the Communist East, between 1958 and 1960, immediately following the erection of Vladimir Mayakosvky's statue in a square in Moscow, Yevgeny Yevtushenko, Andrei Voznesensky and other poets stood beneath the new monument and gave poetry readings to vast audiences of tens of thousands of people, openly defying the Soviet authorities.[13]

Between 1961 and 1964, when I was a student at Cambridge University, we often gave and attended live poetry readings. It seemed an

[11] See 'Edinburgh Festival', *Wikipedia.*

[12] See 'Cheltenham Festival', *Wikipedia.*

[13] See 'Interview with Yevgeni Yevtushenko' (online; English slightly corrected): "I was the first poet who after Stalin's death began to recite poetry openly in the schools, in the factories, in the colleges, everywhere, in offices, in little cafés. Sometimes I recited more [...]. I had more readings than days in the year. And we organized a giant poetry reading in the Mayakovsky Square once; there were about 35 or 40,000 people there."

entirely natural thing to do. The *International Poetry Incarnation* held at the Albert Hall in London, on June 11, 1965, with Allen Ginsberg as the motivating figure, attracted an audience of 7,000 people.[14] A year later, on 18 June 1966, Jonathan Boulting spent his paternal inheritance on hiring the Albert Hall for a single night, for his *New Moon Poetry Carnival.* This event included readings by Robert Graves, Patrick Kavanagh, Stevie Smith, Spike Milligan, Michel Deguy, Godofredo Iommi, Vanessa Redgrave and others.[15]

Many long-standing literary events began in the 1960s, including: *Writers' Week* in Adelaide, Australia, founded in 1960; the Struga *Poetry Evenings*, and Sarajevo *Poetry Days*, both 1962;[16] the biennial *Lahti International Writers' Reunion*, Finland, 1963; the Vilnius *Poetry Spring*, Lithuania, 1965; *Poetry International*, London, 1967; the *PEN International* conference at Bled, Slovenia, in 1968;[17] the Zagreb *Literary Talks* and Rotterdam's *Poetry International*, both in 1969; and the Smederevo *Poetry Autumn*, 1970.[18] So the founding of the Belgrade *Writers' Meeting* in 1964 situates this event firmly in an international tradition of public literary celebrations.

ᔕ

Five of the international literary events mentioned above began in former Yugoslavia and two of them in Serbia, a disproportionately huge number. Why was this? Here I suggest some correlated factors: political, socio-economic and historical-cultural.

First, in the wake of the Second World War, Yugoslav president Josip Broz Tito's increasing disagreements with Joseph Stalin involved political tension, which eventually led to Yugoslavia's schism with the Soviet Bloc in the late 1950s and the so-called *ruska blokada* (Russian Blockade). In 1961, the Non-Aligned Movement of Nations was initiated in Belgrade by Josip Broz Tito, Indian president Jawaharlal Nehru, Indonesian president

---

[14] See Whitehead. The four-part video of this event on YouTube reveals insights into Beat poetry and the atmosphere of the 'Swinging Sixties'. Forty-four years later, the only poet whose work still has any quality is Adrian Mitchell. The rest without exception come across as inflated narcissists.

[15] Email from Jonathan Boulting, September 21, 2019.

[16] See 'Izet Sarajlić', *Wikipedia*.

[17] See also 261-262 below.

[18] 'Zagrebački književni razgovori' (online), and *International Literary Festivals.*

Sukarno, Egyptian president Gamal Abdel Nasser, and Ghanaian president Kwame Nkrumah. As a result, Yugoslavia gradually opened itself to wider influences and contacts. The international cultural events promoted in the country during the early 1960s took on a key role both in shaping local and national cultural life and in creating good will by welcoming and in turn influencing international participants.

By the early 1980s, Yugoslavia's leading role in the Non-Aligned Movement was the main reason that, in its heyday, the annual autumnal *Writers' Meeting* enabled writers from many different countries to get together in a relaxed and unstrained atmosphere. From my own experience in the early to mid-1980s, I can't think of any other city where anything like this would have been possible. What's more, in those years, the October *Writers' Meeting* was hugely popular in Serbia itself. Both indoor and outdoor events attracted huge audiences. The two photos overleaf are proof of this. In the UK, I for one could never have dreamed of reading my poems before such large audiences.

Second, in 1964, Yugoslavia lifted emigration restrictions, and the number of émigrés going abroad increased rapidly, particularly to Germany as guest workers (*Gastarbeiter*).[19] Not only was a spirit of internationalism in the air in Yugoslavia at that time but so too was the sense that innovative political, social and cultural patterns were being shaped that challenged previous restrictions and opened up new possibilities. Economic conditions were still tough, but as travel became easier, new opportunities for work, dialogue and discovery became available. *Sve je moguće*, goes the Serbian saying ('Everything is possible'), and an optimistic feeling was paramount, especially among the curious and adventurous young.

Third, thanks to former Yugoslavia's specific location in a geographical, cultural and political zone connecting East and West, and bordering both but belonging to neither,[20] from the early 1960s on, international literary meetings of this kind, especially in Belgrade and Struga, were among the most dynamic and interesting in the world.

---

[19] "By the early 1970s, Yugoslavia had Europe's second-highest emigration rate, and 20 per cent of the country's labor force was employed abroad. In 1973 about 1.1 million workers and dependents were living and working outside Yugoslavia's borders; 900,000 of these were living in Western Europe" ('Yugoslavia Guest Workers', *Mongobay* (online).

[20] For wider interpretations of history and culture in terms of the geography of the zone, see Stoianovich 1994, Todorova 2009, and East.

An open air poetry reading in Republic Square, Belgrade, October 1984

Fourth, in a lecture delivered in 1988, not long before the collapse of the Federation, Ivan V. Lalić offers a further clue, even if this seems obsolete following the fragmentation of the country. Here he broaches the complexity, variety and richness of literary traditions across Yugoslavia:

> Yugoslav literature. Literature in Yugoslavia. Yugoslav literatures. You may have your choice; all these terms are valid. However, I personally prefer to think of this literary nexus in terms of a specific and unique totality. That is why I prefer to say: Yugoslav literature, particularly when bearing in mind the contemporary literary scene in Yugoslavia. Saying that we have to deal with a *mixtum compositum* is not necessarily a paradox; it is just one specific trait more. For writing in Yugoslavia has a long and rather rich tradition, or, if you prefer, a set of different traditions: a fact which might go some way towards explaining the very quality of its richness and variety.[21]

For all these reasons, from the mid-1960s to the late 1980s, Belgrade was able fully to live up to its claim of being a crossroads, a junction, a meeting point that transcended ideologies. In those days, in bringing together a spectrum of writers from East and West in a convivial atmosphere, the role of the *Writers' Meeting* was incomparable.

ꟹ

There's a fifth and deeper reason too. In at least four of the republics of Yugoslavia – Serbia, Bosnia/Hercegovina, Montenegro and Macedonia – these modern events had roots in a time-honoured tradition of oral and communally delivered poetry, whose lineage was traceable back to the sung Serbian epics.

Albert B. Lord's ground-breaking study of the composition and performance of the long Serbian oral poems rooted in the Kosovo cycle, entitled *The Singer of Tales*, wasn't published until 1960. It was based on Milman Parry's sound recordings of oral bards in the 1930s. These recordings were made, first on wax cylinders and then on phonograph discs, in towns and villages of Bosnia, Croatia, Montenegro and southern Serbia, such as Bihać, Kijevo, Bijelo Polje and Novi Pazar. Here, the tradition of singing old epics in the *kafana* (coffee-house) was still alive until the mid-twentieth century, especially on market days. Most singers were analphabetic. So singing a long narrative poem was a considerable feat of memory and improvisation, and some of these composer-performers commanded extensive repertoires of material and had masterly skills in oral epic techniques. "When our collecting began in the nineteen-thirties," writes Harry Levin in his preface,

---

[21] Lalić 1993. He wrote this piece in English for a lecture for a conference in Lisbon (May 4-8, 1988), organised by the Wheatfield Foundation, New York. I helped him polish it.

"the Yugoslav oral epic was accessible, alive, and distinguished."[22] Lord elaborates, using the present tense:

> Among the Muslims in Yugoslavia there is a special festival which has contributed to the fostering of songs of some length. This is the festival of Ramazan, when for a month the men fast from sunrise to sunset and gather in coffee houses all night long to talk and listen to epic. Here is the perfect circumstance for the singing of one song during the entire night. Here also is an encouragement to the semi-professional singer to attain a repertory of at least thirty songs. It was Parry's experience that such Muslim singers, when asked how many songs they knew, frequently replied that they knew thirty, one for every night of Ramazan. Most Muslim kafanas engage a singer several months in advance to entertain their guests, and if there is more than one such kafana in the town, there may be rivalry in obtaining the service of a well-known and popular singer who is likely to bring considerable business to the establishment.[23]

Similarly, thirty years before Parry, writing in her first of many books about the Balkans, Edith Durham describes an enthusiastic bout of epic-singing at a patriotic festival in the village of Andrijevica, Montenegro, in summer 1903. Her account of a gathering on the evening of a market day is an enthusiastic, energetic, indeed almost rapturously infatuated portrayal, which she delivers in detail. This quotation is part of a much longer passage:

> The musical talent of the neighbourhood flocked to the guest-room at the bakers', the *gusle* passed from hand to hand, and each man in turn vied with his comrades in long historic ballads. Those who meant to go home brought their rifles with them, "for it is dark"; those who meant to stay hung up their revolvers and took their belts off. How those fellows sang! – sang till the sweat glistened upon their brows, their faces flushed, and the veins stood out upon their throats. Nor did there seem to be an end to the number of verses each man knew. [...] They sang of Kosovo and of the Servo-Bulgarian war and of the border fights of the neighbourhood. The song often ended on a yell of triumph, and the singer threw himself back exhausted by the emotions he had lived through.[24]

---

[22] Levin xiii. Parry (1902–1935), Lord (1912–199) and Levin (1912–1994) were all Americans.

[23] Lord 15. See also Parry.

[24] Durham 2015 [1904]: 205. However, see also 101 above, for her revised attitude to these heroic songs.

Durham goes on to describe how Djoka, her guide – who was a Muslim – joined in this company by singing a song about "the sorrows of a Turkish woman whose husband the Montenegrins had killed".[25] She adds that he was the most accomplished *gusle*-player present, and concludes, "When everyone had sung himself hoarse we suddenly discovered it was one o'clock in the morning."

☙

For centuries, among the Southern Slavs, as elsewhere, home-life in agricultural communities held few privacies and involved few personal possessions. These old epic poems were traditionally sung not only at festivals or on public occasions as described by Lord and Durham, but also inside the communal dwellings of extended families, usually built around an open compound. The name for this kind of communal building, and for this kind of living, was the *zadruga*.[26] The American anthropologist Joel

---

[25] *ibid.* 205. The word *Turkish* here means 'Muslim'. When Djoka is asked whether he's "Christian or Mohammedan?", he replies, "By God, I know not." While *Djoka* is a pet-name for *Djordje* (Serbian, 'George'), his religious affiliations are as uncertain as his ethnicity, whether this is Montenegrin or Albanian. I'm grateful to Vesna Goldsworthy for drawing my attention to this nuance. This instance draws attention to the fact that the tradition of singing the Serbian epic poems belonged as much to Muslims as to Christians, and also that there was a good deal of friendly 'sportsmanlike' mingling among ethnic and linguistic groups. See also Parry, Lord. For another example of a similarly complex Balkan identity, but made explicit by Durham, see 79 above.

[26] This word is cognate with South Slavic noun *drug* 'companion, friend' and, in the Communist period, 'comrade', as well as with the adjective *drugi* (*-a, -o*) meaning both 'second' and 'other'. The idea and practice of *društvo* 'society' (in all its English senses) is strongly loaded with positive attributions. In a separate context, Emile Benveniste offers relevant and fascinating insights:

> In Old Slavic and in the modern Slav languages […] *drugŭ* signifies 'friend, companion'. The notion of a bond, of friendship is so strong that the adjective, when repeated, may render the notion of reciprocity, 'the one, the other': Russian *drug druga*. (Benveniste 1973: 89)

Benveniste also connects these words with **dreu-*, which has a plethora of outcomes in Indo-European languages, including Slavic *sŭdrava* 'salvus, healthy'. This becomes *zdrav* in all modern South Slavonic languages, leading also, for example, to *zdravo* 'hello'. Similarly the cognate adjective **dru* 'strong, resistant, hard' "[…]

Halpern, who lived in a Serbian village in Šumadija in the 1950s, has a great deal to say about this way of life, which he observed at first-hand. His simple definition of the *zadruga* is "an extended family group characteristic of the South Slavs, consisting of a man, his wife, and their married sons and families, sometimes including the man's brothers and their families".[27]

An article on the Serbian village community, originally published in German one hundred years earlier by the Jewish Austro-Hungarian ethnographer and traveller Felix Philippe Kanitz (1829–1904) gives a detailed description of the *zadruga* and the role of the *starešina* (etym. *star* 'old, aged'), its elected headman or house-father. Although Kanitz's picture is clearly based on Romantic projection, he clarifies that the sing-ing of epic poems was a regular social event:

> Evening finds the family by the household hearth, by the bright-burning fire in the house of the stareshina [*sic*]. The men cut and repair the agricultural tools and house vessels. The elders rest from their labours, smoke, and discuss what is to be done next day or the events of the village and the country. The women group themselves, quietly working, in a circle near them; the merry little ones play at the feet of their parents, or beg the grandfather to relate to them about Czar Troyan or Marko Kralievitch. Then the stareshina, or one of the other men, takes the one-stringed gusla from the wall. To its singular monotonous accompaniment are sung legends, heroic songs, and such as in burning words relate the need of the fatherland and its wars of liberation. Thus the house of the stareshina becomes the social gathering point of the whole family. At his hearth is kindled the love of individuals for the old traditions of the family and people, and the inspiring enthusiasm of all the freedom and prosperity of their native land.[28]

Despite Kanitz's idealised emphasis on the 'fatherland' and his attempt to assimilate a South-Slavic tradition to a Germanic stereotype, this account

---

has become the word for 'tree'" (*ibid.* 88). Modern Russian *дерево* (*derevo*) and Serbian *drvo* belongs to this nexus, as do words in Germanic languages embedding the idea of 'fidelity', such as modern German *Treue* 'loyalty' and English *true.* If this analysis is accepted, as proposed by Benveniste and others, in Indo-European languages the notions of society and sociability, strength and sturdiness, and friendship and fidelity, appear to have a fascinating common origin.

[27] Halpern 22, n. 2, and see 134-150; also Mackenzie and Irby, vol 2: 329-331. Halpern's archive is held at the University of Bradford. See *Joel Martin Halpern Balkan Archive* (online).

[28] Kanitz, quoted in Mackenzie and Irby, vol 2: 351.

is based on first-hand witnessing.

Interestingly, too, in writing of his own experience of the *zadruga* in 1875, the young English journalist Arthur Evans (1841–1951), later internationally renowned and knighted for his archaeological excavations at Knossos, emphasises its democratic character:

> [T]he house-father, who represents the family in dealings with the authorities, and the house mother who shares with her consort his patriarchal sway over the house community, are elected. [...] [T]he domestic government is thrown out if it does not continue to give satisfaction to its constituents. In short, this is their little Parliament house, and these the earliest germs of Constitutional Government.[29]

Elsewhere in the same book, Evans connects the *zadruga* as a model of communal living with his separate perception of an "'*égalitaire*' spirit" among the Bosnians he meets. This involves an informality which, he, as a snobby Harrow-and-Oxford-educated and immensely Victorian English gentleman, finds it particularly hard to swallow, especially when it comes to finding *himself* being addressed as "'*brat*' or brother" or "'shija' – *neighbour*":

> It is part and parcel of a democratic habit of mind common to the whole Serbian, and indeed the whole South-Sclavonic race. [...] [F]or one need not be enamoured of *liberty coupled with equality and fraternity* not to perceive that, when the choice lies between it and tyranny, freedom, even in such companionship, is to be infinitely preferred; and a man must be either blind or a diplomatist not to perceive that in the Sclavonian provinces of Turkey *the choice ultimately lies between despotism and a democracy almost socialistic.*[30]

By connecting the informality he meets and the tradition of the *zadruga* and by deploying the explicit terminology of revolutionary French republicanism, here Evans's finding of "a democracy almost socialistic" isn't far from implying an 'inherent' communistic tendency among the southern Slavs. Oddly, and perhaps contradictorily, Evans's superior, snobbish and racist attitude doesn't blind him here to accurate analysis.

The *zadruga* tradition has been widely interpreted as a precursor of communist Yugoslavia, as well as one of the suggested background reasons to explain why and how communism took root in the country from the

[29] Evans 1876: 60-61; see also 56-61, including a sketch, 57; and Evans 2005 [1878]: 16.

[30] *ibid.* 309-310; emphases added.

1930s on, and for more than forty years, from 1945, came to dominate it as a state-system.

It should be added here, however, that the role and interpretation of the *zadruga* have been debated by recent scholars. Maria Todorova argues that "this esoteric sounding term"[31] was a nineteenth century invention, probably by Vuk Karadžić,[32] and a kind of Romantic idealisation of the "extended" or "multiple family", which wasn't typical of Balkan society.[33] She even suggests that there should be "a symbolic ban" on use of the term among historians.[34] Traian Stoianovich ripostes that in "the western half of the Balkans [...] extended family households were the rule, except along a narrow Adriatic and Aegean fringe from at least the sixteenth until the mid-nineteenth century[...]".[35]

ᔕ

The national liberation movements in the Balkans during the nineteenth century involved a relatively sudden shift to capitalism and modernism from a society whose rigidly inflexible hierarchical structure had been based on a kind of feudal caste system, which itself was rooted in foreign occupation. In the wake of four centuries of Ottoman rule in the Balkans, this transition took place over a much shorter period than in Western Europe. Much of the peninsula had had little or no opportunity either to enjoy or to benefit from anything like gradual bourgeoisification, let alone a Renaissance or an Enlightenment.[36] Of course, there was international trade, and there were educated intellectuals and wealthy city-dwellers, but most of the population was involved in agriculture.

Particularly in south and central Serbia, Bosnia and Hercegovina, Montenegro and Macedonia, the longevity of the tradition of singing old epic poems needs to be understood precisely within this social and political context. From medieval times until well into the twentieth century, these

---

[31] Todorova 1989: 37.

[32] *ibid.* 38.

[33] *ibid.* 74.

[34] *ibid.* 76.

[35] Stoianovich 1992, vol. 2: 147.

[36] Stoianovich's essays entitled 'Factors in the Decline of Ottoman Society in the Balkans' and 'The Social Foundation of Balkan Politics, 1750–1941' give detailed analyses of the processes involved. See Stoianovich 1995, vol. 3: 103-110 and 111-138.

songs bound agricultural communities together and instilled and maintained a heroic sense of cultural, linguistic and national identity.[37] Until relatively recently, some of the deep roots of modern poetry in the territories of former Yugoslavia were rural, communal, oral and analphabetic rather than city-based, educated, individualistic, or 'literary' in any narrow sense.

In complete contrast, however, in western Croatia, especially along the Dalmatian littoral, a thriving and articulate literary culture developed during the fifteenth and sixteenth centuries, above all in the Republic of Ragusa (Dubrovnik), but also further north, for example in Zadar, Split and some of the Dalmatian islands. Here, Venetian cultural models were imitated. Italian was widely spoken.[38]

Gradually, then, mingling with these very diverse traditions, the subsequent influences of successive waves of European literary Romanticism in the nineteenth century, and of international Modernism in the twentieth, moulded a uniquely complex amalgam of traditions for twentieth century Yugoslav poets, who were therefore able to draw on and choose from among an unusually wide and rich range of models, all of which could be immediately available and any of which might be pertinent.

৩

Until the break-up of the Yugoslav Federation, I believe this combination of widely disparate factors actively stimulated a commonly held belief: that literature, especially poetry, resonates with a relevance to people's lives, and even a central importance in them. *For poetry, like song, belongs to everybody*. In the various south Slavonic languages, even the words *pesma*, *pjesma* and *pesna* mean both 'song' and 'poem'.[39]

Poetry, then, like song, was meant to be shared communally and publicly, as well as being enjoyed in the intimacy of private silent reading. Nor did its performance belong mainly or merely to the select ambience of the educated family, genteel salon or scholarly lecture, as for example it did in nineteenth century England. By 1990, when I left Belgrade to return to Cambridge, thinking back over the numerous poetry festivals

---

[37] They also instilled a heroic warrior-ethos into each one of the various traditions of ethnicity in the Balkans. This surfaced powerfully among all sides in the wars that broke up Yugoslavia in the 1990s. See 'Edge-dwellers, Bandits and Heroes' 113-116 above. For Edith Durham's changing views on these poems, see 79, 236 and 237 above.

[38] For a study of interpretations of Dalmatia by Venetians and others, see Wolff.

[39] Respectively, in Serbian, Croatian and Bosnian, and Macedonian.

and readings that I'd regularly attended in Yugoslavia in that decade, I had the vivid sense that the particular qualities of energy that writers such as Kanitz, Evans, Durham, Parry and Lord had experienced directly from the oral tradition were still simmering under the surface.

That was one reason, among many, why I was sad to leave.

ᔕ

It's October 2005. I'm due to travel to Serbia once again for the Belgrade Writers' Meeting. I receive a message asking me to arrange my trip so that I can stay an extra few days. To my surprise, I'm told that I'm to receive an international award, entitled the *Povelja Morave* ('Morava Charter'),[40] for Vera Radojević's Serbian translation of *In a Time of Drought*.[41] The prize is to be presented in Mrčajevci. For English-speakers, this name is a tongue-twister. Its pronunciation is something like *Myrrh-cha-yev-tsi*. I learn that the name belongs to a village near the town of Čačak (*Chachak*) in central Serbia. It has a population of around 3,000. My prize will be in one category among several. Others will be for a well-known Serbian poet, a children's poet, a local amateur poet, and local children. I've never got to learn exactly how and why this village has decided to award an annual suite of poetry prizes.

I'm driven to Mrčajevci from Belgrade in a car with my friend Slobodan Rakitić,[42] who is to receive the Serbian poet's prize. The drive takes under two hours. The formal parts of the event will be in the local elementary school. On arrival, we enter the school dining hall, where around a hundred adults of all ages sit at long trestle tables, eating lunch, drinking, and smoking. I recognise some of them from the Writers' Club in Belgrade, but have the impression that many of them are local and would have attended this school in childhood. The long-buried schoolboy in me reawakens. It occurs to me that they wouldn't have been allowed to smoke in this hall then.

The prize-giving ceremonies take place in the main hall, which also serves as a gym, with a basketball-basket and a pair of vertical wooden-slatted climbing ladders fixed to each end-wall. These walls are gloss-

[40] Named after the River Morava. Vesna Goldsworthy has kindly reminded me that this award involves the engraving of prize-winners' names on a local monument, the *Pesnička Stena* ('Poets' Stone').

[41] See RB 2004.

[42] For a short sketch, see 393-394 below.

painted: the place looks like any primary school in England. Much to my own surprise, I manage an impromptu speech in Serbian. The atmosphere is cheerful. Nobody seems to mind my mistakes.

Then we're driven to a grassy slope outside the village, where a large porker has been roasted on a spit. Everyone is treated to yet another large meal, sitting on benches and trestle tables in a packed marquee, accompanied by a pair of accordion players singing *stare gradske pesme* (Old Town Songs), after a local choir dressed in folk costume has delivered traditional songs in plaintive Balkan harmonies.

Once the meal's over, everyone goes outside again. Then, spontaneously, people cluster into small gaggles to listen to one another reciting poems. There's no order or organisation about this procedure and people take it in turns to start reciting as the mood takes them. I can't resist joining in with an English poem. I don't remember which one, perhaps a Shakespeare sonnet, something like that. This foreign poem is accepted along with all the others as part of the fun, even though few if any understand it. Here, then, are the grass roots of Serbian poetry. As of old, poems are recited, not just read. *And still, poetry belongs to anyone, everyone.*

ဖ

Just as in the plastic arts, especially sculpture and architecture, in Serbian poetry and fiction from the late 1940s to the late 1980s, there was a huge flowering. At one time or another, at the Belgrade *Writers' Meetings*, there was the opportunity to meet Serbian and Yugoslav writers of the stature of Ivo Andrić, Miloš Crnjanski, Desanka Maksimović, Oskar Davičo, Vasko Popa, Meša Selimović, Miodrag Pavlović, Danilo Kiš and Ivan V. Lalić, to name but a few.

Reciprocally, distinguished writers from other countries were drawn to Serbia. Some of those who attended the Belgrade meetings included (in alphabetical order): Ernesto Cardenal, Michel Deguy, Allen Ginsberg, William Golding, Günter Grass, Robert Graves, Lars Gustafsson, Ferenc Juhász, Arthur Miller, Czesław Miłosz, János Pilinszky, Edoardo Sanguineti, Josef Škvorecký, Aleksandr Solzhenitsyn, Wole Soyinka and John Updike. Moma Dimić's anthology of guest-writers who had attended the Belgrade *Meetings* in its first forty years contains poems by around three hundred and fifty writers from all over the world, translated by around one hundred and fifty Serbian contributors.[43]

---

[43] Dimić 2005.

In 1982, when I first attended the Belgrade *Meeting*, one of the great points of excitement was the opportunity to meet writers from countries that were still behind the Iron Curtain. It was a particular pleasure, for example, to meet the Russian poet Vyacheslav Kupriyanov, and to be able to invite him to the Cambridge Poetry Festival. At that time, meeting a Russian writer on simple, equal and friendly terms seemed little short of miraculous.

ᔕ

My first invitation to the Belgrade *Writers' Meeting* came about through an unexpected offer of reciprocity. In 1973, I founded the first international Cambridge Poetry Festival, a large biennial event that ran from 1975 to 1985.[44] In 1981, Vasko Popa was our guest.[45] After meeting him in Cambridge, and following an unexpected invitation from the British Council to lecture on a seminar for English language teachers in Arandjelovac, in the summer of 1982 I visited Serbia for the first time. At the conclusion of that seminar, I took the opportunity to spend a few extra days in Belgrade, staying at the Hotel Slavija. I rang Vasko, who invited me for a coffee and promptly introduced me to his friend, the poet and editor Ivan Gadjanski.[46] Together, they asked if I might like to come to the International Writers' Meeting that autumn. This was the first time I'd heard of this event. As I'd hugely enjoyed my stay in Arandjelovac and was curious to find out more about Serbia, I immediately said yes.

That was the beginning of my immersion in Serbian literary life. My return that October turned out to be the first of many occasions when I spent time in Belgrade, meeting writers from Serbia and other countries, giving poetry readings, and running bilingual poetry writing workshops for children and teenagers.[47] The Belgrade *Writers' Meeting* and other similar events yielded a wealth of new acquaintances, some of whom later became close friends. The atmosphere was usually stimulating, surprising, and full of new information, and always richly hospitable and convivial. This was a highlight in the calendar that I always looked forward to. Over the years, I also persuaded my hosts to invite several other poets: Walter Perrie, John

44 See RB 2009a.

45 In 1983, Ivan V. Lalić also attended the Cambridge Poetry Festival; and in 1985, Miodrag Pavlović.

46 For memoirs on these two poets, see 314-316 and 317-322 below.

47 See 270-275 and 276-280 below.

Matthias, and Peter Russell (1921–2003) as well as the novelist Moris Farhi (1935–2019).

ᔕ

Arandjelovac in summer 1982 is buzzy, fresh and vibrant. There are concerts in the Sculpture Park and I'm impressed by the adventurousness of the town's modernist architecture. At the hotel where our course for language teachers takes place, there are parallel seminars in English, French, German and Russian. The Russian course attracts few Serbian participants, and the Russian lecturers, always besuited, over-formal and uncomfortable-looking, are closely watched over by accompanying political commissars to ensure they don't stray out of line. These people are so stiff they seem almost to parody a stale Stalinism.

By now, the large majority of Serbian teachers teach English. Many arrive with family-members, so people get together in the evenings for dances and other events, in a holiday atmosphere. I quickly make friends among some of the Serbian teachers and, after a request for suggestions for "evening activities" from my British Council host, an affable man on the point of retirement who sports a naval-style captain's beard and looks and speaks rather like the English actor James Robertson-Justice, but doesn't speak a word of any Slavonic language. I offer a poetry reading and he seems to accept this with some relief. Around eighty to a hundred people turn up in the hotel's largest conference room. I'm surprised at how many there are.

At its end, I ask if anyone has questions or comments. An elderly woman stands up and in perfectly enunciated English delivers these words: "Mr Burns, you will forgive my poor English accent. You have just read us your poem about walking with your children in an English garden, and remembering your Jewish father. I wish to say one thing." And here she pauses. "You have the soul of a Serb."[48] After delivering this bombshell of exquisitely courteous sweetness in my direction, she quietly sits down. Hairs quiver on my goose-pimpled arms. Nobody has ever addressed me in this way, in public or in private. "Who *are* these people," I think to myself, "who are capable of such directness, welling straight up from the depths?"

---

[48] I later learned that this woman, whose name I never found out, had studied in Oxford before the Second World War. The poem was 'May', which I'd recently completed. See *For the Living* (RB 2011a): 177-184.

That woman's words were the turning point. From that moment on, Serbia had me hooked.

ɞ

By contrast, Belgrade that October exudes an atmosphere of grand, dignified melancholy, epitomised for me by the city's magnificent autumnal plane trees, by my first exposure to *stare gradske pesme* (lit. 'old town songs') at the *Tri šešira* and *Ima dana* taverns in Skadarlija,[49] and by a long walk through Kalemegdan, which Rebecca West accurately describes as "the special glory of Belgrade and indeed one of the most beautiful parks in the world".[50] At 7 Francuska Street, headquarters of the Writers' Association, I make new friends among poets, especially Ivana Milankov, Duška Vrhovac, Adam Puslojić and Ratko Adamović. And I do all the sort of things that every newcomer to Belgrade does. I drink Turkish coffee in Trg Republike (Republic Square), saunter past bookstalls on Studentski Trg (Student Square), and stroll along Knez Mihailova, a pedestrian street in the heart of the old town. On its continued path into the park-fortress of Kalemegdan, I buy crunchy roasted chestnuts from a gypsy who stands tending her brazier alongside hawkers of pistachio nuts, nougat, raisins, cheap toys and lace. I walk to the high parapets overlooking the river-bank far below and survey the Sava emptying into the Danube, and watched gaggles of elderly men on park benches playing chess, arguing about moves, and mothers hovering over toddlers on tricycles and scooters.

ɞ

The structure of events at the *Writers' Meetings* was similar in the 1980s and 1990s to that of today. There was a good deal of variety between large and small events and formal and informal ones. I found all of them hugely interesting, all the more so because they disrupted many preconceptions and prejudices, and provided me with a stream of constantly new perspectives. Each year, writers were present from many different countries, from Morocco to Hungary, Italy to Israel, Algeria to Argentina, Syria to Spain, Cyprus to China, so there were always new people to meet and new

[49] Names of taverns: *Tri šešira*, 'Three Hats'; the name *Ima dana* is based on the title and first line of a well-known song in the *Stara gradske pesma* genre: "*Ima dana kada ne znam šta da radim*" ('There are days when I don't know what to do.').

[50] West, *op. cit.* 466.

things to learn. This was all the more exciting because I'd never met such an international spread of writers before.

Under the umbrella of the Serbian Writers' Association, the Belgrade *Meeting* was a loose-knit conglomeration of events, operating through the participations of many different organisations and venues, and spilling over into other Serbian cities. This variety has always been and still is one of the most invigorating features of the Belgrade *Meeting*. As at the best conferences of any kind, it has a blurry-edged quality, with the most valuable and memorable contacts often occurring either on the fringes and edges of formalised events, or as spin-offs, entirely outside them.

The typical pattern of the *Meetings* changed from one year to another. In the 1980s, after an informal evening reception at the Writers' Association at Francuska 7, there was a plenary meeting in the National Library, with simultaneous earphone-translations of speeches into French, Russian and English. Moving into the large hall, picking up my earphones, and twiddling the knobs between languages, for a moment or two I swelled with phoney self-importance, half-fantasising that I was some kind of *significant delegate*, able to make (or at least influence) global decisions, perhaps at the United Nations [...]. Topics for these plenary sessions provided templates for wide-ranging, free-flowing and apparently never-ending blue-sky discussion: for example, the myth of the culture hero; the literature of exile; the end of Utopia; poetry at the close of the twentieth century, and so on. Then a formal reception hosted by the Mayor of Belgrade in the Serbian *Skupština* (National Assembly) building. On the next day, separate, small round-table sessions in Serbian, Russian, French and English at 7 Francuska Street, each moderated by a Serbian writer. The final day involved another plenary session, at which these smaller discussions were reported back. And alongside more receptions and interspersed between these events, evening and daytime poetry readings at various sites in Belgrade, including venues like *Dom omladine* (House of Youth) and the Vuk Karadžić Library, and large open-air readings in Trg republike, Skadarlija, and Kalemegdan – all culminating in a marathon poetry reading at Kolarčev Popular University, during which every participant would deliver a poem. This was the only tedious event.

After these days in Belgrade, tours were organised to various towns in Serbia. Groups of writers, consisting of both Serbs and visitors, travelled together by bus, mini-bus or car, to deliver poetry readings at a wide variety of venues, varying year by year, and including Novi Sad, Sombor, Pančevo, Kruševac, Zaječar, Vršac, Smederevska Palanka, Kragujevac, Valjevo, Novi

Pazar (taking in the stupendous frescoes in the monasteries of Studenica and Sopoćani), and down the Ibar valley to Leposavić and Kosovska Mitrovica, returning via Raška. In different years, I went on one or other of most of these excursions. In this way, over the years, I had the chance to travel to parts of Serbia that otherwise I might never have visited. The scents and flavours of many of these places have surfaced in my poems, especially in the collection *Under Balkan Light*.

In the 1980s and 1990s, the Belgrade *Meeting* was scheduled in October, which meant that it coincided with 'the Great School Lesson' (the *Veliki školski čas*), which commemorates the 1941 Nazi massacre at Šumarice on the 21st of that month. So a bus trip to Kragujevac was incorporated into the overall programme. I first visited Kragujevac for that event in 1982. I remember a young German woman, a prose writer, weeping uncontrollably.

Šumarice would later play a deeply significant role for me, in the inspiration and formation of *The Blue Butterfly*.[51]

August 2013; revised, August-September and December 2019

[51] See 25-40 above.

Above: The festival roast
Below: Celebrating poetically
Mrčajevci, Central Serbia, October 11, 2005

Above: In the poets' marquee
Below: Impromptu poetry recitals
Mrčajevci, Central Serbia, October 11, 2005

The Belgrade Writers' Meeting in the wake of Slobodan Milošević

In 2013, my aim in writing the first draft of the previous piece was to document the history of the Serbian Writers' Association for publication on its website in Serbian and English. But fulfilment of that informal invitation never transpired, and even as I've embellished the essay since then and, six years later, have done more research, and added more material, the website still states: "*English version of web site is still under construction. Thank you for patience and understanding*" (*sic*). Writing this follow-up piece in 2019–2020, I'm conscious of a double need and desire: to celebrate the historical achievements of the Serbian Writers' Association and its October *Writers' Meeting*, but also to outline at least some aspects of what happened during Slobodan Milošević's rule and as a result of it; and, even if sketchily, to contextualise that story.

ൾ

Unsurprisingly, before the break-up of the Yugoslav Federation in the 1990s, every possible shade of political opinion could be found among writers in Serbia, just as it's likely to do at any time in any other country. But Milošević and his regime (1989–2000) at first eroded and eventually destroyed whatever cultural consensus there might have been, including any tacit agreement to disagree, just as they destroyed so much else of value. During the disastrous period of his leadership, the views, attitudes and positions taken by Serbian writers ranged from direct ideological opposition, through a tacit, uneasy acceptance, to dynamic, wholehearted and programmatic advocacy. The response of some writers may well have been an impossible wish for it all simply 'to go away', a longing for escape, and/or a sense of futility and depression, resulting in a kind of stunned silence, or even a silence that was self-imposed. But I don't believe many Serbian writers felt or believed that quietude or resignation was a viable option. I'm reminded of the attitude simultaneously expressed and contradicted by W. B. Yeats in 1915 in his poem 'On being asked for a War Poem', and especially of its opening lines: "I think it better that in times like these / A poet's voice be silent [...]."[52] Contradicted, simply because in claiming the prerogative of silence, Yeats actually broke silence, and did so with succinct yet devastating effect. To put it another way, in not being silent by the very act of writing this poem, *he silenced his own silence*.

In Serbia at the end of the twentieth century, it was hard, if not impossible, for any writer to stay under the radar, to retreat into privacy, to remain politically indifferent, and, less still, to try or pretend to be 'above it all'. As for the Serbian Writers' Association, it contained widely divergent attitudes and positions and, in the early to mid-1980s, it reflected a relatively wide range of opinions. But as that decade wore on, things changed, and this was marked by the Serbian nationalist poet Matija Bećković (b. 1939) being elected as the Association's President. He served from 1988 to 1992: that is, precisely during the years in which Yugoslavia collapsed. A supporter of Slobodan Milošević and propagandist for him, he took every possible opportunity to celebrate what he saw as the superior glories of Serbia, even to the extent of declaring his support for the Red Star football team (*Crvena zvezda*) at a time when some of its supporters were committing atrocities in Slavonia and Bosnia under the command of the gangster Arkan.[53] His administrative committee consisted of other nationalists. Also a leading member of the Serbian Academy of Sciences and Arts (*Srpska akademija nauka i umetnosti*, SANU), Bećković used both these roles to promote Serbian nationalism as actively as possible. In an astonishing outburst, at the second Serbian Unity Conference in Chicago in 1991, he scornfully dismissed the bombardment of Dubrovnik by saying, "It seems that if Hitler had sought refuge in Dubrovnik he would have been protected by UNESCO."[54]

---

[52] Yeats 175.

[53] Čolović 2000: 381.

[54] Quoted by Vujović 133, among similar statements by other Serbian writers at the time. Some of these were astonishingly vitriolic, and ethno-nationalist stereotyping turned into racist hatred: for example, the historian Radovan Samardžić, who was also a member of SANU:

> The situation is not dangerous for Dubrovnik. It is a prostituted city of hotel keepers visited by American grandmothers, British queers, stupid Frenchmen and German typists. We don't need the Allies because the US is corrupt, the English are stupid, the French are right-wing and Russians are poor. (*ibid.* 133)

Other nationalists included the novelist and political theoretician Dobrica Ćosić (1921–2014) and the novelist Vuk Drašković (b. 1946), both of whom became even more influential as politicians in the melee of Serbian politics in that period. Ćosić, like Bećković, was a member of SANU and was regarded as one of the main authors of its 1986 'Memorandum', which argued that the Serbs had long been discriminated against in the constitution of Yugoslavia. This document was instrumental in the rise of Slobodan Milošević.[55] As one of the latter's supporters, following the Croatian and Slovenian declarations of independence in 1992, Ćosić was fully rewarded. He became the first President of the rump Yugoslavia, the so-called 'Federal Republic of Yugoslavia' (SFRY). As for Drašković, he founded his National Serbian Renewal Party (*Srpski Pokret Obnove*, SPO) in January 1990. A non-Communist, he opposed Slobodan Milošević, but was no less a Serbian nationalist and, at the time, was just as responsible for fomenting inter-ethnic conflict as any other leading Serbian intellectual. In the same year, he was reported as saying: "The Serb people are close to finding out something which is true, that the main indicator of all conspiracies against the Serb people and in the Balkans is the Zagreb Kapitol [the residence of the Catholic Archbishop]."[56]

ဢ

In my time in Serbia, I avoided people such these. On the other hand, they wouldn't have been interested in meeting me either – an internationalist and a foreigner. I had many writer-friends in Serbia, of various shades of opinion, from communists to devoted conservative Christians. I recognised them all, broadly speaking, as humanists and internationalists, whose world-views had been shaped, as mine had been, not only by national and linguistic identities, but in the broader traditions of European literature, culture and history. And as far as my friends were concerned, whatever their particular backgrounds or individual political leanings, at the time I believed that by and large they saw themselves simultaneously as patriotic Serbs, as loyal Yugoslavs, and as 'European', with all the connotations implied by each of those broadly brushed identity-markers. In retrospect,

---

[55] For a detailed study of the role of SANU in perpetrating ethno-nationalism, see Milosavljević.

[56] Marković 602-603, quoting *Duga*, No. 432, April–May, 1990. For Drašković's volatile shifts of mood and policy, see also Stojanović 463-465. At one time he had his own militia.

I believe that my own predilections led me to make friends with political moderates and with advocates of peace and tolerance. This was a matter of elective affinity. However, I now also realise that more of these writers were Serbian nationalists than I recognised at the time.

For those who lived to witness the break-up of the Yugoslav Federation in chaos and barbarism, the collapse was all the more shameful and shocking. That period of political confusion was also one of soul-searching, of moral stress, of psychological trauma, for anyone who went through it. I believe it's no accident that during Milošević's rule, as well as immediately before it, and in its wake, many fine writers and intellectuals in Yugoslavia died, and some of them well before their time.[57]

Although I came to be moderately well-informed about Serbian literary politics when I lived in Belgrade in the late 1980s, after returning to England in 1990 I knew I was no longer up-to-date and, from a distance, struggled to understand what was going on.

ᔓ

When it comes to international relations, it's a well-established practice for cultural friendship-visits to precede political rapprochement. In earlier times, invitations that were issued to foreign writers to attend the annual October Writers' Meeting had often themselves been indicators of which way political winds might be blowing. For example, in 1987, for the first time since the foundation of the event in 1964, an Israeli writer, Jakov Orland, was on the guest-list. In the following October, I met two more Israeli writers, Abraham Hus and Aviv Ekroni. These visits turned out to be forerunners of a political rapprochement between Serbia and Israel. By contrast, six years earlier, in summer 1982, as I'd walked from the Hotel Slavija along Marshal Tito Boulevard to Terazije, to drink a coffee with some of the new friends I'd met in Arandjelovac, on my way I nearly got caught up in a large and noisy demonstration in support of the Palestinian Liberation Organisation, which was going on in *Trg Marksa i Engelsa* (Marx and Engels Square).[58] This demo had clearly been officially sanctioned and

---

[57] See also 311-312 below.

[58] Renamed Trg Nikole Pašića (Nikola Pašić Square) in 1992. Dubravka Ugrešić describes the identical syndrome in Zagreb, and points out that changes in place-names during and in the wake of regime transition, inculcate memory loss and disorientation:

possibly actively approved.[59] But only seven years later, the presence of Israeli writers marked a radical shift in official policy and popular attitudes.

At the time, this kind of deep-layered government influence seemed unremarkable, and typical of the behaviour of many countries. I saw this as a sign of changes in international affiliations.

But when I attended the Writers' Meeting in October 1999 for the first time since my departure from Yugoslavia in 1990, a new, more arrogant and openly interfering kind of political pressure was in stark evidence. Along with other international guests, I was invited to meet the then-Minister of Culture, a Milošević stooge whose name I don't remember, for what turned out to be an opportunity for him to exploit his TV exposure with us for crude propaganda. This was a deeply unpleasant experience.

ꕥ

More than a decade earlier, in the mid-1980s, after accepting several return invitations, I gradually learned about the complexity and variety of ethnicities and languages in Yugoslavia. Even before the collapse of the Federation, I'd come to realise that one of the drawbacks to the Belgrade October Meeting was that while I'd regularly met Montenegrin and Macedonian writers at its events, as well as Bosnians from both Orthodox and Muslim backgrounds,[60] I very rarely came across a Slovene, and *never* a single Croatian or Albanian-speaking writer from Kosovo. Despite the 'external' internationalism of the *Writers' Meetings*, these absences from other parts of Yugoslavia struck me as being odd, and a pity, even then. Nor did our hosts ever convey any sense at these meetings that anyone might have been 'missing'. A hypothetical comparison might have been

---

> The streets have changed their names: the Square of the Victims of Fascism has become the Square of our Great Croatian Forbears, Republic Square is Ban Jelačić Square [...] Never mind, I'll learn, I think, but I notice with horror that I can't remember either the new or the old names. And I become very anxious: I'll have to learn, I'll buy a new map of the city. I'll learn the streets, because if I need something, a doctor, or a lawyer, how will I find them [...] (Ugrešić 107)

[59] "The Yugoslav foreign ministry at the time was headed by a Muslim who was also the leader of a powerful pro-Arab lobby. In addition, the Yugoslav government had many investments in Iraq and Libya, and therefore didn't wish to alienate these countries. Officials in Belgrade continued to demonstrate their solidarity with the Arabs." (Abadi 300)

[60] For example, Andjelko Vuletić and Izet Sarajlić, see 403-406 below.

a poetry festival in Dublin or Limerick, say, avoiding sending invitations to Protestant poets from Belfast or Derry, and excluding any guests from England other than fellow-Catholics.

A group defines its literary culture in reciprocal contra-distinction to those of its neighbours, even when the same or a similar language is spoken. Like any form of affiliation, literary identity is social: relative, contrastive and often oppositional. Nor is contiguity a guarantee of neighbourliness. When there's actual or potential conflict between groups, the usual pattern is for foreigners from countries that are relatively distant geographically to be given safe hospitality and warm welcome, and even to be allowed some degree of inclusion, but not the perceived *others* who live adjacently, whose proximity might signal potential threat or danger if they were to be invited to come *too* immediately close. Undeniable subliminal vulnerabilities and insecurities surface in antagonism.

☙

Writing as early as 1996, Drinka Gojković, editor of the literary journal *Mostovi* ['Bridges'] and an authoritative and astute Serbian critic of the Serbian Writers' Association, introduces her essay on its changing role in the 1980s and 1990s, from upholding free speech to nationalistic propagandising, as follows:

> [T]he Association [...] managed to run the gamut between two completely opposite poles of political involvement [...] at the beginning of the 1980s, offering resistance to the ideology of the old government. The end of the 1980s found it helping the new government to put into place a new ideology. This was a complete surprise: the energy of democratic changes was replaced by an eruption of nationalism.[61]

And she concludes:

> Instead of apportioning blame, it is more useful to talk about responsibility for the public word. The *anti-modern, anti-intellectual, anti-literary trend* in the AWS (Association of Writers of Serbia] increased, by means of its victim ideology, the field of irrationality, in which various forms of aggression became psychologically acceptable and politically 'inevitable' and 'justified'. That this did not happen in Serbia alone does not diminish the damage done by its main cultural institutions. They are a salient part of the picture of Yugoslavia's collapse.[62]

[61] Gojković 327.

[62] *ibid.* 346-347.

The wars that broke up Yugoslavia involved savage brutality and atrocity. As a result, whatever mutual acceptance, tolerance and reciprocity had existed before it among writers living in different republics was bound to decrease dramatically. Twenty years later, I don't think this acute suspicion and distrust has shifted markedly towards literary neighbourliness, other than possibly among younger writers. There are contemporary exceptions, such as the annual *PEN International* Meeting in Bled, Slovenia, directed by the poet Ifigenija Simonović, which has consistently maintained its multicultural and ecumenical vision.[63] And perhaps the movement for *rapprochement* that has begun to emerge in the wake of the 'Declaration of the Common Language' in 2016 will also have positive results.[64] A recent outcrop of literary events with similar aspirations includes the two-day *Think Tank Town Festival* in the south-Serbian town of Leskovac, launched in 2007 by novelist and essayist Saša Stojanović, founding editor of *Think Tank* magazine in 2005, who was imprisoned in 1994, for his opposition to Milošević.[65]

However, movements such as these, which aim to rebuild genuine pan-Balkan and international understanding among intellectuals, remain in opposition to prevailing centripetal tendencies. They run directly counter to the official educational policies of governments in Bosnia-Herzegovina and Croatia, which for the last twenty years have aimed to inculcate linguistic differences in both grammar and vocabulary and so to render what had been accepted as 'Serbo-Croat' or 'Serbo-Croatian' as

---

[63] In 2019, the guest of honour at this annual conference was the Serbian poet Dragan Jovanović Danilov.

[64] See 63, n. 13 above and the *Wikipedia* entry on this declaration, which has been signed by many leading writers from Bosnia and Hercegovina, Croatia, Montenegro and Serbia, and thousands of citizens. The declaration grew out of the activities of the 'alternative' Belgrade literary festival *Krokodil*, founded in 2009. See Milekić (online) and the next footnote.

[65] Email from Saša Stojanović, January 8, 2020: "The aim of this festival," he writes, is "to bring together creative people who have their lost own selves" and "to promote creative individuality and present the finest aspirations and achievements of Balkan and world literature". He also cites several other similar events involving young writers: in Serbia, the *Festival poezije mladih* ('Youth Poetry Festival', Zaječar), *Na pola puta* ('Halfway', Užice), *Krokodil* ('Crocodile', Belgrade) and *Kikinda Short* (Kikinda); in Croatia, the Pula Book Fair; and in Bosnia-Herzegovina, *Dani književnog kluba* ('Literary Club Days', Mostar), *Zeničko proleće* ('Zenica Spring', Zenica), *Cum grano salis* ('With a Pinch of Salt', Tuzla), and the *West Herzegovina Fest* (Široki Brijeg).

both despised and obsolete. The same kind of investment in nationalistic separatism prevails too in all religious authorities in the region: Catholic, Muslim and Serbian Orthodox. The Jewish population is far too small to have had any significant effect.[66]

ഗ

In 1987, I walk around the large annual Belgrade Book Fair at the *Sajam* (exhibition centre) with the novelist Hanifa Dalipi. At her suggestion, we stop at an enclosure where a publisher from Kosovo is displaying books written in Albanian, and look around. Apart from us and the Kosovan writer-publisher from Priština who's manning it, it's empty. We see no-one else come anywhere near it.

ഗ

Under Milošević, the situation of the Serbian Writers' Association embedded an insoluble contradiction. On the one hand, it had a tradition of freedom of speech, tolerance and internationalism, which reached its acme in the early 1980s, a time which, fortunately for me, coincided with my first visits to Yugoslavia. On the other, as a state-sponsored and state-financed organisation, it was tacitly expected to support the status quo. Previously, combining these two functions hadn't appeared to be especially problematic, because the status quo had meant acceptance of a relatively stable Serbian Republic within a relatively stable Yugoslav Federation. In 1981, the Association spoke up for Gojko Djogo, a Serbian poet who was imprisoned for criticising Tito.[67] This was a *cause célèbre* at the time, but by the 1990s, the Yugoslav Federation had ceased to exist in all but name, and in the wake of its collapse, while the Serbian government itself grew increasingly extremist, exploitative and corrupt, many Serbian intellectuals whose perspectives were broadly humanistic and internationalist – and possibly also *jugonostalgik* (nostalgic for the former Yugoslav Federation) – gradually but inevitably came to view the Writers' Association itself as a source of crude nationalism and to deem it as directly complicit with corruption and supportive of inhumane and repressive policies. Many grew to hate and despise it and to find its role pernicious, obsolete and irrelevant.

---

[66] To comprehend these patterns from a psycho-social perspective, C. J. Jung's theory of the shadow-archetype is relevant and helpful.

[67] See Gojković 327-328.

Among Serbian writers, strains led to cracks and, eventually, to schism. In the later years of that decade, if there was any factor that continued to exert any appearance of unity among intellectuals, it was opposition to the bombing of Serbia by NATO, which started on March 24, 1999. In that year and the two that followed, my aim as a sympathetic foreigner was consistently to criticise the NATO bombing and support cultural life in Serbia, while in no way supporting or condoning Milošević.[68]

In the wake of a series of large demonstrations in Belgrade in 1996 and 1997, usually referred to as the *studentski protesti*, and a huge one in October 2000 when the parliament building was stormed, Milošević was toppled by his own people.[69] In March 2001 he was transferred to the international court at The Hague.

In the same year, a group of Serbian writers finally and formally split off from the Serbian Writers' Association. The divorce was bitter and rancorous. A breakaway group was formed, which included some of my good friends, including the poets Ivana Milankov and Jelena Lengold. They and others set up an alternative association, the *Srpsko književno društvo* or SKAD (Serbian Literary Society), which was legally registered in 2001. This name is almost identical to that of Serbia's very first literary association,[70] founded nearly a century before, in 1905.

ᔓ

As a result, today Serbia has two competing literary associations. In a democracy, there's no reason why various literary organisations, reflecting different viewpoints, shouldn't exist alongside one another, whether amicably or not. Controversy can be creative; diversity, healthy; variety, interesting; and multiplicity, productive. But in Serbia, while some of the wounds of the Milošević era may have healed, individual memories are still scarred and sore. And while there have been some rapprochements, and many individual writers have friends in both clubs, I don't see any likelihood of the two associations joining together again, or needing to do so.

The reality is that there's no equivalent today of the one single literary organisation in Belgrade that somehow managed to bring together all the best writers between the very early 1960s and the mid to late 1980s.

---

[68] See 297ff below.

[69] See Makić, *Foto Dokumenti*, and RB 1999a.

[70] See 229 above.

Whatever the future holds for the two associations and for international festivals in Belgrade, I know I was lucky to have experienced Serbian literary life at its best and to have attended the international *October Meeting* towards the end of that extraordinary period.

September 2019–January 2020

A Note on 'Poetry Autumn' in Smederevo

Smederevo's *Pesnička jesen* ('Poetry Autumn') is another major Serbian literary festival.[71] It was inaugurated in 1970, six years after the Belgrade 'Writers' Meeting'. Smederevo is an ancient city of around 100,000 inhabitants on the Danube. In 1430–1439 and in 1444–1459, it served as the last capital of the independent Serbian state, immediately before the Ottoman conquest of the country, which lasted for four centuries.

In recent years, while the Belgrade event has been in decline, Smederevo's *Poetry Autumn* has gradually become the most important poetry event in Serbia. Held annually in October, this international festival began in 1970, shortly after the poet Risto Vasilevski (b. 1943) moved to the city with his family. Born on the borders of Serbia, Macedonia and Albania, Vasilevski writes in Serbian and Macedonian. Following his arrival, he gathered around himself a group of writers, who together founded the Smederevo Literary Society. Under its auspices, and working with an organising committee, he quickly set up and directed this annual event.

At the outset, like the *Struga Poetry Evenings* in Macedonia, and probably influenced by its success, the Smederevo *Poetry Autumn* was pan-Yugoslav. Gradually, it became international, and since that time it has hosted more than 500 poets from more than fifty countries. From the mid-1980s to 2020 the event was directed by the Serbian poet Goran Djordjević, a member of the original committee of 1970 while still a secondary school pupil. The five-day-long programme now includes everything one could wish for in a poetry festival: readings by home and international poets, discussions, performances of classical music and folksong, a large poetry performance for and including children, visits by poets to schools, and events for the disabled. Under the stamp of *Meridijani* ['Meridians'], it publishes between six and ten bilingual books annually, by poets attending the festival in that year. So far it has published around 150 poets in this series. Its prizes include the international *Golden Key*, as well as awards for

[71] Literally 'Poetic Autumn'; also translatable as 'Poets' Autumn'.

well-known Serbian poets, for first books by new poets, and for children's writers. Recipients of the *Golden Key* have included Manolis Anagnostakis, Homero Aridjis, Yves Bonnefoy, Erich Fried, Peter Handke, Mateja Matevski, Miodrag Pavlović and Stevan Raičković. In 2009, a prize for translation was established, in memory of the Serbian poet and translator, Zlatko Krasni.[72] Goran Djordjević, who directed this festival for thirty years, retired in 2020. In 2021 Miljan Guberinić took over, assisted by Marina Milenković. The Festival celebrated its fiftieth anniversary in 2019.

My only criticism of the event is that, just as at the Belgrade Writers' Meeting and, I suspect, all other events of this kind in Serbia, one still isn't likely to meet a Croatian or Slovenian poet.

ᔓ

In the 1980s and 1990s, I had several opportunities to visit Smederevo and to present poems there. On October 20, 1983, my reading was introduced by Ivan V. Lalić in the Hall of Culture. Afterwards, Ivan, his English translator Francis Jones, the novelist Hanifa Dalipi and I walked on the battlements of the medieval fortress, with its commanding view of the Danube. Images from that experience stayed with me and resurfaced years later in the poem 'On the qualities of light in the Balkans'.[73] At the 2012 Belgrade *Meeting*, I read this poem in memory of Ivan at a reading at Kolarčev University in Belgrade. A prose-poem of mine, 'Fish soup', is also located in an experience in Smederevo.[74] In 2017, I returned to take part in the forty-eighth *Poetry Autumn*. In the same year, with Vera Radojević, I translated a short book by the Serbian poet Petar Pajić (1935–2017) and published a bilingual book of my own poems, also translated by Vera,[75] both in the *Meridijani* series. I also attended Maja Herman Sekulić's launch and reading of *Our Lady of Vincha* in a performance on the fortress battlements.[76]

Smederevo occupies a special place in my affections. I think of the city as one of the main 'sites' of the qualities that I image as 'Balkan light'.

August 2019, April 2021

---

[72] For my memoir on Jan Krasni, see 382-383 below.

[73] RB 2011d: 34-35.

[74] *ibid.* 33.

[75] RB 2017c.

[76] See 206 above.

PART 5

A LIVING EMBROIDERY

The three pieces presented in this short selection on education and culture are included mainly for their documentary and historical interest.

In the 1970s, and 1980s, before I lived in Belgrade, and in the 1990s after my return to Cambridge, I was active in running poetry workshops for children and teenagers in English primary and secondary schools, as well as in training teachers at educational centres. 'Chains of Freedom' (1984), which I wrote for the *Times Educational Supplement*, records the first bilingual writing workshop of this kind. It took place at the Centre for Foreign Languages, Belgrade, thanks to its Director, Branka Panić. At that time, the idea of running bilingual poetry workshops for children and teenagers was itself original. From the points of view of language teaching and acquisition, cultural transmission, and encouragement of children to accept and value imaginative thinking, the experiment was successful, and highly popular with both pupils and teachers. This event provided a blueprint for similar sessions in other countries too; and in Serbia itself, it led to the tour of central area of Serbia in the following year (1985), mentioned in 'A Synchronistic Experience in Serbia'.[1] Between 1982 and 1989, as well as on later visits, I ran teacher training workshops for teachers in Serbia, Croatia, Slovenia and Macedonia; and in subsequent years, a number of Yugoslav teachers took up some of these classroom approaches.[2]

The second piece, 'Such Stuff as Dreams' (1992), presents two practical and adaptable classroom creative writing games, with examples, which can be used to teach literacy skills, verbal inventiveness, emotional self-confidence, and trust in one's own imagination, to children and adults alike, whether writing in their native language or learning a foreign language. Being simple in structure, these are easy to translate into many languages other than English. They're one category of creative writing

---

[1] See 25-35 above.

[2] These teacher-training workshops took place at seminars on the island of Brač, and in Maribor, Belgrade, Skopje, Split and Zagreb, the first four of which were organised by the British Council in co-operation with Yugoslav organisations. I also ran numerous workshops for children and teenagers in Belgrade, Čačak, Kragujevac, Maribor, Split and Tršić, organised by Yugoslav teachers and their schools. The publisher Dečje novine sponsored some of the Serbian events.

activities, among many others that I've either invented or borrowed and adapted. The short poems here resulting from the games are formulaic but, I think, effective.

ᔓ

When living in Belgrade, I also occasionally sent news-items and cultural reports to *The Jewish Chronicle* in London. Ephemeral though these were, I include one here, 'Jewish Exhibition in Belgrade' (1989), mainly because its focus on philo-Semitism counterbalances the extensive record of persecution of Jews in Yugoslavia under the Nazis and Ustaše during the Second World War. The mutual importance of the Balkans in Jewish history, and vice-versa, can scarcely be underestimated. Here are three examples.

First, the so-called Sarajevo *Haggadah* is a medieval Hebrew masterpiece, "handwritten on bleached calfskin and illuminated in copper and gold".[3] Written to accompany the *Seder*, the celebratory meal that opens the Passover festival, and originating in Spain around 1350, this book is believed to have been taken out of the Iberian Peninsula by Sephardic Jews on their way into exile, following their expulsion by Queen Isabela I of Castile and King Ferdinand II of Aragon in 1492.[4] The volume found its way to Sarajevo, where there was a strong Sephardic community until it was all but wiped out by the Croatian *Ustaše* during the Second World War.[5] During the war, the book was carefully hidden. A facsimile edition was co-published in Sarajevo and Belgrade in 1983, edited by the Serbian-Jewish Hebraic scholar Eugen Verber, who gave me a copy in 1989.[6] Following the Dayton Accord of 1995, which effectively ended the three-year-long Bosnian war, Bosnian Muslims and Bosnian Serbs wrangled over where the *Haggadah* should be housed. In 1998, the Bosnian Serbs argued that it should be exhibited for one third of each year in Banja Luka, the capital of Republika Srpska. In 1998, The leader

[3] See 'Sarajevo Haggadah', *Wikipedia*, for the book's fascinating history. There's a double error on this page, however, which states that the book was published in Ljubljana in 1985. As my copy of this edition attests, it was co-published in Sarajevo and Belgrade and printed in Ljubljana in 1983.

[4] See 'Alhambra Decree', *Wikipedia*; and also 326 below.

[5] See also 388ff below.

[6] See the memoir on Eugen, 323ff below.

of the Sarajevo Jewish Community, Jakob Finci,[7] comments:

> The *Haggadah* is proof of the multi-ethnicity of Bosnia. It is a testament that even in [the] worst times, other people's values were not destroyed.[8]

As a second example: on *Yom Kippur*, or the Day of Atonement (September 17, 1676), and shortly after his fiftieth birthday, the self-proclaimed Jewish 'Messiah', Sabbatai Zevi, died in Ulcinj on the Adriatic coast of Montenegro.[9] Ten years previously, he'd converted to Islam. Thanks to the apparently paradoxical interpretations of the Kabbalah that his unusual and lifelong patterns of behaviour explained and justified to his followers, this public act of apostasy surprisingly served to convince them all the more seriously of his authenticity. His extraordinary life-story, thoroughly explored in Gershom Scholem's mammoth-sized biography,[10] marks a turning point in the long history of Jewish mysticism. What Scholem doesn't emphasise, however, is that the contrarieties and contradictions of Zevi's life-story are typical of Balkan history itself, especially vis-à-vis the effects of Ottoman rule, and the constantly shifting intersections and blurred borderlines between ethnicities and religions throughout the region.

A third equally fascinating aspect of later Jewish history in the Balkans is the life, work and influence of the Sephardic rabbi of Zemun, Judah Alkalai or Alkalay (1798–1878), who was born in Sarajevo and died in Jerusalem.[11] He became one of the prime instigators of the international Zionist movement, which itself drew inspiration from the Kabbalah, and in particular from the apocalyptic and millenarian flights of hope and projection that had found earlier expression in the Sabbatian cult.[12] Zemun, which was one of the frontiers of the Austro-Hungarian Empire,

---

[7] Finci would have run for the Presidency of Bosnia and Hercegovina had it not been for a discriminatory flaw in the post-war constitution that was foolishly overlooked in the Dayton Accord. This didn't allow Jews to be considered as eligible – a major American and NATO-sponsored gaffe, considering that the aim of the Accord was to ensure inter-ethnic and inter-religious tolerance. See 'Jakob Finci', *Wikipedia*.

[8] See Tanner.

[9] Known as Ulqin in Albanian and Dolcigno in Italian, on the coast of modern Montenegro, 65 kms from the Albanian border. See Scholem 1973: 917.

[10] Scholem 1973 [1957].

[11] I'm grateful to Jonathan Boulting for pointing this out to me.

[12] See Scholem 1978: 376 (index).

lies on the Danube and is separated from Belgrade by the River Sava. I spent a year living there in 1989–1990.

ꙮ

These three stories in turn suggest two more general recurring themes in this book. First, they're typical examples of the vitality of permeable border-zones, both generally and in the Balkans particularly, thanks to the greater opportunities provided by open access and ease of movement for the cross-fertilisation and interbreeding of 'strains' in such areas, including the ecologies of genes, myths, traditions, customs, and languages.

Second, from the seventeenth century onwards, as the Ottoman empire grew increasingly decadent, millenarian tendencies in the Balkans developed not only among Jews but also among Christians and even within Islam itself. These various millenarian beliefs and movements were underlying factors in the formation of ideologies that eventually materialised in the making of new nations.[13]

ꙮ

The final piece in this section, 'A Living Embroidery: English Teaching and Cultural Contacts in Yugoslavia' (1992) was written in Cambridge in late 1991, soon after the end of my three-year stay in Belgrade. Since Yugoslavia had fallen apart by that time, the end of an era had also come for co-operative English language teaching across all its six republics, and I wanted to put on record at least some aspects of the international cultural practices that I'd known and been part of as a teacher and teacher-trainer in previous years.[14]

The 1970s and 1980s were exciting decades for English language teaching in Yugoslavia. Thanks to the enthusiasm of many teachers and professors throughout the country, and the active co-operation of Yugoslav educational institutions with the British Council and the USIA,[15] regular in-service teacher-training seminars, many of them residential, encouraged and developed effective techniques and modern approaches. This was all

[13] See 'Les Structures millénaristes sud-slaves aux XVIIe et XVIIIe siècles' in Stoianovich 1995, vol. 4: 1-13.

[14] Under the title 'Bare Ruined Choirs', a version of this piece also appeared in *The Times Educational Supplement*, as did 'Chains of Freedom'.

[15] United States Information Agency (1953–1999).

part of the wealth and variety of cultural visits and exchanges with English-speaking countries in that period. In my own case, my first interest in Yugoslavia was first sparked by involvement as a lecturer at seminars of this kind.

November 2018–January 2019; revised, September 2019

Chains of Freedom: An Experimental Poetry Workshop for Children in Yugoslavia

The scene: sixty youngsters, aged nine to fifteen, equipped with ball-points, paper, clip-boards. A scattering of adults, one of whom announces: "Welcome to the poetry workshop. Today you are the poets. It doesn't matter if you've never written a poem before. Anybody can learn to write a poem, just as anybody can learn to swim, type, make a cake or drive a car. You can get satisfaction from it yourself, and if you do it well, others can enjoy what you've written too. Your poem may live on after you, and be translated into other languages. The words may change but your poem lives on."

"Poems are news, your own news: not the kind you see on TV or read in the papers, but good news, even when full of pain or anger. Poems tell the truth: your truth, about you. In a poem, your words can have a special power. We're going to start by playing with words. Making poems begins with word-games, and expressing your thoughts and feelings clearly and honestly. These are the only rules. Ready?"

A buzz of voices, mingling interest, suspicion, resistance and curiosity, choruses a jaded, "Yes." The workshop is under way. This scene, or something like it, is familiar enough in Britain. Having a poet into school is increasingly valued by teachers as an aid in all aspects of language development. I recently had the chance to run a children's writing workshop in Yugoslavia, where the idea is catching on too.

It took place in Belgrade on October 20, 1984, fortieth anniversary of the city's liberation from the Nazis, during the period of the 21st annual 'International Meeting' of the Association of Serbian Writers. Set up by Branka Panić and her colleagues at the Centre for Learning Foreign Languages, in collaboration with a children's publisher, Dečje novine, the workshop lasted through a Saturday morning, and around sixty children came voluntarily.

I spoke in English, teachers took turns in translating, and the children wrote in Serbian. The dual-language situation was the main challenge and involved close teamwork and careful pre-planning with the teachers. They were experienced and enthusiastic, but this was as new to them as it was to me. Not knowing more than a few words in Serbo-Croatian meant I had to work blind much of the time, particularly when it came to children reading their poems aloud. Inevitably, this slowed things down, allowing less spontaneity than in a workshop when I could understand what the children were saying.

As it turned out, the novelty of being addressed by a foreign language speaker and being involved in consecutive translation was more fun than hindrance to the children, who generously forgave procedural hiccups, often to hoots of laughter. Many were interested because they were learning English at school.

In all other respects, I ran the workshop just as for a group of English children, starting with games to stimulate word-play, and moving gradually into imaginative exploration of deeper feelings and observation-exercises. Games included cut-ups, guided fantasy, mime, role-play, and work on simile and metaphor.

I had been worried that the whole thing would fall flat or misfire, but it worked. Responses of children and teachers alike were positive to an unexpected degree. In the following week, poems were polished and collected. Some turned out witty, subtle, delicate and heartfelt. Radio Belgrade's 'Children's Hour' part-recorded the workshop and based a programme on it, and some poems were published in a magazine. Here are two samples, translated by Branka Panić:

My city is like a birthday cake

My city is like the most beautiful cake
in the whole cuisine of world cakes,
Like the sweetest city,
Like the happiest man,
Like the funniest clown,
Like the prettiest girl,
like eternity.

Kosta Ladavac (aged 12)

My Fear

I fear for birds making their way south
I fear for birds which the north casts into ice chains
In the sun-golden desert sand hopes dry up
I fear for the world while hot tempests are born
I fear for my childhood while wars break out
I fear while before my eyes icy rains fall yet again
I fear before myself I cannot recognise in others
Bird I am, migrating from my south to someone else's north
Earth I am, from which shoots the rosy corn
I fear deep down to these roots branching human fears inside me

Tatjana Ignjatović (aged 13)

In English workshops, 'process not product' is usually the key. Turning out budding Bards can happen occasionally, and is a bonus when it does but not the main aim. Children quickly catch on, if they don't know already, that this is partly a power-game too: using language inventively can confer prestige and privilege simply by having this ability recognised by others. That's how most stand-up comics begin, and that's what street-wise means.

In a writing workshop, every child participating should be given the chance to have access to this power, and wield it. This is why I prefer to work with large mixed-ability groups. Children labelled 'unimaginative', 'difficult', or with some other such institutionalised put-down, often produce poems that shine with wit, commitment and warmth. Dylan Thomas and Alan Bleasdale were both just that kind of model bad boy, hating everything about school except the chance to write. In Britain, regional arts associations and education authorities are actively sponsoring Writers in Schools schemes now. We need more of them and more funding for them.

But the Belgrade dual-language experiment could have other implications too: that poetry is indeed a metalanguage, and the spirit of poetry truly international, transcultural, universal. By using such approaches in language-teaching, there might be practical applications. Students or pupils could be encouraged to explore the resources of their first language *through* the medium of the second. This could help strengthen bridges between source and target languages simply by the teacher according equal dignity to both. It could be particularly useful in teaching English as a Second Language and in schools with multicultural intake.

photos: Branislav (Vlaja) Vlajinić

Bilingual poetry workshops in Serbian schools, 1985
(above) Indoors (below) Outdoors

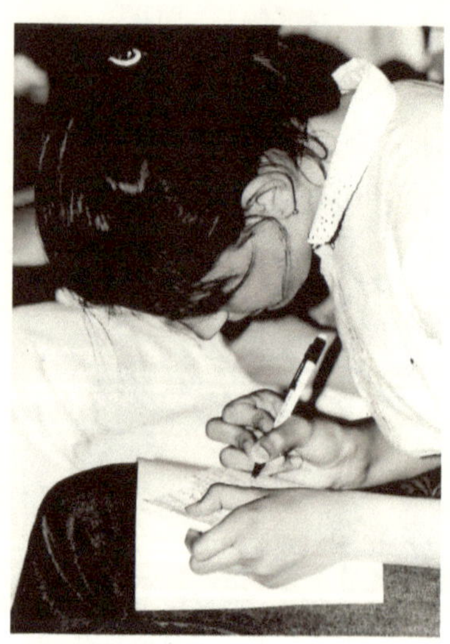

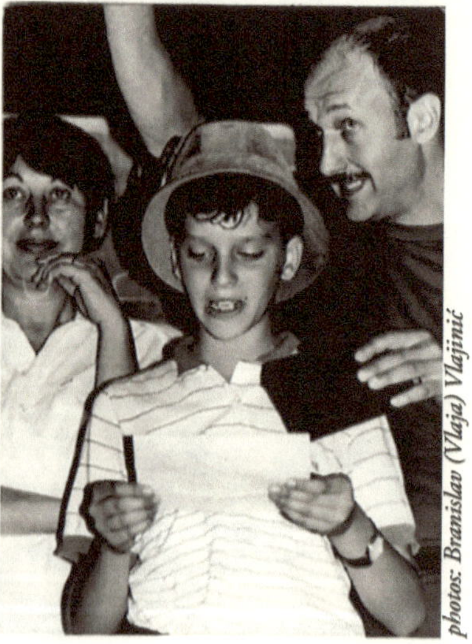

photos: Branislav (Vlaja) Vlajinić

Bilingual poetry workshops in Serbian schools, 1985
(above) Explaining (below left) Writing (below right) Performing

More workshops of this kind need to be tried out among communities whose languages have grammars very different from our own. An international anthology of children's poems emerging from such workshops could help link speakers of all languages. Poems demystify prejudice and deconstruct the very power they confer. They bind us in chains of freedom.

1984

Such Stuff as Dreams

It goes without saying that language teachers are *ipso facto* transmitters of consciousness. Whenever one gets bored, tired, discouraged, overworked, it's surely not a bad thing to remember that. *Without language: no thought, no ideas.* So in teaching a language, any language, we're necessarily teachers of imagination, fantasy and awareness too; and any techniques, methods, tricks, games, ruses, strategies, that can open up these areas, quickly, simply, and even for only a few minutes, need no further justification. Teachers may or may not wish to use them in the classroom though some can be learned effortlessly, to enliven the occasional lesson.

In the USA and Britain, creative writing workshops have become widely available over the last ten years or so to all age groups from six-year-olds to pensioners. In such workshops, spaces are opened up for the participants to range, dive, soar, into and through language, further, deeper, higher – and, maybe even more important, to enjoy the experience. These activities, of course, take place among native speakers. In Yugoslavia over the last four years, the teaching profession has been quietly pioneering creative writing workshops in a different context: that of English as a foreign language. This is a small but possibly significant achievement, and there's vast scope here.

Some of the work done on these occasions is presented below, together with tips, where relevant, on how to adapt the games used to your own classroom practice. Names of individual authors aren't given, first to emphasise that these were group activities, and second to respect the reticence and privacy of participants.

Clearly, there's a difference between reading such work in print, and that of 'vocational' writers, in verse or in prose. How then, as readers, are we to approach these texts? The following are suggestions only.

First, for pleasure. I believe that genuine writing talent is displayed here: sometimes in the occasional line or image, sometimes in a whole piece. The reason is simple*: language is part of being fully human.* To use language effectively isn't the privileged prerogative of so-called professional or vocational writers. Perhaps we need to erode the confidence barrier that most people hide behind, built on protestations such as "I'm not imaginative" and beliefs that writers, true writers, are 'born, not made'.

Second, as records of a process: linguistic, imaginative, intellectual, emotional. *Writing is an act that integrates and orders experience.* Each text is a record of such an act, and the reader may openly enter in too, if the text is even to a partial degree successful ('achieved', 'realised', 'communicative').

And third, for possible use as teachers.

Gifts for a New-born Child

An easy game to run, which appeals to all ages.
Humanistic aim: to contact and express feelings.
Linguistic aims: practice of simple structures and extension of vocabulary.
Poetic aim: to develop the faculty of fantasy, leading on to metaphor.

Technique: write the title, 'Gifts for a New-born Child' on the board, followed by the key phrase, 'I bring you'. Then ask "What would you bring a new-born child? Think of special things – exciting, impossible, magical." To get associations moving, simple everyday categories can be suggested, e.g. something to eat, to drink, to wear, to make music, to help the baby sleep; something precious; a line with a colour word in it; something mysterious; and so on. The first four poems that follow are by Yugoslav teachers of English. The fifth is by a native speaker of English, aged 7. The last two are by non-native speakers, aged 5 or 6, with rudimentary writing ability.

1. I bring you a moonbeam on my palm
I bring you a sunray in my eye
I bring you a fresh breeze with my smile
I bring you glittering stars in my hair

2. I bring you beauty to charm the world
I bring you wisdom to see through the dark
I bring you love to fill your heart
I bring you music to give you peace

3. I bring you the music of waters
I bring you the dance of the reed and the nightingale
I bring you the voice of silence
I bring you the heart of the
Happy Prince with diamond eyes

4. I bring you a shining star
to lead you through your life
I bring you a magic flying carpet
so you can fly high
I bring you a magic hat
to be invisible against the world

5. I'll bring you a magic wand
I'll bring you a magic clock
I'll bring you love
I'll bring you my favourite toy
I'll bring you a bleeding heart
I'll bring you all the things that I can
And the most love I can
I'll bring you the best thing in the world – Love!

6. I bring you a magic star
I bring you a magic golden marching suit
I bring you treasure
I bring you happy luck

I bring you a golden dress
I bring you a golden baby
I will bring you a happy toy
I will bring you a magic apple
I bring you a good life

'Who is he/she?' and 'If' games

Equally easy to run and adaptable to different levels. For the simpler version, write up the title, 'Who is he/she?' Then suggest simple categories: e.g. a plant (tree, flower); something to eat, drink, wear; a jewel; furniture; a building; a holiday; a machine; and so on. Categories can be varied as one wishes (e.g. according to topic work), but it's best to choose ones that (a) are general and (b) stimulate the imagination.

Students then describe somebody in terms of these categories. It's a good idea to ask students/participants to think of somebody they're particularly fond of: "Someone in your family, or a good friend, someone you feel warmly about." No need to press for 'romantic' attachments – these will come out of their own accord if they're in the participants' minds. Here, as always in running creative writing workshops, it's important to respect thresholds of privacy, and potential sources of shyness or embarrassment. Good results are never obtained by 'pushing' or 'pulling': people will automatically close up.

The first poem that follows is by a Yugoslav teacher of English. The second and third are by non-native speakers aged 6, in the first grade of school.

1. *Who is she?*

She is wheat in August
She is grass in spring
She is a rough sea in autumn
She is always a new present for my birthday
Who is she? She's my daughter!

2. *Who is he?*

He is a leafy tree
He is a red rose
He is Pepsi Cola
He is a toy whale
He is a gold chain around my neck .
He is a small cosy bed
Who is he?
He is my grandfather

3. *Who is she?*

She is a cherry tree
She is a red rose
She is orange juice
She is a peanut butter sandwich
She is a pretty sofa
She is a gold diamond
Who is she?
She is my sister

This game helps develop the ability to play with metaphor.

The more complex 'if' version practises the conditional mood, and encourages fantasy. Write up "If you / he / she were [...] you / he / she would be [...]" After 'were', list the chosen categories. The 'if" poems that follow are by Yugoslav teachers of English.

1. If you were a scarlet rose, you would be in my room
If you were an orange, you would be in my mouth
If you were a plane, I would be on you travelling to the moon
If you were a man I used to know, you would be in my heart

2. If she were a building, she would be a temple surrounded by
millions of roses
If she were a tree, she would grow as high as a mountain
If she were a flower, she would blossom throughout the year

3, If you were a tree, you would be a birch, wet from the rain,
and full of singing nightingales
If you were a bird, I would destroy all the cages in the world
If you were a flower, I would try to become the sun
If you were a building, I would plant a garden around you

1992

Jewish Exhibition in Belgrade

A major exhibition, 'Jews in Yugoslavia', has been opened here by the Mayor, Aleksandar Bakočević, and Lavoslav Kadelburg, president of the Federation of Yugoslav Jewish Communities, at the Belgrade Cultural Centre. Launched last year in Zagreb by the Museum Gallery Centre, the exhibition was described by the Museum's Director, Ante Sorić, as "the cultural event of the year". It then went to Sarajevo, and the organisers hope it will also travel to London, New York and Jerusalem.[16]

With its 23 sections, this first exhibition of its kind to have been shown in Yugoslavia, charts the history of Jews from archaeological evidence, through religious ceremonies, festivals and architecture, to secular customs, family life, education and the arts. It focuses on contributions to Yugoslav culture, and deals with the Holocaust, the struggle against the Nazis and the rebuilding of the country after the Second World War.

"Jews have lived in this country since Roman times," said Professor Vidoslava Nedomački, the exhibition co-ordinator. "It's a testament to the daily struggle of generation after generation, not only to survive, but to live with dignity."[17] A curious facet of this exhibition is the unique blending of Sephardi and Ashkenazi communities. Another, which is the greatest source of self-respect for Yugoslav Jews today, is the active role they played in the war. Before the 1941 Nazi invasion, 75,000 Jews lived in Yugoslavia. Of these, only 15,000 survived, over half of whom later emigrated to Israel. But 5,000 Jews fought as partisans or were members of resistance organisations, that is, six to seven per cent of the pre-war population, a marginally higher proportion than for the country as a whole. This not only helps explain the high regard accorded to Yugoslavia's Jewish community today, but also gives the lie to the myth that Jews in Nazi-occupied Europe simply went like lambs to the slaughter.

Belgrade 1989

---

[16] For the catalogue, see Goldstein.

[17] For detailed accounts of Jewish populations in the Balkans in the seventeenth and eighteenth centuries, including statistics, see Stoianovich 1992, vol. 2: 10-13.

A Living Embroidery: English Teaching and Cultural Contacts in Yugoslavia

> "In Yugoslavia," suggested my husband, smiling, "everybody is happy."
>
> "No, no," I said, "not at all, but…" The thing I wanted to tell him could not be told, however, because it was manifold and nothing like what one is accustomed to communicate by words. I stumbled on. "Really, we are not as rich in the West as we think we are. Or, rather, there is much we have not got which the people in the Balkans have got in quantity. To look at them you would think they had nothing. The people who made these dresses looked as if they had nothing at all. But if these imbeciles here had not spoiled this embroidery you would see that whoever did it had more than we have."[18]

So wrote Rebecca West of some hand-embroidered dresses which she had bought from peasant women in Macedonia in 1936, after her doctor had insisted they be washed and disinfected. Now, once again, the rich embroidery of peoples, languages, and customs that was Yugoslavia itself is ruined. As Rebecca West realised all too well, generalisations are odious, especially about Yugoslavia, country of contradictions.

When I first went there, as a British Council visiting lecturer on a summer seminar for teachers in 1982, these lay deep below the surface. In the following five years, I returned again and again, and then between 1987 and 1990, I worked as a *lektor*. I taught English, lectured to teachers, ran writing workshops for children, attended language conferences and literary festivals, or gave poetry readings, in every republic. So, on and off for nearly a decade, all aspects of my work and consciousness have been ineradicably marked by Yugoslavia.

This is why I find it hard to remain detached from what's going on now. It isn't just that I've many close friends there in each republic: I fondly used to believe that Yugoslavia had the chance of serving Europe and the world as a model for a multi-ethnic, pluralistic, freedom-aspiring society; a variegated, living embroidery. That chance, it now seems to me, has gone for good, and the thought fills me with sadness, gloom and

[18] West 23.

alarm. Many think and feel as I do. Whatever the political outcome, this war simply has to stop. Peace is necessary, not just for every person in each of the republics, but because the whole of Europe, including Russia, and America too, are implicated in the Yugoslav tragedy. For these reasons, in what follows, I want to assert that there are other aspects to this land than the horrors of war. This sketch on English language teaching and cultural contacts until 1991 is offered as a counterbalance to despondency, in the modest advocacy of hope and reason.

∽

In 1918, a young Serb by the name of Vladeta Popović, who had been wounded in the Great War, was granted a scholarship at Cambridge. He graduated from Peterhouse in 1921 and completed his Ph.D. thesis at London in 1925. The title was 'Shakespeare in Serbia'. Together with his British wife, Mary Stansfield Popović, he then returned to Belgrade.

In the years that followed, the couple effected a quiet revolution in English teaching. Mary Stansfield Popović published her *First Course in English* in 1927, a textbook which inaugurated the use of the International Phonetic Alphabet in Yugoslavia, and in 1928, she began running regular English classes for all comers at Kolarčev People's University. In 1929, the husband-and-wife team founded the first English department in Yugoslavia, at the Philosophical Faculty in Belgrade, with Dr. Vladeta Popović as its first chairman. Until then, undergraduates had only been able to take English as a subsidiary subject, with French or German as their major. Mary Stansfield Popović went on to publish her *Second Course in English* in 1934 and her *Third Course* in 1935. This contained selections of literary texts from Chaucer to Galsworthy and an overview of the grammar, with exercises. Professor Naum Dimitrijević, who at the time of writing holds the Chair in Methodology of English Language Teaching at the Philological Faculty in Belgrade, describes this book as "excellent and systematic in its general conception, much of which is still valid today".

In 1939, two years before the Nazi invasion, the British Council set up its first offices in Yugoslavia, employing locally recruited teachers to run English classes. The Council officers managed to escape via the Dalmatian coast and were repatriated to England after various scrapes and adventures: the serving Representative's official report on this has been unearthed recently from the Council's archives and published in the journal of the British-Yugoslav Society in London. Others weren't so lucky:

as a prominent Anglophile and Shakespearean scholar, Professor Vladeta Popović was one of the first to be arrested by the Germans in April 1941. Along with many others, he was deported. He survived four years of camps, including Dachau, and returned to Belgrade to resume his work. He died in 1951. Professor Mary Stansfield Popović, who had become a Yugoslav citizen, was also interned in Germany. After the war, she too devoted the rest of her life to her students, a personal embodiment of all that has been best in British-Yugoslav friendship and cooperation. She died, a grand old lady, in 1989. In language teaching circles throughout the republics, Vladeta and Mary Stansfield Popović are remembered with pride and respect as pioneers who maintained their integrity as teachers and scholars through tragic and difficult times.

☙

The development of English following the Second World War fully mirrors the complexities of Yugoslavia's political, economic, and cultural history. The central contradiction might be summed up as follows: while the country was inexorably opening itself up to the world, it was simultaneously hampering itself from doing so. Between 1945 and 1948, an atmosphere of xenophobia was officially encouraged and the learning of foreign languages other than Russian was regarded as ideologically suspect. It's a mistake, though, to attribute the deep-rooted mistrust of foreign interference to communism alone. Centuries of annexations, invasions, and occupations have shaped the mentalities of all the peoples of the Balkans, where ancient codes of prodigious hospitality by ordinary people and wariness of strangers by officialdom are two sides of the same coin. Even after Tito's death in 1980, anachronistic laws still existed which required Yugoslavs to report any professional meetings with foreigners to the authorities, although in practice a blind eye was often turned, and interpretation of the law varied from region to region and official to official.

On the other hand, the factors tending to openness and liberalisation were more numerous and powerful. The turn towards the West following the Russian Blockade in 1948 inaugurated a chain of economic conferences and meetings that has continued steadily ever since. Whatever the merits of Tito's banding with Nehru, Nasser, and others to form the Non-Aligned Movement, English was the international language needed for this kind of diplomacy; and following the summit conference in Belgrade in September 1961, when Yugoslavia was the only European member among the fifty-one nations represented, the teaching of English in schools gradually began to catch up on Russian through the 1960s and to overtake it over the next two decades.

Meanwhile, the steady growth of tourism, particularly along the Adriatic coast, made international contacts at home not only inevitable but desirable. Visa formalities were removed as far as possible both for foreigners coming in and Yugoslavs going out; and Yugoslav guest-workers, especially in Germany, and emigrants to Australia, Canada, the USA and elsewhere, sent their savings back home to help their families. Yugoslav engineers worked on government contracts in Iraq, Libya, Kuwait, Algeria, Uganda, and other developing countries. Easy travel regulations also meant tourism and study abroad for those who could afford it. Western commodity culture and all its concomitants slithered easily into even the remotest mountain villages on TV soap commercials and pop-music, and skiing resorts flourished. The Eurovision Song Contest, the European and World Cup, the Olympic Games, and countless other similar smaller events played the same internationalising role.

Since 1948, all these factors combined with more specific and deeply rooted cultural patterns, too, to make people all over Yugoslavia warmly receptive to outside influences and strongly resistant to any laws inhibiting contacts with foreigners. The vast majority in every republic are freedom-loving, have a healthy disrespect for bureaucracy, and delight in side-stepping regulations: an art perfected under miscellaneous foreign occupations. They're addicted to *kafana* jokes and gossip, and have a massive curiosity about other countries and cultures, as well as an insatiable appetite for poetry and song, sharpened by breathing the air of a long and vital demotic tradition.

☙

Strange though it may sound in England, where poetry has always been bound up with class and privilege, and perhaps in North America too, this art form has played a key role in the cultural hospitality offered by Yugoslavs, and not just among literati or specialists. In 1963, Jean-Marie Domenach and Alain Pontault published an unusual and perceptive tourist guide-book in the *Petite Planète* series in Paris. "In Yugoslavia," they wrote, "poetry has never stopped being taken seriously. It's certainly the country with the highest density of poets in the world [...]. This is the sign of a people who love their language with a new love, who have not finished playing with all their words."[19] What these French writers are describing here, as a kind of popular craving for poetry, is the tip of a tradition that's very different from anything in Western Europe or North America. In all the South Slavonic languages, the word for 'poem' and 'song' is identical (*pesma, pjesma, pesen, pesnata*): it belongs not just to educated people, but to everyone in the community, and isn't necessarily book-bound. In 1961, only a year after the Harvard publication of A. B. Lord's masterly study of oral epics sung by analphabetic bards in Bosnian villages, *The Singer of Tales,* a group of Macedonian poets inaugurated a convivial and boozy annual summer get-together in Struga, on the shore of Lake Ohrid. It soon went all-Yugoslav, and then turned into a huge international jamboree. In 1971, W. H. Auden received the Golden Wreath Award, followed by Neruda, Montale, Senghor, Lundkvist, Alberti, Enzensberger, Stanescu, Voznesenky, Ritsos, and Ginsberg: an impressive list.

From the 1960s on, poetry festivals sprang up in each republic, and it became quite common for even small towns to stage an annual event, often to commemorate a local poet, as in Čačak in Serbia or Bijelo Polje in Montenegro. In many cases, following Struga's example, the various internationalising tendencies spilled over into invitations to large numbers of poets from abroad. Some events, like the Serbian Association of Writers' Annual October Meetings, or the Slovenian PEN meetings at Bled, served as key instruments over the years in mustering international support for writers orchestrated against censorship. Others were rooted in commemoration of wartime sufferings and atrocities, like the 'Goran's Spring' Festival in Zagreb or the 'Great School Lesson' in Kragujevac, which involved choral performance before a massive open-air audience, even in pouring rain. Others, like the Balkan Writers' Conference in Bor and Negotin, the Danube Writers' Meeting in Smederevo and the annual event in Vršac, near the Romanian border, implicitly advocated groupings with Yugoslavia's neighbours, which may well yet have bearings on international politics. Others, like the Budva Summer Festival on the Montenegrin coast, and Struga too, developed into major tourist attractions.[20]

One major result of this spate of international festivals, and of their wide, and frequently national TV and press coverage, is that large numbers of Yugoslavs, even if not regular 'readers', came to know something of other cultures through foreign writers. Clearly, the implications of this for cultural exchange have been enormous. Meanwhile, there has been

[19] trans. RB.

[20] For more on literary festivals, see 229ff.

an equal profusion of international events for other arts, notably the Dubrovnik Theatre Festival, the Split Song Festival, the Pula Film Festival, and Belgrade's Film-Fest and International Theatre Festival (BITEF), as well as its Jazz Festival, where in 1989 I heard Art Blakey for the last time. It's a shame that the rich and generous spirit of so many of these events should have been either broken or undermined by propaganda. It's hard to see how they'll resume when even phone links have been cut between the warring republics and the all-Yugoslav TV service has disappeared. The best one can hope is that they'll eventually be revived as forums for articulate discussion and rapprochement.

∽

Even so, these varied factors, mixed together, have turned Yugoslavia into fertile ground for the steady current of English-speaking literary scholars, critics, linguists, ELT experts, textbook writers and teachers, as well as poets, novelists, actors, and musicians, who have streamed into the country from Britain and the USA ever since the early 1950s. While the list is all impressive one, their reception by Yugoslav hosts and audiences has always been attentive and hospitable, frequently enthusiastic, and sometimes rapturous, even if in the early days such visits somehow 'failed to be reported' in the press. Word, after all, gets around. Here are some names: Sir Herbert Read, Stephen Spender, Sir Laurence Olivier, Paul Scofield, Lawrence Durrell, Dame Helen Gardner, Allardyce Nichol, Saul Bellow, Leslie Fiedler, Ralph Cohen, Barre Toelken, Dorothy Mason, Vivien de Sola Pinto, Katherine Anne Porter, Graham Hough, David Daiches, W. Pitt Corder, Stephen Ullmann, Angus MacKintosh, Tony Tanner, A. C. Gimson, Randolf Quirk, Henry Widdowson, Randall Stevenson, and Alan Sillitoe. Conversely, writers, scholars, and researchers from Yugoslavia have regularly received grants to work in America and Britain, respectively through the Fulbright Commission and British Council ELTECS scheme. Visitors to Britain have included writers like Vasko Popa, Ivan Lalić, Miodrag Pavlović, David Albahari, Jelena Lengold, Antun Šoljan, Dubravka Ugrešić, and Tomaž Šalamun.

As for continuous language teaching, the overall pattern since 1948 has been one of steadily increasing liberalisation, cooperation between Federal and Republican authorities, agencies like the British Council and the USIA, and universities and schools.

Zagreb University's English department was founded by Professor Josip Torbarina in the 1930s, Ljubljana, Sarajevo, and Novi Sad launched departments in the 1950s, followed by Priština, Skopje, Zadar, Niš, and Osijek. In the 1960s, reforms were instigated in updating English studies in line with international developments in literature, critical theory, linguistics, and methodology, especially under the chairmanship of Professor Vida E. Marković at the English Department of Belgrade University's *Filološki fakultet* (Philological Faculty), who set up frequent academic visits and exchanges, despite difficulties. In Zagreb, Professor Rudolf Filipović established new approaches, especially in linguistics. All this fostered the high motivation and professionalism among teachers today. Other leading professors in the Belgrade English department included the Shakespearean scholar Veselin Kostić and Ranko Bugarski, an expert on language and linguistics who had studied under David Crystal and Randolf Quirk at University College London.

In recent years, about ten to fifteen lectors from both Britain and the USA have been employed on renewable annual contracts and attached to universities and at least one independent language school. Some lectors have stayed on to marry and settle permanently. Charters for setting up language schools as workers' cooperatives were in force by at least 1967, and such centres sprang up in Belgrade, Zagreb, Split, Skopje, and other cities, actively fostering more modem teaching approaches than the universities, since these were hidebound by state legislation, academic constitutions, traditional curricula, and the baneful obligation of organising up to six sets of examinations a year, faithfully attended by resit students with little hope of passing.

The past two years have seen a second wave of fee-paying language schools, run on West European lines, with direct input from qualified native-speaker teachers. Standards of teaching to children in schools vary, as they do anywhere, but are often excellent, even in far-flung villages, though the quality is usually higher in large centres. Each republic has its own association of English language teachers, as do most cities, which are active in staging one-day workshops and lectures.[21] Residential teacher-training

[21] Notes added in 2019: In Belgrade, many cultural visits and literary evenings have been organised by Branka Panić, first at the Centre for Learning Foreign Languages between the early 1970s and 1990, and since 1991 at the Yugoslav-British Society School and the Serbian branch of the English Speaking Union. Meanwhile, the Yugoslav-British Society was founded by Dr. Brana Vuković.

Since the break-up of Yugoslavia into different national states, a branch of IATEFL (International Association for Teachers of English as a Foreign Language) has been founded in each one.

seminars and ESP[22] conferences involving lecturers from abroad have been regularly organised by both Republican and Federal authorities, with strong input from successive British Council English Language Officers and Gordana Krstić at the USIA, a greatly respected administrator who has recently retired after years of service to the English language teaching profession throughout Yugoslavia.

Most recently, thanks to the efforts of the last two British Council English Language Officers, Marilyn Robertson and Susan Leather, and local language school organisers, University of Cambridge examinations were introduced at six centres in 1991, with a total of 1,075 candidates in June and about 1,300 in December, numbers which are likely to expand. The June pass rate of 81 per cent was 16 per cent higher than the average for other countries. Both Oxford and London Chamber of Commerce exams have started in Slovenia too, and will soon do so in Belgrade, where a branch of the English Speaking Union, founded by Branka Panić, also opened in 1991. However, neither privately run language courses nor foreign exam fees are cheap, and at least since the troubles started, English has been valued not only for employment and status at home, but as a potential emigration ticket.

While the toll taken by the civil war has been devastating in terms of people killed or maimed, families broken, consciousnesses of children permanently scarred, home, property, and industries devastated, jobs lost, and inflation, the teaching profession has struggled on, attempting wherever possible to maintain normality for students and pupils. The British Council and USIA have adopted the same approach and earned respect for maintaining even-handed distribution of resources. Whatever political shapes emerge, all the obvious long-term predictions are that English teaching will flourish with the establishment of market economies and, as a key factor in their development.

This survey began with contradictions and ends with them. As a teacher, I look forward. As a poet, I look down, up, down, and remember. As a human being I'm torn between hope and mourning:

> Watch where you walk. You think you tread on stones'?
> You're wrong, my friend. It is your brother's bones.[23]

December 1991–January 1992

---

[22] English for Special Purposes.

[23] 'War Again : Yugoslavia 1991': RB 2011c: 16.

PART 6

BOMBS OVER SERBIA, 1999

While political issues run inexorably through all of this book, this part presents two pieces, both written in 1999, in which politics is the dominant thread. Although this kind of writing is more likely to suffer from obsolescence than most others, I include these two, both as documentation and for the wider historical, economic and psycho-social issues they raise.

As I write these notes twenty years later, I recall vividly that these pieces, among others that I wrote at the time, were engendered by my dissatisfaction with the stereotypical mind-sets and political processes evident in Western countries vis-à-vis Serbia just before the Millennium. Mass-produced projections were manifested in many ways and transmitted by multiple channels, for example: the eagerness of Western governments, and the disingenuousness of their ministers and agents, in actively provoking and abetting the dissolution of Yugoslavia; NATO's bombing of Serbia in spring 1999; the factual distortions and lies presented about Serbian life in the official Western media; the apparently cultivated ignorance of Serbian culture; the popular stereotyping of Serbs as villains in British and American films and TV dramas; and the lies about Serbs and Serbia perpetrated by Western political leaders, whether deliberately or unconsciously, or both.

To oppose NATO at that time, however, didn't mean supporting or condoning the leadership of Slobodan Milošević. Far from it: I viewed him as a dangerous and cynical opportunist, and was critical of all his policies and believed them disastrous both politically and economically, for Serbia and for Yugoslavia. My position involved a double opposition.

☙

In 1999, Serbia was increasingly isolated, largely through the policies of its own government. But a government isn't a population; and that October, in particular, it seemed to me important to attend the International Writers' Meeting in Belgrade, if only to offer whatever small moral support I could, and to demonstrate that there were articulate people elsewhere who hadn't forgotten Serbia or Serbs. As the sole British participant at this large event, I gave a prepared address to a packed plenary session, in which I broached the topic of ethnicity by attempting to analyse terms like *narod* and *narodnost.*[1] Although my plea for multi-ethnic tolerance received enthusiastic applause, it was clear that this wasn't a time for such points to be absorbed with any degree of analytical coolness. This is the first piece included here.

The second, 'Letter from Kosovska Mitrovica' (2000), records a minibus trip made by a small group of Serbian and foreign writers, organised by the October Writers' Meeting and led by the Serbian poet Predrag Bogdanović Ci. We travelled from Belgrade down the bombed Ibar valley to northern Kosovo, where we watched French and Russian troops on patrol. This piece was published by *The Times Literary Supplement.*

I wrote several other polemical piece in 1999. Although I don't include these in this book, here I add the story of the composition of one of them, and its sudden and unexpected circulation.

ൾ

During the nights before NATO's bombing of Serbia started, between March 22 and 24, 1999, I was at home in Cambridge. Hours before the first bombs were dropped, I sat up writing an angry piece, which I entitled 'Is NATO Right to Bomb Yugoslavia? A personal view'. In opposing all aspects of NATO's provocation and war against Serbia, I also opposed the economic blockade and the demonisation of Serbs by NATO governments and media. As soon as I'd dashed this piece off, I faxed it to several friends, including the poet Ivan Gadjanski in Belgrade.[2] Without my knowing, he took my polemic straight into the offices of *Politika*, the leading Serbian daily. As a result, while the bombs were actually falling, the piece was serialised in the paper in five daily instalments, between March 28 and April 1.[3] By being published in Serbian translation even before similar condemnations had been articulated by foreign intellectuals such as Noam Chomsky, Harold Pinter and Peter Handke, this set of articles represented the first protest on behalf of Serbs and Serbia to be voiced by any western writer. The piece was also circulated in English and published, without my

[1] These words *narod* and *narodnost* embed similarly complex etymologies, connotations and overlays to those of their English equivalents, *nation* and *nationality*. Both sets relate directly to birth and being born (Srb. *roditi*, Lat. *nascī*, etc.), as well as to concepts such as ethnicity. See also 301 below, especially note 8.

[2] Email wasn't widely available then. Today it's hard to imagine, let alone remember, what life was like before it. For my memoir on Ivan, see 317ff below.

[3] RB 1999b.

knowing, on the Internet, where it's still available.[4]

In preparing this present book twenty years after these events, I've held several detailed arguments with myself about whether to include this piece or not. My arguments in favour of doing so were rooted in a desire for inclusiveness of documentation and accuracy of representation. Among those against were my reservations about the quality of the writing, my sense that the piece probably wouldn't travel well outside its time, and the fact that it was angry, off-the-cuff and one-sided. With twenty years' hindsight, I also think that if I'd had the clearer perspectives then on the faults and failings of *all* sides in the Yugoslav wars that I have now, especially in the light of fuller evidence of brutalities and atrocities committed by all parties in the conflict, I'm not sure that I would have defended Serbia quite so unequivocally as I did then.[5] However, I believe now that what I said in that piece needed saying at that time, and that its core arguments about the arrogance endemic in the Western mindset – and, what's more, the self-righteous assumptions about the *right* to arrogance – still hold good.

But this book isn't about polemics. Nor is it about anger, or sustaining, provoking or projecting it.

ꟿ

Even so, if I was 'right' to express my anger about the NATO bombing of Serbia, I also ask myself now why I didn't do so too about the gangs of Serbs from Belgrade who forayed into Bosnia and Slavonia on weekend murder-sprees, or about the immediate trigger for the NATO bombing, the militarily-organised Serbian attempt to displace hundreds of thousands of ethnic Albanians from Kosovo into neighbouring Macedonia, Albania and Montenegro?

---

[4] RB 1999a (online).

[5] On retrospective political accounts and analyses of the collapse of Yugoslavia, hundreds of books have been written in many languages and there is no consensus. Those I have found particularly helpful are Popov (ed.), Judah 2008 and 2009, Beloff, Glenny, and Wachtel. As a good collective example of varied interpretations by historians, see also the essays in Naimark. On critical and scholarly analysis of stereotypical attitudes to the Balkans and the Slavs, see for example: Stoianovich, 1994: esp. 342-354; Goldsworthy 2013 [1998]; Todorova 2009 [1997]; and numerous writings by Bakić-Hayden and Hayden. The last three listed are influenced by Edward Said's *Orientalism*, even though, as in Said himself, the underlying theory of projection in Freud and Jung remains unanalysed.

Now, it seems to me, to have been partially 'right' wasn't good *enough*. I should have condemned these brutalities too. And I should have subjected my own anger to examination.

But this book isn't about retrospective guilt, either.

ᔕ

In the context of *sustaining* anger, I think it's worth adding here that the procedures and motivations of the International Criminal Tribunal for the Former Yugoslavia (ICTY) in the Hague have been queried and criticised on precisely these grounds. In a lucid and convincing essay, Robert Hayden argues that, rather than serving either the genuine ideals of disinterested justice or the human and political need for meaningful reconciliation, the main beneficiaries of these long-drawn-out trials have been three distinct entities: first, the agencies, organisers and employees of the court itself, which all have vested interests in its perpetuation, that is to say, their own financial security through continuing employment; second, the most extremist nationalist politicians in all the former republics of for-mer Yugoslavia; and, third, NATO itself:

> [F]ar from being an instrument of reconciliation, the ICTY is instead *a mechanism for continuing the war by other means.* For the NATO powers, the wars seem to have been utilized primarily as a way to expand NATO and exclude Russia from the Balkans the first time since 1878.[6]

December 2019 and January 2020

[6] Hayden 2007: 324; and 2013: 281; emphasis added.

Address to the Plenary Session of the 36th International Meeting, organised by the Serbian Writers' Association, 1999

Introduction

Most of us who are present as foreign guests at this 1999 Belgrade International Writers' Meeting have come here in a very different spirit from that of other years. I personally decided to attend this year, come what may, because I believed it my duty as a man and as a poet to be here with you. A Writers' Association should represent freedom of speech for every citizen. For this reason, at this dreadful and difficult time for your country, I should like to ask you, the writers of Serbia, to hear and pass on at least one simple message from me: that there do exist people abroad who continue to hold your culture and history in very high regard and who love your country.

All of us here recognise this is a terrible time for Serbia and Yugoslavia. Emotions are running very high. The entire infrastructure of the country has been decimated by NATO's bombs. NATO found that it could afford the massive investment in war, but when it has come to the so-called peace, that's a different matter. There is massive pollution, and no-one can really estimate what will be the effects of the depleted uranium used by NATO. Innocent people have been killed and are still being killed. Countryside and cities teem with refugees. Unemployment is rife. Many people haven't enough money to buy the basic necessities for survival. And the future of Kosovo has never been more uncertain. Clearly, this is a time of enormous danger. I believe it's a time of very deep crisis, which will come to be seen by later generations as a crucial turning point in your history, and possibly in world history.

Along with the devastation, so many declarations, threats, attacks, defences and justifications have been made, and there has been so much blame and guilt, and such spurious and questionable motives have been revealed, and we've all heard so many lies – on all sides – that most people have become heartily sick of it all. Through the whole of this last decade, since Yugoslavia began to collapse, I wonder if we can remember a single year in Europe when we've been bombarded so intensively as in 1999, by so much verbal rubbish, so many deliberate distortions, such a spate of pernicious doublethink ('spin'), grossly affronting the most basic elements of ethics and morality in each of us, and the most fundamental principles of reason and logic?

I don't wish to add to this flood, worthy of the satires of Huxley and Orwell. Loud protest against political injustice and moral wrong is of course necessary. But my own intention here will be to speak with a quiet and critical yet constructive voice. So, in what follows, I propose to participate with you in the attempt towards formulating not answers but questions. My talk will be divided into three parts. First, I'll present you with several personal facts. Second, I'll ask some practical and theoretical questions about four issues for Serbia, arising out of this war. Finally, I'll make a single practical proposal for our hosts. Unfortunately, I've no time to present my perceptions of the frightening global issues raised by NATO's actions. I'm willing to engage in discussion outside this chamber afterwards with anyone interested.

Some Personal Background

Here is a cool summary of the lived experience underlying what I have to say. I've been involved in Yugoslavia since I launched the International Cambridge Poetry Festival in 1975. In successive years, we invited leading Yugoslav poets to this biennial event: Vasko Popa, Ivan V. Lalić, and Miodrag Pavlović. In 1982, I received my first invitation to the Belgrade October International Writers' Meeting. This year, 1999, represents the eighth time that I've been a guest at this Meeting. So, in seventeen years, I think I've been your guest more often than any other writer from the whole of the English-speaking world. This humbles me and places a considerable responsibility on my shoulders.

For three years, between 1987 and 1991, I lived in Belgrade. I wrote poems and attended literary and educational events all over Serbia, Croatia, Bosnia and Hercegovina, Macedonia and Slovenia. I'm fairly sure that during that time I was the only English-speaking and even foreign poet who had chosen to live and work in Yugoslavia. Between 1989 and 1990, I even considered making Yugoslavia my permanent home and applying for Yugoslav citizenship. Of course, my timing couldn't have been worse.

My long but incomplete sequence of poems entitled *The Blue Butterfly*, translated in part by Danilo Kiš, Ivan V. Lalić and others,[7] springs from sufferings in Serbia during the Second World War; and the open questions posed in this text are rooted in Yugoslav experience. So, my life and work as a man and as a poet continue to be profoundly marked by this country.

Days before the NATO planes began to attack, between 22 and 24 of March this year, I wrote a 5,000-word article entitled 'Is NATO Right to Bomb Yugoslavia?'. This article was published in *Politika*, incidentally without my knowledge, over a period of five days, between March 28 and April 2, and it was also circulated on the Internet. I rigorously opposed the bombing of Serbia by NATO, and all aspects of NATO's provocation and war against Serbia. Now as then, I oppose the continuing economic blockade of Serbia, and the demonisation of Serbs by NATO governments and media.

I oppose *all* the atrocities against people of *all* ethnic groups that have taken place in this country.

Four Issues for Serbia

ONE

In the course of my work I often travel to countries like Poland and the Czech Republic. Ten years ago, the standard of living in Yugoslavia was seen as a model to be emulated by those countries. But even last year, before the NATO bombing, those countries had overtaken Yugoslavia; and the comparison now, after the NATO destruction, shows the Yugoslav situation to be far worse. Politically, Serbia is now excluded from the rest of the world's affairs. About as much notice is taken of Serbia as of Byelorussia. Not so long ago, Yugoslavia led the Non-Aligned Movement. What's to be done to reverse this situation – to bring Yugoslavia back into the international community, to encourage inward investment, to open up the airports, roads, rivers and trade routes, to inaugurate conferences and exchanges, to help young people fulfil their aspirations to a good education and a fuller and happier life? *Formulating these questions more accurately and understanding their full implications surely provide the principal task for all of us here today.*

[7] When this speech was made, Vera Radojević hadn't yet started working on her translation of the book.

TWO

Most of us who have witnessed and been involved in the collapse of Yugoslavia in the last ten years are still suffering from a kind of shock. Every worst, darkest and most inhumane scenario we'd envisaged in our fantasies as a remote but unlikely possibility took real and actual shape. It's as though we were forced to witness one bad outcome after another unrolling before our very eyes, in slow motion, and with the kind of insane inevitability of nightmare. At times it seemed, perversely, as though what everybody wanted *least* was the *only* thing that could or would happen. We kept saying and thinking – it surely, surely can't get any worse – but it did, progressively and, it seemed, in defiance of any notion of moral or ethical goodness.

So it's hardly surprising that it has become fashionable these days for commentators to state glibly that Yugoslavia was an 'artificial construct' and 'was bound to' disintegrate. However, *all* nations are 'artificial constructs', and none last forever. *I maintain that I don't personally believe that Yugoslavia need necessarily have fallen apart.* Time and time again, wiser, less short-sighted and more intelligent decisions could have been made, *by everyone concerned*, and on every side. My own view is that for all its faults, the old united Yugoslavia was a far better place than any or all of the smaller units that have replaced it.

To understand why and how the country did crumble is a job that needs to be painstakingly undertaken by historians. There are many layers of analysis and it isn't likely that the full truth will be known until the 'official secrets' have been divulged by all the governments concerned – i.e. in about fifty years' time. By then, of course, much of the evidence will have been lost, buried or destroyed. However, the task needs to begin immediately. Those outside the country tend to blame internal contradictions and those inside tend to blame external conspiracies. I submit that both versions of this analysis are true, and I should like to examine one aspect from each perspective.

THREE

Not just people, and not just governments, but also *concepts* and *symbols* can be set to the purpose of producing and waging wars. With regard to internal contradictions, I'd like to draw your attention to one particular complex factor: I submit to you that the various terms in your language relating to *ethnic identities, distinctions and differences* are now more than ever in urgent need of clarification and analysis. I refer especially to the group of terms *'narod'*, *'narodnost'*, *'nacionalnost'*. *'nacionalna pripadnost'*, etc.[8]

Only you, who have lived through the official codification of such terms within the institutions of the former Yugoslav Federation, can be fully competent to decode their layerings of meanings, and their complexities, ambiguities and confusions of associations. And only you, who have witnessed and experienced the descent from 'Brotherhood and Unity' (*Bratstvo i jedinstvo*)[9] into ethnic hatred and killing, can really determine how genuinely or effectively these terms ever fitted Yugoslavia's rich ethnic mix. It's not hard, however, for even a foreigner like myself, who can't fully grasp the nuances between '*nacionalnost*' and '*narodnost*', to see that *all the conflicts that have broken Yugoslavia up have been fought along lines of thought and borders of belief which have been drawn by such terms as these.*

Furthermore, on a theoretical level, I submit to you that these terms are *constructs*, that they've always been conceptually imprecise, and that, especially in view of what has happened over the last ten years on this territory, the notions embedded in all of them now need *deconstructing*.

In this context, I ask you to consider whether the former Federation of Yugoslavia could have been configured in some other way that might have worked better. *And what lessons can be learned now? Isn't the central question: how is Yugoslavia to be configured in future?* I said at the outset that I intended to participate in the formulation of questions, and I submit to you that critical examination of this complex issue of *narodi*, *narodnosti*, etc. isn't just a matter of detached academic interest. *It can show a way forward.* Surely this is no small task. My belief is that it's one that calls for an unusual blend of intellectual clear-sightedness and vision, political realism and moral courage, determination and magnanimity.

---

[8] *narod*, 'people, nation, race'; *narodnost*, *nacionalnost*, 'nationality', 'ethnicity'; '*nacionalna pripadnost*', lit. 'national affiliation' (i.e. ethnicity). In addition to their inherent ambiguities and associations, these terms acquired further resonances – not to mention complexities and confusions – by being enshrined in the bureaucratic distinctions of the constitution of Communist Yugoslavia. The term *narod* (pl. *narodi*) was applied to Serbs, Croats, Slovenes, Montenegrins, and Macedonians, that is, to the larger nations or ethnic groups with republics of their own. After 1971, this term was extended to Bosnian Muslims too. *Narodnost* (pl. *narodnosti*) in effect meant 'ethnic minorities': that is, groups with 'motherlands outside of Yugoslavia', e.g. Hungarians, Albanian-speakers, and Jews. See Judah 1998: 53-54.

[9] A popular slogan in Communist Yugoslavia.

I should like to add a quiet personal note here. To my mind, the best and finest of former Yugoslavia consisted in the multi-ethnicity of its population. Tolerance and appreciation of the qualities of the individual – perceived with the full force of the word '*čovek*'[10] – over-rode *narodnost, nacionalnost*, etc. I experienced these qualities time and time again, and I still do. And such experiences and perceptions inform, underlie and inspire all my own writings connected with Yugoslavia with a quality which I can describe only in terms of *images of light*: as a sudden kind of wholly human, and wholly delightful, and always wholly astonishing *clarity and brightness*.

I therefore ask my hosts, after the horrors of these inter-ethnic wars, what has happened to that honourable, humane, decent, kind, inclusive, peculiarly Yugoslav vision of the '*čovek*'? Is it not time, now, again, to reinvoke a more humane and generous vision for the children of this country than the narrower view of individual, social and cultural identity based on the more limited scope of *narodnosti / nacionalnosti*? *Narodnost* and its fellows love to divide the world into '*Us*'es and '*Them*'s. The vision of the '*čovek*' involves full recognition of every *Other*, of every *Thou*. *Narodnost* pluralises and turns its face away. Recognition of the '*čoveka*' individuates by looking each single *Other* in the eyes.

However, you may well ask, what's the use of talking about the individual as '*čovek*' if you've no choice but to walk every day along the main street of Priština, or Belfast, or the Bronx, or Freetown, or East Timor – or any other location of tribal, religious or ethnic conflict? This all goes to show that these problems aren't just those of Serbia, and that Serbia's problems are symptomatic of patterns of events all over the world. In such a chaotic world, none of us can pretend to occupy the high protected ground of a holier-than-thou morality, and we're right to view anyone who claims to do so with extreme suspicion. We're all in this mess together. It's surely also essential, wherever we live, to endorse and approve of cultural, religious and ethnic differences, to allow full scope to every single individual to express and develop pride in his/her origins; and this necessarily involves both the freedom to treasure and cultivate one's own '*nacionalna svest*'[11] and the obligation to treasure that same freedom in others.

Thus, unless we invoke this quality of '*čovečnost*', and do so over and above our manifold human differences, *how can we possibly even begin to live together*? What may be needed here at this point, I submit, is the vision of a man like Bishop Tutu in South Africa.

[10] *čovek, čoveka*' (genitive): 'man' in the sense of ἄνθρωπος (*ánthropos*), 'human'.

[11] *nacionalna svest*: 'national awareness or consciousness'.

FOUR

With regard to external conspiracies, it would hardly be surprising if, mentally and psychologically, an attitude of 'Fortress Serbia' did not now prevail among the country's rulers and population, if we consider for a moment the massive disbelief and shock which the bombing by former allies produced. It's tragic that the 'Fortress Serbia' attitude has been reinforced so strongly by the NATO bombing.

However, I would simply like to submit to you that the traditional Serbian virtues of self-reliance should *not* involve a shutting of doors to foreigners. Why? Because the best in the Serbian spirit – in history, politics, religion, poetry, art and science – in fact in every sphere – has always gone beyond *narodnost* / *nacionalnost* – has always tended in aspiration and practice, to generosity, openness, internationalism, and universalism.

Serbia *does* have friends 'outside' who recognise this. In this connection, I think people in Serbia ought to know that despite the massive propaganda from NATO and the British government, opinion in Britain was very heavily divided about the morality or justification for the war – and here I'm speaking of the quiet voices of huge numbers of people from all walks of life who expressed their opposition, worries and doubts.

Anti-war groups sprang up in many places, as in my own town, Cambridge. The people who came together in these groups were of all ages and backgrounds and all political and religious persuasions. And while everyone here knows that indictments have been set out at The Hague against President Milošević and others here, let citizens of Serbia also note that an international indictment has been issued accusing President Clinton and Prime Minister Blair, together with the politicians and generals directly under them – of committing war crimes and atrocities against Yugoslavia. This indictment has been prepared by lawyers in Britain and the USA. Several Cambridge people have been instrumental in formulating this indictment. In this connection I bring a letter of greetings to you from the Cambridge group who have opposed the NATO bombing.

A Practical Proposal

Arising out of my last point, I should like to offer a proposal for the consideration of our hosts. If there *are* indeed 'friends outside' the country whom you can trust, can your authorities not set up a series of voluntary international advisory bodies, to meet here in Belgrade and other Yugoslav cities and internationally on a regular basis? These bodies could be connected to your professional organisations. Their function would be to work with Serbia to renew and develop its potential in all fields: to name a few, social welfare, medicine, education, research, technology, industry, finance, commerce and law. I'm speaking of attracting by invitation the best of international intellects and experts, not to impose ideas, but to engage in dialogue. If this can't be done directly through governments, then couldn't an independent organisation be set up to put this in place

This International Writers' Meeting may perhaps serve as a model which could be applied and developed in many other fields. Sure, it's the job of writers to write, and to articulate and clarify ideas and values. And let us admit, all writers love talking, not to mention listening to the sounds of our own voices. But many other different kinds of skills than ours are needed to solve a country's practical problems.

Cambridge and Kazimierz Dolny
September and October 1999

Letter from Kosovska Mitrovica

Our driver winds down his window to provide answers in gruff German to the French KFOR soldiers guarding the so-called frontier between Serbia and Kosovo.[12] His snorty *Jawohls* are deliberate. In Zvečan we arrive over an hour late but sixty people have waited to hear our poetry reading, despite the complete absence of heating, including a choir of schoolgirls who start the proceedings with two folk songs in a sort of haunting plain chant. In Kosovska Mitrovica, I especially enjoy Vitaly Shentalinsky's recitation. It's hard to believe that this quiet, elegant, unassuming man, with his Ezra Pound-style goatee beard and swept-back silvery hair, is the one who got the KGB to open up its archives on Mandelstam, Babel and many other persecuted and/or murdered Russian writers.[13] Throughout our trip, Vitaly keeps jotting things down in his journal. I suppose he's been well-disciplined by his Lubyanka experiences. Sometime, I'd like to read his report on this improbable literary cabaret, if he ever gets around to writing it.

After the reading, we venture out to the bridge that divides ethnic Serbian and ethnic Albanian communities, and in pouring rain I chat with the French soldiers on guard there – one from Strasbourg and one from Toulouse. I ask about crossing the bridge. The one from Strasbourg answers in good Franglais. Monsieur, since you're from the EC, you would be entitled to cross if so you wished. But I wouldn't recommend it, because you might get your head blown off. The one from Toulouse is a Georges Brassens fan. Everyone I meet around here seems to manage to get along by insisting on keeping a twinkle in the eye. Just a small one, mind you. It reminds me of the ironic points of light Auden claimed for "the just" who exchange their messages in 'September 1, 1939'. And what have the 1990s been but another "low dishonest decade"?[14]

---

[12] KFOR, a "NATO-led international peacekeeping force which was responsible for establishing a secure environment in Kosovo". See 'Kosovo Force', *Wikipedia.*

[13] Shentalinsky 1995.

[14] Auden 86, 89.

Back in Zvečan for the night, we wake next morning to find Russian soldiers climbing out of two armoured cars and a truck. We wander out and take photographs, and someone interprets for me to ask an officer how well they're getting paid. The officer seems genuinely surprised, not even offended, at my question. "Good pay", he answers, and shrugs. Why do we believe the stuff newspapers tell us? The soldiers stroll into the restaurant at the inn while I blearily finish off my breakfast. I suggest to Vitaly that he might stand up and recite his poems to them. He's a modest man as I've said but eventually he's persuaded. While to me, this event seems like reality surpassing the surreal, these Russian soldiers don't seem to think it at all unusual. They clap and go on sipping their tea.

In one photograph, I'm standing with three other poets – a Russian, a Greek and a Serb, our hands sort-of-defiantly joined above us – on a bombed metal railway bridge somewhere along the Ibar valley between Kraljevo and Mitrovica. Seen from the side, the bridge crumples drunkenly at one end into the lower river bank. But as we step gingerly onto it, with the river twenty metres below, the rails at the other end twist like brackets or quotation marks, as in a Dali painting, towards a now unusable tunnel. At the dipped end, the uprooted rails have been jerked up to point skywards. Predrag Bogdanović Ci[15] grins wryly and mutters, in Serbian, "The bridge to the skies?" – an ironic reference to the epic Kosovo cycle.

In fact, most of the bridges over the Ibar are down; most bombs have hit their targets. Big boys' computer-games. I'm reminded of Stanley Milgram's 1974 experiments at Yale into thresholds of willingness to inflict pain. According to Zygmunt Bauman: "Perhaps the most striking among Milgram's findings was the inverse ratio of readiness to cruelty and proximity to its victim. It's difficult to harm a person we touch. It's somehow easier to inflict pain upon a person we only see at a distance. And it's still easier in the case of a person we only hear. It's quite easy to be cruel towards a person we neither see nor hear."[16]

The next stop is different. It's an old stone bridge and its bomb smashed half of it but it's already being repaired. The monument reminding passers-by that it was erected in 1885 now has a fresh marble plaque fixed onto it, recording that it was rebuilt in August 1999 following the NATO aggression. So much, then, for the claims of exponents of official Anglo-American ideology, like Timothy Garton Ash, who says that the Serbs are stuck in a "victimhood complex". None of the behaviour I've seen

---

[15] Ci, born 1944, dies of Covid in April 2021.

[16] Bauman 1989: 155.

suggests a society sunk in misery or victimhood. There is poverty, shock, anger, disillusionment and disgust – but also stamina and a determination to get on and surmount problems, despite uncertainty and foreboding. As for behaviour towards me as an Englishman, wherever I've been, I've experienced no animosity, only curiosity and hospitality, just as I used to, ten or twelve years ago, when I lived and worked here and travelled all over the country. Many people I've met on this trip have been at pains to distinguish governmental policies from the attitudes of ordinary citizens. I'm not referring to intellectuals or professionals, but people who talk to me in streets, kiosks, taverns, shops, hotels and restaurants. "Come back in any time so we can talk some more," said the owner of a corner shop I'd gone into to buy some biscuits, in the village of Pazarište, not far from the monastery of Sopoćani…

One of the members of our ten-poet-strong group whose company I find myself enjoying perhaps more than any other is eighty-four-year-old Branko Branislav Ćirlić, a professor of Slavonic languages who has lived in Warsaw for the last thirty years. His oldest child is fifty-four, the youngest fifteen. There's not an ounce of pomposity in him, and he doesn't miss a trick. He's always cracking wry, understated, ironic jokes. About five feet six, he has a discerning eye for the ladies but is never smarmy or crude. He deploys his barbs only to keep a sense of *društvo* (camaraderie) going. He has a fine tenor voice and a huge repertoire of folk songs, and whenever he remembers one, he'll ask the others to sing their versions and then, of course, perform himself and argue that his version is best. "I never went in for the English much," he teases me, "but *you* might be all right." He won't let anyone help him up steep slopes or down steps but insists on managing by himself. I'd like to be like that at eighty-four, I think; and, to prove that even the English have their uses, I translate one of his poems, an affectionate piece, in which the exile expresses his love for the homeland he has left, about the relativism of us and them, of here and there.

In Novi Pazar ('New Market'), a town inside Serbia, ethnic Serbs, Muslims and Albanians mingle in the streets as they've done for generations. There are streets full of little shops tucked under the minarets that have hardly changed in decades – with plenty of silversmiths, and the mingled smells of coffee, slabs of meat hung out to dry, newly sheared wool and *ćevapčići* (the original hamburger?), and the blare of wailing music from radios and cassettes. Last time I was in this town in the mid-eighties, on an identical bus tour from Belgrade for guests at the annual Serbian October Writers' Meeting, there was a much larger group of Yugoslav and foreign writers, and a light, exuberant, jamboree atmosphere. This year, the keynote is intensity and poignancy, and the people we meet seem to have a special need, an exaggerated hunger, a craving, for poetry. Before a packed, ethnically mixed audience of Serbs and Muslims, the lights go out in the library because of the shortages, and under a huge portrait of Shakespeare we read on by candlelight.

As for refugees from southern Kosovo, we meet plenty of them in the area north of Mitrovica up to the border, especially in Leposavić, where the Serbian cultural centre from Priština has set up its temporary headquarters. One wonders how soon temporary will turn into permanent. These are all Serbs and from all walks of life. We hear of atrocities, not the kind profusely reported in the Western press, that is, by ethnic Serbs against ethnic Albanians, but the other way around. Since the war, under the eye of KFOR, there has been a relentless exodus of Serbs and Romanies from Kosovo. One can't help wondering whether, at this rate, only ethnic Albanians will be left there. Later, back in Cambridge, my email brings me an article by Malcolm Fraser from *The Australian*, dated December 28, entitled 'The West's Policy: A Catalyst for Balkan Terror'.[17] "In Kosovo," writes Fraser, "the West's failure is ever more apparent. The overwhelming majority of Serbs have fled the province because KFOR, NATO's Kosovo peacekeeping force, couldn't supply security and the number of international policemen has never reached the original target, which was in any case almost certainly too small. According to the International Contact Group, murders have been running at around 30 a week, the majority of the victims Serbs, since KFOR entered Kosovo in mid-June. If the level of killings estimated by the International Contact Group continues, by Christmas about 800 people will have been killed in Kosovo since KFOR's occupation."

What's so depressing is that most of the people I communicate with regularly knew in advance that this would happen – all of it.

2001

---

[17] John Malcolm Fraser (1930–2015), Australian politician, and twenty-second Prime Minister of Australia. See 'Malcolm Fraser', *Wikipedia*.

PART 7

SKETCHES FROM MEMORY

This final part of the book consists mainly of reminiscences of some Yugoslav writers I was lucky enough to know as friends. Some of them are likely to be entirely unknown to English-speaking readers, so here and there I've appended versions that I've made of poems. I now wish I'd translated many more. I intend each one of these small sketches as a personal tribute.

While my main purpose here is to record friendships, I'm in little doubt that, whatever the criteria, among these writers at least half a dozen would qualify for the epithet *major* and several of them *great*. Among them were men and women whose breadth and depth of learning and culture, knowledge of languages and customs, and understanding of the intricate twists and turns of history, beggared my own. In such company, I often felt ignorant, insular and provincial. And if some of these mini-portraits may be so slight as to fall far short of doing full or fair justice to their subjects, I hope they'll at least serve as glancing insights, even if not as adequate introductions.

To set contexts and chronologies, both personal and political, I've included anecdotes and commentaries. The result is an amalgam of sketches and autobiography.

ശ

In adding this part to the book, I've found myself limiting its portraits to writers who have died. This self-selecting procedure dictated itself immediately and spontaneously, and without conscious decision, plan or query on my part.

Because some of these men and women died well before their time, a further issue arises. It's not in doubt that the protracted collapse of Yugoslavia, the ubiquitous aftermath of its wars and conflicts, and their economic, intellectual, emotional and psychic shocks and repercussions – all combined to create a noxious atmosphere of insecurity and danger. Nobody in the Yugoslav Federation was unaffected. So I think it's more than likely, too, that this vicious context accelerated many illnesses and deaths, even if indirectly. Here, I'm not thinking of the immediate horrors and atrocities of war itself, nor of suicide, but of so-called 'natural' causes –

among which, cancer must be included. Most writers I knew in Yugoslavia were also heavy smokers. I'm not a statistician and have no proof of anything so specific as post-traumatic stress disorder (PTSD), which in any case wasn't a widely-known term in Europe in the late 1980s even though it had been coined in the USA in the 1970s. Nor do I mean to suggest that individuals who possess or are possessed by a so-called 'artistic temperament' are any more susceptible to such influences and pressures than anybody else. Even so, the fact that so many fine writers of many different ages died in such a short period, and some – I repeat – well before their time, does seem significant. I find it hard, not to feel sad and bitter about this, for some of these writers were dear friends of mine. They had more in them, much more, to give to the world.

∽

The sketches that follow were written in Cambridge between August and November 2018, with the exception of an earlier feature on Desanka Maksimović (written for *Zavičaj* in 1988), and three obituary notices: on Oskar Davičo (for *Politika*, in 1988); and on Ivan Lalić and Ned Goy (in 1996 and 2000 respectively, both for *The Times* of London). I quickly decided against even trying to write memoirs about Ivan or Ned for this book. They were such close friends that to do so would have seemed a discourtesy, or worse. Instead, I include brief personal notes here.

Ivan and I often found ourselves finishing each other's sentences. I respected and loved him as if he were an older brother. He died, aged only 65, as he was approaching the height of his poetic powers. These, I believe, were of the order of those of George Seferis. The hospitality that he and his wife Branka showered on me and my family was phenomenal. I remember many fine evenings in their company, together with their other friends, such as the poet, playwright, teacher and theatre and drama critic, Jovan (Vava) Hristić, and the translator and editor Bernard Johnson.[1] Ivan's poems, like those of Seferis, have inspired many of my own, not only the elegiac sequence for him in *Under Balkan Light*, but

[1] For my note on Vava Hristić, see 370 below. Bernard Johnson (1933–2003) was a lecturer in Russian and Serbo-Croatian at the Language Centre of the London School of Economics, and a prolific editor and translator. His many publications include the pioneering Penguin anthology, *New Writing in Yugoslavia* (1970), and he translated selections of poems by Miodrag Pavlović (1985, 1989) and Jovan Hristić (2003). I learned a great deal from this kind and gentle man in our all-too-few conversations.

others in that book too.[2]

Edward Dennis (Ned) Goy is the only non-Yugoslav included in these mini-memoirs.[3] I met him in the mid-1990s, after my return to Cambridge from Belgrade, when he'd already retired from teaching at Peterhouse, the oldest of the Cambridge colleges. A gentle, wise man, with a huge gusto for life and a quick sense of humour, Ned was a scholarly expert on Serbian and Croatian literature and a lover and admirer of the entire culture – or rather, cultures – of the South Slavs. He shared my dismay at the collapse of Yugoslavia and the enthusiastic support of its dismemberment by NATO allies, above all by the USA and Germany, followed sheepishly by the UK and others. Towards the end of his life, Ned and his wife Jasna Levinger-Goy spent many evenings together with Melanie and me.[4]

August 2019, January 2020

---

[2] See 'On the Death of Ivan V. Lalić, in *Under Balkan Light* (RB 2011d): 97-118. Other poems I've written in direct response to poems by Ivan, and collected in the same book, include: 'Whose voice?' (69), 'Who can I ask'? (70), and 'The voice in the garden' (71). Poems more pervasively influenced by Ivan's writings include 'On the qualities of light in the Balkans' (34), 'Silken thread: gypsy's song' (90), 'Silken thread: poet's pages' (91), 'The face of light' (92), and 'The voice of light' (93). Since influence works subliminally too, there may well be others.

[3] For my elegy and tribute, see 'Ned Goy has gone out' in *Under Balkan Light*: 80-82.

[4] Melanie Rein, my partner since 1999 and wife since 2013.

Vasko Popa (1922–1991)

photo: Horst Tappe

It's June 1990, not long before I'm due to leave Belgrade. My three years are up. I can't find another job here. I've no choice but to go back to my house in Cambridge.

I call Vasko from the apartment in Zemun. We've met only rarely since I've been living here. But he's been a constant background presence. It was he who first invited me to the October Writers' Meeting, back in 1982. I've known him since the year before that, when he was our guest at the fourth biennial Cambridge Poetry Festival in 1981.

Can we meet for a coffee, I ask, to say goodbye? As usual, we talk in French. I know and he knows this will be our last meeting. He also knows I know it. Vasko has cancer. His time is nearly up. Of course, there's no need for explicit acknowledgement of this from either of us.

He suggests we meet at the *Poslednja šansa* kafana and restaurant in the centre of Tašmajdan Park in the centre of Belgrade. I shiver. *Poslednja šansa*, 'Last Chance'.

At times like these, when truths burst, stark, through ragged appearance, I think I'm living in a myth. That's what life is like in the Balkans. That sense of living in a myth keeps happening to me, again and again. What could be called 'archetypality' – or perhaps 'archetypicity' – keeps radiating into and through the commonplace. Here, ancient pagan gods seem to be alert and going about their business all around me and in me, as *part of the fabric* of everyday reality.

Even so, it's always a surprise. It shakes and shocks me each and every time. It takes my breath away. Living in the Balkans means constantly holding that awareness open, ready and available for filling, in every fibre of one's being. Like a thirsty traveller unexpectedly coming across a stream or a spring and drinking with cupped hands.

ര

Vasko has a guttural voice, basso or baritone. As always, he talks to me in sonorous and deep-throated French. "C'est comme ça, tu vois, Richard [...]." But he trills his 'r's against his alveolar ridge. He doesn't speak English, and my Serbian still isn't good enough to enable me to converse about anything interesting, even though by now I often get the gist. As is always the case for a foreign language speaker, my listening skills are better than my speaking skills, which are adequate at least for practical needs and superficial conversation.

On this occasion, we don't talk much about poetry, but about politics and politicians in the various Yugoslav republics, of the ways that petty nationalisms and local and regional vested interests have ripped through the country's fabric. "Mais on ne pourrait pas vraiment attendre autre chose, tu vois." He cuts to the chase and suddenly I'm a student again. He quickly sketches out how the vision of Yugoslavia as a federated state incorporating diverse cultures and traditions has been misconstrued, distorted, abused. His tone is quiet, his speech measured and objective, his political analysis crisp, accurate, unsentimental.

We drink our morning coffees and our goodbye is low-key. Again, I shiver slightly as I walk away from him.

ര

Vera Radojević knows a man somewhere in Šumadija who is a beekeeper and natural healer. He produces a kind of honey that's more richly imbued with royal jelly than normal honey. Behind the scenes, I suggest to Vera that she approach Vasko's wife, Haša, and tell her that we're trying to get some of this honey for Vasko. A last throw of the dice? A last chance? We manage to get a huge pot of this honey to Vasko, via Haša.

ര

In January 1992, I've been back in England for eighteen months. I hear that Vasko has died. I feel an emptiness. He's lived long enough to see Yugoslavia fall apart. I find myself thinking: *I'm glad that he didn't have to live to see the total collapse.* I had exactly the same feeling about Oskar Davičo in 1989. I'm a *jugonostalgik.* I can't help it.

ᔓ

Nine years after my farewell to Vasko, in October 1999, I revisit Belgrade with Melanie for the October Writers' Meeting. One of our hosts and an old friend is Moma Dimić, a leading member of the Writers' Association and director of its international programme.[5] He takes a small group of writers, including Răzvan Voncu from Romania and us, to the huge city cemetery on Mije Kovačevića Street. We're about to witness a simple ceremony. The urn containing Haša's ashes is to be placed on Vasko's grave. Several people give short speeches. Somewhere else in the vast cemetery, tubas, trombones and trumpets sound out the sombre march of another funeral.

Then Moma takes us across to the Jewish cemetery on the opposite side of the street.

September 2018

---

[5] See also 371 below.

Along Balkan Street: Ivan Gadjanski (1937–2012)

photo: Literaturen svyat

Ivan Gadjanski is the first writer I meet in Serbia after Vasko, who introduces us on my first visit to Belgrade in summer 1982. Vasko has been our guest at the Cambridge Poetry Festival in the previous year. He picks me up from the Slavija Hotel and Ivan is with him. We stroll to a coffee place nearby.

Ivan speaks fluent English, having lived in the USA. I quickly discover that he's knowledgeable about American poets and, later, that his poetry is influenced by American models. With his deep-lined, slightly careworn face, his presence carries a sense of acute intelligence, tinged with a wistful humour that blends sadness and irony. In private life, I also gradually discover, he's gentle and soft-spoken, though he's capable of addressing large literary audiences with engagement, conviction and zest. A poet, translator, literary scholar, and authority on Balkan oral culture and folk traditions, he's influential in the Serbian Writers' Association and the *Pesnička jesen* (Poetry Autumn) festival at Smederevo.[6] In 1996, in the large theatre at that city's *Dom kulture* (House of Culture), I see him give an eloquent introduction to the Greek poet Manolis Anagnostakis, winner of the city's Golden Key award for poetry that year.

[6] See 261-262 above.

When I move to Belgrade from Cambridge in 1987, Ivan and I become firm friends. He and his wife Ksenija Maricki Gadjanski, a distinguished Hellenist, live with their daughter Ivana (later a biologist, and a poet herself) in a spacious flat in the high converted roof-space on the top floor of an old apartment block on Mihaila Bogićevića Street. With its sloping rafters and crossbeams, it's what we would have called a *pad* in the 1960s. Every cranny contains shelves brimming with books. The apartment, a stone's throw from the main railway station, is around the corner from Balkanska ulica (Balkan Street), which slopes all the way down from Terazije in central Belgrade towards the River Sava and, later, I learn, has a central role in Ivan's oeuvre. When I live in Belgrade in the late 1980s, this street is still lined with tradesmen's workshops and small family-run shops and businesses. This is where I get my hair cut, relishing the chatter of the moustachioed barber and his local customers. Ivan's poems draw richly on the textures and flavours of life in this neighbourhood, in a similar way, perhaps, to William Carlos Williams in *Paterson*. Ivan's *Balkanskom ulicom* ('Along Balkan Street') makes this street famous and the book runs into many editions. "The poet's pen," says Shakespeare, "gives to airy nothing / a local habitation and a name." Ivan's poems universalise the locality they're rooted in.

Quite apart from her gifts as a scholar, Ksenija's cuisine is exquisite. She specialises in traditional Serbian dishes. Over many years, she and Ivan are hugely hospitable to me and my family.

ℰ

On one of those evenings, Ivan tells an anecdote, probably apocryphal, about Milman Parry's research into the traditional singing of Serbian epic poems in the 1930s. In Bosnian coffee houses during evenings in the month of Ramadan, Parry and his fellow scholars discover rich sources of material among the analphabetic male bards who still sing their own variants of the old Serbian narratives from the Kosovo cycle. Aside from the intrinsic literary and documentary value of these recordings, Parry has an ulterior motive: to compare modern renderings of oral ('primary') epic with Homer, and, in particular, to explore how individual contemporary bards build up their repertoires and patterning techniques, especially through formulaic insertions – the equivalents of such time-worn phrases as "wine-dark sea" and "ox-eyed Athene". His research in Yugoslavia pioneers a revitalised study of oral poetic traditions all over the world.[7]

[7] See Lord; Parry; and Milman Parry Collection.

The joke goes like this. In a Bosnian village, word gets around that a large group of wealthy Americans are due to arrive, loaded with fancy modern sound equipment. These are phonograph cylinders. For whatever reason, unbeknownst to the villagers and of little interest to them, these Americans are interested in making recordings. The rumour is that the rate for singing a single song will be a dollar a line. So all the local bards agree to make their recitations as long and complex as possible. To milk the cash-cow, they adorn and amplify the songs with every improvisation they can possibly think of, adapting motifs from one song to another with even more creative freedom than usual.

ᔕ

In 1997, with Ivan's help, I translate his long poem, 'Balkan Destiny', which he then publishes in a multilingual edition.[8] The first stanza moulds casual conversational diction into a composite picture of a dystopian city. This produces a raw urban lyricism, almost in the manner of a French *chansonnier*:

> one of those days bright and early
> the dog got itself fed and
> was as they say chained in fact
> holed up altogether in some kind of cage
> in a small courtyard cluttered to overflowing
> with things from bygone times
> stuff maybe we might still find some use for
> to help us remember yes even get by

Following its gentle first line, beguilingly reminiscent of folk songs, the deadpan, matter-of-fact tone of this opening stanza, with its lack of punctuation and its cummings-like exclusion of capital letters, isn't just manneristic. Maintained throughout, this offhand flattened tone masks stark ironic juxtapositions, while gradually, surreptitiously, almost filmically, the poem moves through apparently trivial details – the drab urban surroundings, the bric-à-brac "cluttered to overflowing", the "fine capillaries of resignation", all "chipped by irony", and images of pets such as cooped up dogs, cats, and chickens – to a shockingly tragic climax:

---

[8] Gadjanski 1997.

[…] and the cracked enamelware that's being used
for something else now and chipped by irony
pots that in fact aren't even pots any more
in this backyard of what was once a communal
productive unit squeezed in between buildings
in which people and kids that is if there are still
any left eat sleep and make merry though

of course now and then some young pup
or kitten is bound to vanish in the course
of the struggle for a better life as they used
to call it and perhaps still do in those primers
for young unformed minds we had to read
in the school canteen as we sat waiting for hot milk
and fresh-baked bread and the 8 a.m. bell when we'd
hear a maiden si-i-ng-ing in the va-a-lley below

which my dear ćopić as i remarked to różewicz
is a song we were not to hear again till the leap
of your limp body into free fall into its own juices
into its own choice into the battle forever lost
on the street under the bridge in front of those
trucks which forever seem to be arriving
out of nowhere empty and ready to carry
everything off into a better and brighter future

Here the phrases "the struggle for a better life" and "a better and brighter future" not only take a sardonic swipe at conventional and official Marxism, but also echo the hilarious late-1980s TV sitcom about a typical Belgrade family, entitled *Bolji život* ('A Better Life') – whose weekly episodes, when I lived in Belgrade, I became addicted to watching. It was as intriguing as the BBC's soap *Eastenders* and as funny as *Outnumbered.*

More significantly, the suicide that's registered in the poem's last stanza, combined with the urban myth surrounding it, provides the key both to this piece's entire seedy atmosphere and to its range of meanings and associations, which are at once deeply personal and broadly political. On 26 March 1984, at the age of 69, the writer Branko Ćopić jumped off *Brankov most* ('Branko's Bridge'), which spans the River Sava in central Belgrade. A brilliant and famous humorist, ironist and children's writer, Ćopić had fought as a partisan from 1941 to 1945. But in the 1950s, he drew increasing and repeated criticisms from the ruling Communist Party, and even from Tito himself, so that eventually he found himself being accused of 'dissidence' and 'heresy'. These official and officious objections were made in response to the wry humour of his writings, and especially his ironic take on 'progress' and official notions of it. What's more, into Ivan's poem, references are woven to both this bridge's name and its reputation: 'Branko's Bridge' is an extension of Brankova Street, originally named after the Romantic poet Branko Radičević (1824–1853). But since some forty people try to commit suicide by jumping off this bridge each year, it has also earned the nickname 'Suicide Bridge'. Following Branko Ćopić's death, many people actually came to believe that the bridge was named after *him* rather than after the earlier Romantic poet Branko.[9] In the poem's last stanza, these associations are deployed to underpin the subtlest and bitterest of ironies. Here, by means of a string of repeated prepositions of direction and placement – "into" (repeated four times), "on", "under" and "in front of" – the pace accelerates vividly, relentlessly, unstoppably, as if itself enacting the velocity of the unfortunate writer's body tumbling into the river below. And here, in a tone that contrives to control lamentation with a levelling anti-Romantic veneer as he personally addresses the dead writer, Ivan not only brings in the first-person voice for the first time but also, by mentioning a conversation on the topic with Polish poet Tadeusz Różewicz (1921–2014), as if thrown in merely casually, he broadens the theme to imply a far-from-merely-localised significance. All these complex and disturbing undercurrents cohere seamlessly, held together by the poem's masterly surface-tension.[10]

ശ

Two years later, Ivan is responsible for passing my essay 'Is NATO Right to Bomb Yugoslavia?' to the editor of Serbia's main daily paper *Politika*, which serialises it over five issues, only hours before the American-led aerial campaign gets under way.[11]

Then, in 2001, while I'm working on the postscript and notes to *In a Time of Drought*, Ivan gives me invaluable leads for references on Serbo-Croatian etymology and Balkan folk customs, especially works by Petar Skok and Špiro Kulišić. In 2004, as General Editor at RAD, he publishes

---

[9] See 'Branko Ćopić'; 'Branko Radičević'; 'Branko's Bridge': all at *Wikipedia*.

[10] For further extracts from *Along Balkan Street*, see also Gadjanski 1993.

[11] For more background, see 294-295 above.

Vera Radojević's translation of this book (*U vreme suše*). Curiously, the Serbian version appears two years before its English original.[12] I also introduce Ivan and Ksenija to the Greek poet Nasos Vayenas, a close friend since 1977, whose poems I translated in 1978.[13] Nasos then edits the Greek translation of Ivan's *Balkanskom ulicom*.

Ivan and I email each other regularly between 1997 and 2007. In 2009, he discovers that he has Parkinson's disease. Not surprisingly, I don't hear much from him after that.

When I think of Ivan, I remember his kindness and hospitality, and how sensitively and accurately he registered the trials and stresses of life in the Balkans. He had his finger on the living pulse.

October 2018

---

[12] This accident of timing turns out to an oddly dislocating experience for me. Paradoxically, it seems almost as if the Serbian version were 'primary' and 'originary', and the English version a 'secondary copy', a translation-of-a-translation.

[13] Vayenas 1978 and 2010.

Eugen Verber (1923–1995)

photos: mediasfera.rs

In the mid-1980s, I'm a regular guest at the International Writers' Meetings in Belgrade, organised each October by the Serbian Writers' Association. The first day always involves plenary sessions in the National Library's conference hall. During the mid-morning break, when thronging delegates mill around in the entrance hall and the atmosphere is clouded in pungent cigarette smoke, a broadly-built man in his mid-sixties approaches and introduces himself. This is Eugen Verber. He's obviously Jewish, speaks good English, and emits a gaze that hybridises a beam and a twinkle – plus, perhaps, an anarchistic hint of being on the lookout for absurdity. I immediately sense a rapport. After chatting for five minutes, we agree to miss the next session and make our way to the café at the back of the building, where we sit on high plastic-covered stools and drink sugary Serbian coffee out of miniature throw-away cups. We talk and talk. First about London, which he knows quite well, then about mutual acquaintances, my Anglo-Jewish background, the Belgrade Jewish community, and Serbian writers, including Jews. In this single conversation, I learn a good deal.

Eugen is magnetic and endearing. His presence improbably integrates the stolidity of a Serbian patriarch with Mittel-European *Yiddishkeit*. Many years later, online photographs show him to have been slim and elegant in his youth, but by the time I meet him he has a squarish face and a bald pate. With his thick-rimmed glasses and bow tie, this gives him the air of a portly and authoritative professor. Eugen exudes an exuberant and confident joviality which at times seems to be able to mingle with the *gravitas* and authoritativeness of a Serbian Samuel Johnson. He appears to be at once deeply solemn and to sparkle with an effervescent lightness of being. This curious combination inspires confidence, affection and trust, and perhaps initial puzzlement too, all of which give him a unique aura.

Following my move to Belgrade in September 1987, I frequently socialise in circles that intersect with his, so I soon discover that everyone else acquainted with Eugen feels a very particular but shared kind of affection towards him too. But as I gradually get to know him better, I soon realise that he isn't merely endearing, but a man of many parts. He's not only a leading committee member of the Writers' Association, but also a polymath, polyglot, internationally eminent Judaic scholar, teacher of Hebrew, and editor of the beautiful illuminated medieval text, the fourteenth century *Sarajevo Haggadah*.[14] He has written on the Talmud and Kabbalah, and translated books from German, Hungarian, Yiddish, Aramaic, and Hebrew.

Born into an Orthodox Jewish family in Subotica, ten kilometres from the Hungarian border, Eugen attended school in Novi Sad. In 1942, the occupying Hungarian army committed atrocities in the city, including a massacre of Jews, Serbs and Roma. Aged 21, Eugen fled to Budapest, where at that time anti-Semitism was less violent. He managed to find work as a dental technician, but in 1943 was conscripted as a forced labourer on the Eastern Front. He escaped in summer 1944, enrolled in the Red Army, and re-entered Serbia via Romania, where he joined the Yugoslav People's Liberation Army. His experience during the Second World War, like that of other Serbian Jews I meet, is one of Odyssean astuteness and bravery in his determination to survive.

In addition to his many other gifts, it comes as no surprise to learn that Eugen is a well-known, well-loved, and versatile character-actor, who has appeared in scores of movies and broadcasts. I occasionally see him on TV playing a minor role in a drama or sitcom. As a fluent German-speaker, he sometimes even takes the part of a heel-clicking Nazi officer in a war film, full of *Jawohls* and *Meine Herren* and raised long-arm salutes. The experience underlying this knowledge, of course, is no joke. Later, I discover yet another side to him, when I sit down with him in his apartment to translate several of his poems. One of these, 'Warmed by a Frozen Seed', is an impassioned lament for the Jews of the Warsaw Ghetto. Informed by

[14] See also 266-267 above.

the twin motifs of shattered vessels and shards scattered in darkness, the poem is richly infused with Kabbalah. I append it after this memoir.[15]

On one occasion Eugen and I have a minor tiff. He accuses me, as a foreigner, of interfering with the selection of guests for the annual October Writers' Meeting. On the suggestion of another committee member, I've recommended two very different writers. One, Moris (Musa) Farhi (1935–2019) is a novelist of Turkish-Jewish origin who lives in London and writes in English. Musa is currently working on a mammoth novel about the fate of Romanies during the Holocaust, to be entitled *Children of the Rainbow*, which I know will be of interest in Serbia. The other suggestion is my old mentor, the English poet Peter Russell (1921–2003), who lives in a valley near the walled village of Pian di Scò, 50 kms from Arezzo, having moved there from Venice in 1983.[16] A polyglot, friend and follower of Ezra Pound, Peter has taught himself Serbo-Croatian, visited Croatia and Bosnia, and translated some poems. I assure Eugen in my best pseudo-diplomatic manner that it hasn't been my intention to meddle, no, not at all, but only to make 'informed suggestions'. He accepts the point graciously and we both grin. Eventually each of these writers receives an invitation, probably thanks to his advocacy. I realise he's been checking me out.

ꕥ

In the same year, I help Gordana Kuić (*aka* Krstić) polish an English translation of the first two chapters of her as-yet-unpublished romantic novel, *Miris kiše na Balkanu* (*The Scent of Rain in the Balkans*). This book turns out to be the first part of a saga, based closely on the story of Gordana's Jewish family in Sarajevo. As a result, I find myself thinking about Ladino, the language of the Sephardic Jews, especially those of Sarajevo and Salonika, ninety percent of whom were murdered in the Holocaust. It suddenly dawns on me that Ladino derives from varieties of medieval Spanish in an almost symmetrically parallel way to the development of Yiddish, the language of Ashkenazi Jews, from medieval German.[17] In the

[15] To the best of my knowledge, Eugen wrote poems only very occasionally and never published them.

[16] In 1965–1966, I lived in Peter Russell's flat in Castello, Venice, thirty metres from the Riva degli Schiavoni. For my memoir on Peter, see RB 1996.

[17] Actually, Yiddish also includes elements from Slavic languages, ancient Romance languages, Hebrew and Aramaic. Its origins, even within German, are a matter of scholarly controversy. See Johnson, George (online).

wake of their expulsion from Spain in 1492, Iberian Jews took Ladino with them wherever they emigrated, including the Balkans.[18] I also discover that the word *Sephardic* originates in the Hebrew word for Spain or Iberia: סְפָרַד (*s'farád*).

I then find myself writing a quasi-Borgesian prose-piece entitled 'Fragment: On the Sepharad'.[19] This emerges in a mock-archaic style. I round off the piece by adding the ponderous 'Salamon Ruben ben Israel of Salonika, 1688'. The pseudonym surreptitiously embeds my own Hebrew name, 'Israel' being one of my father's two given names. The date marks exactly three centuries before that of the piece's actual composition; and the location, Salonika, perhaps even enmeshes a hint that Salamon Ruben *might* have been a member of the secret *Dönmeh* sect, a follower of the 'false Messiah', Sabbatai Zevi. According to Gershom Scholem, members of this cult practised orgies on Yom Kippur (the Day of Atonement).[20]

Shortly after writing 'On the Sepharad', when I visit Eugen's apartment to work on a translation of one of his poems,[21] I decide to play a mild prank on him, partly to find out if this *jeu d'esprit* of mine might seem even remotely plausible. Casually, I mention that I've come across a "rather unusual" piece of Hebrew prose, and add that I happen to have an English translation with me.

"Might you be able to tell me anything about it?" I ask. I hand over the typescript.

He scans it quickly. "That's extraordinary," he says, shaking the two pages at me. He disappears into another room to consult various reference books and encyclopaedias.

He comes back after ten minutes, nonplussed. "*Neverovatno*," he says. "Unbelievable. I can't find a single reference to this author."

Neverovatno is one of my favourite Serbian words. It makes me think of Never-Never-Land.

---

[18] The Alhambra Decree, which expelled all Jews from Spain, was an edict issued on 31 March 1492 by the joint Catholic Monarchs, Isabella I of Castile and Ferdinand II of Aragon. The Sephardic diaspora then spread into North Africa, many parts of Europe, and the countries of the Ottoman Empire. Ladino today is recognised as a minority language in Bosnia and Hercegovina, France, Israel, and Turkey. See: 'Alhambra Decree', *Wikipedia*.

[19] See *Under Balkan Light* (RB 2011d): 38-39.

[20] Scholem 1978: 148ff. See also 267 above.

[21] See 327-330 below.

I hesitate, but decide not to let the joke fester. "*I* wrote it. It's a hoax."

He curses me. And bursts out laughing.

ℰ∽

Eugen was seventy-two when he died. There was a Protean bounty about him. He was uniquely gifted in both magnanimity and modesty. I've never met anybody remotely like him, before or since.

I've a copy of his edition of the *Sarajevo Haggadah*, a gift from him, which I treasure.

The following poem hasn't been published before. And, why I don't know, I can't find the Serbian original.

September 2018

Warmed by a Frozen Seed

The German Kommandant ordered that the Warsaw Ghetto should be destroyed, bulldozed, and rolled flat. Today all that remains in the huge square is a memorial to the fighters of the Ghetto Uprising

In this square
light no candle,
ignite no torch,
kindle no memorial.
In this square
where, once, there was no square,
a mass of voices roared:
Fire!
Fire!
Fire!

In this square
where, once, there was no square –
what gleams now
instead of candles, torches, memorials,
from pulverised stone,
from shattered vessels,
from smashed glass,
is their eyes.

In early spring
I stand in the square
where, once, there was no square
and watch the sky
which once watched
those same eyes,
as blue then
and cold as today.

In this square
where, once, there was no square
there are no trees,
no leaves,
no falsely weeping willows.
Here the slavering *Ritter*[22]

decorated with his oak leaves
passed with tank and bulldozer.
There are no oak leaves now
to cover those eyes
in autumn with a warm shroud.
There is nothing. Nothing.
My mouth is dumb.

Step by step,
step by step
among rubble and shards,
horrific wreckage.
Step by step,
and I stand still:
that scattering of crimson shards
was not blood,
but the red bricks of homes where once
lived Yidl or Avromele or Motche
and laboured like slaves
for their tribes of children.

---

[22] German, 'knight'.

That early spring,
from a house standing here
built of blood coloured brick,
Motche or Avromele or Yidl
or maybe some other yid
heeded neither himself,
nor his wife, nor his children,
but defended the name
of his human honour,
spat on always, and reviled,
and to these same cold blue skies
man, woman and child
arose in flame.

Eyes, let me take
just one more step
to pass among you,
the fairest eyes
among fair eyes of Jewish women,
and let me drink you,
and let me share you
as a potion, among the humbled.
For you are the balm
and you are the milestone
and you are the conscience
and the torch
and candle
and memorial flame
and the tree
in this square
where, once, there was no square.

It's cold today
and this cold blue sky
watches me
as it watched them.
I stop   I listen.
Yidl mitn fidl is playing

his melody, his warm *nigun*[23]
by the waters of eternal Babylon
I catch the song's silken thread
which shimmers, like a springtime spiderweb
then dissolves   disappears
I am utterly stilled.

I'm cold in this square
where, once, there was no square
and there are no warm rooms
where I can hide
from pulverised stone,
from shattered vessels,
from smashed glass,
but only the cold arrows
of a bloody sun
beats down

and into my hands
I take these freezing
pulverized shards of horror
and with these icy grains
I warm my breast
and I sow
I sow
I sow
In myself
and in you
the germ of life
conceived in the womb
of this square
where, once, there was no square.

Translated, Belgrade, 1988

[23] Hebrew, ניגון, 'tune, melody, religious song'.

Bogdana (Boba) Bobić (1937–1996)

photo: Branislav (Vlaja) Vlajinić

Boba Bobić reading from her translation of Black Light *(Crna svetlost). Seated, RB and Miodrag Pavlović. Ethnographic Museum, Belgrade, April 1985.*

My second trip to Belgrade takes place in October 1982. I'm to be a guest at the October Writers' Meeting. This is the first of many subsequent invitations. I write to Branka Panić, whom I've met that summer in Arandjelovac, to ask if she'd like me to put on an extra event with her. Branka, who is Director of the Centre for Learning Foreign Languages on Vase Pelagića Street, immediately invites me to run a daytime poetry writing workshop for children and teenagers and to give a poetry reading on the same evening.

The poetry workshop has to be bilingual because I don't yet speak a word of Serbian. Three teachers of English at the Centre interpret, so that the children can understand me and then write their poems in Serbian. This event turns out to be a humming success, partly because of the high motivation of children and teenagers to learn English, and partly because the whole idea is entirely new. Nobody has ever tried out anything like this before in regular schools in Yugoslavia. We get newspaper and TV coverage, and three English teachers at the Centre are actively involved in running the workshops: Branka herself, Nada Popović and Bogdana Gagrica (Boba) Bobić. As for the audience at the evening reading, this turns out to be very different in make-up from the typical acolytes and devotees of events at the Writers' Association. The considerable number of those present on this occasion are motivated not only by interest in literature but also by the opportunity to hear and practise spoken English. I don't know it at the time, but between 1987 and 1989, I'll spend two happy years teaching English here, mainly to adults attending evening classes.

Boba, I quickly discover, has already translated several of my poems from *Black Light*, and wants to work on more. We get on immediately; and she becomes my first Serbian translator. Her husband, Djordje, is the Belgrade manager for an international car hire firm. On later occasions, whenever I visit Belgrade, he arranges a rental car for me. Boba and Djordje often come to meet me at the airport on arrival and see me off at the end of my stay. They have two teenage daughters, Anabeli and Lana. I visit their apartment, and a great deal of eating, drinking, talking, and laughing gets done. They're hugely hospitable. Together with Branka and her husband Joca (pron: *Yotsa*), and both families, we sometimes go to eat at one of the tavernas in Skadarlija, in the city centre.

In 1985, Boba completes her translation of *Black Light* into Serbo-Croatian: *Crna svetlost* is jointly published by Dečje novine and the Centre for Learning Foreign Languages, mainly on the initiative of Branka, who in her typically generous fashion organises a launch-event at the Centre. This coincides with the start of our poetry workshop tour in Central Serbia. Both Branka and Boba are key to the success of this tour, working with me as translators and interpreters.[24]

∽

[24] See 25 and 270-280 above.

Boba is a Serb who was born in Drvar, western Bosnia, near the Croatian border, and brought up in Knin, a city in the Dalmatian hinterland. Knin was part of the northern Military Frontier (*Vojna krajina*) that separated the Austro-Hungarian Empire from what many nineteenth-century travellers described as 'La Turquie d'Europe' ('Turkey-in-Europe', 'European Turkey').[25] Boba is a true Yugoslav, tolerant of all ethnicities; and later I learn that because she aims to draw on the entire resources of both Serbian and Croatian in her translations, she sometimes includes unusual and even archaic literary diction, which can seem remote and artificial to Serbian ears. Her translations are definitely Serbo-Croatian rather than Serbian.

Boba also translates my two long poems 'Angels' and 'Tree'.[26] The second of these is a chant-poem of 365 lines. At poetry readings, we explore varying styles of performance for the second of these poems, aiming to find the most effective ways of delivering extracts from the poem to audiences. We soon hit on a mode that turns out to be effective and original. In counterpointed duet, as if making a kind of verbal jazz, we alternate short bursts of English and Serbo-Croatian by reciting groups of lines in each language, sometimes speaking solo, one after the other, and sometimes overlapping and overlaying the two languages. The effectiveness is partly thanks to Boba having a rich, husky, sonorous voice, and partly because the balance between male and female voices in itself sets up a dynamic interplay.[27] On one of these occasions, in 1985, we read with Miodrag Pavlović at the Ethnographic Museum, at an event organised by Branka before our 'travelling poetry workshop' tour.[28] Later, when I move to Belgrade in 1987, Boba and I become teaching colleagues at Vase Pelagića, and we often meet at her apartment to work on more translations of poems for an

---

[25] See 80 above.

[26] 'Andjeli' and 'Drvo'. *Književnost* 12: 2081-2089 (RB 1987). A second version of 'Drvo', translated by Vera V. Radojević, was published online in April 2019 (RB 2019a).

[27] In many later bilingual readings of this poem, I've followed the model that Boba and I first developed together. I've combined readings of *Tree* with versions in other languages: for example, Chinese, Irish, Italian and Spanish. For an example of a reading in English and Irish, overlaid with a visual rendering in Italian, see 'Tree, a Video' (RB 2017g, online). For translations of *Tree* into many languages, see 'The Albero Project' and 'A Forest of Trees' (RB 2017e and 2017f, both online). A second Serbian version of 'Tree' by Vera V. Radojević is included in this online collection. See RB 2019a.

[28] See 25 and 265 above.

edition contracted by the publisher KOV in Vršac.[29]

In the mid-eighties, during a freezing winter, Boba visits me in Cambridge with Anabeli, her elder daughter. She has been experiencing severe headaches. I arrange a consultation in London for her with Robert Maurice-Williams, a distinguished brain surgeon. Robert and I were fellow-students at Pembroke College, Cambridge. He kindly agrees to see Boba without charge. Boba is eventually diagnosed with a tumour. She dies in 1996. Then Djordje dies, and so does Anabeli, very young.

ഗ

The place I most think of in connection with Boba and her family is Skadarlija, where we went to drink and eat with family and friends. Skadarlija is a little pedestrian cobbled street, tree-lined, full of taverns, that slopes down from a corner of Trg republike (Republic Square) in Belgrade's city centre to the Bajloni fruit-and-flower market on the other side of George Washington Street, in the direction of the Danube. It's a place where, if you go for a meal in the evening, alone or in company, a costumed band will still come to your table with violins and accordions, and sing you rich, sentimental songs in haunting minor keys – like 'Ima dana',[30] and patrols of Roma children may accost you, trying to sell you roses or carnations. At the turn of the twentieth century Skadarlija was a bohemian area, a mini-Montmartre or Plaka; but unlike those districts in Paris and Athens, it's still unspoilt and charming, with its own unique and authentic Balkan flavour and sweet, sad smell. Especially in October. Skadarlija is specific, unique, unrepeatable, uncopiable.

Boba was too. In retrospect, it seems to me that sadness and happiness were always subtly mingled in my friendship with Boba and her family. I remember them with huge affection.

September–October 2018

[29] For reasons I never find out, this book never materialises.

[30] See 246, n. 49 above.

Arrival, 1987

In May 1987, the British Council takes me on as a lector to teach English at the Centre for Learning Foreign Languages in Belgrade. My preliminary contract is to be for one year. Thanks to various short visits since 1982, I'm already familiar with parts of Serbia, Croatia and Slovenia,

Before departure, my garage mechanic in Cambridge agrees to help me purchase a reliable car. We find a dealer in London specialising in left-hand-drive vehicles. After taking the train down, we see a sturdy second-hand white VW Golf and take it for a spin. On his advice, I buy it on the spot and drive it back to Cambridge. In early July, I let out my house for the year and pack the Golf with basic items I think I'll need, including a smart new electronic golf-ball Olivetti typewriter, a plentiful supply of ribbons, an electric kettle, an electric toaster, and a second-hand suit that I've picked up for £10 from the Salvation Army shop in Mill Road.

I spend the summer in Split as the guest of Daša Marić. I drive to the Dover-Ostend ferry, and from Ostend to Bruxelles. There I set my Golf on the auto-train to Ljubljana, and spend the night in a more-or-less comfortable sleeper. Daša meets me at Ljubljana station the next morning, and we drive down the winding and dramatically beautiful Jadranska magistrala (Adriatic Highway) to Split. We visit the island of Hvar, the coastal towns of Šibenik, Omiš, and Zadar, from which I've memories of white-painted buildings with flat roofs where you can sit and sunbathe. Then the ruins of ancient Salona, whose Roman columns lie scattered at all angles in long grass. And then the Ivan Meštrović museum, north of Split. I've already seen several of his sculptures at the University of Notre Dame, Indiana, and his Caryatids on the summit of Avala, a hill surmounted by a telecommunications tower, ten miles south of Belgrade, as well as what Rebecca West calls a "glorious naked male figure", perched high on a column Kalemegdan Park, looking out over the river Sava, a statue erected in 1928, celebrating eventual victory over the Ottomans.[31]

[31] West 469-470. I don't share her enthusiasm for Meštrović's sculptures, most of which I find craggily crude, bulky and unsubtle. Never mind.

In Split, on the eastern slope of Marjan hill, a promontory overlooking the city and the sea, Daša and I walk around the old Jewish cemetery. We eat *seppie in umido* (squid in their own ink, which leaves the tongue blackened), a good deal of fish, and tender saltmarsh lamb. We also visit an aunt of hers in the small town of Sinj, sheltered among the hills behind Split, to watch the *Alka*, an ancient lance-spearing contest in which the competitors – burly, moustachioed, costume-clad men – in turn gallop on horseback along a prepared track, as they aim to spear a metal ring suspended on a wire while riding at full tilt, in a ritualised phallic celebration of the warrior-spirit.[32]

In this way, I get a taste of life in Dalmatia, begin to learn a little Serbo-Croatian, and acquire at least a basic understanding of the complex interactions and tensions between Croats and Serbs – including the rifts between Catholicism and Orthodoxy, the Roman and Cyrillic scripts, and the cultural influences westward to Rome and north-westward to Venice on the one hand, and eastward to Russia and southward to Greece on the other. I learn a good deal about the history of Yugoslavia, especially of the Communist Party. An uncle of Daša's was prominent in the movement in the 1920s, when the party was banned and membership an offence punishable by prison. For his pains, he was imprisoned by Tito on Goli Otok ('Naked Island, Bare Island') in the 1940s.[33] Daša also introduces me to the poems of Tin Ujević and together we start translating some of them.[34]

ᔕ

Very early one morning at the end of August 1987, I set out to drive non-stop through the deep-set valleys of Bosnia and across western Serbia to Belgrade. For some reason I don't understand, I don't feel comfortable in these valleys: to me they somehow feel eerie and I've a sense of claustrophobia. I take only necessary stops. I manage to arrive the same evening at Branka Panić's house in the hilly suburb of Voždovac. After staying at her place for a few days, I rent a small ground floor flat on nearby Gostivarska Street, off Vojvode Stepe. In the spring I'll hear an

---

[32] The *alka* is the name of the metal ring. This tilters' tournament takes place annually on the first Sunday in August, to commemorate the victory over the Turkish army in 1715. The tilter who scores the highest number of points (*punat*) is declared the victor".

[33] See 343 below.

[34] See 161-196 above; and Ujević 1993, 2005, 2010, 2011, 2013.

unseen nightingale's songs brilliantly flooding moonlit gardens that are scented by blossoms of a huge variety of trees.[35]

Located on the corner of tree-lined Vase Pelagića and Koste Glavinića in the suburb of Senjak, the Centre for Learning Foreign Languages offers part-time courses. Organised as a co-operative and directed by Branka, this is where I'm to work. From my involvement in events here on several previous short visits,[36] I've already made friends with some of the teachers, including Boba Bobić. Quite often, after evening classes, some of us teachers go to the Šešer restaurant across the road, especially Vera Valok, Nada Popović and Boba, to have a drink or snack with students.[37]

September–October 2018

---

[35] See the opening lines of 'Do vidjenja Danice, Goodbye Balkan Belle' in *Under Balkan Light* (RB 2011d): 3.

[36] In the 1980s, I recommend several Anglophone poets to the Writers' Association as guests for the international October Meeting, including John Matthias from the USA and Walter Perrie from Scotland. I arrange with Branka for these poets to give readings at the Centre for Learning Foreign Languages, as well as another guest, English poet Carol Rumens.

[37] Since then the restaurant has been renamed 'Fenjer' ['lantern'].

At the Yugoslav Drama Theatre

One morning in early September 1987, only days after settling into my small flat in Gostivarska Street, I get an unusual commission, which suggests that my life in Belgrade may well turn out to be more interesting than I'd anticipated. The next three years amply fulfil that promise.

I receive a phone-call from the British Council office. The director of the Yugoslav Drama Theatre on Marshal Tito Boulevard needs help with an English translation.[38] I go along to the theatre to meet him. Jovan Ćirilov (1931–2014) is a slim, elegant man who impresses me by his professional authority and brisk courtesy.[39] Later, I learn that long before the Gay Lib movement, he has been a leading campaigner for acceptance of same-sex relationships. Serbia in the 1980s is still a country where deeply ingrained prejudices make life very difficult for homosexuals.

Ćirilov is looking for a native English speaker to train two actors to speak some lines that need to be delivered in English. Slobodan Selenić (1933–1995) has written a drama set in the Second World War.[40] A minor scene involves two British officers who've been flown out from London to liaise with Tito's partisans. In the play, neither of these two characters knows Serbian. They speak only English. They eventually disappear in

---

[38] The Yugoslav Drama Theatre was destroyed by fire in 1997 and not opened again until 2003. *Bulevar Maršala Tita* (Marshal Tito Boulevard) was renamed *Bulevar Srpskih vladara* (Boulevard of the Serbian Monarchs) in 1992, and later reverted to its original name, *Kralja Milana* (King Milan). One of the main thoroughfares in central Belgrade, it runs from Slavija Square to Terazije.

[39] See 'Jovan Ćirilov', *Wikipedia*.

[40] Several weeks later. I meet Slobodan Selenić (1933–1995) for a drink at the bar of the Yugoslav Drama Theatre, but only on one occasion. He's gentle, quiet and affable, and speaks perfect English. Years later, I read two of his novels in English translation, *Fathers and Forefathers* and its sequel, *Premeditated Murder*. These are works of very high quality. Set respectively in the first half of the century including the Second World War and during the break-up of Yugoslavia a generation later, these books are masterly explorations of both periods.

mysterious and questionable circumstances, never to be heard of again.

I think of Churchill's three famous emissaries to Tito during the War: the astute William Deakin, in 1942, later Warden of St. Antony's College, Oxford; Fitzroy MacLean, in 1943, who became a close friend of Tito and a key supporter of his regime; and then Randolph, Churchill's only son, who was parachuted out in 1944. The first two were later knighted and played key roles in the transference of British support towards Tito in preference to Colonel Dragoljub (Draža) Mihailović's royalist *četnici* (Chetniks). Randolph, whose bouts of drunken incompetence were well-documented, was less effective.[41] Unlike the fictional characters in Selenić's play, all three survived the war.

My job is to train the two young actors to speak their lines in authentic-sounding English. As it happens, the real situation inversely mirrors that of the play: neither of them actually speaks any English at all. First, I read the script and slightly revise the lines to reflect the dated upper-class inflections of British officers during the Second World War. Then I rehearse the actors. The phonetics course I'd taken at UCL (University College London) in the 1970s comes in handy, and I make a cassette recording for them. They practise assiduously, syllable by syllable, phrase by phrase, until they're word-perfect and get the intonation exactly right.

When I go to see the play, since my Serbian is minimal, I understand far too little. But I'm impressed by the quality of the acting and have at least a small insight into the quality of theatre in Belgrade. And I'm deeply proud of 'my' two actors.

September 2018

[41] See: Deakin; Maclean 1949 and 1957; Lees; and 'Randolph Churchill', *Wikipedia.*

'Our man'

The same October, I once again attend the international Writers' Meeting. The final poetry reading winds up with participants having a late-night meal together in a large restaurant in central Belgrade. I've particularly enjoyed the event this year because there's a radical difference in my own involvement. For I'm not just a visitor on a short trip. I'm actually a resident here. And I'm exhilarated to be living in Belgrade.

I feel expansive and have far too much to drink and get excessively chatty. Apart from the poet and novelist Ratko Adamović, one of the October Meeting's organising hosts, and a friend I've known since my second visit to Belgrade in 1982, I find I'm the last person to leave. I'm still, let's say, effusive, and have every intention to go on drinking and talking.

The staff clear the tables and empty the ashtrays. Ratko waits patiently. Eventually, gently but firmly, he ushers me out of the restaurant to help me find a taxi. I assure him that I can manage perfectly well by myself, thanks very much. But he won't let me go until he finds a cab. He escorts me, one arm around my shoulder to steady me, as I wobble along the pavement.

Just before I get into the cab, he says, *Sve je u redu, Ričarde.* And bear-hugging me, he adds, *Ti si naš čovek, znaš.* This means, literally, "Everything's OK, Richard. You're our man, you know." But this literal English version does little to impart the flavour of *naš čovek*. A translation closer to the spirit would be "You're one of us." And the implication, at least as I read it: *We accept you. You're at home here.*

April 2019

Danilo Kiš (1935–1989)

photo: Daily Beast

In late 1987, soon after my arrival as a resident in Belgrade, Boba Bobić takes me to meet the editor of *Književnost* ('Literature'). They're going to publish her translations of my two long poems 'Angels' and 'Tree'. Danilo Kiš happens to be visiting their office and we're introduced. That's one of the things I like about Belgrade, the fact that it's small enough to bump into people. It makes for an informal, chatty intimacy.

A tall, slim, craggily built man, with a shock of dark, wavy hair, Danilo emits a wholly individual magnetism. When he enters a room, you can't help notice. Conversation pauses or dies away and the atmosphere suddenly undergoes an indefinable, subtly nuanced shift. If you're facing away from the door, you find yourself turning around, without even registering that you've done so.

Danilo immediately asks me to call him and arrange a time to visit. If I'm free, he says, could he ask for some help with a translation? I feel surprised and honoured. He's a writer whose books I admire enormously: *Garden, Ashes* and *A Tomb for Boris Davidovich*.[42] I sense a controlled, leashed power in him, almost crackling with delicate, nervous energy.

---

[42] *The Encyclopedia of the Dead* doesn't get published in English until 1989, two years after this meeting.

I visit his apartment several times to help him proofread and correct an English version of one of his stories, which has been poorly translated from French. His partner and French translator, Pascale Delpech, is with him. We chat in French peppered with English. I warm to them both. As is the norm among writers in Belgrade, Danilo is informal, friendly, and doesn't stand on ceremony. He's a heavy smoker, as I am too at this time.

When I'm with him, I feel the need to be ever-so-slightly more alert than usual: this arises, I think, not out of any need for reticence but from the sense of being in the presence of a bracing and acute intelligence, an acutely attuned sensibility. I can't help wondering what's the source of this charged quality. It's as though he's always brimful of more energy and ideas than any single time-and-space bound situation could be capable of containing or constraining. I give him a copy of *Crna svetlost*, Boba's translation of *Black Light*, my sequence of poems set in Greece, dedicated to the memory of George Seferis.

I learn later that in 1939, when he was three years old, Danilo's Jewish family in Novi Sad took the precaution of having him and his sister Danica baptised into the Serbian Orthodox church, to enable him to have certified proof of Christian identity. This turned out to be a wise and fortunate premonitory safeguard. In 1942, his father Eduard miraculously survived a massacre of Jews in the city by the Hungarian army, and then escaped with his family to a small town in south-west Hungary, where there was less immediate risk of atrocity or persecution. But in 1944, Hungarian policy towards Jews shifted and Eduard was deported. He perished in Auschwitz in 1944, along with many of his relatives. The survival of Danilo and his mother and sister was largely due to the baptismal certificates. These early experiences left an indelible imprint on Danilo.[43]

ഗ

At the time I meet him, Danilo is working on a TV documentary about Yugoslav citizens who, from 1949 until 1956, were arbitrarily incarcerated by Tito's secret police. In the wake of disagreements with Stalin and the departure of Yugoslavia from the Soviet Bloc in 1948, institutionalised paranoia became even more the political norm than in the immediate wake of the Second World War. Tito deployed imprisonment without

[43] See 'Danilo Kiš', *Wikipedia*; and Mark Thompson's *Birth Certificate: The Story of Danilo Kiš*, which blends biography with literary interpretation.

trial to remove all potential challengers to his authority from within the pro-Russian Communist Party; and any person, whether a party member or not, could be arrested for the tiniest misdemeanour – even for an ironic hint that might seem to slight the regime and its leadership, or for simply telling some harmless joke. The two most infamous prisons for citizens even faintly suspected of dissidence were the tiny Adriatic islands of Goli Otok (Naked Island) and Sveti Grgur (Saint Gregor), with areas of 4.5 and 6.7 square kms respectively. According to Peter Heylyn's *Cosmographie* (1652):

> Along the Coasts of Sclavonia, lie a Cluster of ISLANDS to the Number of a thousand, as is said by Plinie: most of which (if indeed so many) are but Rocks, not Islands, and not inhabitable at all, nor of any note.[44]

In 1949, these inhospitable rocky outcrops were turned into high security labour camps. Conditions were harsh and primitive and only the strong survived.[45] Located between the larger populated Dalmatian islands of Rab and Krk, Goli Otok was reserved for male prisoners and Sveti Grgur for females.

Usually Danilo lives in Paris. He is an internationalist who finds the bickering and cliquishness of the of Belgrade literary circles stifling. When we meet he's preparing for a short trip to Israel, accompanied by a film crew, to interview several Jewish women, former prisoners of Sveti Grgur. Later, when I watch this moving documentary on TV, I recognise sweeping shots of his apartment in Belgrade, and can't help noticing that among the books scattered on a table is a copy of my *Crna svetlost*. The camera pauses an instant on its black cover and white lettering. As I see this, I feel inordinately proud to have occupied even a short moment in the life of this great European novelist.

I feel even prouder when, with Ivan Lalić, Danilo co-translates the title-poem of my book *The Blue Butterfly*, based on the rough translation made by Ivan Gadjanski and Moma Dimić on a communal trip to Bor and Negotin.[46]

---

[44] Heylyn 1669 [1652], Book 2: 162.

[45] See Popov 1996b: 92

[46] In 1987 or 1988, the Serbian Writers' Association organises a weekend trip from Belgrade to these south-eastern towns for a busload of Serbian writers. They generously include me, the only foreigner. The trip involves impromptu poetry readings and a good deal of convivial and sometimes raucous drinking.

At the time I meet Danilo, he has a nasal problem. He's constantly sniffling from one nostril. He doesn't say anything about this. But I don't think this is just a common cold.

He dies two years later of lung cancer, at the shockingly young age of fifty-five, the same age his father Eduard died in Auschwitz. Dubravka Ugrešić calls him "the last 'Yugoslav' writer".[47]

September and December 2018

---

[47] Ugrešić 41, 161.

Desanka Maksimović (1898–1993)

photo: Poezije Ljubovi

photo: pinterest.com

It's summer 1988. Desanka Maksimović has been awarded the Struga poetry prize. At the age of 80, she's the grand old lady of Serbian poetry. A short, slim woman with a high-pitched voice, she always wears a broad-brimmed hat. These big hats are her trademark. Her poem about the schoolboy victims of the 1941 Kragujevac massacre, 'Krvava bajka' ('Bloody Fable'), a lament written in Belgrade in 1941 immediately after she heard news of the Nazi massacre, is known to every schoolchild and adult in Serbia.[48] She's also famous for her poems for children. Her poems deploy the Serbian language in a rich but simple colloquial way to register personal content that resonates immediately. Thanks to these combined qualities, she's hugely popular in a very specific way that includes affection, admiration and respect. She has the genuine gift of the common touch.

Shortly after my arrival at Struga, one of the festival organisers suddenly asks me to translate Desanka's famous poem of old age, 'Nemam više vremena' ('I've no more time'). It's needed urgently for the award ceremony, which is tomorrow. As I've already learned, this kind of last-minute frenetic improvisation is typical of organisation in the Balkans.

[48] 'The blue butterfly' has been referred to as 'engleska krvava bajka' ('the English Bloody Fable'): see Raketić and Radišić.

It's a rather different way of doing things from the more controlled, long-term, phlegmatic kind of planning that I've been used to in England but, at least so far, in my experience, things nearly always tend to work out right in the end. With crucial help from my partner Jasna Mišić,[49] I manage to cobble together a preliminary translation, and on the next day I read an English version before a packed audience and TV cameras at the prize ceremony in the cathedral-church of St. Sophia in Ohrid. Here's the article I wrote at the time, followed by the translation of the poem.

August 2019

Time to Spare: Desanka Maksimović at Struga, 1988

The Golden Wreath Award at the Struga Poetry Festival (Struga Poetry Evenings) this year went to Serbian poet Desanka Maksimović. Widely translated into a dozen languages, and into Russian by none less than Anna Akhmatova, she has published fifteen full collections since her first in 1926. Independent of schools and fashions, she has remained true to a simple, almost childlike vision: her themes are human generosity and suffering, the transitoriness of life, the ups and downs of Balkan history, and landscape and nature. In 1923 she wrote: "I could give my heart to everyone / and still have plenty left over for myself." She's deservedly loved throughout Yugoslavia: the kind of poet anyone can approach.

And she has time for everybody, though little left of her own. Still pert and spry at the age of ninety-one, she indefatigably autographed her way through the five days of the Festival, cheerily chatting to journalists, poets, children, everyone, without once losing her energy, temper or smile. That in itself was a lesson in manners and modesty. In her work, beneath the apparent homeliness and informality, there is durability, dignity, and a minutely organised modernist patterning of detail. On August 28, as always wearing her broad-brimmed hat, she stood, five feet two, on the narrow bridge where Lake Ohrid gurgles into the River Drim, and under the camera glare, surrounded on the podium by poets from forty countries, received her award before a milling, relaxed holiday crowd of around seven thousand. That night, her prize preceded both politics and sport on Yugoslav TV news bulletins. Previous winners of the award have included Auden, Montale, Neruda, Enzensberger, Ginsberg,

[49] And later my wife, from 1989 to 1996.

Artur Lundkvist, Yannis Ritsos, Rafael Alberti and Andrej Voznesensky.

The Struga Festival started as a Macedonian poets' informal summer get-together in 1961. Soon it extended to all of Yugoslavia, and after a few years it went international. Though criticised for not being 'serious' enough, it's now the doyenne of literary festivals, a national institution in Yugoslavia, and the most important showpiece for poetry in Europe.

This year, over eighty poets from forty countries took part in the official programme, as well as at least fifty more, who simply turned up, from all over Yugoslavia. There's no stuffiness, little one-upmanship, and the organisation is often improvisational: the seriousness, of course, is *in* the fun, not despite it. The whole atmosphere is informal, the hospitality generous, and the setting, by a blue lake surrounded by mountains, breathtakingly beautiful. I found myself hobnobbing with poets from Australia, Belgium, Canada, Cuba, Cyprus, Greece, Malaysia, Norway, Sweden, USA and USSR, usually at the bar of the Hotel Drim, and, on one night, discussing Gramsci, Lukács, Walter Benjamin and Raymond Williams with a young Macedonian philosopher at 2 a.m. Again, of course, at the bar. A memorable and delightful occasion.

Next year?

Belgrade, 1988

I've no more time

I've no more time for long sentences
and I've no time to negotiate,
I tap out messages like telegrams.
I've no time to fan the flame,
now my hands just scrabble burnt embers.
I no longer have time for pilgrimages,
all at once my route to the estuary shrinks,
I've no time to glance back or turn back,
nor have I time for little bits and pieces,
now I need to think of the everlasting and boundless.
I've no time to think about crossroads,
I can only get to places nearby.
I've no time to study anything new,
and no time for analyses,
for me water now is just water

as when I drank it from the pure spring;
there's no time for me to dissect the sky into bits,
I see it just as children see it.
I've no time for strange gods,
I haven't even explored my own properly.
There's no time left to adopt new commandments,
even the old ten commandments are too much for me.
I've no more time for togetherness
even with those who keep striving to prove the truth.
I've no more time to fight against the hunters.
I've no more time to dream, to stroll along.

translated with Jasna B. Mišić, Struga and Belgrade, 1988

It's autumn 1989. I receive a call from Miron Grindea.[50] He's just arrived from London and he's staying at the Hotel Slavija. And he's in a hurry. "Richard, I want to meet *everybody*," he says. "I know you can fix this for me, can't you?" I don't know how Miron has got hold of my phone number. Probably from our mutual friend Tony Rudolf. Miron is a literary fixer on a huge scale and he hasn't lost one iota of his zest, charm or nervy *chutzpah*. Then I remember, he was born in Romania. That means he's a Balkan. So, even though not a Serb, perhaps he can be excepted to fit in here, at least to some extent.

I take him to see Desanka. She was born in 1898, which makes her just over ninety, maybe ninety-one. Miron was born in 1909, which makes him eighty. I've never been to her apartment before, but she greets us warmly, remembering me from Struga the previous year when she'd received the prize in the cathedral.

Miron bows deeply and kisses Desanka's hand. She accepts graciously. Immediately, they're conversing in easy French and exchanging genteel *plaisanteries*. And Desanka is suddenly charming, coy, even coquettish. Her eyes twinkle and her glances distinctly *prance*. Imperceptibly, some long-dormant trigger has clicked, and she's transformed into a girl again, mildly flirting with an admirer. Totally unexpectedly, a time-window creaks open, and even though this offers no more than a momentary

[50] Miron Grindea, OBE (1909–1995), Romanian-born literary journalist and editor of the London-based literary journal, *ADAM*, from 1940 until his death. See 'Miron Grindea', *Wikipedia*.

aperture before it slams shut again, we're transported back into the 1920s. Through this unforeseen close-up, I'm endowed with an intimate view of the manners of a bygone age which, previously I've only glimpsed in period movies. I realise, too, that I've already met hints of this *ambience* through one of Desanka's early lyrics, 'Strepnja', which I've loosely translated, along with two others.

September–October 2018

Anticipation

No, don't come close. Allow me from afar
to love, adore and worship your two eyes.
For joy is finest in anticipation
rather than in achievement of her prize.

No, come no closer. Anxiety is sweeter
when it combines expectancy and fear.
Pleasure is best when journeying towards it
and happiness is promise and foreboding.

No, don't come closer. Shall I tell you why?
All things maintain their quality and shine
like stars, when they keep distant. Do not dream
of letting those two eyes of yours touch mine.[51]

translated, Belgrade, 1988

[51] The English word *anticipation* doesn't really do justice to the Serbian title *strepnja*, which means something like a blend of 'anticipation' and 'anxiousness, anxiety'.

Speak softly

Speak softly. The trees are wide awake tonight and it saddens me that they should overhear how short life is.

Speak softly. The birds are singing beside us tonight and it saddens me that they should overhear the weeping in our voices.

Speak softly. The crickets are mating in the next meadow and it saddens me that they should overhear love's grief in our hearts.

Speak softly. The sky is stretched to infinity tonight and it saddens me that the overhearing stars should suffer because of us.

Nobody knows

Nobody knows we were a single stream, which the hills divided into smaller channels.

Nobody knows we were a single elderwood flute, which a grief-flooded shepherd broke in two pieces.

Nobody knows we were an island in the ocean, which the water-currents of night separated in two halves.

translated, Belgrade, 1988

Miodrag Pavlović (1928–2014)

photo: Dragoljub Kažić

Three Serbian poets have been guests at the biennial Cambridge Poetry Festival, which I founded in 1975: Vasko Popa in 1981, Ivan V. Lalić in 1983, and Miodrag Pavlović in 1985. During my stay in Belgrade between 1987 and 1990, I keep up with all of them.

Miodrag and I often meet at the *Ruski car* (Russian Czar)[52] on Knez Mihailova Street, off Trg republike (Republic Square). We usually sit at an outside table. Sometimes his partner Nada Šerban comes with him. I always think of them both in connection with central Belgrade. This large pedestrian zone is the heart of the city. It's a wonderful area, buzzing with life, cheerful and friendly, and because Belgrade isn't a destination for mass tourism, it hasn't been spoilt. Whenever I think of Knez Mihailova and Trg republike, I'm filled with longing to be back in Belgrade.

Mija is a quiet man, slightly reserved if you don't know him, but when you do, he's relaxed, charming and considerate. He wears a stylishly long, belted fawn-coloured raglan raincoat. His manners are immaculate and his English is perfect, as is his German. Erudite on all aspects of Serbian culture, he sometimes gives me advice about Serbian etymologies,

---

[52] In the 1990s, during Milošević's rule, the once-famous restaurant closed in the wake of various shady deals and financial scandals. See 'Ruski car', *Wikipedia*.

history, literary references and folklore. On one occasion, after coffee at the *Ruski Car*, he escorts me around a fine exhibition of figurines from Vinča[53] at a nearby gallery in Knez Mihailova, introducing me caringly to this Neolithic culture and explaining the provenance of the artefacts. On another occasion, in 1985, Branka Panić organises a joint poetry reading for us at the Ethnographic Museum on Studentski trg (Student Square) in Belgrade, with Boba Bobić.[54]

ഗ

Early in 1988, Mija and I are invited to give a reading in the small town of Požarevac, about 60 kms from Belgrade. It's an afternoon event and I drive us there in my Golf.

When we arrive at the venue, we get shown into the private room of a restaurant. A dozen or so burly and ruddy-faced men and a couple of well-built women have been indulging in a meaty late lunch. They all look well-sated. We assume they're local politicians and dignitaries. They seem entirely uninterested in us, and neither of us quite follows what possible connection there might be between these people and a discussion or reading of poetry. Puzzled, we're as unimpressed by them as they (obviously) are by us. We too grab a quick bite of lunch.

The poetry reading is in a room next to the restaurant, and some of these people attend, with a small sprinkling of others. There aren't more than a dozen present, including the local poet who has invited us there, Aleksandar Lukić. We wonder if he realised what he was letting himself in for, or us. Nobody at the event looks in the slightest bit interested.

Driving back to Belgrade, Mija and I wonder about this bizarre, almost surrealistic event. What was the point of it? What was the subtext? Only in the light of subsequent political events do we realise that it was a minor piece of cultural *dressage*, designed to add frills to the mustering of local support among politicians for Slobodan Milošević (1941–2006). Like his wife, Mirjana Marković (1942–2019),[55] Milošević was born in Požarevac and has a large and loyal following there.

October 2018

---

[53] See also 208ff above.

[54] See the photo, 331 above.

[55] Mirjana Marković dies in exile in Moscow as I'm putting the final touches to this book (April 14, 2019).

Slobodan Milošević and the Red Hat (1988)

Like Desanka Maksimović, I too have a hat. I've been wearing it for several years, usually as a prop when running children's poetry workshops. When I run these events, I style and introduce myself to the children as *Mister Hatman*. This isn't entirely a gimmick. The hat has its own surreptitious educational usefulness, because a child who has written a poem and wants to recite it gets to wear Mister Hatman's hat. While the promise of putting on the hat encourages the children to engage in the game of writing a poem, actually wearing it means that they forget to feel shy or embarrassed. Children *want* to write a poem so that they can get to put on the silly hat. There's a dressing up, clowning element to this game. Scores of children have tried it on.[56] And I sometimes wear it at adult literary events too.

The hat is a Trilby-cum-Fedora-style felt thing, with a soft crown, so that the crease can easily be pinched into a variety of positions, depending on mood and whatever effect I'm aiming to create. If I want to pretend to look vaguely like an old-style Hollywood hoodlum, the brim is broad enough to be worn down.

But what stops me from looking Bogart-cool, and what's unusual about this hat, is that it's bright red, which makes it faintly ridiculous. By now it's also got somewhat bedraggled.

ᔓ

The Struga *Poetry Evenings*, summer 1988. Desanka is to receive the international prize. There's a poetry book exhibition in a small hall at the theatre, and I wander in to take a peek. It's mid-afternoon, off-programme, and hardly anyone else is around. I happen to be wearing the red hat. And even though it's quiet, suddenly I sense a hush, or perhaps

---

[56] In my first two years in Belgrade, I ran weekly poetry workshops at the city's International School. The school was run on American lines, mainly for children of foreigners living in Belgrade. The hat was regularly worn at these workshops.

something like a change of air pressure or temperature. I turn around to see three poker-faced, muscular giants standing behind me, clad in black suits so shiny that their gloss seems metallic. Each one is between six feet four and six feet seven tall. Very tall people aren't unusual in Yugoslavia. But these three are built even more like armoured robots than animated cartoons of top-notch American football stars or second-row international rugby players. Their biceps swell through their tight-sleeved suit jackets, and their shoulders are so bulky that their bodies look like elongated isosceles triangles with the short horizontal side uppermost, each topped by a head like a cannonball with square jaws. They've entered the hall in complete silence. Bodyguards. Or as the Serbs call them, *majmuni* (pron. *my-moony*). That is: Apes.

Then, to my astonishment, in struts the Serbian president, Slobodan Milošević. He's about the same height and build as me. Momentarily, in this quiet space, with absolutely nobody else present other than his guards, we size each other up. He stares at me, expressionless, and his eyes take in my red hat, pausing on it. Cursorily and with coolly curious eyes he peers around the hall, realising that there are no literary celebrities or official personages here with whom it might be even mildly advantageous to pump hands, and that this place is of no importance or use to him whatsoever. Only some foreign fool bizarrely wearing a red hat. Obviously some poet. But clearly not a Serb, or even a Macedonian. Presumably he's expected somewhere else by a throng of journalists and acolytes, and has gone to the wrong room by mistake. He's probably in Struga because Serbian Desanka is to receive the prize. That's not her fault, I find myself thinking. Or at least, I hope it isn't.

He turns on his heels. Vanishes. Followed by his Apes.

September 2018

Ease and Unease in Serbia

From the moment I arrive in Yugoslavia in 1982, I discover that I'm peculiarly at ease with myself, and when five years later I come to live in Belgrade, I feel as if at home. I say *as if,* only because this isn't my birth-country and at the beginning my knowledge of the language is less than basic. All the same, I experience minimal difficulty in settling in, settling down, making friends, and – apart from a year's experience teaching at the university – in working with colleagues. The Belgrade life-style suits me. In general I find the ways people behave to one another convivial and enjoyable.

Some aspects of myself that have lain dormant or hidden in England even begin to edge their way towards recognition and expression. For example, because I'm relaxed here, at least for the time being, I gradually lose much of the habitual wariness and edginess I've always felt among literary people in Cambridge and London, where (so it seems to me) everyone of 'importance' or 'significance' is dead set on creating an artificial impression and on cultivating and marketing an image, posture, reputation, platform or following, or all of these together. In England, inevitably, I find myself falling into doing this myself, as a kind of defensive strategy.

Perhaps we all suffer from a kind of conspiracy of distancing and self-distancing which imprisons us all. Here, though, I don't need to cultivate any armour of this kind and it's a relief to discover that I can entirely dispense with the need for it. Perhaps this is in part because a composite ready-made image has already been carved out for me to fit into, fully and neatly, simply *because* I'm a foreigner *and* a poet. But when on reflection I ask myself, *Is this change in me no more than the product of receiving hospitality, of being privileged as a foreign guest?* My reply to myself is, *I don't think so – or at least not entirely*. I sense that it's equally an effect that the place itself and its way of life have on everybody born and bred here too. Is this an illusion or a sentimentalised projection on my part? I'm still not sure. In any case, for myself, at some visceral level, I sense that it's as a 'person in my own right' and not just as a 'foreigner' that I'm accepted here: for who and what I am.

As for poetry, I've always started from the assumption that sincerity and integrity on the one hand and consumerism on the other, being natural enemies, will never combine either comfortably or effectively, let alone blend, and that to try and persuade them to do so isn't just to waste time and energy on an inevitable misfit, but to play a stupid game that'll eventually consume its players in sell-out or self-destruction, whether partial or complete. In the Western world, since at least the time of William Blake – which is to say, since the Industrial Revolution – there can be no straightforward tally between poetic popularity and quality. This view accords with Erich Neumann's argument in his essay 'Art and Time': that art 'compensates' for the unconscious collective values that have become the cultural canon and hegemonic dogma in the age in which it's made[57] – even though I don't think that idea tells half the story and am suspicious of a psychological theory that tries to 'explain' art.

At any rate, in unpicking the lineaments of my own situation in Serbia, I find myself paradoxically entertaining the condition of being *doubly* an outsider. For my residence here not only locates me *outside the outsider-status* that, according to the above argument, is automatically conferred on English poets who live 'at home' in England. But it also screens me by means of the respected status accorded to a foreign guest in a country which, despite conforming to a kind of Communism, still partly upholds the values of a poetic culture belonging to an age prior to the Industrial Revolution.

What's more, my Jewishness, or rather, what Albert Memmi calls *judéité*, also comes into play here: a condition several thousand years older than any patterns instigated by the Industrial Revolution.[58] Zygmunt Bauman designates the Jew as "an ubiquitous and constant concomitant of Christianity, a virtual *alter ego* of the Christian Church",[59] and therefore as the perpetual stranger in the midst, "always on the outside even when

[57] Neuman 1959: 90.

[58] According to Memmi, *Judeity* designates "[…] exclusively *the way in which a Jew is a Jew*, subjectively and objectively: the manner in which he feels himself Jewish and reacts to the Jewish condition." He elaborates: "*Judeity is the fact and manner of being a Jew*: the ensemble of the characteristics, experiences and objective, sociological, psychological and biological which make a Jew; the manner of living of a Jew [….]" (Memmi 6; emphases in original text). I prefer the Gallic precision of *Judeity* to the woollier English notion of *Jewishness*.

[59] Bauman 1989: 37-38.

inside".[60] I go along with that.

ᔓ

As for the practical difficulties of living that I encounter, for example with bureaucrats or garage mechanics, I've little difficulty in finding Serbian friends and allies to step in and offer immediate help through their informed understanding of how to operate the complex *veza* system, for example to stop me being overcharged because I'm a foreigner, and quickly to sort matters out for me. The word *veza* means 'link, contact, connection'; and by describing it as a *system* I mean the Balkan version of the universal exchange code that Marcel Mauss has defined in *The Gift*. This consists of an elaborate set of unwritten social rules that requires the giving and receiving of favours, with the firm expectation of later reciprocation in some shape or form. From what I've seen of the way this works in Yugoslavia, the *veza* system functions vertically (i.e. hierarchically), especially in working life *and* horizontally (equably) among friends.

For me, in Serbia, then, exile *is* home. I'm where I want to be, and I know it.

ᔓ

I live in a relatively small world, writing poems, meeting friends, doing my best to learn Serbian. And while teaching and attending literary events both sometimes involve travelling. I begin to manage quite well conversationally. When living in Italy in my early twenties, I learned Italian quickly and effortlessly. But Serbian – with its case-system, its aspect-system for verbs, its rules on word order, its enclitics, and its wholly unfamiliar vocabulary – is altogether harder and more distant. My progress is painfully slow. At this time I'm not fluent enough to read newspapers without a dictionary, and I don't understand the TV news well enough to get the full gist of events, even though I soon find I can follow snippets, and eventually, chunks.

But even though I've little conscious conception or even intuitive premonition of impending political and social collapse, beneath my gladness to be living here – which is considerably deeper than my difficulties – it's impossible *not* to sense anxiety and unrest stirring. The wider political world keeps encroaching

ᔓ

[60] *ibid.* 53.

Some of my students and teaching colleagues are wildly enthusiastic about Slobodan Milošević. They seem to believe that he embodies some kind of Serbian national *Rinascimento*. At first, out of ignorance, I simply don't get this, and just find it curious. I've no historical background. I listen. Then, in Spring 1988, out of curiosity I go along to listen to Milošević addressing a huge cheering crowd at a rally in a park on the bank of the *Ušće* (the confluence of the Sava and the Danube).

Ne damo / Kosovo ('We won't give / Kosovo'), they roar, with the rhymed three-syllable stress chanted on the last vowels. Everyone present is a supporter. The mood is friendly but reeks of nationalistic fervour. I keep my foreign mouth firmly shut. I also go along to several demonstrations in central Belgrade, one outside the Federal *Skupština* (Parliament), where I meet my friend Niki, a mild-mannered waiter at the Writers' Club restaurant. Has he come along, like me, to see what's going on?

Around the same time, at the Centre for Learning Foreign Languages, on two afternoons a week over a short period, I'm appointed to give one-to-one English lessons to a mature student, a freelance journalist. A fervent nationalist, this man writes pot-boilers, and his latest is an exposé of the Albanian Mafia. I do my best to treat him as I would any other student. I've never come across anyone quite like him before or since. To him, nationalism is both belief and business. He treats me politely and tries to convince me of his world-view. I manage to teach him English effectively only by avoiding the subjects that concern him the most passionately.

Later, in one of my regular evening classes at the Centre for Learning Foreign Languages, I make a more serious mistake, one that has repercussions. To practise my students' English conversational and vocabulary skills, I decide, foolishly, on a 'Current Affairs' lesson. Casting around for a topic, I invite the students to talk about Kosovo. This class consists of adults of varying ages, apart from one teenager. It's an advanced group whose English is already accomplished. I'll be on safe ground here, I tell myself, as this is my favourite group. Its fifteen or so students and I have socialised on several occasions, and we seem to like and trust one another. But my idea turns out to have been a huge blunder. With the exception of the teenager, a clearly-spoken and independent-thinking young woman, the conversation turns into an outpouring of vitriolic condemnation of all Kosovars and everyone and everything Albanian. Though I don't show it, I'm shocked at the ubiquitous and passionate intensity of this reaction.

Several days later, the school administrator, a humanist who's very far from being a nationalist of any kind, asks me to come to the main office. A group of students have been to see the administrator to deliver an organised complaint. They've been very angry and have sardonically asked if I'm some kind of *špion* (spy). The administrator, who I know has a sense of humour, isn't amused on this occasion. We go on, politely, to discuss my teaching methodology. The affair blows over but leaves a bad aftertaste.

Not until many years later, as my reading about Yugoslavia widens and deepens, do I understand how far back one has to go to acquire even the slightest understanding of these prejudices and their centuries-old history.

In 1989, the Pan-Yugoslav annual English language teaching conference organised by the British Council and its American equivalent, the USIA (United States Information Agency), takes place in Slovenia. The venue is a hotel with a beautiful view overlooking Lake Bled. This annual event is attended by British and American lectors and Yugoslav teachers of English delegates from all the republics. But this year, the usual professional cordiality among teachers from different republics is entirely missing and the atmosphere is decidedly suspicious and frosty.

Yugoslavia is about to implode.

March–April and June 2019

Oskar Davičo (1909–1989)

photo: from Branka Davičo

The Bosnian poet Andjelko Vuletić has come to Belgrade from Sarajevo for the 1987 international October Writers' Meeting. He wants to introduce me to Oskar Davičo. Andjelko tells me that Oskar is the greatest Yugoslav poet alive today. He's also a novelist, Jewish, and a Communist.

When we arrive at his apartment, a strikingly beautiful woman in her late thirties or early forties answers the door. His daughter, I assume. No, it turns out to be Branka, his third wife, who used to be an air hostess and speaks quite good English. I also meet Branka's and Oskar's daughter, Jana, aged 10. Oskar is short and even in his late 70s seems strong and wiry. His eyes twinkle with quick, alert intelligence. He's gentle and hospitable, but beneath that I sense a steely toughness. He and I talk in French, which Oskar speaks fluently.

I visit again several times, always welcomed, and once with Daša Marić, who has come to visit me from Split. Oskar and Daša belong to different generations and branches of the old Yugoslav Communist establishment. Daša's uncle had been a party member in the 1920s, well before Tito's arrival on the scene. He regarded Tito as an upstart opportunist and, after 1945, spent time incarcerated on Goli Otok. According to Daša, after his release he never spoke a word about this. Clearly, Oskar and Daša like each other.

On one occasion, Oskar holds up his fingers to show me that they're twisted and maimed, the result, he says, of being tortured by the Royalist police in the early 1930s, when he was imprisoned for illegal Communist activity. "It didn't stop me writing," he grins.

I mention to him that I lived in Greece in 1967 during and after the military *coup d'état* instigated by 'the Colonels', Pattakos and Papadopoulos, and that I wrote a satirical poem about the coup, which I published under a pseudo-Greek pseudonym.[61] He was in Greece twenty years earlier, he tells me, during the Civil War, when he joined the Communist leader Markos Vafiadis and his Democratic Army. "I thought we Yugoslav partisans were tough," he says, "but we were nothing compared with those men. The way they fought [...]." He doesn't go into detail, and his eyes glaze a little, suggesting that momentarily he's in memory-land. I don't ask further questions. But one of the reasons Oskar fascinates me is that I've never met a dedicated Communist revolutionary before, let alone one who's Jewish. Even in his old age, the proletarian fire burns strong in him.

On another occasion, I get invited to a meeting of writers in central Belgrade for a conference on Oskar's oeuvre, which he attends himself. After it, I drive him home. There have been recent ructions in the Serbian Writers' Association, and in the car, he tells me how disillusioned he is. Things are falling apart, he says disgustedly, and the new committee are all *četnici*, Chetniks. He loads this term with disgust.

From a factual point of view, irrespective of his value-judgements, Oskar's analysis was essentially correct. In the late 1980s, major shifts of perspective were occurring not only in the Serbian Writers' Association but in the country as a whole. Anti-Federalist and anti-Communist nationalism took many forms. Evidence of a marked swing towards ethnic nationalism in the Serbian Writers' Association was marked by the presidency of the poet Matija Bećković between 1988 and 1992.[62] In retrospect I realise that, like Vasko, Oskar foresaw the possible break-up of Yugoslavia.

ɞ

[61] '*The Easter Rising 1967*' (RB 1968 and 1969), by 'Agnostos Nomolos'.

[62] See also 252 above.

Later, I learn more about Oskar's extraordinary and adventurous early life. He was born in 1909 into a Jewish family in Šabac in central Serbia. His father was an accountant, atheist, and socialist. Oskar began writing as a teenager, and edited a self-published magazine. By all accounts he was something of a firebrand even then. In 1926, aged only seventeen, after being expelled from high school in Belgrade for criticising religion, he ran off to France and enrolled at the Sorbonne, but left two years later without taking any exams. In Paris he supported himself by working as a waiter, cobbler, boxing trainer and 'paid companion' to several wealthy women. He returns to Serbia in 1928 and two years later graduated from Belgrade University's Philosophical Faculty, with honours in French language and literature. Later, his mature poems filtered motifs of French Surrealism, especially in their linguistic playfulness and deliberate contradictions of conventional perceptions. After being sacked from a teaching post in Šibenik, Dalmatia, and leaving another post (at his old school) in Belgrade, he was appointed to teach French in a high school in Bihać, western Bosnia. There he secretly founded the local committee of the Communist Party, which was then illegal; but following his betrayal by a fellow-member, he was imprisoned for five years, during which time he was tortured. After release, his literary and revolutionary activities continued until the outbreak of war, after which he went on working underground for the Party. In 1941, he was imprisoned by the Italians in Split and interned, first in a prison for Jews on the Dalmatian island of Korčula, then in Lombardy. In 1943, he managed to escape, make his way back across the Adriatic to Dalmatia, and join the Partisans. He saw gruelling action in Bosnia, Montenegro, the Sandžak, Mount Tara, and Durmitor,[63] and took part

[63] The most compelling and authoritative contemporary eye-witness account in English of the trials and deprivations of life among the Communist partisans in 1943 is *The Embattled Mountain* by Sir William Deakin, Churchill's emissary to Tito in that year. This soldier, scholar, historian, and political analyst was Churchill's literary assistant from 1936 to 1940 and, during the war, a member of the War Office's 'Special Operations' division. In 1950, he became the first Warden of St. Anthony's College, Oxford. Deakin's reports from wartime Yugoslavia were among the key-factors that gradually weighed Churchill's mind in favour of switching support to Tito's pan-Yugoslav Communist movement rather than Draža Mihajlović's Serbian Royalist 'Chetnik' fighters. Churchill later came to regret this switch and see it as one of his gravest errors. See Milan Stojilović (online), 1993, quoting David Martin, 1946: "Concerning his handling of the Yugoslav situation, Churchill has already informed the Press that he considers it his greatest mistake. Churchill is reported to have said, 'I was deceived and badly informed'"

in the final offensive to liberate Belgrade. After the war, as a journalist, he covered the Nuremburg Trials and the Greek Civil War, and in his forties, he settled into the life of a full-time writer.[64]

ᔓ

Together with Daša, I translate some of Oskar's poems from the 'Hana' series, published in 1939, nearly fifty years previously. Into their tightly-rhymed structure, Oskar has poured a richly assonantal and alliterative sound play, seasoned by French Surrealist touches. There's a delight in the rich sonic capacities of the Serbian language, almost like that of a dervish dance, combined with a zany, nervy, and sometimes frenetic, rebellious energy. I manage to get several versions out in English, including two sonnets, which I think are close enough in spirit to reveal at least something of Oskar's poetic personality.

ᔓ

In June 1989, after teaching English for two years at the Centre for Learning Foreign Languages, I'm about to move to a new job at the Philological Faculty. On May 19, I give a farewell poetry reading at the Centre, introduced by another good friend, the poet Ivan Lalić. Oskar is in the audience, and my translator Boba Bobić recites several of his poems, which I deliver in my English versions, including one of the best known, the title-poem 'Hannah'. So we illustrate the fact that translation is a two-way current.

In October of the same year, the poet Duška Vrhovac phones to tell me that Oskar has died, aged 80. I write an obituary note for *Politika*.[65] At the funeral, I'm the only non-Serb there.

So far as I know, nobody else has yet translated any of Oskar's poems into English, and I've rendered fewer than a handful.

September–October 2018

For documentation by a British officer appointed to work with Mihajlović's Royalist fighter, also Michael Lees, *The Rape of Serbia;* and see also 112 above, n. 165.

[64] 'Oskar Davičo', *Wikipedia*.

[65] Bernz 1989.

Obituary note for Oscar Davičo

The poet is dead but the work lives on. Although my native language is different, I believe that Oskar Davičo's poems will live as long as there are human beings in the world who speak the Serbo-Croatian language. He was a wordmaker and a word-wizard. He opened up new doors and gates and windows in the language for others to walk through with ease. He dug and built those spaces out of his individual genius and his common dream for humanity – the vision of a poet-revolutionary and a revolutionary poet. To me, newly arrived to work in Belgrade, he was consistently kind, encouraging and hospitable, and he even honoured me by attending a poetry reading of mine, only four months before his death. He treated me on equal terms, as a fellow-poet: there seemed to me no trace of condescension or pomposity in his character, only commitment to poetry, to human beings, and to the secret spaces of his beautiful mother language. I'm proud to have translated into English several poems from his major cycle, *Hana,* though it's hard in another language to convey both the virtuosity of wordplay and the tight formal structure that exist together in the originals. For the combination of a marvellously woven verbal texture with a pure lyrical gift, exploited to the full, he reminds me of the greatest Anglo-Welsh poet of the twentieth century, Dylan Thomas. For his range, depth, intellectual rigour, daring and outspokenness, he reminds me of the greatest Scottish poet of the twentieth century, Hugh MacDiarmid. Yugoslavia and Serbia should be proud of him. The poet is dead but his work lives on. It belongs now to you, to me, to all of us.

Belgrade, October 1989

Hannah

I, son of a rotten hunter, ram and otter,
fell for refugee Hannah, only daughter
of a widowed Jew, who'd made his shabby haven
down by the graveyard – opened up shop and tavern.

As a crackling rocket shatters pines and firs,
she woke me – and my chirpy nature's spoiled.
Love loves alone yet loves full of the world –
Love is both lighthouse and saved mariners.

My eyes blaze bright now – streetlamps, on a mob –
now sea, nets, fish and fishermen grow tall –
eels thread the needles of the waterfall.
That crook? A sparrow cheeping, not a slob.

Whatever I had dreamed or been or spoken,
one eyed, cock-eyed, and twice expelled from school,
whatever I had drunk, whatever broken –
out of my childhood, I've paid up in full.

But now from heaven – into these hands – love sails,
and with love I drag drowned men from the deeps,
pump engines, and recover crates and bales –
my brow breaks dungeon bars and castle keeps.

Skies, awnings, villas, open up their soul,
this hand has stripped whole halos from the sun.
Come, all of you – sun, bones, gravedigger, mole,
and all, being me – come drink my barmaid's wine.

Translated in Belgrade and Split 1988–1989

Two sonnets

No, I'm not double-barrelled. Family trees
are for sound sleepers, who wake up alert.
I come from a long line of nobodies
who spat out blood – and loved. That was their lot.
My folks' huge hopes for love couldn't be dashed
at lowdown stakes or from the heights of gallows –
and when their mouths got split and jawbones smashed
they sealed lips tight and, well, forgave the blows.
In love, they swallowed smiles, took hurried steps,
avoided high noons, honeymoons and homes,
quivering with fear at every shadow's shapes.
Inheriting tough, hunched up, crooked frames
they misfired every arrow from hope's quiver
and all they longed for floated off down river.[66]

Nor is my blood of tsars or petty kings,
who loved their bloodsports – and battled, pillaged, burned
their ways through wars and orgies. My poor makings
were folks who earned their salt – and paid – and yearned.
I come from bitter nothingness, from nowhere,
from those who dig the grain and plough the mine.
So, here's my youth – for freedom! Should I care?
Why not stake all when not a crumb is mine?
Without a single soul in this wide world –
from caves of wolves, where no planks line the floor –
with empty hands, with furrowed brow, I'm thirled
to search out just one man – brave, strong and sure –
a comrade, unafraid, though darkness bleeds,
to sneer at death, and carry out great deeds.

Translated in Belgrade and Cambridge

[66] For an earlier version, see *Notness* (RB 2015): 19.

E. D. (Ned) Goy (1926–2000): An Obituary

photo: Jasna Levinger-Goy

Dr. Edward Dennis Goy – affectionately known to his friends as Ned – died suddenly at Addenbrookes Hospital, Cambridge, on March 13, 2000. He was the leading expert on Croatian and Serbian literature in Britain and one of the foremost authorities on South Slav culture and history throughout Europe. Despite the collapse of Yugoslavia during the 1990s, admiration for his work continued unstinted in both Belgrade and Zagreb. In 1999, he was recommended for election to both the Serbian and the Croatian Academies of Sciences.

Brilliant and startling contrasts were keynotes to his life and achievement. Born in Enfield, Middlesex, on September 22, 1926, Ned Goy was brought up by his mother, a strong-minded woman who was the eleventh child of a Sunderland miner and later built up her own business as a clothes designer. His father, a Hull silk-trader, was descended from a long line of Huguenot merchants. Ned was brought up in Hampshire and attended Churches College in Petersfield. After a spell as a teacher at private schools in Devon and Woking, he returned to Hampshire to finance the remainder of his own secondary education, and passed his Higher School Certificate in English, History, Art and Russian, after only seven months' preparation. On his army call-up in August 1945, he was sent to Cambridge to complete the Joint Services Russian Course. In

1946, with the rank of corporal, he was sent to Poland and Germany as an interpreter for the British Liaison team. After demobilisation in 1948, he went back to Queen's College, Cambridge. He also joined the Territorial Army, rose to the rank of Major, and in later years remembered the camaraderie of his army days with affection.

In Cambridge, the leading Slavonic scholar Elizabeth Hill recommended that he should read Serbo-Croatian alongside Russian. His first teachers of Serbo-Croatian were Miodrag Stajić and Irinej Djordjević, former Orthodox Bishop of Dalmatia. He graduated in 1951 with a starred First. Much of the research for his Cambridge PhD thesis – on 'Russian influences on Serbian Thought and Literature' – was completed between 1951 and 1954 in Belgrade libraries, and he also frequently visited Zagreb. Numerous personal friendships with leading Yugoslav writers began in this period too, and such contacts multiplied throughout his life: for example, with Miroslav Krleža, Miodrag Bulatović, Radomir Konstantinović, Marijan Matković, Dragutin Tadijanović and Vladan Desnica. His literary correspondences with several of these writers are well-known in former Yugoslavia.

From 1954 to 1990, he was Cambridge University Lecturer in Slavonic Studies, concentrating increasingly on Serbian and Croatian Literature rather than Russian. In the 1960s, Russian teaching at Cambridge was unexceptional, and Goy's innovatory, Leavis-influenced approaches to textual analysis aroused his department's suspicion and hostility – albeit unofficial and unstated. But when he saw colleagues penalising his students in examinations for approaches and views which they had acquired from him, he beat a tactical withdrawal and refused to teach Russian again. At least in Serbo-Croatian he had more freedom to infect his students with his own passionate love of literature, his devotion to open critical methods, and his refusal to accept humbug. Throughout his time at Cambridge, he was loved and admired by undergraduates as a great and inspiring teacher – humanistically generous and personally kind, verbally witty and intellectually demanding, unfailingly critical of intellectual faddishness and prepared to stick his neck out over issues of principle. Students of his who went on to achieve distinction include two British ambassadors to former Yugoslavia, Sir Andrew Wood and Sir Peter Hall, and the literary and linguistic scholars and translators Celia Hawkesworth and Francis Jones.

From the 1960s on, Ned Goy consistently refused to visit Yugoslavia, despite many invitations, owing to his disapproval of Tito and Titoism. Still, the twin realities of a Yugoslav literature and a Yugoslav culture always remained meaningful to him, and he kept in close contact with unfolding events. Coinciding with the imminent break-up of Yugoslavia, his retirement from lecturing in 1990 was unfortunately the signal for Cambridge to remove Serbo-Croatian from its syllabus. During the 1990s, when there was a proliferation of new British 'experts' on Yugoslavia, many of them unable to speak a word of any of its languages and ignorant of the country's history, Ned Goy was never invited to offer views or analyses by the British Foreign Office, let alone newspapers, radio or television. A modest, just person, he would never have dreamed of putting himself forward. However, he was a leading and articulate British opponent of the bombing of Serbia by NATO in 1999.

His literary-critical work was wide-ranging and influential, but in typical Goy-fashion, was circulated in the most modest of ways. He wrote more than forty essays and monographs on Croatian and Serbian literature, which still await a collected edition. He was also a prolific translator of fiction, poetry, and folk literature. Ned wrote extensively on literature in Serbo-Croatian and Russian, and translated works by, among others, Ivan Gundulić and Dragutin Tadijanović (1993), and with his wife Jasna Levinger-Goy, by Meša Selimović (1999) and Miroslav Krleža (2004).[67]

Already twice a widower, in February 1997 he married Dr. Jasna Levinger, a linguist from Sarajevo, and with her began a series of new translations, including Meša Selimović's novel *The Fortress* and Miroslav Krleža's *The Banquet in Blitva*. They had just started translating Miloš Crnjanski's *Roman o Londonu* (*A Novel of London*), when he collapsed and died.[68] Those of us who were lucky to know him, whether as teacher or friend, already miss his unfailing intellectual speed, the accuracy of his pinpointing in analysis, his energetic and sometimes zany sense of humour, his compassion for the suffering, his refusal to accept conventional black-and-white explanations, and his deep understanding of every side, angle and aspect of the Balkan kaleidoscope.

March 2000

---

[67] See also Djidić.

[68] Miloš Crnjanski (1893–1977), a significant Serbian poet and novelist, has had only two books translated into English (*Migrations*, New York, 1994, and *A Novel of London*, Princeton, NJ, 2020), although he's been widely translated into other languages. In the UK, his work has attracted the attention of only a few Slavists in a single critical volume: see Norris.

Jovan (Vava) Hristić (1933–2002)

photo: pdfzone.pw

I often meet the poet, playwright, teacher and critic of theatre and drama, Jovan (Vava) Hristić at Ivan Lalić's apartment. They're old and close friends and belong to the same generation. Vava deserves much more than this brief note. But I don't know him well.

A quiet and reticent man, and a poet of fine intellect and classical distinction, he writes sparingly, but always with a perfect sense of diction, pitch and rhythm. He manages to combine high lyricism with delicate irony. His poems combine an exquisite finesse of diction with clarity and resonance. Major influences on his poems include Cavafy and T. S. Eliot. Hs work is full of echoes of classical Greek. I think he'll come to be remembered as one of the finest Serbian poets of his era. He has a collection in English translated by Bernard Johnson, simply entitled *Poems*.

He speaks perfect English. I remember several evenings with him and Ivan when I try out a new poem of mine on them. Sometimes their response is positive. But on one of these occasions I deliver an inferior piece. Vava takes pains to explain why. He does so carefully, gently and in few words, getting to the point with unerring swiftness and quiet courtesy. I'm impressed by the speed of his intuition, the incisiveness of his intellect, his perfect sense of taste, his dismissal of the spurious, and his passion for the genuine.

Moma Dimić (1944–2008)

photo: knjizara.com

Moma (Momčilo) Dimić is a versatile novelist, poet, essayist, and editor. For many years, as artistic director of the Belgrade International Writers' Meetings he's known to all non-Serbian writers visiting Belgrade.

Together with Ivan Gadjanski, he makes the first draft translation of the title poem of *The Blue Butterfly*, which Ivan Lalić and Danilo Kiš then polish. Moma is my kind, courteous and cordial host on many occasions, always hospitable and attentive. He edits several anthologies for the Serbian Writers' Association, including *Kletva* ('Curse') (1999), which includes poems by more than a hundred writers protesting against NATO's bombing of Serbia.

In 1999, he takes Melanie and me to the ceremony transferring Haša Popa's ashes to the grave of her husband Vasko.

October 2018

Out of the Shatter Zone

I continue to work as a British Council lector in Belgrade for three years until June 1990, after which date my annual work contract can't be renewed. So I write to friends in France, Italy, Spain and Greece, to see if they can help me find a teaching job in any one of those countries, but without success. I give a farewell poetry reading at Francuska 7, headquarters of the Serbian Writers' Association. It's time to leave Belgrade, with Jasna and our one-year-old daughter Arijana. Destination: England. Jasna's eleven-year old daughter Jelena is on holiday and will join us later.

We drive overnight in a convoy of three cars, loaded with belongings, thanks to three Serbian friends who kindly offer to be supporting drivers, sharing the driving between us. Under drizzle somewhere in Bosnia, we stop to fill up with petrol. Around midnight, as we get out of our cars, blinking under the bright lights of the petrol station forecourt, we see a man's corpse, fully clothed, lying stretched out on glistening tarmac. A tall, well-built young man, he lies soaking in the rain, face down, arms angled upwards in a surrender position, next to a stationary truck. A crowd of onlookers is half-encircled around him at a distance of three or four metres, as if approaching any closer might be disrespectful. There's no sign of police or ambulance. We don't stop to enquire whether this death involved a crime or an accident.

This is the last image of Yugoslavia I take back to England with me. I'm sad, gloomy. I comfort myself with clichés and simultaneously irritate myself. We'll just have to make the best of things.

ᔕ

We reach the Austro-Slovenian border early in the morning and enter Austria. Stopping for breakfast at a sub-Alpine roadside inn tucked neatly into a green-clad slope, we might have driven into a kitsch postcard. I'm taken aback at the sober tidiness of the place, the hygienically spick-and-span washroom, actually equipped with loo seats and loo paper, the polished orderliness of the ranks of cars that swish by, the pristine upkeep of the roads, the tended, tailored landscape. It all seems filmic, unreal, cleansed not just of dirt and muddle but of humanity. After driving all night in shabby cars with laden roofs, we don't fit. I've been *Serbified, Balkaned* – thought not Balkanised. I like it that way. Being back in Western Europe is a shock.

I cheer up a little as we reach Ostend and then board the ferry. Crossing the Channel for the first time in many years is pure pleasure. I think of Blake's 'Jerusalem'. As we sit in one of the ferry's saloons, a young American woman on the deck outside takes a snapshot of Arijana, who has recently learned to stand, her head and hands pressed against a glass window as she sees the cliffs of Dover for the first time. The woman approaches me to tell me about her photo, and to take my address. Later, when the photo arrives, it's a clever double-image, simultaneously showing Arijana through the glass and the cliffs' reflection upon it.

Once arrived in Cambridge, we unload and get an Indian takeaway. Our three Serbian friends stay the night. The next day, they set out back to Belgrade in two of the cars.

❧

Meanwhile, *perestroika* is well under way. Cambridge, which has always attracted international students as a congenial place to learn English, has an increasingly large influx of mature students from Eastern Europe and Russia, including a new breed of 'business-person'. After working for some months at a language school in nearby Sawston, I start off my own small English language teaching outfit, specialising in training business-people working in large companies that are making the transition to supply-and-demand economies. Brought up in a Communist command economy, they know next-to-nothing in practice about supply-and-demand business or international competitive markets. Over the next few years, this line of work will take me to run language-training courses in the Czech Republic, Poland, Latvia and Russia, going as far east as Yakutsk. While this will bring in just about enough money to live on, it'll afford no time at all for writing for almost a decade.[69]

[69] Eventually, these experiences fed into a book-length poem, *The Manager* (2001). An incomplete Serbian version *Menadžer* was published eleven years earlier in Montenegro, just before my departure from Yugoslavia, trans. Jasna Mišić and Vladimir Sekulić.

While Yugoslavia crumbles into full-scale ethnic war, in Cambridge Jasna and I make friends with Serbs, Croats and Bosnians, most of whom have fled the country, and several of whom are in mixed marriages. For example, we meet a Serbian doctor who has been called up to fight against his Croatian wife's people. They've managed to get out and arrive in Cambridge with their children, where they're quickly settled into a Council house.

We get involved with 'helping' refugees. I may be in England physically, but mentally, emotionally and spiritually, I'm still in the Shatter Zone.[70]

ᔕ

Late one evening in 1991 or 1992, we receive a phone-call asking us to drive down to Saffron Walden, fifteen miles away, to do some on-the spot interpreting. A plane has just arrived unannounced on an unscheduled flight from Priština. An aid centre has been set up in a local church hall, and by the time we arrive, the place is already swarming with volunteers. It boasts camp beds, blankets and sleeping bags and, on a long table, a tea urn, water dispenser, and plastic cups and plates full of English biscuits. Sandwiches are being made. As we await the plane's arrival, piles of second-hand clothes and toys appear as if by magic from local charity shops. An entire organisation develops quietly, coolly and matter-of-factly. Many local individuals and organisations are involved, including several parish councils and the Red Cross. It's the kind of situation when so-called ordinary people pull together and get on with whatever needs to be done in a simple, kind, effective way.

The passengers drift in, bleary-eyed, off a bus that has brought them directly from the airport. The Serbs, Croats and Bosnians on board turn out to be easy to converse with and help. They're few in number and keen to move on and get settled. Some already have contacts, friends or family

---

[70] Coined by the English geographer Gordon East in 1961, the 'Shatter Zone' is a little-known term designating an area that's more usually described as 'Central Europe' or 'Eastern Europe'. As the title of East's essay suggests, 'The Concept and Political Status of the Shatter Zone' is a particularly valuable and insightful idea, especially in the light of the political upheavals across the Balkans and Central Europe during the 1990s, not to mention the oscillating patterns of centripetal and centrifugal movements over a much longer period. The metaphor perfectly fits what happened to Yugoslavia in that period. For further discussion of this term vis-à-vis the Balkans as a 'crossroads between East and West', see also Stoianovich 1994: 296-297.

members in London or Manchester. Several are quite canny about this. But the majority of passengers are ethnic Albanians from Kosovo who, as a matter of principle, absolutely refuse to admit to anyone that they understand or speak a word of Serbian, the language of their arch-enemy, even though we know they've learnt it at school and speak it fluently. Sadly, we don't speak Albanian, so we can't help.

Everybody on this flight seems to have been allowed to land and pass through immigration control without question, and I wonder if British visa controls have been waived, and if so why, how and by whom. This astonishes me at the time and even more so when immigration regulations to the UK for former Yugoslavs quickly become more stringent and visas get harder and harder to come by. I also wonder how much these passengers have to had to pay for their one-off flight, who has organised it, and how much money the organisers have made out of it. I don't realise that the instigator of this aerial excursus is a precursor of the criminal enterprises that will later profit from the plight of refugees and migrants to Western Europe, by arranging whatever means may be available, from hiding them as stowaways in the backs of trucks to perilous sea-crossings in inflatable dinghies. The phrase *people traffickers* isn't yet current. Perhaps it hasn't even been coined.[71]

ɞ

Meanwhile, Slovenia and Croatia both inch towards independence from the Yugoslav Federation, and within a year, both achieve it, co-ordinating their declarations for the same date: June 25, 1991. The Berlin Wall has been pulled down in October 1990, nine months previously, and among the first European governments to recognise both these entities as creditable states is the recently re-unified Germany. Again historians' clichés apply: the weaker one's neighbours – and the neighbours of one's neighbours – the stronger a country is likely to be. Divide and rule: a policy tested thousands of times; and Germany is good at it. Sheeplike, the other EU countries follow the example of the Power-House of Europe.

In the Krajina, Slavonia, Bosnia and Kosovo, interethnic wars rage. Within the overall pattern of Balkan splintering, there's movement and counter-movement, as if within and beneath the horror, a plethora of mini-chess-matches were being played, all parts of a single, complex, overall

[71] Later I find that the phrase *people trafficking* first occurs in print in 1977 (*OED*). The next entry after that is dated 1999.

multidimensional tournament consisting of leagues and a super-league. In a pocket of the now-independent Catholic Croatia, the Orthodox Serbs of Knin in the old Krajina[72] set up a micro-state that declares its own micro-independence, which is soon crushed by the Croats in what they call *Operacija Oluja* ('Operation Storm'). More refugees travel to Bosnia and Serbia on blocked highways. In Kosovo, Albanians attack Serbs who attack Albanians who attack Serbs and it's impossible to work out who 'started it' and almost doesn't matter anymore.

It's the same in Bosnia. Its capital, Sarajevo, a city once loved and lauded for its tolerance, splits along ethnic lines and is under siege from the surrounding hills, with Moslems, Serbs and Jews alike inside the city and Bosnian Serbs shooting down into it, led by the politician-psychiatrist-poet Radovan Karadžić[73] and their military general, Ratko Mladić. Thanks to an organisation calling itself *La Benevolencija*, the Jewish population of the city organises an escape programme, and some refugees eventually settle in North West London, where I was brought up. There they publish a regular community newsletter in English and Bosnian, entitled *SaLon*, which I later contribute to and receive.[74] International Mujahedin are attracted from all over the world to the fields, woods and villages of Bosnia, including British Muslims, and the zone becomes a testing ground for the movement that will later be known as Al-Qaeda.

These debacles start several years before the World-Wide Web and email revolution. But in the late 1990s, the unregulated Internet gets under way and war videos begin to surge through Western households in a series of waves so imperceptible, rapid and unstoppable that, later, it's hard, if not impossible, to remember exactly when it started or what life had been like before it. It isn't long before a single or double search-click produces graphic images on screen, including live videos of atrocities committed on Orthodox Serbs by Muslims and on Muslims by Serbs. Memories of Ustaša atrocities at Jasenovac fifty years earlier are revived. But this time it gets increasingly hard to see who's doing what to whom, because fabricated texts accompany shots of victims who are anonymous. We don't know it at the time, but this is a precursor or pioneer of what will later get called 'fake news'. Reactivating what they see as the *hajduk* tradition,[75] warlords from Serbia organise private bands and militias of

[72] See also 80 and 333 above.

[73] See 404-405 below, note 108.

[74] 'Fragment, on The Sepharad', 1999; see RB 2011d: 38-39.

[75] See 61-116 above.

armed nationalists, who travel to Bosnia by car or minibus for weekend jaunts that involve thuggery, pillage and murder.

In Summer 1991, on a quick visit to Belgrade, by chance I get to meet one of these scoundrels, the husband of a friend of a friend, whose apartment I visit for dinner. The man is eager to show me his revolver, tucked into a wardrobe, and he tells me in brazen confidence that he drives off to Bosnia at weekends with a bunch of cronies. God knows what he gets up to there. I don't ask, and he goes out rather than joining his wife and friends for the meal she has cooked. Later, I learn, she divorces him.

Thanks to Federal conscription laws, all mature men throughout Yugoslavia have had to serve in the JNA (Yugoslav National Army), so the entire male population has received weapons training. Gradually, more and more graphic videos of skirmishes appear on the Internet, including severed heads of warriors tossed into buckets, and each side claims they're the victims. Years later, I write:

> As for Bosnia-Hercegovina, an international Mujahedin regiment was assiduously assembled to fight in the Bosnian war, which lasted from 1992 to 1995. Their presence was welcomed by Bosnian president Alija Izetbegović and there are plentiful records of his meetings with Mujahedin, including members of al-Qaeda. Those Mujahedin who rallied to Bosnia included radicalised Moslem students born and educated in various European countries and bearing passports of EU member states, including the UK. Al-Qaeda leaders were clear in their policy towards the Bosnian war: they treated it as a preparation ground for international Jihad. Ayman al-Zawahiri, Osama Bin Laden's second-in-command, is reputed to have co-ordinated several Mujahedin operations in Bosnia-Hercegovina through the fronts of charity organisations, and to have visited Sarajevo. His brother Zaiman al-Zawahiri is thought to have worked for the CIA against the Serbs in Kosovo. The most superficial browsing of the Internet indicates accumulated evidence of this kind, even bearing in mind the necessity for caution about the reliability of such material.[76] The financing for Izetbegović's overall war effort and in particular for Moslem extremists in Bosnia also needs further investigation and identification. Fairly reliable Western investigations point to banks and NGOs operating in Bosnia, with funding sources in Islamic countries including Saudi-Arabia, Qatar, Kuwait, Egypt, Algeria, Iran and Sudan, and with links ranging from al-Qaeda, Hamas, Hezbollah, the Egyptian terrorist group Al-Gama'a al-Islamiyya and other Moslem organisations

[76] The most violently graphic material has since been taken down from the Internet, though not entirely purged.

> identified in the USA as "suspected of terrorism", to the Saudi royal family and the Iranian Ministry of Intelligence and Security.[77]

Not until many years later do the Western news media begin to catch up retrospectively with the fact that the Bosnian conflict has served as a training and recruitment ground for Radical Islam and for both Al-Qaeda and ISIS. At the time, though, it's the Serbs who are predominantly configured as villains.

ᔕ

Throughout the 1990s, helplessly and from afar, I watch the entire country crumble. There are brutal and senseless killings and trains of refugees, including Serbs from Knin fleeing Croats into Bosnia and from Bosnia into Serbia (1992–1993). Later, thousands of ethnic Albanians from Kosovo fleeing from the Serbian army stream across the border into Macedonia (1999), and this is the trigger for NATO to bomb Serbia. Concealed and congealed resentments, buried for generations but never forgotten, are dug up, loosened and resuscitated. Still living memories of old injustices, especially from the Second World War, seethe, bubble to the surface and boil over. But the deepest roots of these traumas go back much further and can be traced as far as the Battle of Kosovo (1389), which was followed, in some regions, by more than four centuries of Turkish rule. The shadows and bogeys of nightmare are fleshed in human form, wearing militia-uniforms, strolling down streets with grenade belts and Kalashnikovs. Ancient revenge stalks village and city, lane and highways. Buildings are torched and bombed. On all sides, criminals thrive on the violence. Admittedly the process of disintegration is piecemeal and gradual but, through the 1990s, little by little we realise that the total dismantling of the state has already taken place and that collapse is proceeding relentlessly and with an inexorable sense of fatality to its ultimate irrevocable full-scale end. Chess game within chess game, perhaps, but no winners other than petty nationalists. We seem to be living *simultaneously* in the particular *here-now* of the end of the millennium, *and* back in a previous century. We keep blinking, almost pinching ourselves as, day-by-day, we wonder *what's real.*

In the early part of the decade before the Internet revolution, I avidly absorb every possible scrap of TV and radio news, I keenly read papers, and filter whatever information I can from faxes, gossip and hearsay. Occasion-

[77] I don't include the essay in this book. See RB 2012c: 27.

ally, I find myself cursing TV commentaries by British reporters with plummy accents, whose bias against Serbs is obvious even though ostensibly they fake an objective neutrality. Gaffes include commentaries that are obvious falsifications of the scenes they claim to witness. For example, on one occasion in 1992 or 1993, the respected correspondent Kate Adie, the BBC's chief foreign news correspondent, and even then a respected pundit, speaks of "the brave Croatian soldiers" on the front line. And while the camera shot reveals a background of a village road, where young men in black neo-Fascist uniforms jump onto the back of a truck, which then roars off around a road-bend, her voice maintains the assured, informed tones of apparent authority and reliability that are always assumed by the British Establishment, even though the picture itself contradicts her statement as a bald-faced lie. Swiftly, through all Western countries, a prevalent anti-Serbian bias transforms into a standardised norm, a programmed trope, and the stereotyped cliché of villainous Serbs assumes the mantle of a truth that nobody around us questions, let alone challenges, except within my own small circle, at least as far as I know.

During this period, I receive an invitation from the linguist and translator Celia Hawkesworth to give a 'poetry reading for peace' at London's School of Oriental and East European Studies, where she's a Senior Lecturer.[78] I read translations I've made from Serbian, Croatian and Macedonian poets, as well as some of my own recent poems on Yugoslav themes, mainly from the as-yet-unfinished book *The Blue Butterfly*. When it comes to question-time, bitter arguments fly between the Serbs and Bosnian Moslems present. Poetry can't possibly bring peace. Could it ever? At the end of that evening, I feel particularly useless. For Yugoslavia, at any rate, it's too late.

Even so, I also take part in a similar group reading at the ICA (Institute of Contemporary Arts) just off the Mall, where apart from my own voice, the mood is universally anti-Serb. Most of these poets are part of the London Literary Establishment, to which I've never belonged, or wanted to, and have always detested. Then, with some other sympathisers and several Serbian students, I manage to get a small group going at Cambridge University, which advocates peace.

---

[78] Celia and I were exact contemporaries as Cambridge undergraduates, 1961–1964. An authority on women writers in the Balkans, she has also written language-study books for learners of Serbian and Croatian, and translated fiction and non-fiction by many Serbian and Croatian authors. For an interview with her, see Peligra.

Meanwhile, in a small, informal group of Bosnian, Serbian and Croatian friends, and with several English people as well who know something about the Balkans, we keep telling one another, "Things can't get any worse, can they." And then: "They've already gone and done *a* and *b* and *c*, not to mention *d* and *e* and *f*. But surely they *can't* be so stupid as to do *g* and *h* and *i* too." And then, when they *do* go and do the unimaginable *g* and *h* and *i*, we repeat the same views about *j*, *k* and *l*. And then *m* and *n* and *o*. ... And so it goes on – as if the overall dramatic plot were being propelled by an invisible, pre-ordained and insane command from some mad *ex machina* god looking down from on high and laughing. No matter what the particular situation, what happens is that the stupidest and most tragic of all solutions are the ones that get enacted. Simultaneously, madness and irrational absurdity accumulate and concatenate. But, as if we were watching a horror movie in chillingly extra-slow motion, the chain reaction seems absolutely unstoppable,[79] so much so that the repeated news of horror after horror and disaster after disaster even seems to grow *monotonous*. It's as if the only functional pattern discernible or operative in this entire train of events were a headlong gravitational slide, an inexorable teleological pull towards the worst and most miserable of all possible conclusions. Yugoslavia tumbles like a house of cards. Total collapse seems not just a destination but a predestination. The collective psyche seems to have caved in on itself, and every involved person suffers, whether responsible or not, whether able to bear it or not. Morale shrinks, confidence sinks, and depression prevails, often burnished into anger. But there's nowhere to vent it. A Bosnian friend in Cambridge, a tall, gentle, quiet man, hangs himself. He came to England with his wife and small son, hoping for a new lease of life. Eventually, unable to countenance living here, his widow returns to Sarajevo with their child.

ഗ

In retrospect, many other older contours reappear, and historical patterns become clearer. It's hard not to forget that on June 28, 1914, on the corner of a narrow street in Sarajevo, Gavrilo Princip shot the Austro-Hungarian Archduke Franz-Ferdinand and his wife Duchess Sophie at close range as they were passing by a cordon of official chauffeured cars. The royal couple knew they were courting danger.[80] Princip was a Bosnian Serb and

[79] See 'A twentieth century dream' in RB 2011b: 66-69.

[80] See West 1174, and 'Gavrilo Princip', *Wikipedia* (online).

a member of an underground cell of nationalists called the *Black Hand*, opposed to the rule of the Austro-Hungarian Empire over any part of the Balkans. This assassination sparked the First World War.

I think back ironically to 1988, when in my political and cultural naiveté I once thought of Federal Yugoslavia as a potential model for a kind of Balkan Switzerland. And I particularly recall Christmas Day 1989, when on Serbian TV, in shock I'd watched the trial and killing of Nicolae and Elena Ceaușescu in Târgoviște, Romania, only 500 kilometres from where I sat in a rented apartment in Zemun. And I remember thinking: "*That couldn't happen here. This is Yugoslavia.*"

November 2018–April 2019

Zlatko Krasni (1951–2008)

photo: sudöst Europa Kultur e.V.

Zlatko was a prolific translator of German literature into Serbian and a committee member of the Serbian Writers' Association. A gentle, generous, unpretentious and immediately likeable man, I met him regularly at the Writers' Club and in particular at the October Writers' Meetings. In 1999, he was active in opposing the NATO bombardment, and wrote a subtly ironic poem with reference to German involvement, which Moma Dimić published in *Kletva*. The Serbian version deploys rhymed doggerel for bathetic effect. My translation follows this note.

In April 2004, Zlatko and I began emailing each other regularly. In May 2007, he took part in the enormous poetry festival in Medellin, Colombia. When I visited Belgrade later that year, he told me how extraordinary the experience was – a huge poetry reading in the city that only a few years previously had been the heart of Colombia's drug culture.[81]

He's already very ill, but makes a point of attending the presentation of my work at the Writers' Association. Afterwards, some of us go to Skadarlija for a meal. He comes along for the *društvo* (company) and out of friendship for me. But he eats nothing.

An annual translation prize has been established in Zlatko's name by his son Jan, in co-operation with Goran Djordjević, director of the Smederevo Poetry Autumn Festival. A fitting memorial.

[81] See Krasni, 'Uzalud'.

Schiller and Miller

There's a major poet by the name of Schiller
and a Luftwaffe pilot by the name of Miller

While Freedom gets praised by poet Schiller
Serbia gets blitzed by pilot Miller

And while mankind gets uplifted by Schiller
Serbia's bridges get smashed by Miller

On a nightly Tornado Miller flies
to split asunder the Belgrade skies

So what am I to make of Schiller
when it's all I can do to cope with Miller?

By day should I now be reading Schiller
and by night be shooting back at Miller?

Man of two faces   Schiller-Miller
by day my delight   by night a blood-spiller

Ah but could there be any Schiller at all
if he didn't have some Miller on call

Once slave to his bloody Führer   and still a
faithful servant   slick NATO-killer

Sure   I can read what the rockets spell
Hitler's in heaven   Goethe's in hell

Translated 1999

Cadik (Braco) Danon (1923–2009), Survivor of Jasenovac

photos: Danon family archive and Dosije

In May 2007, I pay a short visit to Serbia from Cambridge to make preliminary arrangements for my part in the Great School Lesson (*Veliki školski čas*) the following autumn. Extracts from my book *The Blue Butterfly* are to be used, in Vera Radojević's translation, as the basis for the oratorio in the annual commemoration of a wartime massacre of nearly 3,000 victims by the Nazi occupiers of Kragujevac. It's the first time a work by a foreigner has been used to shape the entire programme, so this is a high honour. Before Vera and I go to Kragujevac, there's to be an afternoon discussion about *The Blue Butterfly* at the Serbian Writers' Association in Belgrade, organised by Predrag Bogdanović Ci, its General Secretary, and an old friend. When Vera and I arrive, we're ushered into the central upstairs room, with its familiar faded leather couches and coffee tables, and busts and portraits of Ivo Andrić, Vasko Popa, Danilo Kiš, and other famous Serbian writers. After a plethora of welcoming speeches, Ci calls on an elderly man I haven't noticed, sitting at the back of the room. A hush falls.

Someone whispers to me that this is Cadik Braco Danon, last living survivor in Serbia of Jasenovac, the notorious Ustaša concentration and extermination camp. I realise immediately that his presence is special and pay close attention. Eighty-four years old, silver-haired, dapper, he stands to speak – formally, eloquently, and pointedly – on the absolute necessity of commemorating atrocities. Afterwards, I thank him and his wife Olga for coming, and we exchange contact details. He gives me two copies of his book, privately published, one in Serbian and an abbreviated English version.[82]

ꕥ

On the way home, on the JAT flight from Belgrade to Heathrow, I settle down in my aisle seat to read his book. It's graphic, gripping, and I can't put it down. It's the most chilling Holocaust memoir I've ever read. Braco's detailed personal account, with all its horrors, is told unflinchingly. Suddenly I wake with a start. I must have fallen asleep over the book, which has dropped from my lap into the gangway. The man in the adjacent seat looks across, puzzled, and helps me pick it up. I don't realise at this moment that I've momentarily passed out.

When I pick up my luggage at Terminal 2, I feel slightly dazed and tired, phone Melanie on my mobile to tell her that I've landed, and catch the airport circuit bus to the car park. I locate my old red Passat and start driving home to Cambridge. But somehow, inexplicably, I manage to lose my way, even though I've driven the route dozens of times and know it perfectly. I find myself driving all around Heathrow airport to the farther exit onto the M25, near terminal 4. Go slow, I tell myself. Focus. I drive onto the M11.

Suddenly I wake in my stationary car at the side of the motorway, at a slight angle to the barrier alongside it. A man is knocking at my window. He has an accent and I ask him where he's from. Italy, he replies, and I cheerfully start talking to him in Italian. But then I realise that I haven't a clue where I am. My mind is hazy and everything around me seems surrealistic. Then it dawns on me – I must have fainted, again. But this time, at the wheel of my car. I feel slightly dazed. I also realise that I've swerved into the Italian man's car and damaged his wing. Then police and ambulance arrive, and I tell them I'm fine and am happy to drive home. But they won't allow this. Obviously, even to me by now, I'm not quite with it. One of the policemen calls Melanie, then passes me his phone. I tell her that I'm ok and not to worry, but that I have to be checked out in hospital. The

---

[82] The Serbian title is *Sasečeno stablo Danonovih, Svedok holokausta, Sećanje na Jasenovac* (lit. 'The Felled Tree of the Danons: Holocaust Witness, Remembering Jasenovac'). The English title is *The Smell of Human Flesh, A Witness of the Holocaust: Memories of Jasenovac* (Danon 2006, 2007).

ambulance takes me to Hitchin, and they send me up to a ward. Melanie and my elder daughter Lara arrive, both very worried. I feel fine, I tell them. But gradually I realise that the accident could have been far more serious, both for me and for the Italian driver. I'm kept in hospital for two nights and am put through various scans. They find nothing wrong. Brain and heart are both normal and blood tests show no abnormalities. Melanie drives down from Cambridge in her car and takes me home. My car is a write-off. My insurance settles the damage on the Italian man's car. I don't lose my driving licence.

Later, I finish reading Braco's book in one sitting. The extract from his story below needs prefacing by a summary of the broader context.

&

Following the Nazi invasion and dismemberment of Yugoslavia in April 1941, the 'Independent State of Croatia' (*Nezavisna Država Hrvatska*, or NDH) was established as a pro-Nazi government. Its ideology was concocted from a mixture of Nazism, Italian fascism, and an extremist local form of Roman Catholic fanaticism. The so-called Ustaša dictatorship inaugurated its racial policies as soon as it came into power. Between August 1941 and April 1945, the systematic annihilation of all Serbs, Jews, and Roma living within the Croatian borders, as well as of anti-fascists of many nationalities, was perpetrated at the extermination camp known as Jasenovac, a complex of five major and three smaller 'special' camps, spread out over 240 sq. kms in south-central Croatia, over 100 kms south of Zagreb and 80 kms north of Banja Luka, Bosnia. The Serbian word *jasen* means 'ash-tree'. Jasenovac is the equivalent of 'Ashtown, Ashton'.

Estimates of the total numbers of men, women and children killed at Jasenovac range from 70,000 to 700,000. The regime so far exceeded the Nazi camps in its barbarism and savagery that even hard-bitten visiting German officials were shocked. If one could imagine some kind of grotesque comparison between kinds or grades of hellishness, it might be said that while the Nazis aimed to reduce the deaths of millions to the status of a quantifiable and depersonalised 'end-product', resulting from a massive co-ordinated industrial programme – and in this way, simultaneously to mask, deny and utterly dissociate themselves from the chaos, horror and terror they had actually inflicted on their victims – the Ustaša consciously aimed to 'experiment artistically' in devising the most bestial and barbaric of individual atrocities imaginable. Indeed, the Jasenovac authorities specialised in vengeful unpredictability, variation and inventiveness in the sadistic application of torture and murder. General von Horstenau, Hitler's representative in Zagreb, wrote in his personal diary for 1942 that the Ustaša camps in Croatia were "the epitome of horror". Arthur Hefner, a German transport officer for work forces in the Reich, wrote on November 11, 1942: "The concept of the Jasenovac camp should actually be understood as several camps which are several kilometres apart, grouped around Jasenovac. Regardless of the propaganda, this is one of the most horrible of camps, which can only be compared to Dante's *Inferno*."[83]

The full scale of the crimes committed at Jasenovac has never been fully admitted by successive Yugoslav or Croatian authorities, let alone systematically investigated. During the Tito era (1945–1980), and the post-Tito period when Croatia was still part of Yugoslavia (1980–1991), as well as since the break-up of the Federation under the presidency of Franjo Tudjman (1991–2000) – who was notorious for his anti-Semitism and his statements of Holocaust denial and revisionism – the pattern of evasiveness was identical. Deliberate and systematic attempts to shroud or whitewash truth, destroy evidence and render the site 'unreadable' were consistently made by successive authorities and regimes, as well as by individual Croatian historians.[84]

Thanks to pressure on Croatia from the European Union, under the presidency of Stjepan (Stipe) Mesić (2000–2010), some progress was made in the direction of admitting that crimes had been committed. But in the climate of increasing tolerance of anti-Semitism throughout Europe since 2016, further revisionist and apologist versions of Jasenovac have increased in number and brazenness.[85]

ᔕ

Braco Danon was born in Sarajevo in 1923. He grew up speaking Ladino as well as Serbo-Croatian. The surname *Danon*, he writes, which is common among Bosnian Jews, is believed to derive from Dan, one of the twelve tribes of ancient Israel.[86] Braco's family moved to Belgrade in 1934. At secondary school he took preparatory courses for a specialisation in architecture. In

[83] See: Jasenovac Research Institute (online); and *Under Balkan Light* (RB 2011d): 148-150.

[84] See e.g. Karge.

[85] See e.g. Rosensaft 2017 and 2018.

[86] Danon 2006: 174.

his teens, he joined the League of Communist Youth of Yugoslavia (*Savez komunističke omladine Jugoslavije*, or *SKOJ*). Following the Nazi invasion of Serbia in 1941, his family fled to Tuzla, Bosnia; but this area was already coming under Ustaša control. Wearing long Muslim gowns, his mother and sister escaped to the Italian-controlled city of Mostar. Braco was imprisoned in December 1941 at the age of eighteen, together with his father; and in the following year he was transferred to Jasenovac and then to another prison in the camp-complex, Stara Gradiška. He got separated from his father, who later perished. But in September 1942, extraordinarily, Braco managed to escape and join the partisans.

At the end of the war, as a seasoned guerrilla warrior aged only 22, and as a member of the Twelfth Slavonian Brigade, he was among the Yugoslav troops who witnessed the surrender of the defeated Croatian army and home guard (*domobrani*) to the British army in Bleiburg, Austria, in May 1945. His astonishing story of his search for the Jasenovac battalion in the lines of the surrendering troops is particularly moving. Single-handedly interrupting their march and pointing his loaded rifle at several officers at chin-point, he ordered them to lay down their arms. They obeyed, unwillingly and resentfully, and so did the entire battalion. But no Croatian soldiers had been allowed to stay too long at Jasenovac, which he describes as "an Ustaša officers' school".[87] All the guards he knew had moved on or been promoted, and he recognised nobody among them from his incarceration three years previously.[88]

He returned to Belgrade, qualified as an architect, and practised that profession until his retirement as General Manager of the design company Jugoprojekt.

ᔕ

[87] *ibid.* 169.

[88] For a memoir on what happened to the Slovene refugees by a British pacifist and medical orderly who served at Bleiburg, see Corsellis. And for diametrically contrasting perspectives on Bleiburg and the subsequent revenge-atrocities committed on war-prisoners by Yugoslav partisans, when Croatian prisoners who had surrendered to the British were callously returned to Yugoslavia, see the essays edited by two Croat emigrés to the USA, Prcela and Guldescu. Since the Croatian and Slovene separation from Yugoslavia in 1991, many untold details of these atrocities have emerged from excavation of caves and pits in Slovenia, where the partisans dumped corpses. See also Popov 1996b: 89.

After our first meeting in May 2007, I email Braco and ask if I may visit him and Olga in October, when I'll be in Belgrade for the International Writers' Meeting. I also ask if he would accept my dedication to him of a group of short poems. These are epigrams commemorating victims of Jasenovac, which will appear in *Under Balkan Light.*[89] He readily agrees.

photo RB

Braco and Olga Danon, 2007

At 11 a.m. on 22 October, I ring the bell of the small fifth-floor apartment on Šafarikova, near the *Politika* offices, in central Belgrade. I receive a warm welcome. The living room table has been caringly set with patterned porcelain coffee cups and saucers, and matching plates piled with cheese- and spinach-filled pastries and sweet biscuits, all neatly laid out on mats over a lace tablecloth. Having so recently read his autobiography, I find this traditional hospitality and homeliness particularly moving. There are blue and white ornamental porcelain vases, two wall-mounted antique clocks in ornate gilt frames, and a grandfather clock. On the dresser, a seven-branched menorah stands in front of a vase of bright, fresh, orange chrysanthemums. Among several family photos, I'm struck in particular by a close-up black-and-white portrait of Olga in semi-profile. It must have been taken when she was in her late twenties or early thirties, a beautiful woman with long wavy hair. From Braco's book, I know how close they are as a couple. They first met in 1949, and even though "it was love at first sight", for reasons unexplained they went their ways into separate marriages, with children. But in 1988, nearly fifty years later, they met,

[89] 'By the Banks of the Sava: Eight Memorial Tablets', *Under Balkan Light* (RB 2008d): 17-26.

fell in love again, and married.[90] In this apartment, I sense quiet lives being lived to the full.

We sit down to talk in a mixture of Serbian and French. I give Braco copies of several of my books and show him the manuscripts of the poems I'd like to dedicate to him, together with accompanying images. These are black-and-white photos of mutilated corpses, including those of named individuals. I've been in two minds about reproducing them. "Should I publish the photos as well as the poems?" I ask. "Definitely," he replies without hesitation. "You *must* publish them."

I ask if he would tell me a little more about his wartime experiences. He agrees, and tells me of his exhaustive eight-hour-long video-interview for the Shoah Foundation in 1998.[91] Before I leave, he gives me a copy of this, on four CDs. As he talks to me, what first comes across is his clarity of mind and deep personal modesty and humility. He tells me about night raids, dug-outs, hunger, living in the wild, being wounded, and hand-to-hand combat. Then, in the strongest possible contrast to the menorah and chrysanthemums, from a drawer he takes out his black wartime revolver, holster, and several medals. He arranges these objects neatly – and incongruously – on a rectangular white doily on a polished coffee table, together with a copy of his book, so that I can take photographs.

He also shows me his tiny five-point Partisan star-pin, presumably meant to be worn in a lapel or on a beret. "That little star lasted me three years," he says. No, he never wears the pin or the medals, he says. Implication: he did what had to be done, but none of this is to be flaunted. I ask if he thinks that *sudbina* (destiny) had anything to do with his survival. "No," he says unhesitatingly and matter-of-factly, "I don't believe in *sudbina.* I'm a dialectical materialist." Thinking of the 'survivor's guilt syndrome' suffered by some concentration camp survivors, I ask, further, how he thinks he managed to survive those three terrible years when so many others didn't. He pauses. "I was faster," he says. And adds: "And I was good at it." He doesn't go into details. There's no need.

He says that writing his book in his old age has been a deeply painful experience, but that he's relieved to have completed it. After all these years, he says, he has only been able to face these memories thanks to Olga. Some of this account is expressed in his book:

[90] See 'Cadik Danon' (online).

[91] See Danon 1998.

photo RB

Braco's medals, book, revolver and holster

> Olga offered me peace and strength as well as the unselfish help and support to write this book. Night after night we were sitting at our table; I would lean my elbows on the table, and would cover my eyes and let my painful reminiscences return, which had been haunting me for almost 60 years. Olga would sit next to me and patiently record every word of mine. Often I would be silent as the tears were suffocating me because of the horrors I was seeing again. I am deeply grateful to her for her heartfelt assistance in writing and completing this book.[92]

But, he tells me, he hasn't finished yet. Since completing this book, there's more that he needs to say and he plans to write another. His difficulty is that he's pursued by terrible memories, headaches and nightmares, often waking in the middle of the night and finding himself overwhelmed. Without thinking, I ask if he might be able to write spontaneously, allowing whatever comes into his head to find its way onto paper, so that he can sort his rough notes later. No sooner have the words left my mouth than I realise how inappropriate and insensitive they are. This is the only time he shows any hint of irritation with me. His brow furrows. "I don't want to do that," he retorts. "It has to *make sense*." And only at this point do I fully realise how disciplined is his entire way of thinking, and how he has carried the silent weight of all these memories for the majority of his life.

Before I leave, I promise to look for a London publisher for his present book, as well for as the next one. On my return to England, I approach several leading firms. Not one of them is interested. I lose heart, and my life gets taken over by other priorities.

---

[92] Danon, *op. cit.* 178.

Then, two years later, I receive the news that Braco has died.

Unless there's a draft of it somewhere, his second book will never get written.

ശ

Now, ten years later, I'm again trying to get his book published in England. By comparison with the Nazi Holocaust, the history of Jasenovac is scarcely known. Braco's testimony is needed.

September 2018

Slobodan Rakitić (1940–2013)

photo: frontal ka

In the 1990s, I meet the poet, editor and publisher Slobodan Rakitić several times at the Serbian Writers' Association. He was president from 1994 to 2005. During the first part of this controversial period, the Association was accused of complicity with the Milošević regime. Inevitably, it aroused strong opposition and its role and reputation declined, so much so that a breakaway association was formed.[93] Steering the Association through and after the Milošević years was a challenging task, which Slobodan met with calm, integrity and dignity.

Slobodan is deeply informed about Serbian cultural and literary traditions. With me, he's usually quiet, reflective and reserved, but in company with more people, he can display a light and ironic sense of humour. In all aspects of his thinking and activities, he has a conservative bias, including devout adherence to the Serbian Orthodox Church.

My first personal contact with him was at the Belgrade launch of Vera Radojević's translation of *In a Time of Drought* (*U vreme suše*) in April 2004. From then on, following his realisation of the Serbian influences on my writing, he encourages and advocates it in every possible way. In retrospect, I believe he was influential in the award of the Morava Charter prize to this book in 2006 and in the selection of *The Blue Butterfly* (*Plavi leptir*), in

[93] *Srpsko Književno Društvo*, or SKAD (the Serbian Literary Society) was founded in 2001.

Vera's translation, for the *Veliki školski čas* in Kragujevac in 2007. He also resources a Belgrade co-publisher for this book and writes an interpretative postscript for it.[94] Later, in 2012, as director of *Srpska književna zadruga* (SKZ, Serbian Literary Co-operative),[95] he co-publishes the bilingual edition of *Do vidjenja Danice: Goodbye Balkan Belle*, and speaks generously at its two launches in Belgrade and Kragujevac, with Slobodan Pavićević.

His death in the following year is sudden and unexpected and comes as a shock and a loss to his many friends.

October 2018

---

[94] Rakitić, 'Poet in the power of a Butterfly', in Jope *et al.* 313-324.

[95] The term *zadruga* here is worth noting. Compare Halpern 22, n. 2 and 134-135; and see also 237, n. 26 above.

Slobodan (Boba) Pavićević (1942–2013)

photo: Nebojša Raus

I first met Slobodan (Boba) Pavićević in the 1980s. A tall, handsome man wearing a black leather jacket, he had long hair and an impressively thick moustache. Like many other Serbian poets, he was a heavy smoker. Warm, gentle, modest, and sociable, he had a delicate sense of humour. In September 1992, at a time of huge political turmoil in the immediate aftermath of the collapse of the Yugoslav Federation, he founded a small press, named after the fourteenth century Serbian poet Jefimija,[96] "dedicated to upholding the Serbian cultural and political heritage, and in particular the past and present of Kragujevac and Šumadija".[97]

---

[96] Jefimija's real name was Jelena Mrnjavčević. She engraved her small poems on the backs of ikons and embroidered them on shrouds and church curtains. The simplicity and purity of one of her lyrics, 'Lament for a Dead Son', makes it a mini-masterpiece of Serbian medieval literature. This poem was written between 1366 and 1371. For an English translation, see Holton and Mihailovich: 22. See also 'Jefimija', *Wikipedia*.

[97] trans. from an announcement written by Boba. The press published around one hundred books until it was formally closed in October 2018 (email, Jovana Pavićević, October 29, 2018).

Nearly two decades later, in 2005, after completing *The Blue Butterfly* in Cambridge, I set to work on a historical postscript. I aim to summarise the background to the Kragujevac massacre of 1941, as well as to the annual memorial event, the *Veliki školski čas* ('Great School Lesson'). I've read accounts of the massacre itself from at least half-a-dozen history books, but am keen to find more recent and authoritative records, as well as first-hand local information, especially about the number of victims, on which there's wide disagreement.

I email Vera Radojević in Belgrade, to ask if she knows anybody from Kragujevac who might be able to answer some of my factual questions. She puts me back in touch with Boba Pavićević, so I email him, renew our old acquaintance, and we enter into correspondence. He helps me refine and correct various facts in the postscript and, in turn, puts me in touch with the Kragujevac historian, Staniša Brkić, head of archives at the 21st October Memorial Museum.[98] While Staniša provides me with even more detailed information, Boba sends me a short poem he composed in 1999, which he dedicated to me following my opposition to the NATO bombing of Serbia. This is the first time I've seen it.

Soon after this, I discover that Boba is the official Councillor for Culture for the City of Kragujevac. Supported by Staniša, he proposes the subsequent invitation I receive for Vera's translation of *The Blue Butterfly* (*Plavi leptir*) to serve as the theme-poem for the 2007 *Veliki školski čas*, a considerable honour.[99] When Vera and I go to Kragujevac for preliminary meetings, we visit Boba's office in his family home, and meet his two daughters Aleksandra and Jovana, both of whom at various times have worked part-time as editorial assistants for *Jefimija*. Then, in 2010, Vera and I co-translate Boba's own long poem based on the Kragujevac massacre, *May Peace be the Name of the Centuries* (*Mir neka je ime vekova*), which is published in a four-language edition. And then, in 2012, I'm invited to become an honorary citizen of Kragujevac, an even greater mark of respect. During the spring holiday period surrounding Djurdjevdan (St. George's Day, May 6), I give my acceptance speech in Serbian in the historic building that served as the country's first Parliament in 1859.[100]

Around this time, we learn that Boba has cancer. But it doesn't prevent him from welcoming Vera and me again in Kragujevac, or co-publishing

---

98 See the next memoir, 398-402 below.

99 See: 'Veliki školski čas za hiljade plavih leptira'; Raketić and Radišić; and '"Veliki školski čas" u Šumaricama'.

100 See: 'Barns počasni građanin Kragujevca'; and Radisavljević.

the bilingual edition of *Do vidjenja Danice: Goodbye Balkan Belle*, under the *Jefimija* imprint, or speaking eloquently at its launch in Kragujevac. Meanwhile, Vera and I co-translate Boba's series of thirty-three haiku, entitled *Dreams of Hilandar* (*Snovi Hilandara*). These gem-like poems on traditional and religious Serbian themes are accompanied by close-up colour photos of chunky pieces of jewellery, designed by Slavoljub Djani Galić, which provide a dramatic counterfoil to Boba's delicate, filigree-like poems.

On January 13, 2013. Boba dies.

Dreams of Hilandar reached page-proof stage shortly before Boba's death. But at the time of writing this memoir, more than five years later, the book still remains unpublished. The first of the following haiku is reminiscent of the tone of Jefimija herself, and in its simple purity, the last in the series returns us to the Serbian Orthodox monastery of Hilandar on Mount Athos. Here, the *Sveta Gora* itself (Holy Mountain) is the full and living symbol of perfection, wholeness, and the Self. This pearl of a poem might well be an apt and modest epitaph for Boba himself

September–October 2018

Grove of the Holy Virgin

through Heaven's garden
shines a cross-shaped
bud of meaning

Sveta Gora, Labyrinth

seeking an exit
I finally found the way
in me myself

translated with Vera V. Radojević, 2013

Staniša Brkić (1950–2013)

photo: Vreme

Staniša Brkić and I start corresponding in January 2006 thanks to an introduction from Boba Pavićević. As a professional historian and as research director of the 21st October Memorial Museum at Šumarice, Staniša has become the recognised authority on the massacres of Kragujevac, as well as on the city's Jewish community.[101] Thanks to his patient and thorough local research, he presents an accurate reassessment of the numbers of victims of the 1941 massacre, which have previously been highly controversial and often wildly inaccurate. His knowledge on both these subjects is unsurpassed.[102] Between 2006 and 2007, in a three-way correspondence with Vera Radojević and myself, he provides invaluable information on factual details about the massacre, much of which I include in the postscript to *The Blue Butterfly*.

Vera and I first meet Staniša on a visit to Kragujevac in May 2007, in preparation for the *Veliki Školski Čas* the following October. A slim, tall man, with a beaming smile, he has a manner that's unassuming to the point of self-effacement. He avoids making public speeches; in official company prefers to remain quiet; in general, dislikes professional administrators; and detests any form of pomposity or pretension. Thanks to his sympathetic sense of humour, while relaxing in his company –

[101] See: Brkić 2007; Brkić and Minić.

[102] See 46-52 above; Brkić undated; Brkić 2007; and *The Blue Butterfly* (RB 2011b): 125-140.

which I can't help doing – I sometimes forget that he possesses the astute critical intellect of a first-class historian and that he's the world expert on a topic that epitomises the spirit of tragedy. At the same time, from his modest demeanour, one can immediately intuit how people with devastating stories to tell about their loved ones would feel fully able to confide in him.

Staniša is a kind, patient and informative host. In 2007, he drives Vera and me to the exact location on the quiet, narrow, winding, hilly road between Kragujevac and Gornji Milanovac, near the village of Ljuljaci, where a platoon of thirty German soldiers was ambushed by resistance fighters on the night of October 16, 1941. The German reprisals for this attack came swiftly. Between three and five days later, nearly 3,000 civilians were shot. Staniša then escorts us on a tour of the massacre sites, including the location in the city where most of the city's Jews were executed, and two of the villages. We also revisit the site of the main massacre in Šumarice, which is now the Memorial Park. I'm astonished to see many blue butterflies there, of exactly the same species as the one that landed on my hand in May 1985.

This is the beginning of a warm friendship between Staniša, Vera and myself. Several times, when I fly to Belgrade but can't fit in a visit to Kragujevac, he makes the trip to see me, so that he, Vera and I can catch up and go out for a meal together.

ꟹ

When I return to Kragujevac in 2013, it's for the award of honorary citizenship of the city. During that visit, Staniša introduces Vera and me to the last living survivor of the massacre, Ljubiša (Ljube) Milanović. We sit in a bright café in the city centre for over an hour, while Ljube tells us vividly of his experiences during the war and after. The son of a rabbi, Ljube was rounded up in Ilićevo, a village near Kragujevac, on October 19, 1941. He faced a firing squad, was left for dead, but survived by lying motionless, to be rescued by his family. When he came to, they discovered that he had been strafed with sixteen bullets and was severely wounded in the thigh.[103] Later, he became the first director of the Šumarice Memorial Museum (1970–1983).

---

[103] See Nedeljković.

When Vera and I meet Ljube, he was 87. At the time of writing this, he's 94 years old.[104]

ᔕ

Staniša chain-smokes so heavily that I worry about him. On August 8, 2013, I receive an email from him, which I translate here:

> Dear Richard,
>
> Unfortunately, I developed cancer two years ago (and the doctors say it has already spread more or less through me). But the good thing is this cancer is highly amenable to chemotherapy, radiation and surgery. I'll be operated on at the end of June or the start of July. For the time being I'm bearing up well enough with the therapy and radiation. When this is over, I'll have a scan to see what the situation is, and then I'll need six weeks for my body to recover, and I'll go for more surgery.
>
> I feel good, am not overwhelmed by being ill, and am still working. My family, all my friends and all who know me are with me, and that means a lot to me.
>
> Your support and thoughts are a joy to my soul.
>
> I send you my warm greetings my dear friend
>
> Staniša

Following my reply, on the next day he writes back:

> Dear Richard,
>
> It's all life – both the bad [evil] and the good. For a long time, all I knew about was the good, but the time has come for the bad [evil] to take its toll [take over]. Thank God all the results have been good and I'm gradually getting better. My courage [spirit] hasn't left me for a single second. My family and friends have given me the strength to fight on. This is my great wealth, this sense of care and support, the feeling I'm not alone in this struggle. It's wonderful to know that I'm in the hearts and minds of my friends and acquaintances.
>
> I send you my warm greetings my dear friend
>
> Staniša

[104] Born in 1924, Ljubiša Milanović died on October 16, 2018, only days after I'd written this piece. He was the final survivor of the Kragujevac massacres.

A few days later (August 13), although very ill, Staniša reminds me without prompting that he hasn't forgotten an idea that we've begun to explore during the last few months. A distinctive feature of Šumarice Memorial Park is its monuments, many of them the work of internationally renowned sculptors. Staniša has come up with a scheme: to see if we might find funding for a commission for a British or Serbian sculptor to create a sculpture for the park. This would be of a male figure, or perhaps just a man's left arm or hand, with a butterfly settled on the forefinger. Our idea is that the sculpture would combine white stone with blue glass, which would glitter in the light. Staniša is especially keen on the idea and in his final email tells me that he even has a particular space in mind, and that he wants to put the idea to decision-makers in Kragujevac:

> Dear Richard,
>
> A couple of days ago, I talked to Vera about you coming to Belgrade. I hope I'll be able to come and see you so we can catch up about everything. The idea of the monument is great, and we've a fine location for it too, right next to the museum, the Peace Park is already up and running and this sculpture would be the first one in it. I'll also run this idea past Saša Milenić and director Zlatko, and they like ideas of this kind.[105]
>
> Your friend sends you warm greetings
>
> Staniša

This was his last email to me. He was too ill for us to meet when I come to Belgrade that September. He died in Kragujevac on October 13.

ശ

It's tragic that Staniša died only two years after the publication of his second book. He had more work to do, and he knew it. In 2011, an interview with him in the Serbian weekly magazine *Vreme* ('Time') carried the title 'Istraživanje nije gotovo' ('The research isn't over'). In that interview he says, "My goal remains to name each and every one of the victims by name and surname. Determining that number isn't yet

[105] Saša Milenić: poet, author and President of the Kragujevac City Council from 2008 to 2014. Zlatko Milojević: Director of the 21st October Memorial Museum at Šumarice in this period.

complete."[106] As for the detailed history of the Nazi occupation in Serbia, including the fate of its Jews – not to mention the disappearances of many non-Communists when Tito assumed full power at the end of the war in 1945 – the facts are still under-researched and now will probably always remain so. It's a pity that there haven't been more historians of this period as scrupulously attentive to detail and as passionately honest and objective as Staniša Brkić.

I'd like to think that, one day, perhaps the park might put up a sculpture of a man and a butterfly. It would be a memorial not only to the victims of Kragujevac, but to Staniša, and to our living friendship.

September 2018

[106] Brkić 2011, extract trans. RB.

Izet Sarajlić
(1930–2002)

photo: *Canzoni contro la guerra*

After the end of the Bosnian War (1992–1996), Izet Sarajlić (pron. *Sar-aye-lich)* becomes deservedly well-known as the poetic voice of the Siege of Sarajevo and the major Bosnian poet of his generation. Born in Doboj, the son of a railway worker, he spent his childhood in Trebinje and Dubrovnik and, when he was fifteen years old, moved to Sarajevo, where he lived for the rest of his life. An older name for Sarajevo was *Saraj*, so even his family-name belonged to this city. After studying philosophy at Sarajevo University, he went on to teach the subject. A prolific, energetic and convivial poet, he published his first book at the age of nineteen. In 1962, he co-founded the international *Sarajevo Poetry Days*.[107]

I met Izet on three very different occasions. The first two were in Belgrade at the 1982 and 1987 October International Writers' Meetings. In the 1970s and 1980s, Izet often visited Belgrade, where he had many friends among Serbian poets and where his books appeared from the major poetry publishers. In those days, his entire character and bearing emanated a charming, relaxed, unpretentious affability, and embodying the easy-

[107] 'Izet Sarajlić, *Wikipedia*.

going ambience he lived in. In that period, before the Bosnian war, the openness and tolerance of Sarajevo's inter-ethnic and inter-religious community were renowned throughout Yugoslavia. The city's cultural mix embraced Muslim, Serbian Orthodox, Croatian Catholic, and Sephardic and Ashkenazi Jewish communities. No-one realised then how fragile this multi-culturalism was. Its destruction has been all the more shocking and sad.

In Belgrade, I spent several evenings together with Izet, and on one occasion we talked and drank into the small hours. Modest, gentle, always interested in other people, he was knowledgeable about American poets, particularly Allen Ginsberg and the Beat generation, who had influenced his work. His poems at that time were mainly records of relaxed inner conversations with himself and other poets, and he liked to dedicate poems to friends. I don't know if he knew Frank O'Hara's work, but Izet's poems are marked by a similarly casual surface-texture that somehow manages to come across as spontaneous and stylishly cultivated at once. His language is colloquial, and his entire approach to poetry, as to life, relaxed and informal. When it comes to the written page, this sense of easy, natural spontaneity may well be harder to accomplish than it looks.

Curiously, Izet dedicated an early poem to his fellow-poet Radovan Karadžić, who, later, as the political leader of the Bosnian Serbs, would lead the forces responsible for the siege of Sarajevo, while Izet himself would live in the city, staying on to suffer the horrors of the siege, and become famous for his wartime diary.[108]

---

[108] A note on the extraordinary story of Radovan Karadžić (b. 1945, Montenegro) somehow belongs here, not only by way of accidental contingency and context, but because it dramatically offsets and contrasts with that of Izet.

A Serbian psychiatrist and poet, Karadžić entered Bosnian politics in 1989 and rose to become leader of the Bosnian Serbs in 1991, and in 1992, first President of the *Republika Srpska*, with its capital in Banja Luka. He was involved in all aspects of the Bosnian War, especially the siege of Sarajevo, and deeply implicated in atrocities. In 1995, he was indicted as an international war criminal, but in 1996 managed to 'disappear' for twelve whole years. In 2008, he was discovered in Belgrade under the semi-disguise of a long drooping moustache overlapping into a thick patriarchal beard, which made his lips entirely invisible. He'd been hiding in plain sight, living under an alias, and working quietly – and improbably – as a psychotherapist. After his arrest by Serbian police in Belgrade, he was immediately sent to the International Criminal Tribunal for the Former Yugoslavia (ICTY) in the Hague. In 2016, aged seventy-two, he was sentenced to forty years imprisonment for war crimes. So his term will end, if he lives that long, when he's 112 years old. He's still regarded as a hero by many Bosnian Serbs.

Somewhere in my library I've an issue of a poetry magazine from Banja Luka

ꕥ

The last time I meet Izet is in March 2001 in Sarajevo, five years after the end of the siege, when I accompany Melanie to Bosnia for a trip in connection with an international consultation-project she's planning. Melanie and I visit Banja Luka and drive back through dramatic mountainous vistas and a military checkpoint where tumbling boulders have crashed onto the narrow road. We pass through Jajce (pron. *Yay-tse*) but don't stop there. Here, in 1943, the second Anti-Fascist Council of National Liberation held its famous convention. Two years later, Tito took full control of the country. Ethnically mixed until around 1990, this town lost most of its population. Between 1992 and 1996, it was the scene of bitter conflict between Serbs, Bosniaks and Croats. By the time we get there, like many other places in Bosnia, it has an eerie, vacant feel.

Back in Sarajevo, we lodge in an apartment owned by a quiet, educated Serbian couple who, despite all difficulties, have bravely stayed on in the city throughout the bombing. A bullet, lodged in an interior wall of their sitting room, which they show us, was fired at them from inside the city, not from the periphery or the surrounding hills from where Bosnian Serb forces were besieging the city. The angle of the trajectory makes that 100% clear. The entire city is in a state of shocked, slow, partial recovery. Many tall buildings are half-shattered and derelict. We visit the market area of Baščaršija (pron. *Bash-char-shi-ya*), which is functioning more or less

---

which includes several of Karadžić's poems. An atrocious poem of his, probably an early one, stuffed with megalomaniac pseudo-Nietzschean rant, is dedicated reciprocally to Izet Sarajlić. But there's no fellow-feeling or magnanimity here. Here's a sample: "Convert to my new faith oh crowd while there is time / Because at the final stroke I am preparing / Things will call out their vague sense to me in fear / And only the most wretched who hope for salvation / Will be silent and seek for shades of mercy in my voice." These lines read retrospectively both as a sample of hyper-inflated self-vaunting and as an uncanny forewarning of the siege of Sarajevo, which he instigated and directed for four long years. Lines in another poem are even more explicit: "Go down to the city / to beat up the filthy / Vuksan, holiday. What a nice name." (Vuksan is a man's name, probably short for Vukoslav, from *vuk*, 'wolf'.) Karadžić also invented his own special diabolic reptilian image for the city: "If we did not hold Sarajevo, there would be no state [...]. Never hold a *snake by the tail,* but by the neck: that's what we had to achieve." (Quoted by Vujović 134 and 135; emphasis added). For discussion of his "fervent messianism", see Popov 1996b: 103. See also 'Karadžić', *Wikipedia.*

normally, though it's still being patrolled by NATO's SFOR troops.[109] We call in at the British Council offices and see the street corner by the Latin Bridge over the river Miljacka (pron. *Milyatska*], where Gavrilo Princip shot Austro-Hungarian Archduke Ferdinand and Empress Sophia on 28 June 1914, triggering the First World War.

Towards the end of our stay, I call Izet. He still has the same phone number. I haven't seen him for fourteen years. He suggests we meet in a coffee bar, which unexpectedly turns out to be upmarket and stylish. This place seems surrealistic compared with the bombed buildings all around, a small haven of warmth, promise and friendship. Izet looks tired and far older than his years. As Melanie and I sit chatting with him for an hour or so, he's as cordial as he ever was, but the shell of his former self. An infinite sadness seems to envelop him in layered wrinkles. He's continually interrupted by admirers and well-wishers, most of them people in their twenties, who respectfully and quietly request his autograph. He's now a popular and respected symbol of the defiant and resilient spirit of the city of Sarajevo under siege.[110] Clearly this is one of his haunts. He seems contented enough here, simply to be surrounded by people who love and admire him.

I sense that the war has at once made him famous and broken him.

He dies, aged only seventy-two, in the following year.

His books are translated widely into French, Spanish and Italian but his writings are hardly known at all in English. They deserve to be.

January 2020

---

[109] SFOR: Stabilization Force.

[110] The word *saraj* (pron. *sar-aye)* derives from Turkish 'palace, mansion, government house' (Hony 305). The Turkish word derives in turn from Persian *sarai, serai* 'palace, enclosed court'. The Turks called the city *Sarai Bosna*. Compare also *seraglio*.

Ivan V. Lalić (1931–1996): An Obituary

photo: Lori Sauer

Ivan V. Lalić was a great Yugoslav and European poet. His work and life stand for what was best in former Yugoslavia. His personal biography shows how the finest Serbian and Croatian cultural traditions blended in him. In this respect, he may be regarded as having been fortunate – that's to say, for so long as those two republics remained united and at peace.

He was born into a cultured Serbian family. His father Vlajko was a journalist and his maternal grandfather, Isidor Bajić, a composer. In 1946, aged fifteen, he moved to the Croatian capital. At school there, in the same class, he met Branka, the talented musician who was to become his wife. He entered the Zagreb law faculty in 1949, and in his graduation year, 1955, published his first book, *Bivši dečak* ('Once a boy', 'Bygone Boy'). After graduation, he joined Radio Zagreb and became an editor. In 1961, he moved back to Belgrade to become General Secretary of the Yugoslav Writers' Union. In 1979 he went to Nolit publishing house, where he worked as an editor until his retirement in 1993.

Although the move back to Belgrade in 1961 was permanent, each summer was spent with his wife and two sons at their second family home, in the town of Rovinj on the Istrian coast. Then in 1989, disaster struck. His first son Vlajko was drowned in a sudden squall on an Adriatic yachting trip, as he bravely sacrificed himself to save his two companions. Lalić confronted this tragedy determinedly in later poems, insisting, despite his loss, on the primacy of vision and the poet's inborn duty to continue assenting. Then war and the collapse of the Yugoslav Federation put a complete stop to his Adriatic summers.

Between 1955 and 1992, he published sixteen books in his own language, including two editions of selected poems. He received numerous Yugoslav awards, from the *Tribine mladih* in 1960 to the coveted *Branko Miljković Prize* in 1985. He has been widely translated into other languages. In English alone, seven volumes have appeared. His poems come across particularly well in the English language, and he has been blessed in having two translators of genius, the Englishman Francis R. Jones and the American Charles Simic. Jones's version of the 1984 collection, *Strašna mera,* rendered as *The Passionate Measure* (Anvil Press Poetry 1989) was awarded the 1991 European Poetry Translation Prize. Other international awards include the Hungarian *Pro litteris hungaricis* (1970) and the USA's *Thornton Wilder Prize* (1990). He was a frequent guest at international literary festivals and conferences, in Cambridge, Aldeburgh, Rotterdam and Lisbon. Jones's fourth selection, *A Rusty Needle*, was published by Anvil Press Poetry in 1996.

Ivan Lalić was a polyglot, with fluent English, French and German, and excellent Russian and Italian. His knowledge of the major world literatures was thorough and deep. His translations from English included editions of Walt Whitman, T. S. Eliot, David Gascoyne, and Christopher Marlowe's *Tamburlaine.* He was deeply fond of England and had a soft spot for our sense of humour. On his first visit to Cambridge, for the 1979 Poetry Festival, he wrote some authentically bawdy limericks, as well as composing his fine serious poem 'Concert of Byzantine Music'.[111] He was a devotee of music, from Bach and Mozart to Italian opera, and from French *chansonniers* to ragtime and musicals. He and his wife were famed among a wide circle of friends for their humour, warmth, kindness and hospitality. During evenings in his flat in Belgrade, especially during the Serbian Writers' Association's annual *International October Meetings,* he would regale English-speaking guests with jokes, wittily alternating between parodies of British and American accents.

Critics delineate many dimensions to Lalić's work, and Lalić himself rightly disliked labels. As a European modernist, he felt completely free to pick and choose his themes and influences from all available traditions. In sensibility, he had much in common with other Mediterranean writers,

[111] Lalić 1989: 81-86.

like the Greek poet George Seferis, with whom he shared a passion for the sea. A poem entitled 'Written in the Silver of the Sea' epitomises this.[112] On at least one recent occasion Lalić said that he considered himself more 'Mediterranean' than 'Serbian' or even 'Yugoslav'. It's possible, however, that this statement may have represented his characteristically understated response to the recent narrowing of perspectives in his own country through war and prejudice.

In an early poem he had written, "Places we love exist only through us [...] Places we love we can never leave" (*ibid.* 24). For Lalić, most of these deeply loved "places" were zones of spirit that are recognisably and specifically Yugoslav – both Serbian and Croatian. He was steeped in the poetry (or rather, all the poetries) of former Yugoslavia, from each of the Republics. His 1988 essay 'Some Notes on Yugoslav Literature: A Historical Approach'[113] respectfully and affectionately outlines the interconnections between these traditions, and clarifies his sense of placement among them, including his debts to the generation preceding his own in Serbian poetry, especially Vasko Popa and Miodrag Pavlović.

His sequence 'Dubrovnik, A Winter's Tale' (Lalić 1996a: 151-162) looks to the sea, to Renaissance culture. Many poems, written at different periods, relate to themes most deeply rooted in Serbian history – especially Byzantium and the Byzantine empire. Both the Dubrovnik and Byzantium poems use personae to scry individual moments in national history, and through these, to offer specific insights which have universal implications. The technique is derived from Cavafy, via Miodrag Pavlović, but Lalić brings to bear his own specific stamp.

Lalić was an inspirational poet who would brood long over his subjects, but when it came to composition, he frequently worked quickly and effortlessly, not wishing to mar or overload his texts with corrections. He was a consummate artist in this respect, since his poems were always highly crafted and, at various times in his life, structured in traditional metrics. To him the act of composition was itself an epiphany. As an Orthodox Serb, it was important to him to compose in Cyrillic. He took quiet pride in the neat, firm writing in his manuscript books, which to him were records of these moments of clarity, these Orphic dictations from his innermost voices.

---

[112] Lalić 1981: 60.

[113] Lalić 1993. *Note added in 2019*: Since the break-up of Yugoslavia, this essay hardly reflects the current situation. But see 'Declaration on the Common Language', *Wikipedia*, and 63, n. 13 above.

Perhaps Lalić's most enduring gift is that these epiphanies are experienced directly by the reader, in sudden, unexpected and extraordinarily radiant images. These frequent moments caught in the poem are by no means 'accidental' flashes of technical brilliance, but spontaneous blossomings of a coherent and informed vision, firmly and sturdily rooted in a specific history. And though he knew that the price to be paid for such a seer's gift must be high in terms of personal suffering, he never flinched from his poet's task, but rejoiced in his destiny: "Terrible is the effort to recognise love / In the waning, and to read the sign / In the nettle between two syllables of stone / […] our task / Is to remember, to deliver blows; / The task of the peach is to blossom."[114]

In breadth and depth, in generosity of spirit and in clarity of vision, his poetry is universal and timeless. In his treatments of human love and passion, nature and landscape, history and culture, perception and memory, he combines faultless precision and vitality of image with an unassuming and compassionate authority, and an uncannily accurate sense of premonition with an ability for unpeeling layers from the present to reveal its core. Taken together, these invoke a uniquely gifted way of seeing.

His sensibility, with its emphasis on memory as witness within transience, was formed in the Second World War. In a BBC interview, he commented: "My childhood and boyhood in the war marked very strongly everything I ever wrote. […] The theme of death in my poetry, or destruction, is very deeply rooted in this war experience."[115] So too, in his end is his beginning. In retrospect, it's now clear that the collapse of Yugoslavia was a personally experienced tragedy, which had a profound effect on him. For these reasons, as for many others, he is a writer of our time, even though his recent work offers no crudely overt commentary on recent political events in former Yugoslavia.[116]

July 1996

---

[114] 'Mnemosyne', Lalić 1981: 72.

[115] "The quotation is from an interview for a BBC Radio 3 programme about Ivan. It was recorded in Cambridge when he was over for the Poetry Festival in the early 80s […]" (email from Francis Jones, August 24, 2018). Ivan's reading in Cambridge took place in the Union Debating Chamber on April 18, 1983.

[116] See 'On the Death of Ivan V. Lalić' in *Under Balkan Light* (RB 2011d): 97-118.

Here's a poem by Ivan I've translated, based on his visit to the tomb of the Talmudic scholar and Kabbalist Rabbi Loew (c. 1512–1609) in Prague, who, according to legend, created the 'magical homunculus', the Golem.

At the Tomb in Prague

Earth, frozen each winter, fingers of snow on the stone,
Judah Loew ben Bezalel, scattered among dust,
The book destroyed, its type broken up.

Mercurius, first firebreath, streaked with verdigris,
Down to Saturnus, down to the black beginning.

A sky of lead and silver heaped on Prague,
Wind crystallised over the bend in the Voltava,
Slowly the rabbi dissolves in his legend,
But again and again the moment returns.

Jupiter, true path, from black to blueness,
Paved with opals of fire – sing on, of planets
Growing under formulas of glass.

Even so, the impossible doesn't exist:
Words travel on, like stars,
Wiser at each return, and even more inquisitive
The graveyard's dust sparkles, invisible flowers of frost
Bloom into perfume upon the skin of air.

Sulphur, mercury, arsenic, but something more too.
What was measured once, is forgotten, but promised still.
No more than the shadow of your truth, Rabbi Loew,

Whose blood gleams like rubies within the frozen earth.
But the passer-by places a pebble on your grave, then leaves
Together with the snow and the wind on the street.

translated in 1985

Another vowel

During my stay in Belgrade, after a while my Serbian friends begin to tease me by calling me *engleski balkanac* (pron. *Balkanats*) – the 'English Balkan' or 'Balkan Englishman'. Somehow, the nickname sticks.

Eleven years after my departure from Serbia, I'm back in Cambridge. It's summer 2001. Melanie and I have just returned from a summer holiday and one of the first things we do after entering the house is check our answering machine. There's a surprise message from Ratko Adamović. He's in town as a guest at the British Council annual International Writers' Seminar, which this year is being held at Downing College. Can we meet? he says. I call back and tell him that he must come over to our house immediately. Could he bring two other friends with him from the conference? he asks. *Of course*, I reply.

Melanie and I drive over to Downing and pick them up. They squeeze into the back of my old VW Passat. One of the other two is the Slovenian writer and poet Istok Osojnik, and the other, an American writer whose name I now don't remember. Melanie and I happen to have a fair supply of *šlivovica* (damson brandy) and *lozovača* (grappa), and out comes the first bottle. Having no food in the fridge because we've been away, we order a Chinese takeaway. Ratko, a Bosnian Serb, and Istok, a Slovene, are both extroverts with a good deal in common but with predictable differences in background and conviction. They've obviously been getting on well already at the conference, and now conversation flows in English and floods over into Serbo-Croatian, which all Slovenes of Istok's generation speak. Its entire tenor, content and style are totally non-English, non-American, non-Western: which is to say, animated, friendly, and in this case full of argument about a whole gamut of post-Yugoslav issues. The American writer is flabbergasted and intrigued at the energy generated. In an aside to me she confesses that she's never come across anything like it. And she's closely attentive. We also have some Serbian *stare gradske pesme* ('Old Town Songs') on CDs and tapes, and I play some tracks. I know in advance that these will set Ratko off. In Belgrade, I've heard him sing traditional Bosnian songs over wine and food on many occasions. He has a fine baritone voice and some of the songs he knows are poignantly beautiful. We go on drinking and talking, with interspersions of Ratko's songs, into the early hours.

Before they leave, Istok asks Melanie and me if we'd like an invitation to the Vilenica Literary Festival, which he directs. *Of course*, we reply.

ɤ

From 5 to 9 September 2001, I attend the international Writers' Gathering in Vilenica, Slovenia. Because of other commitments, Melanie isn't able to come, so I go alone. The programme is ambitious and beautifully organised. Around eighty or ninety writers participate from thirty-five countries, as well as translators. Most of those present are poets, with a sprinkling of essayists and novelists. Each poet reads from his/her work in one of half-a-dozen international events that take place at different venues, some of them historic. I try out a canto of *In a Time of Drought*, my long poem based on the Balkan rainmaking rituals, which I've just completed. The theme is both mythical and topical, because its *raison d'être* is the current collapse of Yugoslavia and how some kind of hope might be renewed. A young Slovenian translator kindly agrees to read the Serbian translation, which I've brought with me; and, after a quick rehearsal, she and I alternate in delivering its seven parts, so that the two languages blend into each other and an interactive dialogue emerges between them, heightened by the differing timbres of male and female voices. This goes down well with the audience and I receive invitations to other international events: in Dornbirn, Austria; in Porto Santo and Funchal, Madeira; and in Lausanne, Paris and Tokyo. In the course of the next two years, Melanie and I will visit all of these places together.

The final poetry reading includes this year's laureate, Jaan Kaplinski (Estonia), Michel Deguy (France) and Casimiro de Brito (Portugal). Atmospherically, its setting is impressive, deep in the vast underground cave, from which the festival takes its name. *Vila* means 'spirit, sprite, fairy, nymph'.

I find myself talking to writers from at least a dozen countries. The most meaningful and memorable meetings are with Mohammed Bennis, Michel Deguy, Casimiro de Brito, Katica Kulavkova and Ban'ya Natsuishi – respectively, from Morocco, France, Portugal, Macedonia and Japan. I also meet the linguist and translator Ana Jelnikar, a graduate student from Ljubljana working for her London-based PhD on Yeats, Tagore and the Slovenian national poet, France Prešeren (1800–1849). Later, Ana translates *Black Light* into Slovenian and the launch event in 2004 involves a return visit to Ljubljana for Melanie and me, when I also run a bilingual creative writing workshop for teenagers.

ᔕ

At Vilenica, I also meet the Serbian poet and translator, Kolja Mićević. He seems to be the only Serb present. He lives in Paris and is dear to Slovenians because he has performed the extraordinary feat of translating Prešeren's sonnets into French.

I mention to him that I lived in Belgrade for three years. He grins and pauses. He asks me to write down my name. He likes word games, puns and anagrams. He spells out *B-U-R-N-S* and mixes up the letter order. "Cela nous donne *S-R-B-U-N*," he says. "Pour arriver à *Srbin*, il faudrait seulement une autre voyelle." *Srbin* means 'Serb'.

Not quite Serb. All you'd need would be another vowel.

July 2019

Postscript

On 10 September 2001, in the wake of the Vilenica festival, I fly back to Heathrow from Slovenia, after chatting to the French poet Michel Deguy at Ljubljana airport, while he waits for his plane to Paris and I for mine to London.

The next day, at home in Cambridge, I take things easy. I wake up late and turn on the TV.

While it's actually happening, I watch suicide flights destroy the Twin Towers and damage the Pentagon.

The Millennium is over. For me, Vilenica has definitively marked the end of an era. A new beast slouches into our sitting rooms. Born in our shadows, it morphs into a billion clones.

August–September 2019

Acknowledgements

My thanks to the editors of books, journals and websites in which many of these essays, prose-pieces and translations of poems have first appeared, sometimes in versions that vary from those in this book. Listed below in the order in which they appear, these include:

'A Synchronistic Experience in Serbia' (2019). *Margutte.* Online at http://www.margutte.com/?p=30557&lang=en. Reprinted: (2019) in Christian McMillan, Roderick Main and David Henderson (eds.) *Holism: Possibilities and Problems*, London and New York: Routledge, Taylor and Francis, 159-169 ; and (2021, June), *Synchronicity, Pari Perspectives* 8.

'The blue butterfly', 'Nada: hope or nothing' and 'The Telling' (2006, 2008). In RB, *The Blue Butterfly*. Cambridge: Salt Publishing. Reprinted: (2011), Exeter: Shearsman Books.

'Gaj kamena i gaj drveća'. (1988). Serbian trans. of 'A Grove of Trees and a Grove of Stones' by Jadrana Veličković. *Oktobar*, year XXIII, Kraljevo, 1 and 15. Reprinted: (October 1988), *Zavičaj*, 27-18. Published in English (1989–1990), *Tel Aviv Review*, no. 2, 408-412. Reprinted: (1993), *Out of* Yugoslavia, North *Dakota Quarterly*, 36-39.

'A model of truth-telling' (2011). Published in English with Serbian trans. by Vera V. Radojević. In Staniša Brkić and Milomir Minić. *Jevrei u Kragujevcu*. Kragjevac: Krug, 188-203.

'Dodola and Peperuda: The Balkan Rainmaking Customs' (2006). *Poetry Review*, vol. 96:1, 65-73.

'Rain and Dust '(2007). *Fulcrum, an Annual of Poetry and Aesthetics*, vol. 6, 321-334. Reprinted: (2008), *Studia Mythologica Slavica*, vol. XI, 217-236.

'A Nimble Footing on the Coals: Tin Ujević, lyricist; some English perspectives' (2011). *sic*, year 2, no. 1. Online at: https://www.sic-journal.org/ArticleView.aspx?aid=117

Tin Ujević, 'Everyday Lament' (2011). RB and Daša Marić (trans.). *sic*, year 2, no. 1. Online at: https://www.sic-journal.org/ArticleView.aspx?aid=139. Reprinted: (2013) in *Twelve Poems*, Shearsman Books, 12-17; and (October 12, 2020) 'Richard Berengarten – The Balkan Collection', *The Cambridge Critique*, online at: https://www.thecambridgecritique.com/home/2020/10/13/richard-berengarten-the-balkan-collection; republished elsewhere online, often unattributed.

'A Medieval Serbian Poem' (1988). Published under the title 'The Torment and the Passion'. *Zavičaj* ['Homeland'], no. 34, 112-113.

'Katica Kulavkova's *Naked Eye*' (2010). Under the title 'Infinite riches in a little room'. Introduction, in Kulavkova, Katica. *Golo oko / Naked Eye*, Skopje: Poetiki, 9-15.

Extracts from 'Arrival 1987' and 'A Nimble Footing on the Coals'. (October 12, 2020). 'Richard Berengarten – The Balkan Collection'. *The Cambridge Critique* Online at: https://www.thecambridgecritique.com/home/2020/10/13/richard-berengarten-the-balkan-collection

'Drawing from the Neolithic: Notes on Maja Herman Sekulić's *Gospa od Vinče*' (2018). In *Književno stvaralaštvo Maje Herman Sekulić* ['The Literary Creativity of Maja Herman Sekulić'], Conference Papers. Belgrade: Alfa BK University 16-34.

'Demons and Daimons: The Dark Vision of Filip David' (January 23, 2018). Under the title 'Fictional exploration of the darkest depths of reality'. *Jewish Chronicle*, 46. Online at: https://www.thejc.com/culture/books/book-review-the-house-of-remembering-and-forgetting-1.457018. Reprinted: (2019), *Serbian Studies* 30, 249-250.

'Belgrade: Poetry Capital' (1988). *Serbian Literary Quarterly*, vol. 2, 91-93.

'Chains of Freedom' (June 7, 1985). Under the title 'Today you are poets'. *Times Educational Supplement*. Reprinted: (1985), *Yugoslav English Language Teaching Review*, no. 7, 71-74; and (December 1985) under the title 'Teaching Poetry Abroad', *Schools Poetry Review*, no. 10, 25-26.

'Such Stuff as Dreams' (November 1989). *Yugoslav English Language Teaching Review*, no. 12, 68-79.

'A Living Embroidery: English Teaching and Cultural Contacts in Yugoslavia', (March 6, 1992). Under the title 'Bare ruined choirs', *Times Educational Supplement*, 34. Reprinted (1993) in *Out of Yugoslavia*, 4-11.

'Address to the Plenary Session of the 36th International Meeting, organised by the Serbian Writers' Association', with Serbian trans. Jasna Levinger-Goy, (1999). Cambridge: Los Poetry Press.

'Letter from Kosovska Mitrovica' (February 11, 2000). *Times Literary Supplement*, 15-16.

'Time to Spare: Desanka Maksimović at Struga' (1988). *Serbian Literary Quarterly*, no. 2, 114-115.

Desanka Maksimović, 'I've no more time' (1988). Trans. with Jasna B. Mišić. *Serbian Literary Quarterly*, no 2, 113. Reprinted: (1988), *Zavičaj* 34; (summer 1991) *New Orleans Review* 66; (1993), *Out of Yugoslavia* 104. 'Anticipation' (January 27, 1990), *Politika*, weekly international edn. 19. Reprinted: (1993) in *Out of Yugoslavia*, 105. 'Speak softly' and 'Nobody knows' (1993), *Out of Yugoslavia*, 105.

‘Obituary note for Oskar Davičo’ (October 7, 1989). Serbian version, under the title ‘Pesnik čudotvoran’ [‘Miraculous Poet’], *Politika.*

Edward Dennis Goy: An Obituary’ (March 23, 2000; unattributed). *The Times*, 25.

Oskar Davičo, ‘Hannah’ and ‘Two sonnets’. (1992), *Tel Aviv Review*, vol. 3, 352-355. Reprinted (1993) in *Out of Yugoslavia*, 55-56. ‘No, I’m not double-barrelled’ (2015), reprinted in RB, *Notness*, Shearsman Books: Bristol, 19.

‘Ivan V. Lalić: An Obituary’ (August 5, 1996; unattributed). *The Times*, 19.

ᔕ

The front cover image is a coloured copperplate engraving of Belgrade made by the German artist Josef Eder (1760–1835). For photographs, cordial thanks and acknowledgements as follows: to the Serbian Ethnographic Museum, Belgrade, for Hajduk Chieftain Micko Krstić with comrades and associates, and for girls dressed as *Dodola*, taken by Dr. Dragić in Banja Koviljača, near Loznica, Western Serbia (1957); to Branislav (Vlaja) Vlajinić, for photos of poetry workshops and of Boba Bobić; to Olga Danon and to Mirko Milićević (Dosije Publishers); for photos of Braco and Olga Danon; to Branka Davičo, for Oskar Davičo; to Jasna Levinger Goy, for E. D. Goy; to Lori Sauer and Peter Jay, for Ivan V. Lalić; to Dragoljub Kažić (1922–1999), for Miodrag Pavlović; to Nebojša Raus and Jovana Pavićević, for Slobodan Pavićević; to Horst Tappe (1938–2005), *Poetry International* and Peter Jay, for Vasko Popa. For online photos, similar grateful thanks and acknowledgements to: *Vreme* for Staniša Brkić; *knjizara.com* for Moma Dimić; *Literaturen svyat* for Ivan Gadjanski; *pdfzone.pw*, for Jovan Hristić; *The Daily Beast*, for Danilo Kiš; *sudöst Europa Kultur* e.V, for Zlatko Krasni; *Poezije Ljubovi* and *Pinterest.com*, for Desanka Maksimović; *Canzoni contro la Guerra,* for Izet Sarajlić; and *mediasefera.rs,* for Eugen Verber.

ᔕ

I should also like to express my appreciation to all those who have helped and encouraged me, both directly and indirectly, in many and various ways, during the long gestation of this book and its component parts, including all the friends and colleagues who influenced me during the time I spent in former Yugoslavia, as well as since then in the countries that emerged from it. Without their valuable advice, information and suggestions, for example in tracking historical facts and sources of information, and in the translation of key passages from languages unfamiliar to me, this book would have contained many (more) errors. These friends and colleagues are too numerous to name. Ideally, I would like to say something about the particular and individual ways in which every one of them has helped me, but I fear that would take too long, so I hope I may be forgiven for simply mentioning some of them here: Ratko Adamović, Radomir Andrić, Oytun Ayberk, Tamara Babić, Florentina Badalanova, Bogdana G. (Boba) Bobić, Predrag Bogdanović Ci, Jonathan Boulting, Staniša Brkić, Richard Cook, Marilyn Cvijić, Braco Danon, Olga Danon, Anthony Davies, Branka Davičo, Moma Dimić, Daphne Dorrell, Goran Djordjević, Nikanor Firat, Ivan Gadjanski, John Gery, Vesna Goldsworthy, George Gömöri, Edward Dennis (Ned) Goy, Miljan Guberinić, Maja Herman Sekulić, Ruth Hawthorn, Jeremy Hooker, Svetozar Ignjačević, Olga Kapeliuk, Danilo Kiš, Vesna Kovačević, Katica Kulavkova, Tomislav Kuzmanović, Dragan Lakićević, Branka (Branca) Lalić, Ivan V. Lalić, Jasna Levinger-Goy, Peter Mansfield, Ksenija Maricki Gadjanski, Roderick Main, Daša Marić, Vida E. Marković, Andrija Matić, John Matthias, Ivana Milankov, Jasna B. Mišić, Brane Mozetič, Dimitrije Nikolajević, Paschalis Nikolaou, Jasna Novaković, Biljana Obradović, Iztok Osojnik, Dušan Pajin, Slobodan Pavićević, Jovana Pavićević, Branka Panić, Miodrag Pavlović, Aleksandar Petrov, Silvia Pio, Aleksandra Popević, Adam Puslojić, Marija Puslojić, Dušan Puvačić, Ana Radović-Firat, Mladen Radulović, Slobodan Rakitić, Anthony Rudolf, Vladimir Sekulić, Resul Shabani, Fatos Shala, Vesna Stanojević, Saša Stojanović, Zmago Šmitek, Anelia Tapp, Maria Todorova, Milena Toftisova Koleva, Radomir Uljarević, Eugen Verber, Branislav Vlajinić, Răzvan Voncu, Duška Vrhovac, Dragutin Vučković, Vladeta Vučković and Clive Wilmer. Over the years, many others have done me countless services that have directly or indirectly helped me in the making of this book. Sadly but inevitably, as I write this, some of these friends have passed away.

ᔕ

Finally, my very special gratitude goes to five people. First, to Paul Scott Derrick, Vesna Goldsworthy and Anthony Rudolf, who, in the generous spirit of friendship, have kindly read and helped me improve a near-final draft of this book. Second, to Vera V. Radojević, to whom this book is dedicated, for her friendship, hospitality and kindnesses ever since we first met in Belgrade in 1987 and, in particular, for translating books, poems and essays of mine into Serbian, and for our always-enjoyable collaborations when translating Serbian poets into English. Above all, I should like to thank my wife, Melanie Rein, for her constant support, encouragement and devotion, and for her profoundly perceptive and helpful comments on the later drafts of this book, and in guiding my attention to the clarification of nuances.

April 2021

References

Until 2008, references to works by the author (RB) appear under the name Burns, and occasionally Bernz, and after 2008, as Berengarten. The title of an original or first edition appears in square brackets, as do titles and names in languages other than English, when translated and transliterated. The following pages do not generally mention RB's writings that are included in the Acknowledgements (417-420 above). Online references were rechecked in March 2021.

Epigraphs

(1) "No, rather let me sing and say something wise, without stirring up any of the city's ills." Lines spoken by Amphion in Euripides' play Antiope, c. 420–406 BCE (fragment 202). In *Euripides VII*, Henderson. Jeffrey (ed.). 2008. Harvard CN: Harvard University Press (Loeb Classical Library 504): 194-195. Translation slightly modified.

(2) William Blake, 'The Marriage of Heaven and Hell. In *The Poetry and Prose of William Blake*. Keynes, Geoffrey (ed.). 1956. London: Nonesuch Library: 131.

(3) Fernand Braudel. 1966 (2nd edn.). *La Méditerranée et le monde méditerranéan à l'époque de Philippe*, vol. II. Paris: Librairie Armand Colin: 223. Trans. and quoted by Traian Stoianovich as: "Events are dust. They are brief glimmers, hardly alight before they return to night and often to oblivion. Each event, nevertheless, however brief, bears testimony, lights up a corner of the landscape and sometimes even deep layers of history." This appears in Stoianovich's *French Historical Method: The Annales Paradigm*. 1976. Ithaca NY and London: Cornell University Press: 230. See also the authorised trans. by Siân Reynolds in the English published version of Braudel's book, *The Mediterranean and the Mediterranean World in the Age of Philip II*, vol II. Berkeley, CA: University of California Press: 902. Stoianovich writes in a footnote that the latter "is not quite faithful to the original as I need for my analytic purposes".

(4) C. G. Jung. 1954. 'Der Philosophische Baum' (1945). In *Von den Wurzeln des Bewußtseins* ['From the Roots of Consciousness']. Zürich: Rascher und Cie: 370. "One does not become enlightened by imagining figures of light, but by making the darkness conscious. The latter procedure, however, is disagreeable and therefore not popular." 'The Philosophical Tree', in *Alchemical Studies* (*Collected Works*, vol. 13). R. F. C. Hull (trans.). 1967. London: Routledge and Kegan Paul: 265-266, §335.

(5) W. H. Auden. 'September 1939'. Online at https://poets.org/poem/september-1-1939

Relevant writings by RB (until 2008, mainly as Burns)

1968 'The Easter Rising 1967' (poster-insert). *The London Magazine*, vol. 7, no. 10. (Agnostos Nomolos)

1969 *The Easter Rising 1967*. Brighton: Restif Press. (Agnostos Nomolos)

1981 *Keys to Transformation: Dylan Thomas and Ceri Richards*. London: Enitharmon Press.

1984 *Crna svetlost*. 1st Serbian edn. of *Black Light*. Bobić, Bogdana Gagrica (trans.). Gornji Milanovac: Dečje novine. (Ričard Bernz)

1987 'Drvo' and 'Andjeli'. Serbian versions of 'Angels' and 'Tree'. Bobić, Bogdana G. (trans.). *Književnost* 12, 2081-2089. (Ričard Bernz)

1990 *Menadžer*. Serbian edn. of selections from *The Manager*: Mišić, Jasna B. and Sekulić, Vladimir (trans.). Nikšić and Titograd: Universitetska riječ and Udruženje književnika Cnre Gore [University Word and Writers' Association of Montenegro]. (Ričard Bernz)

1996 'With Peter Russell in Venice, 1965–1966'. In Hogg, James (ed.), *The Road to Parnassus: Homage to Peter Russell on his Seventy-fifth Birthday*. Salzburg: University of Salzburg, 107-123.

1999a 'Is NATO Right to Bomb Yugoslavia? A Personal View'. Online at: http://www.yurope.com/kosovo/articles/Richard_Burns.htm

1999b 'Is NATO Right to Bomb Yugoslavia? A Personal View'. Serbian version in five instalments; translators' names unspecified. *Politika*, March 28-April 1: year 96, nos. 30683-30687.

1999c 'Address to the Plenary Session of the 36th International Meeting of Writers, organised by the Association of Serbian Writers, Belgrade, October 1999' / 'Pozdravna rečupušena plenarnoj sesiji, 36. Međunarodnog susreta književnika, u organizaciji Udruženja književnika Srbije, Beograd, oktobar 1999'. Bilingual English and Serbian edn. Levinger-Goy, Jasna (trans.). Cambridge: Los Poetry Press.

1999d 'Senovit bunar'. Serbian version of 'The Shadow Well'. Mitrović, Srba (trans.). In Dimić, Moma (ed.). 1996. *Kletva* ['Curse']. Belgrade: Udruženje književnika Srbije [Serbian Writers' Association], 118-119.

2001 *The Manager*. 1st edn. London and Bath: Elliott and Thompson.

2001a 'Posle suše ['After the Drought'] and 'Za Dodolu' ['For Dodola'], (extract from *U vreme suše* (*In a Time of Drought*): Radojević, Vera V. (trans.). *Dodola*, vol 1. No. 1 (February-March).

2004 *U vreme suše*. Serbian edn. of *In a Time of Drought*: Radojević, Vera V. (trans.). Belgrade: Rad [Work]. (Ričard Bernz)

2005 'Za dodolu' ('For Dodola'). In Dimić, Moma (ed.). *Ostali svetlosti, strani pesnici (1964-2004) / Remnants of Light, Poets from Abroad (1964-2004). Belgrade International Writers Meeting*: Belgrade, Udruženje književnika Srbije [Serbian Writers' Association], 182-185.

2006a *The Blue Butterfly*: 1st English edn. Cambridge: Salt Publishing.

2006b *In a Time of Drought*: 1st English edn. Nottingham: Shoestring Press.

2007 *Plavi leptir*. Serbian edn. of *The Blue Butterfly*: Radojević, Vera V. (trans.). Kragujevac and Belgrade: Spomen Park, Kragujevački oktobar with Plava tačka [Kragujevac October Memorial Park with Blue Spot].

Relevant writings by RB (from 2008, as Berengarten)

2008a *For the Living: Selected Longer Poems 1965–2000*. 2nd English edn. Cambridge: Salt Publishing.

2008b *The Blue Butterfly*: 2nd English edn. Cambridge: Salt Publishing.

2008c *In a Time of Drought*: 2nd English edn. Cambridge: Salt Publishing.

2008d *Under Balkan Light*: 1st English edn. Cambridge: Salt Publishing.

2009a 'The Cambridge Poetry Festival 1975: 35 years after'. *Cambridge Literary Review 1*, 148-160.

2009b 'Volta Project, The' (ed.). *International Literary Quarterly* 9. Online at: http://interlitq.org/issue9/volta/job.php

2009c. 'Border/Lines: An Introduction' (to 'The Volta Project'). *International Literary Quarterly* 9. Online at: http://interlitq.org/issue9/berengarten/job.php

2011a *For the Living: Selected Longer Poems 1965–2000*. 3rd English edn. Exeter: Shearsman Books.

2011b *The Blue Butterfly*: 3rd English edn. Exeter: Shearsman Books.

2011c *In a Time of Drought*: 3rd English edn. Bristol: Shearsman Books.

2011d *Under Balkan Light*: 2nd English edn. Bristol: Shearsman Books.

2012a *Do vidjenja Danice (Goodbye Balkan Belle)*. Bilingual English and Serbian edn. Radojević, Vera V. (trans.). Belgrade and Kragujevac: Srpska književna zadruga [Serbian Literary Association] and Jefimija.

2012b *Do vidjenja Danice: Lunch Poems at Berkeley*. Poetry reading, April 5. Hass, Robert (intr.). Online at: represinthttps://www.youtube.com/watch?v=mafUBRR9dIY

2012c 'Observations on Serbs, Jews and Israelis: A Plea for Understanding'. *Jewish Affairs*, 26-30 (Burns)

2013a *Crna svetlost.* 2nd Serbian edn. of *Black Light*: Radojević, Vera R. (trans.). Vršac: KOV.

2013b 'I Must Try This Telling'. Interview with Sean Rys. *International Literary Quarterly* 21. Online at: http://interlitq.org/issue21/sean-rys/job.php

2013c *Imagems 1*. Bristol: Shearsman Books.

2015a *Notness: Metaphysical Sonnets*. Bristol: Shearsman Books.

2015b *O voar da bolboreta azul* ['The Flight of the Blue Butterfly']. Bilingual English and Galician selection from *The Blue Butterfly* and other poems: Riviero Álvarez, Loreto and Lavandeira, F. R. (trans.). Auliga: Espiral Major.

2017a 'Extraits du *Papillon bleu*' ['Extracts from *The Blue Butterfly*]: Huynh, Sabine (trans.). In Bonhomme, Béatrice (ed.). *L'œuvre poétique de Richard Berengarten* ['The Poetic Oeuvre of Richard Berengarten']. *NU(e)* 65, 87-112.

2017b *Igra plavog leptira / The Dance of the Blue Butterfly*. Selections from *The Blue Butterfly*. Bilingual English and Serbian edn. Radojević, Vera V. (trans.). Smederevo: Meridijani [Meridians].

2017c 'I Must Try This Telling'. Interview with Sean Rys. In *A Portrait in Inter-Views*: Nikolaou, Paschalis and Dillon, John Z. (eds.). Bristol: Shearsman Books, 110-146.

2017d *The Albero Project. Margutte*. Online at: http://www.margutte.com/?p=23972&lang=en

2017e *A Forest of Trees*. Translations of 'Tree' into various languages (an ongoing project). *Margutte*. Online at: http://www.margutte.com/?p=22640&lang=en

2017f 'Tree, a Video'. Guetemme, Geneviève (film and montage); Rosenstock, Gabriel (Irish trans.); Pio, Silvia (Italian trans.); Ball, Derek (soundtrack). 'The Albero Project' *Margutte*. Online at: http://www.margutte.com/?p=25449&lang=en

2019a 'Drvo'. Serbian version of 'Tree'. Radojević, Vera V. (trans.). In 'The Albero Project'. *Margutte*. Online at: http://www.margutte.com/?p=22640&lang=en

2019b *Imagems 2*. Bristol: Shearsman Books.

2019c Three poems from *The Blue Butterfly*. *Margutte*. Online at: http://www.margutte.com/wordpress/wp-content/uploads/2019/06/Richard-Berengarten-Three-poems-from-The-Blue-Butterfly.pdf

2020a *Lakeside / Ob jezeru / Au bord du lac*. Trilingual edn., trans. into Slovene, Simonovic, Ifigenija; and into French, Chabbert, Marie and Huynh, Sabine. Ljubljana: Slovenski center PEN/ Slovene PEN Centre.

2020b 'Five Sonnets in Honour of Sir Walter Raleigh'. *Oxford Magazine* 426, 14

Relevant writings on RB

'Barns počasni građanin Kragujevca' ['Burns an honorary citizen of Kragujevac']. 2012, April 9. *Danas* ['Today']. Online at: http://www.rts.rs/page/stories/sr/story/57/srbija-danas/1079400/barns-pocasni-gradjanin-kragujevca-.html

Bonhomme, Béatrice (ed.). 2017. *L'œuvre poétique* de Richard Berengarten. *NU(e)* 65.

'Britanski pesnik počasni građanin Kragujevca' ['British poet an honorary citizen of Kragjevac']. 2012, May 6. *Blic* [Blitz]. Online at: https://www.blic.rs/kultura/vesti/britanski-pesnik-pocasni-gradanin-kragujevca/8qgm1dd

'Dvojezična poema "Do vidjenja Danice" Ričarda Berengartena' ['Richard Berengarten's bilingual poem *Do vidjenja Danice*']. 2102, May 3. *Glas novosti* [Voice of News] (*Tanjug*). Online at: http://www.glas-javnosti.rs/aktuelne-vesti/2012-05-03/dvojezicna-poema-do-vidjenja-danice-ricarda-berengartena

Frisardi, Andrew. 2016 [2011]. 'Black Suns on the Scales: on Richard Berengarten's *The Blue Butterfly*'. In Jope *et al.* 337-346.

Huynh, Sabine. 2017. 'Donner des ailes au *Papillon bleu*'. ['Giving wings to the *Blue Butterfly*']. In Bonhomme, Béatrice (ed.). *L'œuvre poétique de Richard Berengarten* ['The Poetic Oeuvre of Richard Berengarten']. *NU(e)* 65, 125-134.

Ignjačević, Svetozar. 2000. 'U znaku plavog leptira' ['At the Sign of the Blue Butterfly']. In *Zemlja čuda u izlomljenom ogledalu (ponovo)* ['Wonderland in a Cracked Mirror (again)']: Belgrade: Filološki fakultet Beograd i Narodna Knjiga [Philological Faculty Belgrade and National Book], 171-186.

——. 2016 [2011]. 'Wonderland Through a Cracked Mirror: An English Poet in Yugoslavia'. Radojević, Vera R. (trans.). In Jope *et al.* 302-314.

Ignjatović, Srba. 2007. 'Neuništevenji spomenik' ['Uninhabited Monument']. In *Plavi Leptir* (RB 2007a), 157-159.

Jones, Francis R. 2016 [2011]. 'In a Balkan Light: Richard Berengarten and the South Slav Cultural Space'. In Jope *et al.* 285-301.

Jope, Norman, Derrick, Paul S. and Byfield, Catherine E. (eds.). 2011. *The Salt Companion to Richard Berengarten.* Cambridge: Salt Publishing. Reprinted, 2016, as *The Companion to Richard Berengarten.* Bristol: Shearsman Books.

Lešović Stanojević, Sofija. 2010. *Moravski susreti i povelje* ['The Morava Meetings/Encounters and Charters']. Čačak, Književno društvo Mrčajevci [Mrčajevci Literary Asociation], 56-57.

Lucas, John. 2016 [2011]. 'Richard Berengarten: The Lyrical and the Political'. In Jope *et al.* 337-346.

Milićević, Ljubiša. 1991, February 1-15. 'Svježi poetski eho' ['Fresh Poetic Echo]', review of Serbian edn. of *The Manager*. *Prosvjetni reč* 3.

Milosavljević, B. 1988, September 9. 'Trag plavog leptira' ['Trace of the Blue Butterfly'] (interview). *Ibarske Novosti*, 4.

Petrov, Aleksandar. 2009. 'The Blue Butterfly Effect'. Radojević, Vera R. (trans.) *International Literary Quarterly* 7. Online at: http://interlitq.org/issue7/aleksandar_petrov/job.php. Reprinted: 2011 and 2016 in Jope *et al.* 347-356.

Radisavljević, Zoran. 2012, May 4. 'Razglednice iz bivše Jugoslavije' ['Snapshots of former Yugoslavia']. *Politika Online*. http://www.politika.rs/sr/clanak/217528/Razglednice-iz-bivse-Jugoslavije#!

Raketić, B. and Radišić, N. 2007, October 22. 'Engleska krvava bajka' u Kragujevcu'. ['English "Bloody Fable" at Kragujevac']. *Blic* ['Blitz']. Online at: https://www.blic.rs/vesti/srbija/engleska-krvava-bajka-u-kragujevcu/my3zjdj.

Rakitić, Slobodan. 2007. 'Pesnik u vlasti leptira, Engleski pesnik na Balkanu'. In *Plavi Leptir* (RB 2007), 151-156.

——. 2016 [2011]. 'Poet in the power of a Butterfly'. Radojević, Vera R. (trans.). In Jope *et al.* 315-324.

Vasić, Ljiljana. January 27, 1990. Belgrade's British Bard'. *Politika*, weekly international edn., 19.

'"Veliki školski čas" u Šumaricama' ['"The Great School Lesson" at Šumarice']. 2007 (October 22). *Politika Online*.

'Veliki školski čas za hiljade plavih leptira' ['Great School Lesson for thousands of blue butterflies']. 2007. *Glas javnosti* [Voice of the Public] Online at: http://www.glas-javnosti.rs/node/7221/print

Vrhovac, Duška. 1987 (December 4). 'Povratak duše' ['Return of the Soul'] (interview). *Intervju*, 30-31.

Wilson, Stephen. 2009. 'Hath Not a Jew Hands'. *International Literary Quarterly* 8. Online at: http://interlitq.org/issue8/stephen_wilson/job.php. Reprinted: 2016. 'Hath Not a Jew Hands?' In Jope *et al.* 357-369.

Selected works translated/edited by RB from South Slavic Languages

Davičo, Oskar. 1993. 'Poems from Hana (1939)'. With Marić, Daša (trans.). In *Out of Yugoslavia*, 55-57.

Gadjanski, Ivan. 1997. 'Balkan Destiny, *il penseroso*'. In *Sudbina balkana / Balkan Destiny.* Six-language edn. Belgrade: Rad, 17-18.

Herman Sekulić, Maja. 2018. *Silna Jerina / The Mighty Irina*, bilingual Serbian / English edn. (trans. with the author). Belgrade: Pešić i sinovi [Pešić and Sons].

Koneski, Blaže. 1993. 'Prayer'. With Marinković, Jadrana (trans. from Macedonian). In *Out of Yugoslavia*, 98.

Kulavkova, Katica. 2010. *Голо око* [*Golo oko*] / *Naked Eye* (trans. from Macedonian). Six-language edn. Skopje: Poetiki.

Lengold, Jelena. 1990. 'Poem'. In Mulford, Wendy (ed.), *The Virago Book of Love Poetry*: London: Virago, 53-54.

——. 2018. 'The Death of an Angel'. In Obradović, Biljana D. and Djurić, Dubravka (eds.). *Cat Paintings, an Anthology of Contemporary Serbian Poetry.* USA: Diálogos, 204-205.

Maksimović, 'Desanka. 1988. I've no more time', trans. with Jasna B. Mišić. *Serbian Literary Quarterly*, no. 2, 113. Reprinted: 1988, *Zavičaj* 34; 1991, *New Orleans Review*, 66; 1993, *Out of Yugoslavia,* 104. 'Anticipation', January 27, 1990, *Politika*, weekly international edn. Reprinted: 1993, *Out of Yugoslavia*, 105. 'Speak softly' and 'Nobody knows', 1993, *Out of Yugoslavia*, 105.

Markovic, Vito. 1993. 'From Analects'. With Radojević, Vera. V. (trans.). In *Out of Yugoslavia*, 108-109.

Out of Yugoslavia. 1993. Ed. with Markovich, Stephen C. Special issue of *North Dakota Quarterly*, vol. 61/1.

Pajić, Petar. 2017. *Izabrane pesme / Selected Poems.* Bilingual Serbian and English edn. With Radojević, Vera V. (trans). Smederevo: Meridijani [Meridians].

Pavićević, Slobodan. 2010. *Mir neka je ime vekova* (*Let Peace be the Name of the Centuries*). Trilingual Serbian, English and German edn. With Radojević, Vera V. (trans). Kragujevac: Spomen Park Kragujevački oktobar [Kragujevac October Memorial Park].

——. 2012 (unpublished). *Snovi Hilandara* (*Dreams of Hilandar*). With Vera V. Radojević (trans.).

Petrov. Aleksandar. 1990. *Lady in an Empty Dress.* Chingford: Forest Books.

——. 1993. Four poems. In *Out of Yugoslavia*, 124-128.

Ujević, Tin. 1988. 'The Necklace (Kolajna) (1926) XXI'. London: Menard Press, Mencard 107.

——. 1991. 'Aubade'. With Marić, Daša (trans.). *New Orleans Review* 18/2, 88.

——. 1993. Six poems. With Marić, Daša (trans.). In *Out of Yugoslavia*, 188-192.

——. 2005. Some Poems. With Marić, Daša (trans.). *South Slavic Literature Library.* Online at: http://library.borut.eu/authors/u/ujevi%C4%87_tin

——. 2010. Some Poems. With Marić, Daša (trans.). *Mediterranean Poetry*. Online at: http://www.mediterranean.nu/?p=1713

——. 2011. *'Twelve Poems'.* With Marić, Daša (trans.). *[sic] - a journal of literature, culture and literary translation* 1. Online at: https://www.sic-journal.org/ArticleView.aspx?aid=139

——. 2013. *Twelve Poems*. With Marić, Daša (trans.). Bristol: Shearsman Books.

Vrhovac, Duška. 1991. *I Wear My Shadow Inside Me*. With Radojević, Vera V. (trans.). Chingford: Forest Books.

——. 1991. 'When a Child Dies'. With Radojević, Vera V. (trans.). *New Orleans Review* 18/2, 83.

——. 1993. Seven poems. With Radojević, Vera V. (trans.). In *Out of Yugoslavia*, 205-208.

——. 1996. Some poems from *I wear my Shadow Inside Me*. With Radojević, Vera V. (trans.). In Vrhovac, Duška, *Blagoslov* ['Blessing']. Belgrade: Trstenik, 65-117.

General References

Abadi, Jacob. 1996. 'Israel and the Balkan States'. *Middle Eastern Studies,* 32/4: 296-320. Online: Taylor and Francis.

Adorno, Theodor. 1967 [1949]. 'An Essay on Cultural Criticism and Society'. *Prisms*. Weber, Samuel and Shierry (trans.). Cambridge, MA. MIT Press.

'Alan Wace'. *Wikipedia.*

'Alhambra Decree'. *Wikipedia.*

Andrejčin, Lubomir; Georgiev, Ljuben; Todorov, Zvetan. 1993. *Български Тълковен Речник* [*Bulgarski talkoven Rečnik*; 'Dictionary of the Bulgarian Language'], 4th edn. Sofia: Bulgarian Academy of Sciences.

'Armatoles'. *Wikipedia.*

Arnaudov, Mikhail, 1971 [1924]. *Студии върху българските обреди и легенди* [*Studii vurhu bulgariskite obredi i legendi*; 'Studies in Bulgarian Customs and Legends'], vol. 1. Sofia: Bulgarian Academy of Sciences.

Aristotle. 1944 [1932]. *Politics*. Rackham, H. (trans.). Cambridge, MA and London: Harvard University Press (Loeb Edn. 264).

Auden, W. H. 1979. *Selected Poems*. London: Faber and Faber.

Bakić-Hayden, Milica. 1995. 'Nesting Orientalisms: The Case of Former Yugoslavia'. *Slavic Review* 54/4: 917-931.

Bakić-Hayden, Milica and Hayden, Robert M. 1992. 'Orientalist Variation on the Theme "Balkans": Symbolic Geography in Recent Yugoslav Cultural Politics'. *Slavic Review*, vol. 51.1, 1-15.

Bauman, Zygmunt. 1989. *Modernity and the Holocaust*. Cambridge: Polity Press.

——. 1997 [1995]. 'Tourists and Vagabonds: The Heroes and Villains of Postmodernity'. In *Postmodernity and its Discontents*: Cambridge: Polity Press, 83-94.

——. 1998. 'Tourists and Vagabonds' (a second variant). In *Globalization, the Human Consequences*: Cambridge: Polity Press, 77-102.

——. 2000. 'Tourists and Vagabonds. Or, living in postmodern times' (a third variant). In Davis Joseph E. (ed). *Identity and Social Change*. New Brunswick, N.J. and London: Transaction Publishers.

Beekes, Robert. 2010. *Etymological Dictionary of Greek*. Leiden: Brill. Online at: https://dictionaries.brillonline.com/greek

Beloff, Nora. 1997. *Yugoslavia: An Avoidable War*. London: New European Publications.

Benson, Morton. 1980. *SerboCroatian-English Dictionary*. Belgrade: Prosveta.

——. 1986. *English-SerboCroatian Dictionary*. Belgrade: Prosveta.

Benveniste, Émile. 1971. *Problems in General Linguistics*. Meek, Mary Elizabeth (trans.). Miami, FL: University of Miami Press.

——. 1973. *Indo-European Language and Society*. Palmer, Elizabeth (trans.). London: Faber and Faber.

Bible, The. 1611. King James Authorised Version (*AV*).

Blake, William. 1956 [1927]. *The Poetry and Prose of William Blake*. Keynes, Geoffrey (ed.). London: Nonesuch Library.

Blount (*aka* Blunt), Sir Henry. 1666 (3rd edn). [1634]. *A Voyage Into The Levant: A Brief Relation of A Journey lately performed by Mr. Henry Blunt Gentleman, from England by way of Venice, into Dalmatia, Sclavonia, Bosna, Hungary, Macedonia, Thessaly, Thrace, Rhodes and Egypt, unto Gran Cairo: with particular observations concerning the modern condition of the Turks, and other people under that empire*. London: printed by T. M. for Andrew Crook.

Boadella, David. 1973. *Wilhelm Reich: The Evolution of His Work*. London: Vision Press.

Bohm, David. 1980. *Wholeness and the Implicate Order*. London: Routledge.

'Bolji život'. *Wikipedia.*

Bosić, Mila. 1996: *Godišnji običaji Srba u Vojvodini* ['Annual Customs of Serbs in Vojvodina']. Novi Sad and Sremska Mitrovica: Muzej Vojvodine, Prometej, and Vojvođanska banka: IKP Monada.

Boué, Ami. 1838a. 'Remarks on the Scenery, Antiquities, Population, Agriculture and Commerce of Central European Turkey; Communicated by the Author in a Letter to the Editor'. *The Edinburgh New Philosophical Journal*, vol. XXIV: 121-131. *Biodiversity Heritage Library*. Online at: https://www.biodiversitylibrary.org/page/15038786#page/137/mode/1up

——. 1838b. 'Geographical and Geological Observations on some parts of European Turkey, namely Moesia, Bulgaria, Romelia, Albania, and Bosnia; Communicated by the Author in a Letter to the Editor'. *The Edinburgh New Philosophical Journal*, vol. XXV: 174–195. *Biodiversity Heritage Library.* Online at: https://www.biodiversitylibrary.org/page/2506134#page/187/mode/1up

——. 1840. *La Turquie d'Europe : ou observations sur la géographie, la géologie, l'histoire naturelle, la statistique, les moeurs, les coutumes, l'archéologie, l'argriculture, l'industrie, le commerce, les gouvernments divers, le clergé, l'histoire et l'*état politique de cet empire. Avec une carte nouvelle de la Turquie d*'Europe.* Paris: Arthus Bertrand.

Bracewell, Catherine Wendy. 1992. *The Uskoks of Senj: Piracy, Banditry and Holy War in the Sixteenth-Century Adriatic.* Ithaca, NY and London: Cornell University Press.

——. 2003. '"The Proud Name of Hajduks": Bandits as Ambiguous Heroes in Balkan Politics and Culture'. In Naimark, Norman M. and Case, Holly (eds.). *Yugoslavia and its Historians.* Stanford, CA: Stanford University Press, 22-36.

'Branko Ćopić. *Wikipedia.*

'Branko Radičević'. *Wikipedia.*

'Branko's Bridge'. *Wikipedia.*

Braudel, Fernand. 1947. 'Misère et banditisme' ['Misery and Banditism']. *Annales* 2: 129-142.

——. 1995 [1972]. *The Mediterranean and the Mediterranean World in the Age of Philip II.* Reynolds, Siân (trans.). Berkeley and Los Angeles, CA: University of California.

Brkić, Staniša. Undated. *Kragujevačka tragedija / Kragujevac Tragedy.* Bilingual Serbian and English booklet. Kragujevac: Kragujevac October Memorial Park.

——. 2007. *Ime i broj: Kragujevačka tragedija 1941* ['Name and Number: the Kragujevac Tragedy 1941']. Kragujevac: Kragujevac October Memorial Park.

——. 2011. 'Istraživanje nije gotovo' ['The Enquiry Isn't Over']: interview with Staniša Brkić. October 20. *Vreme* 2085. Online at: https://www.vreme.com/cms/view.php?id=1015564

Brkić, Staniša and Minić, Milomir. 2011. *Jevreji u Kragujevcu* ['The Jews of Kragujevac']. Kragujevac: Krug [Circle].

'Brotherhood and Unity'. *Wikipedia.*

Buber, Martin. 1986. *I and Thou.* Smith, Ronald Gregor (trans.). New York: Scribner.

'Alhambra Decree'. *Wikipedia.*

'Buccaneer'. *Wikipedia.*

Bujas, Željko. 1999. *Veliki hrvatsko-engleski rječnik / Croatian-English Dictionary.* Zagreb: Nakladni Zavod.

Burkert, Walter. 1987 [1985]. *Greek Religion: Archaic and Classical.* Raffan, John (trans.). Oxford: Blackwell.

'Cadik Danon'. *centropa.org.* Online at: www.centropa.org/biography/cadik-danon

Cavendish, Harrie. 1940 [1589]. 'Mr. Harrie Cavendish His Journey to and from Constantinople, 1589, by Fox His Servant'. Wood, M. A. (ed.). In *Camden Miscellany*, vol. XVII.

Cavell, Stanley. 1979. 'What a Thing is (Called)'. In *The Claim of Reason*: Oxford: Oxford University Press, 65-85.

Celan, Paul. 1980. *Poems.* Hamburger, Michael (trans.). Manchester: Carcanet.

'Cheltenham Literature Festival, The'. *Wikipedia.*

Chevalier, Jean and Gheerbrant, Alain. 1996 [1969]. T*he Penguin Dictionary of Symbols.* Buchanan-Brown, John (trans.). London: Penguin Books.

Chou, Eva Shan. 1995. *Reconsidering Tu Fu, Literary Greatness and Cultural Context.* Cambridge: Cambridge University Press.

Ćirković, Sima M. 2004. *The Serbs.* Tošić, Vuk (trans.). Malden, MA and Oxford: Blackwell Publishing.

Coleridge, Samuel Taylor. 1887. 'The Rime of the Ancient Mariner'. In *The Poetical Works of S. T. Coleridge*: London and New York, Frederick Warne: 92-110.

Čolović, Ivan. 2000. 'Football, Hooligans and War'. In Popov, Nebojša (ed.). 1996. *The Road to War in Serbia: Trauma and Catharsis.* Budapest: Central European University Press, 373-396.

——. 2002. *The Politics of Symbol in Serbia.* Hawkesworth, Celia (trans.). London: C. Hurst.

Corsellis, John and Ferrar, Marcus. 2005. *Slovenia 1945: Memories of Death and Survival after World War II.* London and New York: I. B. Tauris.

Crnjanksi, Miloš. 1971. *Roman o Londonu* ['Novel About London']. Belgrade: Laguna.

——. 2020. *A Novel of London*. Firth, Will (trans.) USA: Diálogos Books.

Crnjanksi: Seobe / Migrations. 1988. In *Zavičaj* [Homeland] XXXV. Belgrade: Matice iseljenika Srbije i Matica iseljenika Vojvodine i Kosova ['Society of Emigrants from Serbia, and Society of Emigrants from Vojvodina and Kosovo'].

Crompton, Richmal. 1927. *William and the Outlaws*. London: Macmillan.

'Danilo Kiš'. *Wikipedia*.

Danon, Cadik (Braco). 1998. 'USC Shoah Foundation Interview'. *United States Holocaust Memorial Museum*. Online at: https://collections.ushmm.org/search/catalog/irn513553

——. 2006. *The Smell of Human Flesh, A Witness of the Holocaust: Memories of Jasenovac*. Janković, Vidoslava (trans.). Belgrade: Dosije [Dossier].

——. 2007 [2001]. *Sasečeno stablo Danonovih, Svedok holokausta, Sećanje na Jasenovac* ['The Felled Tree of the Danons: Holocaust Witness, Remembering Jasenovac']. 2nd edn. Belgrade: Dosije [Dossier].

Davičo, Oskar. 2001 [1939]. *Hana i druge pesme* ['Hana and other poems']. Belgrade: Zavod za udžbenike [Textbooks Institute].

David, Filip. 2017. *The House of Remembering and Forgetting*. Pribichevich Zorić, Christina (trans.). London: Peter Owen.

Davie, Donald. 1952. *Purity of Diction in English Verse*. London: Chatto and Windus.

Deakin, F. W. D. 1971. *The Embattled Mountain*. Oxford, London and Toronto: Oxford University Press.

'Declaration on the Common Language'. *Wikipedia*.

Deleuze, Gilles and Guattari, Félix. 2004 [1980]. *A Thousand Plateaus: Capitalism and Schizophrenia*. Massumi, Brian (trans.). London and New York: Continuum.

Derrida, Jacques. 1995 [1992]. *The Gift of Death*. Chicago, IL: University of Chicago Press.

Dimić, Moma (ed.). 1996. *Beogradski susreti pisaca, 1964-1996* ['The Belgrade Writers' Meetings/Encounters']. Belgrade: Udruženje književnika Srbije [Serbian Writers' Association].

—— (ed.). 1999. *Kletva, Srbija, proleće 1999* ['The Curse, Serbia, Spring 1999']. Belgrade: Udruženje književnika Srbije [Serbian Writers' Association].

——. (ed.). 2005. *Ostali svetlosti, strani pesnici (1964-2004) / Remnants of Light, Poets from Abroad (1964-2004)*, Belgrade International Writers Meeting. Belgrade: Udruženje književnika Srbije [Serbian Writers' Association].

Djidić, Ljubiša; Lazić, Dragomir; Hawkesworth. E. C.; and Johnson, B. S. (eds.). *Liber Amicorum in Honour of E. D. Goy*. London and Kruševac: School of Slavonic and East European Studies, University of London.

Djordjević, Dragutin M. 1958 [1901]. *Život i običaji narodni u Leskovačkoj Moravi* ['Life and Folk Customs Around Leskovac on the River Morava' Belgrade: Srpski etnografski zbornik ['Serbian Ethnographic Collection'], vol. lxx. Belgrade: Srpska akademija nauka ['Serbian Academy of Sciences'].

Djurić, Dubravka with Obradović, Biljana. 2016. 'Introduction: The Political and Poetic context in which the Poetry from the Anthology was Created'. In *Cat Paintings, an Anthology of Contemporary Serbian Poetry.* USA, Diálogos: xviii-xli.

Dokumenti o izdajstvu Draže Mihailovića ['Documents about the Treachery of Draža Mihailović] (2 vols.). 1945. Belgrade: Demokratska Federativna Jugoslavija: Državna: Komisija za utvrčanje zloćina okupatora i njihovih pomagaća [Democratic Federative Yugoslavia: Commission for Determining the Crimes of the Occupiers and their Collaborators].

Domenach, Jean-Marie and Pontault, Alain. 1960. *Yougoslavie*. Paris: Éditions du Seuil.

'Down by the Salley Gardens'. *Wikipedia.*

Dragić Kijuk, Predrag R. (ed.). 1987. *Medieval and Renaissance Serbian Poetry.* Belgrade: Serbian Literary Quarterly.

Durham, M. Edith. 2015 [1904]. *Through the Lands of the Serb*. Elsie, Robert (ed.). London: Centre for Albanian Studies.

——. 2000 [1909]. *High Albania*. London: Phoenix Press.

——. 2015 [1914]. *The Struggle for Scutari*. Elsie, Robert (ed.). London: Centre for Albanian Studies.

——. 1920. *Twenty Years of Balkan Tangle*. London: George Allen and Unwin. Undated reprint, Champaign, IL: Book Jungle.

——. 2014. *The Blaze in the Balkans: Selected Writings, 1903–1941*. Elsie, Robert and Destani, Bejtullah D. (eds.). London: I. B. Tauris.

Duridanov, Ivan *et al.* (eds.). 1996. *Български Етимологически речник* [*Bulgarski Etimologicheski rečnik*, 'Bulgarian Etymological Dictionary'], vol. 5. Sofia: Institute for the Bulgaran Language, Bulgarian Academy of Sciences.

East, Gordon. 1972 [1961]. 'The Concept and Political Status of the Shatter Zone'. In Pounds, Norman J. G. (ed.). *Geographical Essays on Eastern Europe.* Westport CT: Greenwood Press, 1-27.

'Edinburgh Festival, The'. *Wikipedia.*

Eliade, Mircea. 1964. *Archaic Techniques of Ecstasy.* Trask, Willard R. (trans.). London: Routledge and Kegan Paul.

Elich, Greg. 'The Invasion of Serbian Krajina'. Online at: http://emperors-clothes.com/articles/elich/krajina.html

Eliot. T. S. 1961 [1919]. 'Hamlet'. In *Selected Essays*. London, Faber and Faber: 141-146.

——. 1922. *The Waste Land.* London: Faber and Faber.

——. 1961. [1936]. 'In Memoriam'. In *Selected Essays*: London, Faber and Faber: 328-338.

Encyclopedia Britannica. 2001. CD edn.

Evans, Sir Arthur John. 1876. *Through Bosnia and the Herzegovina on foot during the insurrection, August and September 1875: with an historical review of Bosnia; and a glimpse at the Croats, Slavonians, and the ancient Republic of Ragusa.* London: Longmans, Green and Co.

——. 2005 [1878]. *Illyrian Letters: A Revised Selection of Correspondence from the Illyrian Provinces of Bosnia, Herzegovina, Montenegro, Albania, Dalmatia, Croatia and Slavonia, Addressed to the Manchester Guardian during 1877.* Elibron Classics [London: Longmans, Green and Co.].

——. 1925. 'The Ring of Nestor': A Glimpse Into the Minoan After-World, and a Sepulchral Treasure of Gold Signet-Rings and Bead-Seals from Thisbê, Boeotia. *The Journal of Hellenic Studies*, vol. XLV: 1-75.

Farhi, Moris. 1999. *Children of the Rainbow.* London: Saqi Books.

Forrest, W. G. G. 1982 [1925]. 'Euboea and the Islands'. In Boardman, John and Hammond, N.G. L. (eds.). *The Cambridge Ancient History*, vol. III, part 3. *The Expansion of the Greek World, Eighth to Sixth Centuries, B.C.* Cambridge: Cambridge University Press.

Fortis, Abbé Alberto. 1774. *Viaggi in Dalmazia.* Venice: Alvise Milocco.

——. 2007 [1778]. *Travels in Dalmatia.* New York: Cosimo Books.

Foster Damon, S. 1973. *A Blake Dictionary.* London: Thames and Hudson.

Frazer, Sir James George. 1911. *The Magic Art and the Evolution of Kings* (*The Golden Bough*, vol. 1). London: MacMillan.

Freud, Sigmund. 1975 [1953]. *Totem and Taboo. Complete Psychological Works*, vol. XIII. Strachey, James *et al.* (eds. and trans.). London: The Hogarth Press.

Gadjanksi, Ivan. 1986. *Balkanskom ulicom: roman o nedovršenoj pesmi* ['Along Balkan Street: Novel about an Unfinished Poem'].

——. 2011. *Οδός Βαλκανίων.* ['*Balkan Street,* Street of the Balkans']. Radulović, Iphigenia; Scopetea, Elli; and Tsitsimelis, Nikos (trans.). Vayenas, Nasos (ed). Athens: Gutenberg Publications.

'Gavrilo Princip'. *Wikipedia.*

Gimbutas, Marija. 1971. *The Slavs.* London: Thames and Hudson.

——. 1982 [1972]. *The Goddesses and Gods of Old Europe, 6500–3500 BC: Myths and Cult Images.* London: Thames and Hudson.

——. 1989. *The Language of the Goddess: Unearthing the Hidden Symbols of Western Civilization.* London: Thames and Hudson.

——. 1991. *The Civilization of the Goddess.* San Francisco, CA: Harper.

——. 1999. *The Living Goddesses*. Berkeley, CA: University of California Press.

Glenny, Misha. 1992. *The Fall of Yugoslavia: The Third Balkan War*. London: Penguin Books.

Godward, Alan. 1999. *A Dictionary of Turkish Etymology*. Derby.

Gojković, Drinka. 1996. 'The Birth of Nationalism from the Spirit of Democracy: The Association of Writers of Serbia and the War'. In Popov, Nebojša (ed.). *The Road to War in Serbia: Trauma and Catharsis*. Budapest: Central European University Press, 327-350.

Goldstein, Slavko *et al.* (eds.). 1989. *Jews in Yugoslavia* (exhibition catalogue). Zagreb: Muzejski prostor [Museum Space].

Goldsworthy, Vesna. 2013 [1998]. *Inventing Ruritania: The Imperialism of the Imagination*. London: Hurst.

Goy, E. D. (ed and trans.) 1990. *A Green Pine / Zelen Bor. An Anthology of Love Poems from The Oral Poetry of Serbia, Bosnia and Hercegovina* (bilingual edn.). Belgrade: Prosveta / Vukova Zadužbina [Vuk Foundation].

Graves Robert. 1961. *The White Goddess*. London: Faber and Faber.

Grimm, Jacob. 1875 and 1876. *Deutsche Mythologie* ['German Mythology'] (2 vols.). Berlin: Elard Hugo Meyer.

Halpern, Joel Martin. 1958. *A Serbian Village*. New York: Columbia University Press.

Harding, M. Esther. 1983 [1933]. *The Way of All Women: A Psychological Interpretation*. London: Rider.

Hass, Robert. 1984. 'One Body: Some Notes on Form', in *Twentieth Century Pleasures*. New York, Harper Collins: 56-71.

——. 2010. *The Apple Trees at Olema: New and Selected Poems*. New York: Harper Collins.

Hayden, Robert M. 2007. 'What's Reconciliation Got to do With It? The International Criminal Tribunal for the former Yugoslavia (ICTY) as Antiwar Profiteer'. *Journal of Intervention and Statebuilding* 5/3: 313-330. Reprinted: 2013, in Hayden: 267-285.

——. 2013. *From Yugoslavia to the Western Balkans*. Leiden and Boston MA: Brill.

Herman Sekulić, Maja. 1993. 'Gumbo'. In *Out of Yugoslavia, North Dakota Quarterly* 61/1, 79.

——. 2015. 'A Genealogy of the Twentieth Century /Une généalogie du 20e siècle'. In *De la terre de désolation / Out of the Waste Land*. Brunazzi, Elizabeth (trans.). Paris: Ailleurs.

——. 2017. *Gospa od Vinče / My Lady of Vincha*. Bilingual Serbian and English edn. Belgrade: Pešić i sinovi [Pešić and Sons].

Heylyn Peter. 1669 edn. [1st edn. 1652]. *Cosmographie in four Bookes: Contayning the Chorographie and Historie of the whole World, and all the Principall Kingdomes, Provinces, Seas and Isles, Thereof* (Book 2). London: Printed for Henry Seile, etc. Online at: *Early English Books*: https://quod.lib.umich.edu/e/eebo/A43514.0001.001?view=toc

Hine, Daryl (trans). 2002. Homeric 'Hymn to Demeter'. *The Chicago Homer*. Kahane, Ahuvia and Mueller, Martin (eds.). Online at: https://homer.library.northwestern.edu

Hobsbawm, E. J. 1959. *Primitive Rebels: Studies in Archaic Forms of Social Movement in the 19th and 20th Centuries*, New York and London. W. W. Norton and Co.

——. 2000 [1969]. *Bandits*. New York: The New Press.

Holland, Sir Henry. 1819 [1815]. *Travels in the Ionian Isles, Albania, Thessaly, Macedonia, &c. During the Years 1812 and 1813* (2 vols.). London: Strahan and Spottiswoode.

Holton, Milne and Mihailovich, Vasa D. 1988. *Serbian Poetry from the Beginning to the Present*. New Haven CN: Yale Center for International and Area Studies.

Hony, H. C. 1976 [1947]. *A Turkish-English Dictionary*. Oxford: Oxford University Press.

Hopkins, Gerard Manley. 1959. *The Journals and Papers of Gerard Manley Hopkins*. House, Humphry (ed.). London: Oxford University Press.

——. 2013. *The Collected Works of Gerard Manley Hopkins, vol. 2. Correspondence 1882-1889*. Thornton, R. K. R. and Phillips, Catherine (eds.). Oxford: Oxford University Press.

Horden, Peregrine and Purcell, Nicholas. 2000. *The Corrupting Sea*. Malden MA and Oxford: Blackwell.

Hristić, Jovan. 2003. *Poems*. Johnson, Bernard (trans.). London and Belgrade: Association of Serbian Writers Abroad and the Serbian PEN Centre.

Hull, Denison B. (trans. and ed.). 1972. *Digenis Akritas, The Two-Blood Border Lord*. The Grottaferrata Version. Athens, OH: Ohio University Press.

'Internal Macedonian Revolutionary Organization'. *Wikipedia*.

International Literary Festivals. 2001. Vilenica: Vilenica International Literary Gathering.

'Interview with Yevgeni Yevtushenko'. *Red Spring*: 'Episode 14, The Sixties'. Online at: https://nsarchive2.gwu.edu/coldwar/interviews/episode-14/yevtushenko1.html

Ivanov V. V. and Toporov V. I. 1974. *Исследования в области славянских древностей: Лексические и фразеологические вопросы реконструкции текстов* [*Issledovaniya v oblasti slavyanskih drevnotstei : Leksicheskiye i frazeologicheskiye voprosy rekonstruktsii tekstov* ['Research in the Field of

Slavonic Antiquities / Folklore: Lexical and phraseological questions in the reconstruction of texts']. Moscow: Издательство “Наука” [Izdaetelstvo 'Nauka'; 'Science' Publishing].

Iz, Fahir. 1992. *The Oxford English-Turkish Dictionary*. Oxford: Oxford University Press.

'Izet Sarajlic'. *Wikipedia.*

'Jakob Finci'. *Wikipedia.*

Jakobson, Roman. 1950. 'Slavic Mythology'. In Leach, Maria and Fried, Jerome (eds.). *Standard Dictionary of Folklore, Mythology and Legend*, vol. 2. New York: Funk and Wagnell, 1025-1028.

——. 1985a. 'Slavic Gods and Demons'. In *Selected Writings*, vol. 7: *Contributions to Comparative Mythology. Studies in Linguistics and Philology, 1972–1982*. Berlin, New York, Amsterdam: Mouton, 6-7.

——. 1985b [1964]. 'Linguistic Evidence in Comparative Mythology'. In *Selected Writings*, vol. 7: *Contributions to Comparative Mythology. Studies in Linguistics and Philology, 1972–1982*. Berlin, New York, Amsterdam: Mouton, 22-23.

Jasenovac Research Institute. Online at: http://www.jasenovac.org/what_was_jasenovac.php

'Jefimija'. *Wikipedia.*

Joel Martin Halpern Balkan Archive, The. Online at: https://archiveshub.jisc.ac.uk/search/archives/b1f6abea-a907-35e8-bdb7-37742d86aa67

Johnson, Bernard (ed.). 1970. *New Writing in Yugoslavia*. Harmondsworth: Penguin Books.

Johnson, George. 1996 (October 29). 'Scholars Debate Roots of Yiddish, Migration of Jews'. *New York Times*. Online at: 'https://www.nytimes.com/1996/10/29/science/scholars-debate-roots-of-yiddish-migration-of-jews.html

'Jovan Ćirilov'. *Wikipedia.*

Judah, Tim. 2008. *Kosovo. What Everybody Needs to Know*. New York: Oxford University Press.

——. 2009 [1997]. *The Serbs: History, Myth and the Destruction of Yugoslavia*. New York and London: Yale University Press.

'Judah ben Solomon Hai Alkalai'. *Britannica*. Online at: https://www.britannica.com/biography/Judah-ben-Solomon-Hai-Alkalai

Jung, Carl Gustav. 1955. 'Synchronicity: An Acausul Connecting Principle'. In Jung, Carl Gustav and Pauli, Wolfgang, *The Interpretation of Nature and the* Psyche. Hull, R. F. C. (trans.). London, Routledge and Kegan Paul, 5-146.

——. 1968 [1959]. *The Archetypes and the Collective Unconscious. Collected Works*, vol. 9, part 1. Hull, R. F. C. (trans.). London: Routledge and Kegan Paul.

——. 2014 [1960]. 'Synchronicity: An Acausal Connecting Principle'. In *The Structure and Dynamics of the Psyche. Collected Works*, vol. 8. Hull, R. F. C. (trans.). London: Routledge, 427-531.

——. 1966. *The Spirit in Man. Art, and Literature. Collected Works*, vol. 15. Hull, R. F. C. (trans.). London: Routledge and Kegan Paul.

——. 1967. *Alchemical Studies Collected Works*, vol. 13. Hull, R. F. C. (trans.). London: Routledge and Kegan Paul.

Karadžić, Vuk Stefanović. 1818. *Srpski rječnik* ['Serbian Dictionary'], 1st edn. Vienna

——. 1841. *Srpske narodne pjesme* ['Serbian Folk Songs' / ' Songs of the Serbian People']. Vienna.

——. 1852. *Srpski Rječnik* ['Serbian Dictionary']: 2nd edn. Vienna.

——. 1867. Život i običaji naroda srpskoga ['Life and Customs of the Serbian People']. Vienna. Reprinted: 1957. In *Vukove zapisi* ['Vuk's Notes']. Belgrade: Srpska književna zadruga ['Serbian Literary Association'].

Karge, Haike. 2016. 'Monuments' Biographies – The Case of Jasenovac'. *Vimeo* recording. Online at: https://vimeo.com/151627151

Kermode, Frank. 2010. 'Eliot and the Shudder'. In *The London Review of Books,* 32/9: 13-16. Online at: http://www.lrb.co.uk/v32/n09/frank-kermode/eliot-and-the-shudder

Kiš, Danilo. 1975. *Garden, Ashes*. Hannaher, William J. (trans.). New York: Harcourt Brace Jovanovich.

——. 1980. *A Tomb for Boris Davidovich*. Mikić-Mitchell, Duška (trans.). New York: Penguin Books.

——. 1989. *The Encyclopedia of the Dead.* New York: Farrar, Strauss and Giroux.

'Komemoracija Staniša Brkić' ['Commemoration of Staniša Brkić']. 2013, October 30. *TV Kragujevac. YouTube.*

'Kosovo Force'. *Wikipedia.*

Krasni, Zlatko. 1999. 'Šiler i Miler' ('Schiller and Miller'). In Dimić, Moma (ed.). *Kletva, Srbija, proleće 1999* ['The Curse, Serbia, Spring 1999']. Belgrade, Udruženje književnika Srbije [Serbian Writers' Association]: 120.

——. 'Uzalud ['En vajo' / 'In Vain']. Reading at the Medellin International Poetry Festival. *You Tube.*

Krleža, Miroslav. 2004. *The Banquet in Blitva*. Goy E. D. and Levinger-Goy, Jasna (trans.). Evanston, IL: Northwestern University Press.

Kulišić, Špiro; Petrović, Petar and Pantelić, Nikola 1998 [1970]. *Srpski Mitoloski Rečnik* ['Serbian Mythological Dictionary']. Belgrade: Nolit.

Kuić, Gordana. 1986. *Miris kiše na Balkanu*. Belgrade: Vulcan.

——. 2012. *The Scent of Rain in the Balkans*. Williams, Richard, (trans.). Denver, CO: Centennial Publications.

Lalić, Ivan V. 1981. *The Works of Love: Selected Poems.* Jones, Francis R. (trans.). London: Anvil Press Poetry.

——. 1988. *Roll Call of Mirrors: Selected Poems.* Simic, Charles (trans.). Middletown, CT: Wesleyan University Press.

——. 1989. *The Passionate Measure.* Jones, Francis R. (trans.). London: Anvil Press Poetry.

——. 1993. 'Some Notes on Yugoslav Literature: A Historical Approach'. In RB and Markovich, Stephen C. (eds.). *Out of Yugoslavia,* 12-17.

——. 1996a. *A Rusty Needle.* Jones, Francis R. (trans.). London: Anvil Press Poetry.

——. 1996b. 'Oblikovanje duha jedne tradicije' / 'The Spiritual Embodiment of a Tradition'. In Dimić, Moma (ed.). *Beogradski susret pisaca, 1964–1996* ['The Belgrade Writers' Meeting 1964–1996']. Belgrade, Udruženje književnika Srbije [Serbian Writers' Association]: 4-5 and 16-17.

Larkin, Philip. 1945. *The North Ship.* London: Faber and Faber.

——. 1992. *Selected Letters: 1940-1985.* Thwaite, Anthony (ed.). London: Faber and Faber.

Lawrence, D. H. 1978 [1915]. *The Rainbow.* London: Penguin Books.

Lees, Michael. 1990. *The Rape of Serbia: The British Role in Tito's Grab for Power, 1943-1944.* San Diego, New York and London: Harcourt Brace Jovanovich.

Leighton, Angela. 2007. *On Form: Poetry, Aestheticism, and the Legacy of a Word.* Oxford: Oxford University Press.

Levin, Harry. 1960. 'Preface' to Lord, Albert B. *The Singer of Tales.* Harvard, MA: Harvard University Press: xiii-xv.

Levinas, Emmanuel. 2000. *God, Death and Time.* Bergo, Bettina (trans.). Stanford, CA. Stanford University Press.

Locke, Geoffrey N. W. 2002. *The Serbian Epic Ballads: An Anthology.* London: Association of Serbian Writers Abroad.

Lodge, Olive. 1941. *Peasant Life in Jugoslavija.* London: Seeley, Service & Co. Ltd.

Longinovic, Tomislav. 1992. 'When the Body Sings Itself'. Introduction to *Red Knight: Serbian Women's Songs,* Weissbort, Daniel and Longinovic, Tomislav (eds. and trans). London: Kings College London and Menard Press, 15-20.

Lord, A. B. 1964. *The Singer of Tales.* Cambridge, MA: Harvard University Press.

Lowenthal, Zdenko (ed.). 1957. *The Crimes of the Fascist Occupants and Their Collaborators Against Jews in Yugoslavia.* Belgrade: Federation of Jewish Communities of the Federated People's Republic of Yugoslavia.

Maclean, Fitzroy. 1949. *Eastern Approaches.* London: Jonathan Cape.

——. 1957. *Disputed Barricade: The Life and Times of Josip Broz-Tito, Marshal of Jugoslavia.* London: Jonathan Cape.

Mackenzie, G. Muir and Irby, A. P. 2005 [1877]. *Travels in the Slavonic Provinces of Turkey-in-Europe* (2 vols.). Elibron Classics facsimile edn. [London: Daldy, Isbister and Co].

Main, Roderick. 2007. *Revelations of Chance: Synchronicity as Spiritual Experience.* New York: State University of New York Press.

Makić, Goranka *et al.* (eds.). 2000. *Foto Dokumenti* ['Photo Documents']: (2) *Beogradski Marathon 1997* ['Belgrade Marathon 1997']; (3) *Studentski Protest 96/97* ['Student Protest '96-97']; (4) *Oktobar u Srbiji 2000* ['October in Serbia 2000]. Belgrade: *Vreme* [Time].

Maksimović, Desanka. 2010. 'Krvava bajka' ['Bloody Fable']: the poet's reading. *YouTube.*

'Malcolm Fraser'. *Wikipedia.*

Malcolm, Noel. 1998. *Kosovo, A Short History*. London: MacMillan.

Malory, Sir Thomas. *Works*. Vinaver, Eugène (ed.) Oxford, London, New York: Oxford University Press.

Mann, S. E. 1948. *An Historical-Albanian-English Dictionary*. London, New York, Toronto: Longmans.

Marković, Zoran M. 1996. 'The Nation: Victim and Vengeance'. In Popov, Nebojša (ed.). *The Road to War in Serbia: Trauma and Catharsis*. Budapest: Central European University Press, 587-607.

Martin, David. 1946 (April 13). 'The Case of Drazha Mihailovich'. *The New Leader*. Quoted online at: https://groups.google.com/forum/#!topic/soc.culture.croatia/L1f8QMaUiBY

Matthias, John and Vučković, Vladeta (trans.). 1984. *The Battle of Kosovo*. Athens, OH: Swallow Press.

Mauss, Marcel. 1954. *The Gift: Forms and Functions of Exchange in Archaic Societies*. Cunnison, Ian (trans.) London: Cohen and West.

Memmi, Albert. 1968. 'Negritude and Judeity'. *European Judaism*, vol. 3/2, 4-12.

Milman Parry Collection of Oral Literature. Harvard University. Online: at: https://mpc.chs.harvard.edu/]

Milosavljević, Olivera. 1996. 'The Abuse of the Authority of Science'. In Popov, Nebojša (ed.). *The Road to War in Serbia: Trauma and Catharsis*. Budapest: Central European University Press, 274-302.

Miłosz, Czesław. 1953. *The Captive Mind*. Zielonko, Jane (trans.). London: Secker and Warburg.

Milton, John. 1958. *Paradise Lost*. In *The Poetic Works of John Milton*. Darbishire, Helen (ed.). London, New York, Toronto: Oxford University Press.

'Miron Grindea'. *Wikipedia*.

Mraović, Dragan. 2013. *Susret sa Beogradom: pedeset godina Beogradskog Medjunarodnog susreta pisaca* ['Encounter with Belgrade: Fifty Years of the Belgrade International Writers' Meetings/Encounters']. Belgrade: Udruženje književnika Srbije [Serbian Writers' Association].

Mylonas, George E. 1942] *The Hymn To Demeter And Her Sanctuary At Eleusis.* Literary Licencing: St. Louis MO: Washington University Studies.

——. 1969 [1961]: *Eleusis and the Eleusinian Mysteries.* Princeton NJ: Princeton University Press.

Naimark, Norman M. and Case, Holly. 2003. *Yugoslavia and Its Historians.* Stanford, CA: Stanford University Press.

Nedeljković, Violeta, 2011 (October 18). 'Sećam se: Ležim, a kuršumi me rešetaju po telu' ['I remember: I'm lying down, and bullets are peppering my body']: interview with Dragoljub Jovanović. *Politika online.*

Neumann, Eric. 1972 [1955]. *The Great Mother.* Mannheim, Ralph (trans.). London: Routledge and Kegan Paul.

——. 1959. *Art and the Creative Unconscious.* Mannheim, Ralph (trans.). London: Routledge and Kegan Paul.

Newmark, Leonard. 1998. *Albanian-English Dictionary.* Oxford: Oxford University Press.

Nietzsche, Friedrich. [1886]. *Beyond Good and Evil: Prelude to a Philosophy of the Future.* Project Gutenberg. Online at: http://www.gutenberg.org/ebooks/4363

Norris, David A. (ed.). 1988. *Miloš Crnjanski and Modern Serbian Literature.* Cotgrave: Astra.

Nožinić, Dražen. 1998. 'Postupci za prizivanje kiše na Kordunu, Banija i Moslavini' ['Rainmaking Rituals in Kordun, Banija and Moslavina'], *Raskovnik*, 91-92.

Nusić, Branislav. 1991 (6th edn.). *Hajduci* ['Hajduks']. Belgrade: Nolit.

Onions, C. T. 1966. *The Oxford Dictionary of English Etymology.* Oxford: Clarendon Press.

'Oral history interview with Sadik Danon' (conducted in Serbian). United States Holocaust Museum. Online at: https://collections.ushmm.org/search/catalog/irn513553

'Oskar Davičo'. *Wikipedia.*

Oxford English Dictionary. Online at: http://www.oed.com/

Parry, Milman. 1987 [1971]. *The Making of Homeric Verse.* Parry, Adam (ed.). Oxford: Oxford University Press.

Partridge, Monica. 1988, 3rd edn. *Serbo-Croat: Practical Grammar and Reader.* Belgrade: Prosveta.

Paton, Andrew Archibald. 2007 [1845]. *Servia, The Youngest Member of the European Family, or, A Residence in Belgrade, and Travels in the Highlands and Woodlands of the Interior, during the Years 1843 and 1844.* BiblioBazaar edn. [London: Longman, Brown, Green and Longmans].

Pavlović, Miodrag (ed.). 1982. *Antologija lirske narodne poezije* ['Anthology of Lyrical Folk Songs']. Belgrade: Vuk Karadžić.

——. 1985. *The Slavs Beneath Parnassus*. Johnson, Bernard (trans.). London and St. Paul MN: Angel Books and Rivers Press.

——. 1989. *Links / Karike*. Bilingual Serbian and English edn. Johnson, Bernard (trans.). Toronto: Exile Editions.

Paz, Octavio. 1967. *The Labyrinth of Solitude*. Kemp, Alexander (trans.). London: Allen lane, Penguin Press.

Peligra, Cristina. 2019 'The Translator's (Inter)View. Celia Hawkesworth on *Singer In The Night*'. Online at: https://inpressbooks.co.uk/blogs/news/the-translator-s-interview-celia-hawkesworth-on-singer-in-the-night-istros-books

'Peter Hall (diplomat)'. *Wikipedia*.

Plotnikova Ana. 1999. 'Dodola'. In Tolstoy, I. (ed.). *Slavyanskie Drevnosti: etnolingvistichenski slovari* ['Slavonic Folk-Customs: An Ethnolinguistic Dictionary'], vol. 2. Moscow: Rossiskaja Akademija Nauk ['Russian Academy of Science'], 100-103.

Polanyi, Michael. 1968 [1952]. *Personal Knowledge*. London: Routledge and Kegan Paul.

Popa, Vasko. 1976. *Vućja so* ['Wolf Salt']. Belgrade: Nolit.

——. 1997. *Complete poems 1953-1987*. Pennington, Anne and Jones, Francis R. (trans.). London: Anvil Press Poetry.

Popov, Nebojša (ed.). 1996. *The Road to War in Serbia: Trauma and Catharsis*. Budapest: Central European University Press.

Popov, Nebojša. 1996a. 'Introduction' to Popov, Nebojša (ed.). *The Road to War in Serbia: Trauma and Catharsis*, 1-5.

——. 1996b. 'Traumatology of the Party State'. In Popov, Nebojša (ed.). *The Road to War in Serbia: Trauma and Catharsis*, 81-105.

Prcela, John and Guldescu, Stanko. 1970. *Operation Slaughterhouse: Eyewitness Accounts of Postwar Massacres in Yugoslavia*. Philadelphia: Dorrance.

Pring, J. T. 1982. *The Oxford Dictionary of Modern Greek*. Oxford: Oxford University Press.

'Radovan Karadžić'. *Wikipedia*.

Ralston, W. R. S. 1872. *The Songs of the Russian People: as illustrative of Slavonic mythology and Russian social life*. London: Ellis and Green.

'Randolph Churchill'. *Wikipedia*.

Reich, Wilhelm. 1975 [1971]. *The Invasion of Compulsory Sex Morality*. Harmondsworth: Pelican.

——. 1973. *The Cancer Biopathy*. London: Vision Press.

Reynolds, Barbara (ed.). 1962. *The Cambridge Italian Dictionary*. Cambridge: Cambridge University Press.

Ricks, Christopher. 1974. *Keats and Embarrassment*. Oxford: Oxford University Press.

Rilke, Maria Rainer. 1963 [1939]. *Duino Elegies*. Leishman, J. B. and Spender, Stephen (trans.). London: The Hogarth Press.

Rimbaud, Arthur. 1966. *Complete Works, Selected Letters*. Bilingual French and English edn. Fowlie, Wallace (trans. and ed.). Chicago, IL: University of Chicago Press.

Rosensaft, Menachim Z. 2017 (October 9). 'Croatia Is Brazenly Attempting to Rewrite its Holocaust Crimes Out of History'. *The Tablet*. Online at:]https://www.tabletmag.com/jewish-news-and-politics/246116/croatia-rewrite-holocaust-crimes-out-of-history

——. 2018 (August 27). 'Croatia Must Not Whitewash the Horrors of Jasenovac'. *Balkan Transnational Justice*. Online at: https://balkaninsight.com/2018/08/27/croatia-must-not-whitewash-the-horrors-of-jasenovac-08-27-2018/

Roethke, Theodore. 1966. *Collected Poems*: New York: Anchor Books.

'Ruski car'. *Wikipedia*.

Said, Edward W. 2003 [1978]. *Orientalism*. London: Penguin Books.

'Sarajevo Haggadah'. *Wikipedia*.

Scholem, Gershom. 1955 [1941]. *Major Trends in Jewish Mysticism*. London: Thames and Hudson.

——. 1973 [1957]. *Sabbatai Sevi, The Mystical Messiah, 1626–1676*. London: Routledge and Kegan Paul.

——. 1978 [1971]. *The Messianic Idea in Judaism*. New York: Schocken Books.

Schrader O. 1909. 'Aryan Religion'. In Hastings, James (ed.). *Encylopaedia of Religion and Ethics*, vol. 2. Edinburgh: T. and T. Clark.

Selenić, Slobodan. 1985. *Fathers and Forefathers*. Elias-Bursać, Ellen, Jelena (trans.). London: Harvill Press.

——. 1996. *Premeditated Murder*. Petrović, Jelena (trans.). London: Harvill Press.

Seferis, George. 1969. *Collected Poems 1924–1955*. Bilingual Greek-English edn. Keeley, Edmund and Sherrard, Philip (trans.). London: Jonathan Cape.

Selimović, Meša. 1999. *The Fortress*. Goy, E. D. and Levinger, Jasna (trans.). Evanston, IL: North Western University Press.

Shelley, Percy Bysshe. 1919. *The Complete Poetical Works*. Hutchinson, Thomas (ed.). Oxford: Humphrey Milford, Oxford University Press.

——. 1923 [1820, 1841]. 'A Defence of Poetry'. In *The Four Ages of Poetry*. Brett-Smith, H. F. B. (ed.). Oxford, Basil Blackwell, 23-59.

Shentalinsky, Vitaly. 1995. *The KGB's Literary Archive*. Crowfoot, John (trans.). London: Harvill.

'Shoshin'. *Wikipedia.*

Škaljić, Abdulah. 1989 (6th edn.). *Turcizmi u sprskohrvatskom jekiku* ['Turkisms in the Serbo-Croatian Language']. Sarajevo: Svjetlost [Light]

Skeat, Rev. Walter. 1898 (3rd edn.). *Etymological Dictionary of the English Language.* Oxford: Clarendon Press.

Skok, Petar. 1971–1974. *Etimologiski rječnik hrvtatskoga ili srpskoga jezika* ['Etymological Dictionary of the Croatian or Serbian Language']: vol. 1, 1971; vol. 2, 1972, vol. 3, 1973; vol. 4, 1974. Zagreb: Jugoslavenska akademija znanosti i umjetnosti [Yugoslav Academy of Sciences and Arts].

Smith, Arthur D. Howden. 1908. *Fighting the Turk in the Balkans: An American's Adventure with the Macedonian Revolution.* New York and London: G. P. Putnam's and the Knickerbocker Press.

Stoianovich, Traian. 1976. *French Historical Method: The Annales Paradigm.* Ithaca, NY and London: Cornell University Press.

——. 1992a. *Between East and West. The Balkan and Mediterranean Worlds.* Vol. 1: *Economies and societies: Lands, lords, states, and middlemen.* New Rochelle, NY: Aristide D. Caratzas.

——. 1992b. *Between East and West. The Balkan and Mediterranean Worlds.* Vol. 2: *Traders, towns, and households,* vol. 2. New Rochelle, NY: Aristide D. Caratzas.

——. 1994. *Balkan Worlds, The First and Last Europe.* Armonk, NY and London: M.E. Sharpe.

——. 1995a. *Between East and West. The Balkan and Mediterranean Worlds.* Vol. 3: *'Material culture and mentalities: Power and ideology.* New Rochelle, NY: Aristide D. Caratzas.

——. 1995b. *Between East and West. The Balkan and Mediterranean Worlds.* Vol. 4: *Land, sea, and destiny.* New Rochelle, NY: Aristide D. Caratzas.

Stojanović, Dubravka. 1996. 'The Traumatic Circle of the Serbian Opposition'. In Popov, Nebojša (ed.). *The Road to War in Serbia: Trauma and Catharsis.* Budapest: Central European University Press, 459-478.

Stojilović, Milan. 1993. 'Winston Churchill on Draza Mihailovic'. Online at: https://groups.google.com/forum/#!topic/soc.culture.croatia/L1f8Q-MaUiBY

Tadijanović, Dragutin. 1993. *Selected Poems.* Goy, Edward and Ward, Dennis (trans.). Zagreb: Hrvatski PEN.

Tanner, Marcus. 1998, December 23. *The Independent.* 'Bosnian Serbs and Muslims wrangle over Jews' holy book', 8.

'Taraf de Haïdouks.' *Wikipedia.*

Tennyson, Alfred Lord. 1896 [1850]. *In Memoriam.*

'Tin Ujević'. *Wikipedia.*

Thompson, Mark. 2013. *Birth Certificate: The Story of Danilo Kiš*. Ithaca, NY and London: Cornell University Press.

Todorova, Maria. 1989. 'Myth-making in European Family History: the Zadruga Revisited'. *East European Politics and Societies* 4/1, 30-76

——. 2009 [1997]. *Imagining the Balkans*. Oxford: Oxford University Press.

'Traian Stoianovich'. *Wikipedia*.

'Trial of Mihailović et al'. *Wikipedia*.

Tylor, Edward, Burnett. 1871–1873. *Primitive Culture: Researches into the Development of Mythology, Philosophy, Religion, Art and Culture* (2 vols.). London: John Murray.

Ugrešić, Dubravka. 1998. *The Culture of Lies: Antipolitical Essays*. Hawkesworth, Celia (trans.). London: Phoenix House.

Ujević, Tin. 1986. *Izabrana djela Tina Ujevića* ['Selected Works of Tin Ujević]' (8 vols.). Čović, Bože (ed.). Zagreb: August Cesarec.

Vayenas, Nasos. 1978. *Biography*. Burns, Richard (trans.). Cambridge: Restif Press.

——. 2010. *The Perfect Order*. Berengarten, Richard and Nikolaou, Paschalis (eds.). London: Anvil Press Poetry.

Verber, Eugen (ed.). 1988. *The Sarajevo Haggadah*. Sarajevo: Svjetlost ['Light'].

'Voivode'. *Wikipedia*.

Vryonis, Speros, Jr. 'Foreword' to Stoianovich 1992, vol. 1, ix-xv.

Vujović, Sreten. 1996. 'An Uneasy View of the City'. In *The Road to War in Serbia: Trauma and Catharsis*. Popov, Nebojša (ed.). Budapest: Central European University Press, 123-145.

'Vuk Karadžić'. *Wikipedia*.

Wace, A. J. B. and Thompson, M. S. 1972 [1914]. *The Nomads of the Balkans: An Account of Life and Customs Among the Vlachs of Northern Pindus*. London: Methuen.

Wachtel, Andrew Baruch. 1998. *Making a Nation, Breaking a Nation. Literature and Cultural Politics in Yugoslavia*. Stanford, CA: Stanford University Press.

Waldman, Anne. 2001 [1974]./ *Fast Speaking Woman: Chants and Essays*. San Francisco, CA: City Lights Books.

Walker, Warren and Uysal, Ahmet E. 1973. 'An Ancient God in Modern Turkey: Some Aspects of the Cult of Hizir'. *Journal of American Folklore* 86. Online at: http://khidr.org/hizir.htm

Weinreich, Max. 1945. 'Der yivo un di problemen fun undzer tsayt' ['The *Yivo* and the problems of our time']. *YIVO Bleter, 25/1, Jan–Feb 1945. Wikipedia.*

Weissbort, Daniel and Longinovic, Tomislav (eds. and trans.) 1992. *Red Knight: Serbian Women's Songs*. London: Kings College London and Menard Press.

West, Rebecca. 1984 [1942]. *Black Lamb and Grey Falcon: A Journey Through Yugoslavia*. London: MacMillan.

Whitehead, Peter *et al.* (eds.). 1965. *Wholly Communion 1965. International Poetry Reading at the Royal Albert Hall, London, June 11*. London: Lorrimer. (See also the series four videos of the event on You Tube: https://www.youtube.com/watch?v=jWdYrd_UH9E)

Wilson, Duncan. 1970. *The Life and Times of Vuk Stefanović Karadžić, 1787–1864*. Oxford: Oxford University Press.

Wolff, Larry. 2001. *Venice and the Slavs. The Discovery of Dalmatia in the Age of Enlightenment*. Stanford, CA: Stanford University Press.

Wortley Montagu, Lady Mary. 1994. *The Turkish Embassy Letters*. Desai, Anita (intr.); Jack, Malcolm (ed.). London: Virago.

Yates, Frances. 1964. *Giordano Bruno and the Hermetic Tradition*. London: Routledge and Kegan Paul.

——. 1966. *The Art of Memory*. London: Routledge and Kegan Paul.

Yeats, W. B. 1961. *Collected Poems*. London: Macmillan.

'Yugoslavia Guest Workers'. *Mongobay*. Online at: http://www.mongabay.com/history/yugoslavia/yugoslavia-guest_workers.html

Zaehner, R. C. 1966. *Hinduism*. Oxford: Oxford University Press.

'Zagrebački književni razgovori' ['Zagreb Literary Conversations']. *Wikipedia*.

Zirojević, Olga 1996. 'Traumatology of the Party State'. In Popov, Nebojša, (ed.). *The Road to War in Serbia: Trauma and Catharsis*. Budapest: Central European University Press, 189-211.

Index

www.ingramcontent.com/pod-product-compliance
Lightning Source LLC
Chambersburg PA
CBHW030911050726
47498CB00003BA/687

* 9 7 8 1 8 4 8 6 1 7 5 3 7 *